RAYMOND WILLIAMS

Facsimile of a page from the Raymond Williams Papers, Richard Burton Archive, Swansea University. Archive Reference: WWE/2/2/1/4.

This page is a list of uncollected essays compiled by Raymond Williams in the late 1970s. Many of the essays listed would appear in *Problems in Materialism and Culture* (London: Verso, 1980) and *Writing in Society* (London: Verso, 1983). At the bottom of the page, Raymond Williams notes 'Others best kept for eventual book of WELSH ESSAYS'. 'Welsh politics and culture' refers to 'Welsh Culture'. 'Dividing Britain' is the essay entitled 'Are We Becoming More Divided'. The other titles are as they appear in this volume. Three envisioned essays are scribbled in Raymond Williams's handwriting on the bottom of the page: 'Planned: The English View of the Celts; Images of the Border; Finding the Border'. It seems that these essays were never written.

Long Revolution

xix	Communications as Cultural Science	Communications,1975 (journal)
xx	New Developments in the Sociology of Culture	Sociology,1976
xxi	Base and Superstructure in Marxist Cultural Theory	New Left Review 82
xxii	Means of Communication as Means of Production	Prilozi,77
xxiii	Class of the Conscious	New Society,Jan 78
xxiv	Adult Education	Adult Education,61.
xxv	Marxism in Britain since 45	New Left Review 100
xxv ½	Problems of Materialism	New Left Review 78

Another group : Occasions

xxvi	Soviet Literary Controversy	Politics & Letters 47
xxvii	...And Traitors Sneer	Politics & Letters 47
xxviii	A Hundred Years of Culture and Anarchy	Spokesman,67
xxix	From Listener: Based on Reality;News Values;What Happened at Munich;The Question of Ulster;China Watching;Judges and Traitors;A Very Late Stage in Bourgeois Art;Personal Relief Time;Pitmen and Pilgrims;Three Documentaries; Careers and Jobs;Crimes and Crimes;Where does Rozanov Come In,;A Bit of a Laugh,a bit of Glamour)	
xxx	Democracy and Heritocracy	Guardian 58

Two floating

Realism and television drama   - Screen 77
Realism and Naturalism   - Edinburgh TV Festival,77
The Screen Policeman   - unpubl;notes only.

Other floating

The Left in Britain   - Esprit,63
Political articles in New York Nation - 61-75;

Others best kept for eventual book of WELSH ESSAYS

Welsh politics and culture   - Plaid Cymru,76
Dividing Britain   - ITV,76 ;script
Welsh Industrial Novels   - lecture tape
Wales and England   - commissioned for 78
The Tenses of Imagination   - 3 Aberystwyth lectures 78

The English View of the Celts
Image of the Border
Making the Border

Professor Raymond Williams was born in 1921 in the Welsh border village of Pandy. Among his seminal volumes of cultural criticism are *Culture and Society* (1958), *The Long Revolution* (1961), *The Country and the City* (1973) and *Marxism and Literature* (1977). He died in 1988.

Professor Daniel G. Williams is Director of the Richard Burton Centre for the Study of Wales at Swansea University. He is the author of *Wales Unchained: Literature, Politics and Identity in the American Century* (2015), *Black Skin, Blue Books: African Americans and Wales* (2012) and *Ethnicity and Cultural Authority: from Arnold to Du Bois* (2006).

THE CENTENARY EDITION

RAYMOND WILLIAMS

Who Speaks for Wales?
Nation, Culture, Identity

Edited by
Daniel G. Williams

UNIVERSITY OF WALES PRESS
2021

Introduction, Afterword and Notes to the volume
© Daniel G. Williams, 2021

www.uwp.co.uk

British Library CIP Data
A catalogue record for this book is available from the British Library.

ISBN   978-1-78683-706-6
eISBN   978-1-78683-707-3

The rights of those declared above to be identified as authors of this work have been asserted in accordance with sections 77 and 79 of the Copyright, Designs and Patents Act 1988.

Typeset by Marie Doherty
Printed by Ashford Colour Press Ltd, Gosport, UK.

I Sioned
am fynd gyda fi i'r Pandy.

Ac er cof am ei thad
Philip Griffith Jones
a ddangosodd inni'r ffordd.

Bydd dyn wedi troi'r hanner-cant yn gweld yn lled glir
Y bobl a'r cynefin a foldiodd ei fywyd e'

(Having turned fifty, a man sees pretty clearly
The people and places that have moulded his life)

—D. Gwenallt Jones, 'Y Meirwon'

Das Vorleben des Emigranten wird bekanntlich annulliert.

(The past life of the émigré is, as we know, annulled).

—Theodor Adorno, *Minima Moralia*

CONTENTS

POLITICS

■ ■ ■

PREFACE

Who Speaks for Wales? first appeared in March 2003. It collected in one place the Welsh-related essays of Raymond Williams (1921–88) and was conceived and compiled in the years following the narrow vote for Welsh devolution in the referendum of 1997. If a distinctive Welsh political culture was to develop, and if devolution was indeed to be a 'process' rather than an 'event' – as the then Secretary for Wales Ron Davies described it – then, as several commentators noted, a sense of common aspiration and interest would need to be forged between the socialist and minority nationalist threads of Welsh political radicalism as embodied institutionally in the Labour party and Plaid Cymru. Raymond Williams's thought and writings offered resources for forging a rapprochement between these traditions, and that is what I was attempting to foster in my emphasis in the introduction (which I have deliberately not updated nor amended for this edition) on the pluralism of Williams's vision, on the questions asked as opposed to the answers offered, and on the ways in which Williams's self-defined 'Welsh-Europeanism' could be seen as a manifestation of his call on socialists to engage in a project – associated primarily with the minority nationalist parties of Europe – of exploring 'new forms of "variable" societies, in which over the whole range of social purposes different sizes of society' could be 'defined for different kinds of issue and decision'.

When the volume was launched, in the company of Raymond Williams's daughter Merryn, at the annual Association for Welsh Writing in English conference in Gregynog, Newtown, the Labour government of Tony Blair was two years into its second term in Westminster and about to follow George W. Bush and the United States into a calamitous war in Iraq. An estimated 151,000 to 1,033,000 Iraqis were killed in the first four years of conflict. Having established, via referenda, a Parliament for Scotland and an Assembly for Wales in 1997, and having brokered the Good Friday Agreement in 1998 that ended most of the violence of 'the Troubles' in Northern Ireland, Blair's Labour government in the new millennium seemed to revert to an ideology of British exceptionalism: courting the Murdoch press; wrapping itself in the Union Jack; embracing a neo-liberal ideology that espoused interventionism abroad and a domestic program characterised by the expansion of privatisation and the adop-tion of the language and values of competitive business capitalism into the public arenas of health and education. The two-tiered system established by the Tories under Margaret Thatcher and John Major was continued under Blair, with richer sectors of society buying themselves into private provision and thus cementing the political base for the rejection of any meaningful redistribution. Raymond Williams had warned in the 1980s that destroying public common interests in the name of private solutions would drive whatever was left of the 'public' sector into crisis, starved of investment. This is what the Thatcherite neo-liberal agenda delivered, perpetuated by Blair's Labour.

Wales registered an early resistance to this neoliberal programme in the first elections to the new National Assembly in 1999. While Blair openly admitted that he regarded the devolved institutions to be little more than 'parish councils', Wales at least now had a vehicle where its political voice could be heard. In the first elections to the new Assembly, Labour won as expected, but Plaid Cymru sur-passed expectations by gaining 30.5% of the vote (outperforming her Scottish sister party, the SNP). Labour learnt its lesson and soon deposed the Blairite Alun Michael, putting Rhodri Morgan in his place as First Minister. While Blair was essentially a post-Thatcherite individualist, Morgan had political roots in the hopes and aspirations of the Labour movement and, as the son of T. J. Morgan, onetime Professor of Welsh at Swansea University, also had a foot in the trad-itions of Welsh language culture. Evoking the legacy of Aneurin Bevan, Morgan set out to create 'clear red water' between 'classic' Welsh Labour and Blairism. Morgan understood that welfare systems have profound effects on the wider social framework. He knew that the principle of 'social insurance' was not only efficient but was also a way of underwriting an evolving sense of Welsh citizenship; that 'universalist' policies (free bus passes, free prescriptions, free school breakfasts) were essential to binding the richer sections of society into collective forms of welfare. Thus, while Blair was reconstructing the Labour Party along the lines of Bill Clinton's neo-liberal Democrats in the United States, Rhodri Morgan was establishing a new Welsh polity based on European social-democratic values. This social-democratic vision informed the period of coalition with Plaid Cymru from 2007 to 2011. The affirmative 'Yes' vote (63.49%) for Wales to have law-making powers at the end of this period of coalition government in the referendum of 2011 seemed to suggest that the 'Welsh European' project was very much on track.

Retrospectively, the low turn-out of 35.2% in that referendum should have been a major cause for concern. The form of 'Welsh welfarism' espoused and developed by a series of Welsh Labour administrations failed, unlike the series of SNP administrations in Scotland following their breakthrough election in 2007, to escape the straight-jacket of British politics. Labour in Wales had to keep its devo-sceptic wing happy, making sure that it never appeared 'too nationalist'. Yet, the party's electoral success depended on the impression that it was 'standing up' for Welsh interests against the Blairite and Conservative agendas of sequential Westminster governments. The way to alleviate these tensions was to trumpet relatively minor state interventions in support of redistribution and social provision as 'standing up for Wales'. Welshness was made equivalent to welfarism, in a process that equated class with cultural identity. The progressive Left's project of common social advancement was largely abandoned by Labour for the administration, alleviation and ultimately – if unintentionally – preservation of relative poverty. This political stagnation led to the rise of the Right-wing populism that was an unfortunate feature of Welsh politics in the 2010s.

The result is that this edition of *Who Speaks for Wales?*, celebrating the centenary of Raymond Williams's birth on 31 August 1921, is appearing at a time when the Welsh European vision that he espoused is arguably further out of reach than at any point in my lifetime. We celebrate Williams's centenary under the dark shadow of the European Union membership referendum of 2016. While Scotland and Northern Ireland voted to remain in Europe, Wales followed England in voting to leave. In the face of a virulent, intolerant Right that felt it had the wind in its sails the Left required robust, inspirational, leadership. Beyond the boundaries of the Tories' internecine war there was space to develop a federal vision in which English, Welsh and Scottish Europeans would rejuvenate the Left – a realisation of the rainbow coalition of green, minority nationalist and socialist forces that Raymond Williams imagined in his final years. Undermined continuously by centrist members of his own party and by virtually all sectors of the British press, Labour's openly socialist leader Jeremy Corbyn failed to initiate a decisive shift in the politics of the United Kingdom. This failure may ultimately be seen to lie in the largely unarticulated, but assumed, 'British' frame of his, and his movement's, politics. The European referendum offered the Left within Labour, the Greens, and within the Welsh and Scottish national movements, an opportunity for a mutual re-imaging of the relationship between the constituent nations of the British Isles within a broader transnational context. The failure to do so will haunt progressive politics for a generation. It remains to be seen whether the writings of Raymond Williams collected in this volume document a vision of a 'Europe of the peoples and nations' that was never to be realised, or whether they become crucial, foundational, texts in the rejuvenation and future fulfilment of that Welsh-European vision. Williams noted that Welsh history testifies to a 'quite extraordinary process of self-generation and regeneration, from what seemed impossible conditions'. This new Centenary Edition has been prepared with these words in mind.

Daniel G. Williams
Alltwen
September 2020

ACKNOWLEDGEMENTS

I noted in 2003 that the stimulus for assembling this collection was the wish to resist the 'danger of withdrawn and resentful enclosure and submission' that Raymond Williams identified as a possible response to the persistent 'cultural indifference' towards Wales and Welsh literature in the Anglo-American academic world. Part of the problem, as Williams noted, is that any attempt at following the internal arguments within a specific culture results in 'the reader from elsewhere' wishing 'that he or she had come in at the beginning, to get the shape of the discourse and to understand all the references back'. The explanatory notes at the end of each chapter, updated for this Centenary Edition, were initially intended as providing a means for that 'reader from elsewhere' to gain a sense of the Welsh context. In the process of teaching Williams at Swansea University, however, it became clear that there was also a case for including some information on figures such as Hoggart, Leavis and Konni Zilliacus, as well as Aneirin, Carnhuanawc and Saunders Lewis. Williams rarely documented the influences and sources of his ideas, but where he included footnotes in the original they appear at the bottom of the page, while my explanatory notes appear at the end of each essay or chapter. Full publication details appear on the first page of each essay.

The sense of affirmation (and indeed vindication, given the sceptical attitude of some to this project) that I experienced upon discovering in 2011 that Raymond Williams had intended compiling a volume of 'Welsh Essays' was only tempered by the regret that he never completed that book nor some of the envisaged essays that he planned to include within it. (The page where Williams noted his intentions appears as a frontispiece to this volume.) That discovery was made in the Richard Burton Archives of Swansea University, where the Raymond Williams papers were deposited by Dai Smith following his appointment as a Research Chair in the Centre for Research into the English literature and Language of

Wales (CREW) in 2005. CREW, under the inspired directorship of M. Wynn Thomas and Kirsti Bohata, has been a hive of activity relating to Williams's writings ever since. Dai Smith published his biography *Raymond Williams: A Warrior's Tale* (Cardigan: Parthian) in 2008 and, as editor of the Welsh Government-funded Library of Wales, reinforced that volume's emphasis on the centrality of fiction in Williams's life and work by bringing the novels *Border Country* and *The Volunteers* back into print. Several volumes in the CREW series 'Writing Wales in English' (by Stephen Knight, Hywel Dix and myself) have offered new readings of Williams's thought and writings, and two outstanding doctoral theses completed by Clare Davies and Daniel Gerke are being prepared for publication as I write. Other PhD students at CREW have drawn on Raymond Williams's writings in strikingly original ways, and I have learned much in particular from Charlotte Jackson, Kieron Smith and Liza Penn-Thomas. The range of publications generated by work in the archive – from Dana Polan's 'Raymond Williams on Film' (*Cinema Journal*, 52/3, Spring 2013) to Stefan Collini's reconstruction of Williams's 'nostalgic imagination' (*The Nostalgic Imagination*, 2019) – has been a continual source of education and inspiration. This work has benefitted from the expertise of the archivists at Swansea University's Richard Burton Archives, especially Katrina Legg – expert cataloguer of the Raymond Williams papers, and dedicated tracker of stray references.

Since the first appearance of this volume, interest in Williams's Welshness and the role that it played in his social and cultural thought has been manifested at conferences from Berlin (Harald Pittel and Michael Krause) to Poznan (Karolina Rosiak), from Regensburg (Peter Waller) to Campinas (Alexandro Henrique Paixão and Anderson Ricardo Trevisan). The Raymond Williams papers have attracted many international scholars to Swansea, with Mingying Zhou (Lingnan University, Hong Kong), Carla Baute (Universidade Estadual de Campinas, Brazil) and Ugo Rivetti (University of Sao Paulo, Brazil) staying for extended periods of research. The most significant and long-standing collaboration has been that between CREW and the Raymond Williams Kenkyu-kai in Japan, resulting in conferences in Swansea, Pandy and Newtown (in Wales), and Tokyo, Osaka and Nogata (in Japan). These events have resulted in a series of publications including a special issue of *Keywords* (Vol. 9, 2011), several issues of the journal *Raymond Williams Kenkyu* (2010–18), and two collected editions of Williams's writings in Japanese with space given to his writings on Wales (*Culture is Ordinary and Other Essays* (2013) and *The Tenses of the Imagination and Other Essays* (2016)). I am indebted in particular to Shintaro Kono and Takashi Onuki for initiating the connection with their visit of 2009 (followed up by a year spent by both as Richard Burton Centre International Fellows at Swansea University from 2015–16), for Yasuhiro Kondo for translating this volume's introduction into Japanese (*Raymond Williams Kenkyu* 2, 2011), and to Asako Nakai, Fuhito Endo, Yasuo Kawabata, Ryota Nishi, Tomoki Takayama, Yuzo Yamada and several others for making our collaborations such profound, joyous and far-reaching events. I acknowledged those with whom I had discussed Williams and Wales, both west and east of Offa's Dyke and on both sides of the Atlantic, in the first edition of this volume. Since then I am particularly grateful to Simon Brooks, Luke Gibbons, Catherine McKenna, Patrick McGuinness, Tony Pinkney, Julian Preece, Werner Sollors, Gauri Viswanathan, Peter Waller, Stephen Woodhams and Huw L. Williams for acts or words of kindness and advice relating to this book, to photographer David Barnes and curator Peter Wakelin for encouraging conversations on the relationship between Williams and visual culture, and to Leanne Wood AM who reached out across the political-academic divide in 2009 as she was developing her Williams-inspired 'Greenprint for the Valleys', initiating what has become a valued friendship. These connections and initiatives testify to the truth of Raymond Williams's statement that 'sometimes ... you find that the most local is also the most general'.

In noting the omissions that had to be made in order for the volume to appear at a reasonable price in 2003, I quoted James Baldwin's observation that you 'never get the book you wanted, you settle for the book you get'. This Centenary Edition is closer to the book that I wanted, and I thank the University of Wales Press for allowing me to include the pieces left out of the first incarnation. I can now say with some confidence that this is a definitive edition of Raymond Williams's critical pieces on Wales. The book exists because of the sterling work of the staff at the University of Wales Press, and I would especially like to thank Dafydd Jones and Sarah Lewis for guiding it to publication. The dedication of the first volume was to my wife

Sioned and daughter Lowri born, as I noted at the time, 'while this book was nearing completion and already embarking on her journey of hope'. Lowri's journey takes her across the border to study Fine Art in London this year, while her younger brother Dewi still has a few years before deciding on the next step. If Sioned and I have celebrated additions to the family since 2003, there have also been losses. A collection of Raymond Williams's writings on Wales seems an appropriate place to remember my father-in-law Philip Jones, a much-loved teacher and headmaster steeped in the history of his native Rhymni and the Black Mountains of Gwent.

Merryn Williams has supported this project from the outset almost twenty years ago, and I thank both the Estate of Raymond Williams and Verso Books for the rights to re-publish these diverse pieces in this format.

THE RETURN OF THE NATIVE

That real perception of tradition is available only to the man who has read about it, though what he then sees through it is his native country, to which he is already deeply bound by memory and experience of another kind: a family and a childhood; an intense association of people and places, which has been his own history. To see tradition in both ways is indeed Hardy's special gift: the native place and experience but also the education, the conscious inquiry. Yet then to see living people, within this complicated sense of past and present, is another problem again. He sees as a participant who is also an observer; this is the source of the strain.[1]

In *The English Novel from Dickens to Lawrence* (1970) Raymond Williams argues that Thomas Hardy's writings emanate from a 'crisis – the return of the native'.[2] In the passage above Williams traces 'the source of strain' in Hardy's writings to a structure of feeling and expression that is prevalent throughout his own engagements with his 'native country', for Williams's writings on Wales are consistently informed by that backward gaze from a formal education to the 'intense association' of family and childhood in the Welsh border village of Pandy. In both his theoretical writings and his fiction, Williams shares Hardy's 'special gift' of relating his own early history to the 'insights of a consciously learned history and of the educated understanding of nature and behaviour', of seeing 'the native place and experience but also the education'.[3]

In discussions of Williams's writings, both before and following his death aged 66 in January 1988, the tendency is for the 'education' to be foregrounded, whilst the 'native place' is either ignored or dismissed. The only 'formative influence' that is of any interest to John Higgins in his recent *Raymond Williams: literature, marxism and cultural materialism* (1999), for example, is 'Cambridge English', and it is therefore not surprising that a book that purports to offer 'the single most comprehensive historical and theoretical account of Williams's work' does not contain a single reference to Wales.[4] The same author's *Raymond Williams Reader* (2001) is intended 'as a survey of the whole body of Williams's work', but here the omission of any writings on Wales is compounded by the symptomatic mis-titling of Williams's unfinished fictional exploration of the history of human settlement on the Black Mountains as *People of the Black Country*.[5] Similarly, in the only full biography to have appeared since Williams's death, Fred Inglis gives Wales a place of some importance as the background from which Raymond Williams came, but makes no attempt to understand or engage with the internal tensions and divisions within Welsh culture. When Inglis does refer to Williams's 'late-come Welshness', he betrays his ignorance of the Welsh cultural and historical debates in which Williams was a significant participant from the mid-1970s onwards.[6] Inglis describes Williams's move 'towards that little group of self-mocking Welsh historians led by Gwyn Williams and Dai Smith, and their sometimes comic, always serious politics in Plaid Cymru'.[7] Even if we put the string of inappropriate adjectives to one side, Dai Smith's historical project has been to fundamentally revise the historical narratives and myths that he believes underpin the nationalist politics of Plaid Cymru – a party whose vision he has consistently opposed. Inglis makes no attempt to engage with the Welsh context, for he ultimately considers the 'return to Welshness' as 'a fit of the kind of fervour which overcame Williams several times in later life'.[8]

Perhaps the problem with describing Williams's engagement with Wales as a 'return' is that it can easily be dismissed as a retreat. Patrick Parrinder's reference to Williams 'withdrawing into the redoubt of his "Welshness"' and James A. Davies's dismissive description of Williams's 'alternative Wales' as 'a Celtic commune under threat but indomitable' are indicative of what has become one of a number of dispiriting clichés which now circulate about Williams and his work as he becomes increasingly regarded as a marginal and outdated figure.[9] Even a sympathetic critic such as John Higgins encapsulates a number of the lazy commonplaces informing contemporary discussions of Williams when he notes that 'throughout, he appears to be constitutively blind to the politics of race and gender, and the dynamics of imperialism'.[10] It is certainly possible to marshal evidence in support of these charges, and there is little in this present volume to contradict Morag Shiach's pithy observation that '[f]eminists can find much of use to them in the work of Raymond Williams; they cannot, however, find many women'.[11] It is my contention in this introduction, however, that an engagement with Williams's writings on Wales forces a reconsideration of the role played by questions of colonialism and imperialism in his writings. Indeed, far from showing him to be the critic described by R. Radhakrishnan as 'incapable of dealing with the subtle nuances of the politics of location', the reviews, interviews and essays collected in this anthology testify to the centrality of 'location, position and travel' in Williams's social and cultural thought.[12]

If Williams's critical writings on Wales have been ignored, so too, on the whole, has his fiction. Few critics support their analyses of the ideas by discussing the way Williams explored many of his key concepts in fictional form. The fact that it was in the fiction that Williams began to explore the meaning of his Welsh experience has proved convenient for maintaining a distinction between the 'international' cultural critic and the 'regional' novelist. In this respect the pattern of Williams's reception has been slightly different in Wales where there has been a more specialist interest in the novels, but here again a separation of the critic from the novelist is generally maintained.[13] This collection of Williams's critical writings on Wales testifies to the fact that the engagement with his 'native place' was never limited to the fiction. Williams insisted on the integral unity of his work, and I discuss aspects of the novels along with the theory in this introduction in order to support my central contention that in his writings on Wales – in which 'place, language and identity' intersect with the older triumvirate 'culture, community, class' – Williams speaks directly to contemporary cultural and theoretical concerns.

This is not surprising given that the move outwards in Williams's personal and intellectual history – from an upbringing in Pandy, to being a student and Professor at Cambridge, to being an intellectual of the European left – is always accompanied by a return to the fundamental experiences that have consistently informed the life and the work. Williams's description of himself as a 'Welsh-European' captures something of this 'paradoxical return', which, as Tony Pinkney notes perceptively, 'temporally coincides with rather than following the move outwards and away'.[14] At several moments in this anthology, Williams notes that the specific arguments animating Welsh cultural and historical debates 'are of much more general significance', and describes how it was his 'more conscious Welshness' that led him towards a greater sense of affinity with 'the people to the left and on the left of the French and Italian communist parties, the German and Scandinavian comrades, the communist dissidents from the East like Bahro'.[15] In order to understand the movement outwards, it is crucial that we do not dismiss the significance of the return. Williams described his increasing engagement with Wales and Welsh issues from the 1970s onwards as giving him 'a very strong sense of retracing a journey and finding that I'd come back to the same place but that place had changed'.[16] If Williams traced the 'source of the strain' in Thomas Hardy's writings to the returned native's ambiguous location 'as a participant who is also an observer', he approached the cultural debates of that changed Welsh landscape by 'seeing the matter in my own living conditions from both inside and outside', a position that perhaps derived from imagining himself a 'returning migrant with all his doubts'.[17]

THE MIGRANT'S RETURN

It could be argued that by describing himself as a 'returning migrant', Williams is repeating a widespread tendency amongst intellectuals to exaggerate their marginality. Contemporary discussions on the role of the social critic tend to emphasise, and generally to celebrate, the critic's role as an 'alienated intellectual', an 'outsider', or an 'exile'. The assumption is that marginality provides a stimulus to insight, that a sense of exclusion encourages an analytical detachment, that a sense of geographical or metaphorical 'exile' allows the critic to address and challenge 'the constituted and authorized power of one's own society'.[18] The following passage from Edward Said's *Representations of the Intellectual* (1994) may be considered indicative of the way in which the intellectual's vocation is currently discussed:

Exile is a model for the intellectual who is tempted, and even beset and overwhelmed, by the rewards of accommodation, yea-saying, settling in. Even if one is not an actual immigrant or expatriate, it is still possible to think as one, to imagine and investigate in spite of barriers, and always to move away from the centralising authorities towards the margins, where you see things that are usually lost on minds that have never travelled beyond the conventional and the comfortable.[19]

Stefan Collini has noted a 'tendency to self-dramatisation among social critics whereby they represent themselves as "marginal" or, more bitterly but also self-importantly, as "excluded"', and argues, in a striking reversal of the contemporary trend manifested in Edward Said's words above, that it 'may be helpful to begin by insisting that it is degrees of "insiderness" that we really need to capture in order to characterize the social critic's role'.[20] Raymond Williams wasn't immune to dramatising his own sense of isolation, and indeed his later use of his Welsh identity could be read as a convenient means of establishing his credentials as a 'modish marginal', rather than a 'compromised metropolitan', intellectual.[21] In the pieces contained in this volume and in his fiction, however, positions of 'exile' or 'marginality' are consistently problematised. Exile is never a position to be simply celebrated in Williams's fictional worlds, for those who leave their communities are invariably at a disadvantage when they return. The 'crisis' of 'the return of the native' that Williams identified in Hardy's fiction manifests itself as a crisis of language in his first novel *Border Country* (1960), where Matthew Price feels that he's been 'away too long … I've forgotten it all, and can't bring myself back':[22]

As he looked away he heard the separate language in his mind, the words of his ordinary thinking. He was trained to detachment: the language itself, consistently abstracting and generalizing, supported him in this. And the detachment was real in another way. He felt, in this house, both a child and a stranger. He could not speak as either; could not speak really as himself at all, but only in the terms that this pattern offered.[23]

Matthew is rendered speechless by his inability to apply the acquired language of academia back to the context of his own 'native country'. This was a challenge faced by Williams himself in his early writings.

In the influential essay 'Culture is Ordinary' (1958), Williams writes as – following his description of Hardy – a 'participant who is also an observer'; an educated man who is drawing the reader's attention to 'a native place and experience' in the 'different idiom' of 'conscious inquiry'.[24] The essay is a remarkably distilled statement of the fundamental values and ideas that continued to inform Williams's thought throughout his life, and begins:

> The bus stop was outside the cathedral. I had been looking at the Mappa Mundi, with its rivers out of Paradise, and at the chained library, where a party of clergymen had got in easily, but where I had waited an hour and cajoled a verger before I ever saw the chains. Now, across the street, a cinema advertised the *Six-Five Special* and a cartoon version of *Gulliver's Travels*. The bus arrived, with a driver and conductress deeply absorbed in each other. We went out of the city, over the old bridge, and on through the orchards and the green meadows and the fields red under the plough. Ahead were the Black Mountains, and we climbed among them, watching the steep fields end at the grey walls, beyond which the bracken and heather and whin had not yet been driven back. To the east, along the ridge, stood the line of grey Norman castles; to the west, the fortress wall of the mountains. Then, as we still climbed, the rock changed under us. Here, now, was limestone, and the line of the early iron workings along the scarp. The farming valleys, with their scattered white houses, fell away behind. Ahead of us were the narrower valleys: the steel-rolling mill, the gasworks, the grey terraces, the pit-heads. The bus stopped, and the driver and conductress got out, still absorbed. They had done this journey so often, and seen all its stages. It is a journey, in fact, that in one form or another we have all made.

> I was born and grew up halfway along that bus journey. Where I lived is still a farming valley, though the road

through it is being widened and straightened, to carry the heavy lorries to the north. Not far away, my grandfather, and so back through the generations, worked as a farm labourer until he was turned out of his cottage and, in his fifties, became a roadman. His sons went at thirteen or fourteen on to the farms, his daughters into service. My father, his third son, left the farm at fifteen to be a boy porter on the railway, and later became a signalman, working in a box in this valley until he died. I went up the road to the village school where a curtain divided the two classes – Second to eight or nine, First to fourteen. At eleven I went to the local grammar school, and later to Cambridge.[25]

This justly famous passage is characterised by a tension between the narrator's simultaneous desire to observe and to participate. Despite noting that the driver and conductress are 'deeply absorbed in each other', Williams goes on to represent the ensuing journey as a shared experience; 'we went out of the city', 'we climbed', 'the rock changed under us'. We are asked to assume that the narrator's historically and geographically informed account of the scene – the 'Norman castles', the 'limestone and the early iron workings' – is shared by the other individuals making the journey. It would seem, however, that the narrator's interest in his environment contrasts the relative indifference of the driver and conductress who are 'still absorbed' when the bus stops and who have 'done this journey so often' that they've 'seen all its stages'. The passage is narrated from the position of one who is familiar with the area, who knows its history, but who is sufficiently distanced from it to notice things anew.

The passage is carefully constructed and is made up of a series of spatial and temporal juxtapositions; the actual duration of the bus journey is juxtaposed to the longer duration of the author's life which is itself juxtaposed to the much longer processes of social history and environmental change. The oppositions informing that dominant tradition of cultural criticism, traced back to the Romantics by Williams in *Culture and Society* (1958) – between elite and popular cultures, city and country, nature and industry, continuity and change – are embedded in a scene which crosses the borders defining each of these binary divisions and foregrounds the interplay of cultural forces that Williams would define later, in a more theoretical mode, as 'residual, dominant and emergent'.[26] Christopher Hitchens is surely right to note Williams's indebtedness to George Orwell in this passage: there is Orwell's love of landscape and countryside and for growing things; there is the sense of being at home in ancient towns and buildings and the attachment to family which informs a view of society based ideally on the same principles of solidarity and of sharing.[27] This comparison can be taken further, for in his study of *Orwell* (1971), Williams notes that both of Orwell's long essays about England and Englishness – 'The Lion and the Unicorn' (1940) and 'The English People' (1944) – begin from 'the viewpoint of someone arriving in England':

> But he is not coming to England in the same way as, say, an Indian or and African student: to a foreign country about which he has only read. He has been educated here; his family lives here. He is aware of the internal structures of English society.[28]

Williams argues that this simultaneous sense of exile and belonging results in a 'very special position' in Orwell's writings, 'a kind of conscious double vision'.[29] This sense of Orwell's 'double vision' resonates closely with Williams's description of Hardy as 'a participant who is also an observer', and both notions are applicable to Williams's own writings. To read 'Culture is Ordinary' with Williams's discussion of Orwell in mind, is to be made aware that another border is unconsciously crossed in the opening of 'Culture is Ordinary', which would become increasingly significant to the development of Williams's thought; the border between England and Wales. If Orwell writes as a 'man coming back to England', Williams is here writing as a man travelling back into Wales, yet nowhere is the transition described in national terms. This is perceived to be a journey not across national frontiers, but rather within the border country of Williams's youth. There is enough information in the piece for those who are familiar with the landscape to follow the journey – we're taken from Hereford where the Mappa Mundi is displayed, through the Black Mountains into the narrow eastern industrial valleys of south Wales – but enough is omitted to give the passage a deliberate sense of generality for it 'is a journey, in fact, that in one form or another we have all made'.

Williams was later to describe the late 1950s as a period in which 'my distance from Wales was at its most complete'.[30] Whilst register-ing the exclusive focus on England in his career-making study *Culture and Society*, Williams argued that 'unconsciously my Welsh experience was nevertheless operating on the strategy of the book':[31]

> For when I concluded it with a discussion of cooperative community and solidarity, what I was really writing about – as if they were more widely available – was Welsh social relations. I was drawing very heavily on my experience of Wales, and in one way correctly locating it as a certain char-acteristic of working-class institutions, but with not nearly enough regional shading and sense of historical distinctions and complications.[32]

'Culture is Ordinary', published in the same year as *Culture and Society*, actually locates those meditations on culture, community and solidarity on the border between Wales and England, and uses that personal history as a basis for the ensuing discussion. Pinkney, in his strikingly original discussion of Williams as a 'postmodern novelist', notes that at 'every moment of his intellectual career he was prepared to return general theoretical issues back to immediate lived experi-ence, to a deeply felt personal history and geography'.[33] The opening two paragraphs of 'Culture is Ordinary' offer an early example of the way in which Williams relates the key theoretical issues of his writing back to the 'deeply felt personal history and geography' of the border country. The opening of 'Culture is Ordinary' supports Williams's later sense of complete 'distance' from Wales in the 1950s, but the years in which he published 'Culture is Ordinary', *Culture and Society* and the other early works of literary and cultural stud-ies also saw the continuous drafting and re-drafting of the novel *Border Country*, which recreates the cultural, political and familial relationships of life lived in – what is consciously identified as – the 'Welsh' fictional border village of Glynmawr. This suggests that what remained 'unconscious' in the critical writings was in some ways already 'conscious' in the fiction.

The novel begins, significantly, with the university lecturer Matthew Price being called back to his native Welsh village from London after his father suffers a heart attack. He returns by train:

> Abruptly the rhythm changed, as the wheels crossed the bridge. Matthew got up, and took his case from the rack. As he steadied the case, he looked at the rail-map, with its familiar network of arteries, held in the shape of Wales, and to the east the lines running out and elongating, into England. The shape of Wales: pig-headed Wales you say to remember to draw it. And no returns.[34]

The change in rhythm of the railway carriage anticipates changes in the rhythms of life, and in the rhythms of speech. Matthew arrives in Glynmawr speaking the 'different idiom' of academic life, but upon phoning home his wife notices that 'Your voice is quite different already ... Changed back ... I prefer it.'[35] As the 'consistently abstracting and generalizing' language of academia gives way to the 'quick Welsh accent', his name also mutates from the 'Matthew' which he has used, significantly, since his student days, to 'Will', the name by which he has always been known in Glynmawr.[36] The relationship between the language of intellectuals and the inherited language of one's 'native country' is a recurrent theme in Williams's theoretical and fictional writings. In a significant and revealing moment in the novel *The Volunteers*, Evan castigates a technocratic intellectual for having 'nothing to say for us. You have plenty to say to us. You beam in from another world.'[37] What gives an individual a right to speak for others, and what is the difference between speaking 'for' and speaking 'to', are questions fundamental to an understanding of Williams's practice as a social critic and are asked implicitly in a number of his writings on Wales.

I have deliberately foregrounded these issues in this volume's title, taken from Williams's 1971 review of Ned Thomas's 'little red book' of the Welsh language movement, *The Welsh Extremist*. It is from this period onwards that Williams begins to grapple self-consciously with the meaning of his Welsh experience, and he adopts a strategy in this review that would be repeated many times in his later writings: he locates himself in the border country of his youth and looks westwards towards the two societies that have formed the bases for the dominant, and bitterly divergent, images of Wales in the twentieth century; the 'powerful political culture of industrial South Wales' on the one hand, and 'the more enclosed, mainly rural, more Welsh-speaking west and north' on the other. Revealingly, in both cases, Williams's knowledge of these Welsh communities derives more from research than experience; he recalls 'focusing first' on the history of south Wales, before turning his attention to the Welsh-speaking west and north that 'in the beginning ... was much more remote'. 'In the beginning' suggests that this remoteness is no longer felt to the same extent as it was in the past, and in placing the defence of Welsh speakers' rights within the context of 'Black Power in the United States, civil rights in Ulster... the student movement, women's liberation', Williams looks beyond the divisions on the ground in Wales to locate the Welsh experience within the wider context of New Left activism.[38]

The same cultural divisions were still stubbornly present in the review article 'Community' (1985). Here, Williams compares Emyr Humphreys's celebration and analysis of the 'continuity of Welsh language and literature ... from the sixth century' with Dai Smith's critique of notions of national continuity in his emphasis on 'the turbulent experience of industrial South Wales'.[39] Attempting to see beyond the bitterness of the debate, Williams seeks to effect that unity of the various Waleses he had encountered in his life and work. He is 'especially aware of the common elements of authenticity in each apparently alternative case', and, despite the divisions, argues that 'the more profound community is its area of discourse'.[40] Williams suggests that this unifying view derives from 'seeing the matter in my own living conditions from both inside and outside', an ambivalent location that lies at the heart of his fictional and theoretical engagements with Wales and Welshness.[41] 'I have been an active participant in the internal Welsh argument', he noted in New Society (1986), 'but, living so much in England, I have thought from an early stage that the issues being explored are of much more general significance'.[42] The 'double-vision' that Williams detected in Orwell is made manifest in a number of the pieces collected in this volume, where Williams insists that we 'remember' that he was 'born on the border, and... talked about "the English" who were not us, and also "the Welsh" who were not us'.[43] That border experience, the feeling of being both 'inside and outside', is, then, firstly a lived experience that mutates into a position from which to speak, beyond the divisions, of the wider, international, relevance of Welsh cultural and political debates.

A POST-COLONIAL CULTURE?

In the past decade, the phenomena of ethnicity and nationalism have emerged as major fields of inquiry in cultural and historical studies, and one might thus have expected Williams's writings on Wales to have received some belated attention. Those writings are currently ignored, however, and any wider relevance that they may have is obscured by the reiterated charge that he was 'constitutionally blind to the... dynamics of imperialism'.[44] When challenged by his *New Left Review* interlocutors in 1979 about the lack of any reference to 'nationalism or imperialism' in *Culture and Society*, Williams responded as follows:

> There are in fact two places in the book which do refer to the imperial experience, although in a way they confirm your general emphasis – the discussion of Carlyle's criticism of emigration as a social solution, and the analysis of the magical function of departures to the empire in the fiction of the period. But otherwise there is nothing about it. [...] I think one of the reasons for this is that the particular experience which ought to have enabled me to think much more closely and critically about it was for various reasons at that time very much in abeyance: the Welsh experience. The way I used the term community actually rested on my memories of Wales as I've said. But the Welsh experience was also precisely one of subjection to English expansion and assimilation historically. That is what ought to have most alerted me to the dangers of a persuasive type of definition of community, which is as once dominant and exclusive.[45]

It is this passage that Edward Said had in mind when he recalled that Williams related the absence of 'Empire' in *Culture and Society* to the 'unavailability at the time of [his] Welsh experience' that wasn't 'as important... then as it later became'.[46] This would seem to suggest that any discussion of Williams's engagement with the question of colonialism should take place in the light of his meditations on his Welsh experience.

Unfortunately, the Welsh dimension of Williams's thought is never referred to by Said in his influential reading of *The Country and the City* (1973) that appeared in *Culture and Imperialism* (1993).[47] In that analysis, Said registers the fact that Williams 'does address the export of England to the colonies' but argues that he does so 'in a less focused way and less expansively than the practice actually warrants'.[48] He proceeds to criticise Williams for having limited his discussion of imperialism to the mid-nineteenth century and after. This is a criticism that could be justifiably made of the entry on 'Imperialism' in *Keywords* (1976), but is less applicable to *The Country and the City*, where, in his chapter on 'The New Metropolis', Williams brings the question of colonialism into the centre of his analysis:[49]

> In 1700 fifteen per cent of British commerce was with the colonies. In 1775 it was as much as a third. In an intricate process of economic interaction, supported by wars between the trading nations for control of the areas of supply, an organised colonial system and the development of an industrial economy changed the nature of British society.[50]

Following this discussion of how the consolidation of the plantation economies was dependent on the slave trade, Williams comments that

> The unprecedented events of the nineteenth century, in which Britain became a predominantly industrial and urban society, with its agriculture declining to marginal status, are inexplicable and would have been impossible without this colonial development.[51]

Dai Smith correctly notes that *The Country and the City* marks the moment in Williams's work when 'the wider, encompassing, anglocentric references are often brought up against Irish, Scottish and, more unknown to his readers, Welsh sources of enquiry', but these Celtic references are themselves supplemented by discussions of Indian and African writers whose names were in more limited circulation in 1973 than they are today: Achebe, Nwankwo, Ngugi and Narayan.[52] *The Country and City* expanded the boundaries of literary study as it was practised in 1973, and can hardly be regarded as the work of a man who, according to Gauri Viswanathan, 'consistently and exclusively' studied 'the formation of metropolitan culture from within its own boundaries'.[53]

It is a characteristic of Williams's work that issues which were given more theoretical formulations in the 1970s had already been explored in fictional form in his novels. In the opening paragraph of *Border Country*, Matthew Price travels by bus:

> The conductress, a West Indian, smiled as he jumped to the platform, and he said, 'Good evening', and was answered, with an easiness that had almost been lost. You don't speak to people in London, he remembered; in fact you don't speak to people anywhere in England; there is plenty of time for that sort of thing on the appointed occasions...[54]

The legacy of empire, embodied in the conductress, is there in the novel's opening scene, and is related narratively to the fact – revealed in the following paragraph – that Price is 'working on population movements into Welsh mining valleys in the middle decades of the nineteenth century'.[55] The opening paragraphs of *Border Country* thus make a connection between those contemporary and historical 'population movements' that Williams went on to explore in a more analytical vein in *The Country and the City*. This opening does raise some problems of representation, for whilst the fact that the West Indian conductress is rendered voiceless in this passage can be defended in that the whole scene is narrated from Price's point of view, the reference to her 'easiness that had almost been lost' is dangerously close to reinforcing a primitivist stereotype. This 'ease' of speech is encountered again, however, upon Price's return to his native border country. The initial tense and formal exchanges between Matthew Price and his father's friend Morgan Rosser give way to the native rhythms of the border as Price notes that 'it was easy at last, and enough had been re-established'.[56] We're told later that Edwin Parry, a local farmer, follows Harry Price back to his railway signal box 'with the local reluctance to turn away from any man just met'.[57] Thus Matthew Price's recognition of the West Indian conductress's 'ease of speech' is not based on the shocking revelation of racial otherness, but is in fact based on the awareness that this is a manner of speaking and being that he recognises from his own upbringing.

The danger inherent in connecting a West-Indian and Welsh 'ease of speech' lies in the construction of a simplistic binary contrast (not wholly absent from Williams's later writings on modernism) between the alienated individualism of the metropolitan centre and the warm communal spirit maintained against all the odds by marginalised peoples – an argument that can be traced (as it relates to Wales) back through D. H. Lawrence's celebration of a primitivist Celticism in *St Mawr* (1924) to Matthew Arnold's earlier celebration of Celtic spirituality in *On the Study of Celtic Literature* (1867).[58] There is evidence, especially in the later writings, that Williams was fully aware of the ways in which the 'marginalised' or 'oppressed' can become fashionable symbols of resistance, most strikingly in the novel *Loyalties*, where Emma, a middle class radical, is seen in the 1980s to replace her picture of 'green heads of miners' with 'an embroidered African landscape'.[59] Against such primitivist pitfalls, Williams emphasises historical change and human mobility. In the movements back and forth between Wales and England, which is characteristic of all the novels in the 'Welsh Trilogy', Williams is arguing that all places and peoples have lives and internal tensions of their own; nowhere exists merely as a static, unchanging and idealised background for something or someone else.[60]

This truth is explored in greater detail in the more ambitious but ultimately less successful novel, *Second Generation* (1964), where the experience of the British working class in the 1960s is increasingly related to the legacies of Empire. This thematic thread reaches its climax at a party where the central character Peter Owen engages in the following conversation with two representatives from the West African Federation.

"I have been having an argument with the Minister," Okoi said. "I have been saying our nationalism is now too evident, and that we are not doing enough in the struggle with poverty."

"The distinction is false," Akande said. "But this is still the class struggle, only now between nations ... Nationalism" he said precisely "is in this sense like class. To have it, and to feel it, is the only way to end it. If you fail to claim it, or give it up too soon, you will merely be cheated, by other classes and other nations."

"I agree," Peter said. "This is what I've been learning."

"Then I wish you luck, Mr Owen."

"I wish you luck, Mr Akande. Both of you," he added, smiling across at Okoi.

"It will be more than luck, it will be struggle, Peter," Okoi said.[61]

What Peter 'has been learning' is arguably reflective of what Williams had himself been learning about the complex relationships between class, nationhood and identity at the time of writing *Second Generation*. Two reiterated positions, which emerge in his engagements with the national question, are implicit in the (rather ponderous) dialogue above. Firstly, that whilst class and nation are distinct social categories, they may both offer possible resources for communal identity and political action. A politics based on 'class' or 'nation' will be partly played out on a terrain defined by one's antagonists, but these forms of identity cannot be circumvented; they must be embraced and worked through towards alternative forms of being and belonging. Secondly, whilst the British left has traditionally been opposed to nationalism in all its forms (whilst being blind to its own national biases), Akande's words suggest that it is in fact necessary to discriminate between nationalism's emancipatory and oppressive forms. In his writings from the early 1970s onwards, Raymond Williams would increasingly apply these issues – discussed here by a second-generation member of Oxford's Welsh community and two representatives of newly independent African nations – to his own Welsh experience.

These themes are expressed explicitly, and related to Wales, in Williams's *Poetry Wales* interview of 1977:

I think the point about nationalism really is this, that we're dealing with an entirely different phenomenon when it is a case of a marginal or absorbed or oppressed nationality, the sense of difference from some particular dominant large nation-state or of course empire. In the twentieth century we've seen so many examples of people breaking free from that kind of sense of domination, and I don't see how any serious socialist in the Marxist tradition could be other than with them. You see it's all right when it's the heroic examples like the North Vietnamese, or the Africans... When it comes back to Europe, there's been such a lot of impatience among traditional Marxists that I found that Sartre writing about the Basques had for me a lot of the right sense of this, that people should determine, since it is the crucial thing for them, the conditions of their own social being. And this is the Marxist project. It is extraordinarily difficult to rule out on abstract grounds some particular project which describes itself as nationalist. I often think that is not what it is, but it is the obvious thing to call it, when it comes up in Wales or Ireland, or Scotland or Brittany.[62]

This passage enacts a simultaneous movement outwards towards nationalist struggles in South-East Asia and Africa, and 'back to Europe' to the struggles of the Basques and the Celtic peoples. By placing the Welsh experience within the context of anti-colonial struggles, and by emphasising the need to apply some of the lessons learnt from those struggles 'back to Europe', Williams offers a useful and timely corrective to the binary terms in which contemporary post-colonial criticism is often conducted. Whilst post-colonial critics have demonstrated an awareness of the dangers of homogenising 'the East' in their writings, they are far less inclined to register the equally disabling tendency to homogenise 'the West'.[63] Whilst it is crucial to note the central role that the Celtic peoples willingly played in Britain's imperial project, the problems that arise from totalising 'the West' as the homogenous centre of imperial power can be illustrated in Edward Said's discussions of Ireland in *Culture and Imperialism*. 'What are some of the non-Middle Eastern materials drawn on here?' asks Said in his introduction,

European writing on Africa, India, parts of the Far East, Australia, and the Caribbean; these Africanist and Indianist

discourses, as some of them have been called, I see as part of
the general European effort to rule distant lands and peoples
and, therefore, as related to Orientalist descriptions of the
Islamic world, as well as to Europe's special ways of representing the Caribbean islands, Ireland and the Far East.[64]

How can it be possible for Said to analyse 'Europe's special ways'
of 'representing... Ireland', or, later, for him to describe the movements of 'armed resistance in places as diverse as nineteenth century
Algeria, Ireland, and Indonesia' as examples of 'the great movement
of decolonization' that swept 'across the Third World'? [65] It seems that
to follow Williams in placing Ireland in Europe, and to see the Irish
nationalist struggle as part of similar minority nationalist struggles in
Europe, would disrupt the binary distinction of East versus West on
which Said bases his discussions of literature and culture. Williams, in
the pieces collected in this volume, relates Wales simultaneously to a
wider colonial context, to other minority struggles in Europe, and is
also always fully aware of the often bitter cultural debates taking place
within and between the diverse communities constituting Wales itself.
    In 1975, before the emergence of post-colonial criticism,
Williams described Welsh culture as 'a post-colonial culture, conscious all the time of its own real strengths and potentials, longing
only to be itself, to become its own world but with much, too
much on its back to be able, consistently, to face its real future'.[66]
The precise meaning of 'post-colonial' in 1970s Wales is somewhat
ambiguous. Indeed, the extent to which the Welsh experience could
ever have been described as 'colonial', let alone 'post-colonial', is a
topic of considerable controversy in Welsh historiography and cultural studies, with the divisions in Wales closely mirroring the more
infamous 'revisionist' debates that have animated Irish cultural studies
in recent decades.[67] The Welsh had historically been avid contributors
to the British imperial project, and Williams registers the fact that a
'large number of Welsh people found temporary effective political
identity in wider movements' such as the 'Empire, in which there was
so much direct interest'.[68] If the Welsh had been colonisers, there is
also considerable evidence to suggest that Williams also conceived of
the Welsh as an internally colonised people within the British State.[69]
Williams notes that colonisation has taken several different forms in

Wales. Politically, colonisation results in 'a newly formalised centralization of government and administration continuously "delegating"
and "devolving" limited kinds of authority'.[70] Culturally, it has led
to 'several centuries of political domination, and of consequent cultural indifference, often punctuated by aggression', resulting in the
lamentable fact that there 'is a vernacular tradition on this island …
which a majority even of literary specialists are content to know little
about'.[71] Psychologically, it leads to a situation in which 'parts of your
mind are taken over by a system of ideas, a system of feelings, which
really do emanate from the power centre. Right back in your own
mind, and right back inside the oppressed and deprived community,
there are reproduced elements of the thinking and the feeling of that
dominating centre.'[72] It seems that Williams is not using the term
'post-colonial' to refer to the demise of British imperialism, nor to
suggest that the effects of England's colonial relationship with Wales is
at an end. Rather, Williams shares novelist Emyr Humphreys's recent
use of the term to describe 'the consolidation of colonial occupation
into a settled state of affairs'.[73]

One of the most heated areas of debate in Welsh cultural studies has been over the Welsh language, with the nationalist account
of decline due to the cultural colonialism of an imposed English
language educational system coming under attack from a school of
revisionist historians who argue that the language 'was not mortally
wounded because of schools in the past', for the Welsh were happily
abandoning Welsh (the language of 'customs, traditions, religion,
language and deference') for English (the language of modernity).[74]
Whilst Williams can typically see some validity in both accounts,
his position on the language question is unambiguous. He notes in
'Welsh Culture', for instance, that

> language wasn't only driven back by the Industrial Revolution
> and its movements of people. It was also driven back by
> conscious repression, by penalty and contempt, and in a late
> phase by deliberate policy in the schools. You can still see,
> as carefully preserved as the old tools, the little boards, the
> 'Welsh Nots', which children caught speaking their mother
> tongue had to hang round their necks, for shame. It is bound
> to be wrong to forget or forgive that. It is bound to be right

to use and teach a language still living, after all the attacks on it.[75]

Similarly, in 'Boyhood' he refers to how his own native border country was 'Anglicized' due to the 'conscious pressure through the schools to eliminate the language, which included punishment for children who spoke Welsh'.[76] Revisionists counter this traditionally nationalist emphasis on the role played by the Welsh Not and on 'punishment for children' in the eradication of the language by noting that the Welsh Not was in very limited usage, that its use was generally supported by Welsh parents, and that when 'it was employed in British schools it was also stamped on by the higher authorities immediately'.[77] Williams would certainly have been aware of these debates – indeed he positively reviews some of the key texts of Welsh revisionism in this volume – but it is surely feasible to accept the revisionists' point that the use of the Welsh Not was not as widespread as nationalist myths suggest, without losing sight of the fact that where it was in use it laid bare in a particularly graphic and symbolic manner the status and position of Welsh culture within the British state.[78]

Williams's support for the Welsh language's continued existence is not based upon, nor does it ever lead him to embrace, a familiar form of cultural nationalism which regards the endangered language as the guardian of the nation's 'spiritual inheritance' and the only basis for national identity.[79] (I shall return to Williams's definition of the nation.) His engagement with the actual history of modern Wales made him resistant to any such totalising narratives. During the past thirty years, a generation of Welsh historians have documented the transformation of an agricultural people of about 500,000 in 1800 into an urban population of 2,500,000 by 1911.[80] The shift from a pastoral country with its population fairly evenly spread throughout its regions into a predominantly industrial nation with its urban majority packed into the southern coalfield was accompanied by significant cultural shifts that were the making of modern Wales: geographically from country to city; politically from Liberal to Labour; linguistically from Welsh to English. None of these cultural shifts was to eradicate wholly what Williams referred to as 'residual' cultural practices (nonconformist religion in the past, for instance, the Welsh language or working-class consciousness today) which continued to have an impact upon the dominant culture and could potentially be turned to as resources for resistance in the emergent future. 'If there is one thing to insist on in analysing Welsh culture', notes Williams when discussing this history, 'it is the complex of forced and acquired discontinuities: a broken series of radical shifts, within which we have to mark not only certain social and linguistic continuities but many acts of self-definition by negation, by alternation and by contrast'.[81] Thus, whilst he often locates Wales within a 'post-colonial' context, Williams resists simplistic, binary accounts of Welsh culture and society, and instead emphasises the complexities and ambiguities of the Welsh experience in order to 'put questions to those simple, confident, unitary identities which really belong to an earlier historical period'.[82]

THE CULTURE OF NATIONS

Williams's critical engagements with Welsh history and culture put significant questions to the prevalent models used for understanding manifestations of national identity. In his 1979 interviews with the *New Left Review*, Williams traced the British left's blindness to questions of national identity to the unconscious tendency in the post-war years to conflate the terms 'state' and 'nation':

> The very idea of 'nationalization', as a key political term, rested on the assumption by the left that the nation was an unproblematic entity. In other words, we were quite insufficiently aware of the post-war capitalist state. The most welcome single introduction into Marxist thought of the last decade has been the decisive re-entry of the problem of the capitalist state. All these terms are no longer so easily elided.[83]

Williams played a part in this 'decisive re-entry of the problem of the capitalist state' into Marxist thought. The first positive reference to the nationalist movements in Wales and Scotland in his writings, for instance, occurs in the context of a critique of the capitalist state in the *May Day Manifesto* (1967), where he noted that 'what the nationalist parties are demanding is a necessary and inevitable challenge to centralized managed politics and to a capitalism which, creating prosperity in favoured regions, creates poverty in unfavoured'.[84]

Whilst this economic defence of minority nationalist movements is a recurrent element in Williams's work, the main focus and emphasis of his writings on Wales and national identity is on the cultural rather than the political or economic dimensions of nationhood. Williams's increasing engagement with Wales in his theoretical writings can be read as a part of the New Left's attempt to think beyond capitalist state formations, and throughout his extensive (but generally ignored) discussions of the national question he seeks to maintain a distinction between the culturally defined 'people' and the politically defined 'state'. This distinction can be traced to Williams's Welshness for, as he notes several times in the following essays, Welsh identity 'was primarily cultural – in language, customs, kinship and community – rather than in any modern sense political'.[85] The problematic status of Wales and Welshness is a persistent theme in Williams's writings where he interrogates the question of 'whether Wales – or, put it another way, the Welsh – is a nation or a people or, as seen from elsewhere, a region'.[86] This historical ambiguity poses a challenge to those who wish to formulate all-encompassing theories of nationalism for, as Adrian Hastings notes in his recent *The Construction of Nationhood* (1997), 'we are still after more than a thousand years not quite sure where the Welsh stand – an ethnicity in Britain or even, as at one time seemed the case, within England, a nation in a multi-nation state, even (still to come) a nation-state of their own?'[87] Typically, Williams does not lament the lack of a coherent, official identity, for

> [o]ne of the central advantages of being born and bred among the presumed Welsh is the profusion of official identities. Wales and Monmouthshire, as it was for me at school, with special force since we lived in the append-age. England-and-Wales: that administrative, legal and even weather-forecasting area. Wales for rugby but All-England for cricket. Welsh Wales and English Wales. Wales and Cymru. To anyone looking for an official status it was a nightmare. To anyone trying to think about communities and societies a blessing: a native gift.[88]

It is this 'native gift' that results in the Welsh ability to question the 'imposed definitions' of '"Britishness" … "the United Kingdom" and "The Yookay"'.[89] In Williams's writings, the state is invariably the vehicle for the enforcement of such 'unitary identities'. These imposed identities are resisted by a 'community'; the cultural sphere which is potentially the location of radical ambiguities and resistance.[90]

In the (often repetitive) analyses of nationalism offered by political theorists and historians in recent years, an atavistic, backward and reactionary cultural nationalism is contrasted with, and is often seen to give way to, a healthy, civic, political nationalism. John Hutchinson has noted how even those theorists who register the importance of authors, poets, historians and linguists in the task of nation building continue to consider cultural nationalism to be a regressive force, 'a product of intellectuals from backward societies, who, when confronted by more scientifically advanced cultures, compensate for feelings of inferiority by retreating into history to claim descent from a once great civilisation'.[91] If a theoretical distinction can be made between ethnic and civic forms of nationalism, Williams notes that in practice these types will frequently overlap, and a given national culture will display both ethnic and civic components in its forms of nationhood.[92] He argues, for instance, that the various forms of 'Welshness' are typically 'simultaneously political and cultural', and thus suggests that whether created in the crucible of culture or formed by the development of political institutions, all nations are to some extent 'cultural' entities.[93]

If Williams's account of national identity offers an useful corrective to those who discuss nationalism merely at the level of politics and statehood, the cultural definition of the nation leads logically to one of two highly problematic positions: an authoritarian monoculturalism where the culture of one ethnic or linguistic group is promoted as the only 'authentic' national culture, or a self-frustrating libertarianism where any claim to national distinctiveness evaporates as the 'nation' is regarded as a vessel in which a limitless plurality of cultures may co-inhabit and co-exist with equal validity. Williams attempts to walk a tightrope between these two positions; he insists that it is 'from recognizing the plurality, instead of insisting on the authority of any chosen (but then competitive) singularity, that we can learn to be open to each other', but then sees that plurality as the basis for making 'the effort to move through to effective new common ground'.[94] The structure of this argument – where plurality forms the basis for a new sense of Welsh communality – is repeated throughout the writings collected in this volume. Williams notes, for instance, that the 'major Welsh response' to what we may identify as the postmodern 'dissolutions of community and identity', is to attempt 'to remake communities and identities which will hold'.[95] Wales may then offer a location for the realisation of Williams's call in *Towards 2000* (1983) for 'a new kind of socialist movement' based on 'a wide range of needs and interests', which can be gathered into 'a new definition of the general interest'.[96]

The deepest desire in Williams's cultural thought, from the 1950s onwards, is towards making connections in the name of a cultural 'wholeness', a 'common culture' or a 'general interest'. Capitalism is to be resisted as a system for it breeds divisions; of classes, of peoples, of nations. Thus, when asking in the late-1970s, 'Are We Becoming More Divided?', Williams was attempting to address the challenge posed by his self-conscious Welshness to his fundamental belief in the possibility of a humanist, universal, culture. The question was answered in the following terms:

> In Wales [...] – and I think this would be even more true of Scotland – we have always been aware of the deep differences between industrial South Wales, rural North and West Wales, and the very specific border country from which I myself come. We don't get past that by inventing a pseudo-historical or romantic Welshness; indeed that would only divide us further. We get past it by looking and working for unity in the definition and the development of a modern Wales, in which the really powerful impulses – to discover an effective modern community and to take control of our own energies and resources – can be practically worked through. That is what I mean by saying that the nationalist movements, while they can be seen from one position as working to divide, must be seen from another position as working to unite.[97]

Again, the 'deep differences' between the different parts of Wales are foregrounded, with contemporary nationalism being valued for its move beyond 'pseudo-historical and romantic' methods of imagining community towards a more materialist attempt at taking 'control of our own energies and resources'. It is not wholly clear what Williams means when he talks of 'discover[ing] an effective community' however. This ambiguity is also present in 'Wales and England', where Williams notes that 'to mistake the state for the real identity, or the projections for the people' won't help 'either side of the border', an insight which he develops further in the chapter on 'The Culture of Nations' in *Towards 2000* (1983):[98]

> All the real processes have been cultural and historical, and all the artificial processes have been political, in one after another dominative proclamation of a state and an identity.[99]

'Effective communities', 'real identities', 'real processes'; the weaknesses of arguments based on such undefined terms are surely almost too obviously apparent. Francis Mulhern, in an early response to *Towards 2000*, noted that the nations produced through the expansion of capitalism are 'more than flag-bedecked marketplaces... They are collective identifications with strong supports in economic, cultural and political histories; they are, as much as any competing formation, "communities".'[100] This pertinent criticism was taken a step further by Paul Gilroy, who in a harsh and influential critique, accused Williams of drawing 'precisely the same picture of the relationship between "race," national identity and citizenship' as Enoch Powell.[101]

In his seminal account of the 'cultural politics of race and nation' in Britain, *'There Ain't No Black in the Union Jack'* (1987), Gilroy argues that Williams's ideas of nationhood are based on notions of racial authenticity, which he detects in the following passage from 'The Culture of Nations':

> ... it is a serious misunderstanding... to suppose that the problems of social identity are resolved by formal (merely legal) definitions. For unevenly and at times precariously, but always through long experience substantially, an effective awareness of social identity depends on actual and sustained social relationships. To reduce social identity to formal legal definitions, at the level of the state, is to collude in the alienated superficialities of 'the nation' which are the limited functional terms of the modern ruling class.[102]

Given the seriousness and severity of the critique, it is worth quoting Gilroy's discussion of this passage at some length. Gilroy refers back to the preceding passage in *Towards 2000*, and notes that Williams's remarks are a response

> to anti-racists who would answer the denial that blacks can be British by saying 'They are as British as you are'. He dismisses this reply as 'the standard liberal' variety. His alternative conception stresses that social identity is a product of 'long experience'. But this prompts the question – how long is long enough to become a genuine Brit? His insistence that the origins of racial conflict lie in the hostility between strangers in the city makes little sense given the effects of the 1971 Immigration Act in halting primary black settlement. More disturbingly, these arguments effectively deny that blacks can share a significant 'social identity' with their white neighbours who, in contrast to more recent arrivals, inhabit what Williams calls 'rooted settlements' articulated by 'lived and formed identities'... His use of the term 'social identity' is both significant and misleading. It minimises the specificities of nationalism and ideologies of national identity and diverts attention from analysis of the political processes by which national and social identities have been aligned ... How these social identities relate to the conspicuous differences of language and culture is unclear except where Williams points out that the forms of identity fostered by the 'artificial order' of the nation state are incomplete and empty when compared to 'full social identities in their real diversity'. This does not, of course, make them any the less vicious. Where racism demands repatriation and pivots on the exclusion of certain groups from the imagined community of the nation, the contradictions around citizenship that Williams dismisses as 'alienated superficialities' remain important constituents of the political field. They provide an important point of entry into the nation's sense of itself. [...] Quite apart from Williams's apparent endorsement of the presuppositions of the new racism, the strategic silences in his work contribute directly to its strength and resilience.[103]

The passage in 'The Culture of Nations' from which Gilroy selects his quotations reads rather differently when placed in its proper context, and when placed alongside Williams's discussions of Welsh national identity. Gilroy chooses to ignore the fact that Williams makes it patently clear in the chapter that he does not deny the indispensability of citizenship rights for immigrants. Indeed, he notes explicitly that 'a merely legal definition of what it is to be "British"... is necessary and important, correctly asserting the need for equality and protection within the laws'.[104] Williams's point is that appeals to abstract legal rights, and to facile and patronising ideas of 'assimilation', are not equal to the social strains of Britain's changing ethnic composition. This argument is in fact in keeping with Gilroy's own analysis, a few pages later, of a Conservative Party election poster of 1983 that set an image of a black male above the caption: 'Labour says he's black. Tories say he's British.' Gilroy argues that the term 'Britain' is being used here to suggest that 'the category of citizen and the formal belonging which it bestows on its black holders are essentially colour-less, or at least colour-blind... Blacks are being invited to forsake all that marks them out as culturally distinct before real Britishness can be guaranteed.'[105] This argument seems to be very much in keeping with Williams's own critique of the ways in which a dominant national identity can be used to obscure economic disparities and legitimate cultural and historical differences. It is precisely this mystifying use of 'Britishness' that Williams is problematising when he questions the validity of the 'standard liberal reply' that 'they are as British as you are' when faced with 'protests at the arrival or presence of "foreigners" or "aliens"'. Gilroy responds to Williams's striking shift of attention from the 'ideology of the protest' to the 'ideology of the reply', by asking him 'how long is long enough to become a genuine Brit' and by suggesting that Williams is denying 'that blacks can share a significant social identity with their white neighbours'.[106]

There are several possible responses to this. Firstly, unlike Enoch Powell and the various ideologues of the new right, Williams is not comparing an unproblematic, rooted 'Britishness' with the newer, less 'rooted' and thus less 'authentic' identities of immigrants. 'Britishness' itself was not only a problematic term for Williams the 'Welsh-European' in the 1980s; it was a term, he notes, which 'was not used much, except by people one distrusted' during his boyhood years on the Welsh border.[107] Secondly, at no point does Williams deny 'that blacks can share a significant social identity with their white neighbours', nor does he ever suggest that the 'origins of racial conflict lie in the hostility between strangers in the city'. Williams prefaces the passages quoted by Gilroy by noting that

> What is from time to time projected as an 'island race' is in reality a long process of successive conquests and repressions but also of successive supersessions and relative integrations... [I]t should be obvious that this long and unfinished process cannot reasonably be repressed by versions of a national history and a patriotic heritage which deliberately exclude its complexities and in doing so reject its many surviving and diverse identities.[108]

Cultural diversity thus predates the arrival of immigrants. Williams reinforces this insight towards the end of the chapter where he typically relates the preceding discussion to Welsh history and his own Welsh experience.

> It happens that I grew up in an old frontier area, the Welsh border country, where for centuries there was bitter fighting and raiding and repression and discrimination, and where, within twenty miles of where I was born, there were in those turbulent centuries as many as four different everyday spoken languages. It is with this history in mind that I believe in the practical formation of social identity – it is now very marked there – and know that necessarily it has to be lived. Not far away there are the Welsh mining valleys, into which in the nineteenth century there was massive and diverse immigration, but in which, after two generations, there were some of the most remarkably solid and mutually loyal communities of which we have record. These are the real grounds of hope.[109]

Far from denying that immigrants can share a significant social identity with the settled population, Williams actually turns to the diversity of the south Walian experience as 'the real ground of hope'.[110] At no point in his discussion does Gilroy make any reference to Williams's writings on Wales, and he thus fails to see that Williams is arguing that the production and reproduction of social life – not always under conditions of one's own making – ultimately determines the variable forms of identity and expression available to a people. It is precisely by drawing attention to the ways in which Welsh history foregrounds people's ability to construct loyal communities out of linguistic, national and cultural diversity that Williams attempts, in the words of Cornel West, to 'anchor socialist politics to the contingent constructions of identities'.[111]

Whilst I believe it to be wholly misleading to argue that Williams endorses the presuppositions of the 'new racism', Gilroy is surely right to criticise the rather simplistic contrast between 'artificial' political communities and 'real' cultural communities in Williams's discussion, and there is no doubt that this undermines the balance of his brief analysis of racism in Britain. The question that we face when engaging with Williams's writings on Wales, and with Gilroy's critique of his ideas of nationhood, is how far is it possible to travel away from an insistence on national authenticity, with its inherent dangers of nativism, racism and xenophobia, before a culture is stripped of any specificity? This is a question of particular importance in Wales where, from the late nineteenth century onwards, a nationalist desire to transcend cultural differences in order to forge a viable (but occasionally culturally repressive) sense of a single national identity has co-existed with an awareness of the cultural diversity of a modern Wales that emerged with the industrial revolution. It is a question that lies at the heart of Raymond Williams's engagement with his 'native country', and forces us to consider what, ultimately, forms the basis for his idea of Wales.

THE UNANSWERED QUESTION

It is important to note at the outset that – despite the accusations of his detractors – at no point does Raymond Williams base his concept of the nation on ideas of race. In his entry on 'Nationalism' in *Keywords* (1976), Williams attempts to separate the term 'nation' from its past associations with ideas of 'race':

> It could be and is still often said, by opponents of nationalism, that the basis of the group's claims is racial. (**Race**, of

uncertain origin, had been used in the sense of a common stock from C16. **Racial** is a C19 formation. In most C19 uses racial was positive and favourable, but discriminating and arbitrary theories of race were becoming more explicit in the same period, generalizing national distinctions to supposedly radical scientific differences. **Racial** was eventually affected by criticism of these kinds of thinking, and acquired both specific and loose negative senses. **Racialism** is a C20 formation to characterise, and usually to criticize, these explicit distinctions and discriminations.) It was also said that the claims were 'selfish', as being against the interests of the nation (the existing larger political group). In practice, given the extent of conquest and domination, nationalist movements have been as often based on an existing but subordinate political grouping as upon a group distinguished by a specific language or by a supposed racial community.[112]

The scepticism towards racial definitions of nationhood expressed in this piece – '*supposedly* racial scientific differences', '*supposed* racial community' (my emphasis) – is reinforced more explicitly in the rejection of racial definitions of the nation in Williams's writings on Wales. In exploring the 'differentials of Wales' in his chapter on 'Wales and England', Williams notes explicitly that

> [w]e need not stay long in one of the most populated regions, that of race. The ethnic history of what is now Wales is one of extreme complexity, from the earliest times. [...] We do not even have wholly to deny some observable clusters of some physical features – trends and emphases within a most complex map – to continue to insist that the significant differentials are not in this region at all.[113]

He proceeds to note later in the same chapter that the modern 'revival' of Welsh nationhood 'is the working through of history, among now radically dislocated as well as subordinated people, rather than the fortunate re-emergence of a subdued essence'.[114]

This shift from 'racial' to 'historical' definitions of nationalism is a familiar strategy employed by those who attempt to formulate liberal and pluralist definitions of the nation. It is arguable, however, that the substitution of 'race' with 'history' is never wholly convincing. Sharing a common national history cannot be a criterion for being members of the same nation, for we would have to be members of the same 'nation' in order to identify with its history in the first place. The American critic Walter Benn Michaels has argued that contemporary discussions of culture and multiculturalism are still based on the racial categories that they seek to reject, and a similar argument could be made with regard to Williams's attempts to distance 'nation' from 'race'. Benn Michaels states that

> insofar as our culture remains nothing more than what we do and believe, it is impotently descriptive. The fact, in other words, that something belongs to our culture, cannot count as a motive for our doing it since, if it *does* belong to our culture we are *already* doing it, and if we don't do it (if we've stopped or haven't yet started doing it) it doesn't belong to our culture... It is only if we think that our culture is not whatever beliefs and practices we actually happen to have but is instead the beliefs and practices that should properly go with the kind of people we happen to be that the fact of something belonging to our culture can count as a reason for doing it. But to think this is to appeal to something that must be beyond culture and that cannot be derived from culture precisely because our sense of which culture is properly ours must be derived from it. This has been the function of race. [...] The modern concept of culture is not, in other words, a critique of racism; it is a form of racism.[115]

Williams's understanding of Welsh culture tends to veer uneasily between the two poles of Benn Michaels's analysis; between an idea of culture as what 'we are already doing', and an idea of culture as what we should be doing given 'the kind of people we happen to be'. Welsh nationalist claims for historical and cultural continuity have, historically, been based on appeals to a language and literature dating back to the sixth century. Williams, as already noted, recognises the 'truth' of that claim and expresses a conditional support for forms of identity based on linguistic distinctiveness. In the

1977 interview with *Poetry Wales*, he recognises that the valuable sense that 'it is possible to be a different people' exists 'very strongly in Wales because there's the great continuity of the language', and in exploring the similarities and differences between Wales and England in 1983 he notes that '[t]he central continuity is of course the language, and this remains critical to cultural identity not only in those who have retained or are reacquiring it, but even in many of those to whom it is now lost or marginal'.[116] To base one's sense of Welshness on the language, at a time when it is spoken by less than 20 per cent of the population, is inevitably to subscribe to an understanding of culture as, in Benn Michaels's terms, 'the beliefs and practices that should properly go with the kind of people we happen to be'. Williams's acceptance of a valuable linguistic continuity is conditional, however, in the sense that support for the maintenance of an endangered language should not result in a definition of the nation that excludes over three-quarters of its non-Welsh-speaking inhabitants. Culture is primarily 'ordinary' for Williams, it is what 'we are already doing', as both Welsh-speakers and English-speakers. Thus, whilst registering the value and validity of a Welshness based in linguistic continuity, at the heart of Williams's engagement with Wales lies 'the turbulent experience of industrial South Wales, over the last two centuries, and its powerful political and communal formations', which lead not to 'the abandonment of "Welshness", in some singular and unitary form', but rather to 'the positive creation of a still distinctively Welsh, English-speaking working-class culture'.[117]

Williams's engagement with the culture of south Wales manifests itself powerfully in his series of seminal lectures and chapters on the English language literature of Wales. These chapters can be read as part of Williams's life-long project of challenging the values and assumptions behind the 'selective tradition' underpinning the teaching of English literature. Long before 'questioning the canon' had become a central preoccupation for literary critics, Williams in works such as *The English Novel from Dickens to Lawrence* (1971) was offering a critique of the taught canon of English literature whilst self-consciously constructing his own alternative to Leavis's 'great tradition'. The very notion of creating literary traditions was problematised in a more radical fashion in *The Country and the City*

(1973), which challenged the recognisable borders of literary study in bringing the dominant English tradition up against Welsh, Scottish, Irish, African and Indian sources of inquiry. This project took on a more explicitly theoretical form in *Marxism and Literature* (1977), where Williams noted the ways in which a selective definition of literature was confirmed by literary criticism in the kind of mutually supportive relationships that underpinned all 'selective traditions' in which

> the 'national literature' soon ceased to be a history and became a tradition. It was not, even theoretically, all that had been written or all kinds of writing. It was a selection which culminated in, and in a circular way defined, the 'literary values' which 'criticism' was asserting. [...] To oppose the terms of this ratification was to be 'against literature'.[118]

At a time when no comprehensive taxonomy of English language Welsh fiction existed in even the most basic bibliographical sense, Williams's essays on Welsh industrial fiction played a key role in establishing the parameters for the study of Welsh writing in English – ignored by English literary critics and regarded with suspicion and disdain by many Welsh language writers. Williams's emphasis throughout is that the vibrancy of Welsh literature, emanating from a fractured history, should never atrophy into a 'tradition'. Thus, whilst engaging in a process of creating a tradition of male, working-class, south-Walian writers in the following quotation, Williams is also drawing attention to the limits of that tradition and expressing a desire to move beyond it:

> From the 1920s, through to the 1940s there was an effective tradition of novels in English about the industrial crisis: Jack Jones, Gwyn Jones, Lewis Jones, Richard Llewellyn. Limited as this was, it is still remarkable in Europe as a form of writing largely by, about and for a conscious working class. But for some of its weaker examples, and from commercial projection and stereotyping, it had an opposite effect, in the end, stabilising a type of writing about Wales which persisted after the major crisis that had given the original validity.[119]

He thus proceeds in a number of the literary essays collected in this volume to move beyond the formal and linguistic boundaries of this realist canon to a discussion of Gwyn Thomas's experiments with realist, mythic and comic forms in *All Things Betray Thee* (1949), and T. Rowland Hughes's explorations of a Welsh-speaking working-class experience in *Chwalfa* (1946).[120]

Christopher Prendergast, in discussing Williams's literary criticism, argues that 'what seems to count most for Williams is, relatedly, an aesthetic of integration and a culture of (relative) settlement, as modes of life and practice in which connections are to be found or can be made'.[121] This, for Prendergast, explains Williams's return 'to the idea of realism' in his literary essays, where he is 'very close... to Lukács' in 'preferring to the art of dispersal and fragmentation promoted by the sanctioned versions of modernism an art that connects, especially... forms that join, as mutually necessary for intelligibility, individual experience and social formation'.[122] Whilst this argument is certainly relevant to *The English Novel from Dickens to Lawrence*, it is revealing that in the case of Welsh literature Williams, despite championing the writings of the 1930s realists, is primarily attracted to two non-representational narratives where the consistent voice of the omniscient realist narrator gives way to a chorus of competing voices, and where the view of the world is coloured by wild hyperbole and black comedy: Dylan Thomas's 'play for voices' *Under Milk Wood* (1954) and Gwyn Thomas's *All Things Betray Thee* (1949). Both works can be seen to illustrate Williams's notion that 'Welsh writers cannot accept the English pressure towards a fiction of private lives'.[123] Dylan Thomas follows Joyce in discovering a 'living convention' that juxtaposes the 'language of dream' to the 'public language of chorus and rhetoric', and Gwyn Thomas creates 'a composition of voices' that will express a historical experience not confined to the 'flattened representations or the applied ideological phrases'.[124] If 'tradition' implies closure, the many-voiced writings of Gwyn Thomas and Dylan Thomas engage with a living history that suggests development.

This celebration of dialogue and plurality in the writings of Gwyn Thomas and Dylan Thomas reinforces Williams's emphasis that Wales 'has been a plurality of cultures' resulting in a situation in which 'any formulation becomes a challenge'.[125] Such statements have been characteristic of the tone and tenor of Welsh literary and historical studies since the late 1970s, with Gwyn Williams *When Was Wales?* (1985) and Dai Smith's *Wales! Wales?* (1984) 'pick[ing] up the tone' of the debates to which Raymond Williams was also contributing.[126] This constructivist view of nations and the emphasis on cultural pluralism may be seen to align Williams with those post-colonial critics working under the influence of post-structuralism who conceive of national cultures in terms of their inherent 'hybridity'.[127] Indeed, the post-structuralist critique of all efforts to speak of origins, collectivities and determinate historical projects seemed to speak directly to the Welsh experience in the 1980s following the collapse of the two dominant narratives of Welsh identity and continuity; the defeat of nationalism in the devolution referendum of 1979, and the failure of the miners in the strike of 1984–5. Williams's works of the last years of his life can be read as attempts at imagining forms of community that gesture beyond these two moments of defeat. His emphasis on plural cultures and internal differences cannot, despite appearances, be unreservedly aligned to the views of postmodern hybridists, for Williams's pluralism always involves a simultaneous gesture towards a community of belief and action which is hardly compatible with the cultural and political relativism of postmodernism.[128] Williams responded to the failures of 1979 and 1985 by attempting to move beyond both the socialist tendency to prioritise 'one kind of bonding – trade unionism, the class bond', and the nationalist tendency to prioritise the bonds of language.[129] The cultural and political climate of the 1980s called for a 'new theory of socialism' that would 'centrally involve place', for 'when capital has moved on, the importance of place is more clearly revealed'.[130] This is essentially a cultural argument; a statement of the ground on which new connections may be fostered in the construction of communities 'that can hold'. In political terms, this search for connections called for a realignment of the left which would open a 'space for some federation of socialist, Green and radical nationalist forces'; a movement that embodied a simultaneous cultural and political 'reaching out for new perspectives and new forms'.[131]

Williams's own self-definition as a Welsh-European reflected his call on socialists 'to explore new forms of "variable" societies, in which over the whole range of social purposes different sizes of society are defined for different kinds of issue and decision'.[132] It is this argument that explains Williams's emphasis on the variable forms adopted by, and ascribed to, the Welsh; 'a nation or a people or... a region'.[133] Whilst following Gwyn A. Williams in believing that the Welsh nation 'is an artifact' produced by the Welsh people 'if they want to', Raymond Williams's rejection of ideas of the nation based on race and language leads to an ambiguity as to what, ultimately, forms the basis for Welshness.[134] The advantage, however, of Williams's rigorous distinction between a culturally defined 'people' or 'nation' and a politically defined 'state' is that it allows us to recognise that the political expression of national identity can take many legitimate forms: state separation ('independence'), federation, confederation or limited sovereignty or rights in a multinational or multi-ethnic state. There is no predetermined shape that Welshness will inevitably take, for that elusive entity – 'Wales' – is not the neutral frame within which any array of forces contend for power, but is, rather, itself the subject of persistent cultural and political contestation. Williams recognises that it is through the possibility and necessity of a shifting diversity of levels – ethnic, regional, national, international – for both individuals and communities that a space is created for the creation of a culturally diverse society based on the acceptance of a necessary ambiguity in cultural and political identity.

CONCLUSION

Williams noted that, from the early 1970s onwards, he could 'relate... not just to my own area but to an entity one was then calling Wales', though he maintained that 'I still find it problematic; and whenever I have a really satisfactory conversation it is always when people raise these questions in the same way'.[135] Indeed, having read the various essays interviews and reviews contained in this volume, perhaps it is not the intricacies (and occasional evasions) of the answers that abide, but rather the diverse and persistent questions: 'What then does Wales mean?', 'What is Welsh or Wales when all is UK or Yookay?, 'Are we becoming more divided?,' 'The imagined nation or the nation imagined?'.[136] Williams's most significant contribution to Welsh cultural debate was his continual transformation of the terms of its questions. The resultant chorus of contested answers offers the safest guard against an invariably disastrous over-emphasis upon a single level of cultural and political community. 'The most valuable emphasis in Welsh culture,' he noted, 'is that everybody should speak.'[137] *Who speaks for Wales?* documents Raymond Williams's engagement with a question that should never be answered in the singular.

Notes

1. Raymond Williams, *The English Novel from Dickens to Lawrence* (1970; London: Hogarth Press, 1984), p. 109.
2. Williams, *The English Novel*, p. 106.
3. Williams, *The English Novel*, p. 109.
4. John Higgins, *Raymond Williams: literature, Marxism and cultural materialism* (London: Routledge, 1999), p. 143, i.
5. John Higgins (ed.), *The Raymond Williams Reader* (Oxford: Blackwell, 2001); comment on back cover, 'People of the Black Country' in the 'Preface', p. ix.
6. Fred Inglis, *Raymond Williams* (London: Routledge, 1995), p. 257.
7. Inglis, *Raymond Williams*, p. 257.
8. Inglis, *Raymond Williams*, p. 258, 66.
9. Patrick Parrinder, *The Failure of Theory* (Brighton: The Harvester Press, 1987), p. 78; James A. Davies, '"Not going back, but... exile ending": Raymond Williams's fictional Wales', in W. J. Morgan and P. Preston (eds), *Raymond Williams: Politics, Education, Letters* (London: Macmillan, 1993), p. 207.
10. Higgins, *Raymond Williams*, p. 170.
11. Morag Shiach, 'A Gendered History of Cultural Categories', in Christopher Prendergast (ed.), *Cultural Materialism: On Raymond Williams* (Minneapolis: University of Minnesota Press, 1995), p. 51. It should be noted, however, that there are moments where Williams does engage with the question of gender in this volume: see 'Boyhood', p. 104; 'Decentralism and the Politics of Place', p. 351; 'The Practice of Possibility', pp. 360–1.
12. R. Radhakrishnan, 'Cultural Theory and the Politics of Location', in D. Dworkin and L. Roman (eds), *Views Beyond the Border Country: Raymond Williams and Cultural Politics* (London: Routledge, 1993), p. 291.
13. See, for example, Jeremy Hooker, 'Raymond Williams: a dream of a country', in Hooker, *The Poetry of Place: essays and reviews, 1970–1981* (Manchester: Carcanet, 1982), pp. 106–15; J. P. Ward, 'Raymond Williams as Inhabitant: the border trilogy', *New Welsh Review*, 1/2 (1988), 23–7; Katie Gramich, 'The Fiction of Raymond Williams in the 1960s', *Welsh Writing in English: A Yearbook of Critical Essays*, 1 (1995), pp. 62–74; Stephen Knight, 'Raymond Williams's *The Volunteers* as Crime Fiction', *Welsh Writing in English: A Yearbook of Critical Essays*, 2 (1996), pp. 126–37. Two articles which do move deftly from the theory to the fiction are Dai Smith, 'Relating to Wales', in Terry Eagleton (ed.), *Raymond Williams: Critical Perspectives* (Cambridge: Polity Press, 1989), pp. 34–53, and Jeff Wallace, 'Driven to Abstraction? Raymond Williams and the Road', *Welsh Writing in English:*

A Yearbook of Critical Essays, 5 (1999), pp. 115–29; here again, however, the focus is primarily on the fiction.

14. Williams describes himself as a 'Welsh European' in 'The Welsh Trilogy and *The Volunteers*', p. 228; Tony Pinkney, *Raymond Williams* (Bridgend: Seren, 1991), p. 12.

15. See 'West of Offa's Dyke', p. 88; 'The Welsh Trilogy and *The Volunteers*', p. 229.

16. See 'The Importance of Community', p. 314.

17. See 'Community', p. 79; 'The Practice of Possibility', p. 362.

18. Peter Osborne, 'Introduction: Philosophy and the Role of Intellectuals', in Osborne (ed.), *A Critical Sense: Interviews with Intellectuals* (London: Routledge, 1996), p. xv.

19. Edward Said, *Representations of the Intellectual: The 1993 Reith Lectures* (New York: Pantheon Books, 1994), p. 63.

20. Stefan Collini, 'Speaking from Somewhere', *Times Literary Supplement*, 15 April 1988, 427–8.

21. Williams talks of himself as being 'exceptionally isolated in the changing political and cultural formations of the later forties and early fifties', in the introduction to *Marxism and Literature* (1977; Oxford: Oxford University Press, 1989), p. 2. This is somewhat curious given that this was also the formative period in the careers of leftist intellectuals such as Richard Hoggart, E. P. Thompson and Eric Hobsbawm, and was the period in which Williams was involved in launching the Oxford rival to *Scrutiny*, *Essays in Criticism*. See Inglis, *Raymond Williams*, pp. 132–3.

22. Raymond Williams, *Border Country* (London: Chatto & Windus, 1960), p. 82.

23. Williams, *Border Country*, p. 83.

24. Williams, *The English Novel*, p. 109. The phrase 'different idiom' comes from 'Culture is Ordinary' in Raymond Williams, *Resources of Hope* (London: Verso, 1989), p. 4.

25. See Williams, 'Culture is Ordinary', p. 2.

26. Raymond Williams, *Culture and Society 1780–1950* (London: Chatto & Windus, 1958); for 'dominant, residual and emergent', see Williams, *Marxism and Literature*, pp. 121–7.

27. Christopher Hitchens, 'George Orwell and Raymond Williams', *Critical Quarterly*, 41/3 (1999), 6–8.

28. Raymond Williams, *Orwell* (London: Fontana, 1971), p. 17.

29. Williams, *Orwell*, p. 18.

30. Raymond Williams, *Politics and Letters: interviews with New Left Review* (London: Verso, 1979), p. 113.

31. Williams, *Politics and Letters*, p. 113.

32. Williams, *Politics and Letters*, p. 113.

33. Pinkney, *Raymond Williams*, p. 12.

34. Williams, *Border Country*, p. 12.

35. Williams, *Border Country*, p. 277.

36. Williams, *Border Country*, pp. 83, 33.
37. Raymond Williams, *The Volunteers* (London: The Hogarth Press, 1985), p. 154.
38. See 'Who Speaks for Wales', pp. 47, 48.
39. See 'Community', p. 78.
40. See 'Community', p. 79.
41. See 'Community', p. 79.
42. See 'West of Offa's Dyke', p. 88.
43. See 'Marxism, Poetry, Wales', p. 171.
44. Higgins, *Raymond Williams*, p. 170.
45. Williams, *Politics and Letters*, pp. 118–19.
46. Raymond Williams and Edward Said, 'Media, Margins and Modernity', in Raymond Williams, *The Politics of Modernism* (London: Verso, 1989), p. 196.
47. Edward Said, *Culture and Imperialism* (1993; London: Vintage, 1994), pp. 98–9.
48. Said, *Culture and Imperialism*, p. 98.
49. Raymond Williams, *Keywords: A Vocabulary of Culture and Society* (1976; London: Fontana revised edn, 1983), pp. 159–60.
50. Raymond Williams, *The Country and the City* (London: Chatto & Windus, 1973), p. 280.
51. Williams, *The Country and the City*, p. 280.
52. Smith, 'Relating to Wales', p. 35.
53. Gauri Viswanathan, 'Raymond Williams and British Colonialism', in Prendergast, *Cultural Materialism; On Raymond Williams*, p. 190.
54. Williams, *Border Country*, p. 9.
55. Williams, *Border Country*, p. 9.
56. Williams, *Border Country*, p. 16.
57. Williams, *Border Country*, 62.
58. Matthew Arnold, *On the Study of Celtic Literature* (1867), in *Collected Prose Works*, Vol. 3, ed. R. H. Super (Ann Arbor, MI: Michigan University Press, 1962); D. H. Lawrence, *St Mawr* (1924), in *The Complete Short Novels* (London: Penguin, 1982).
59. Raymond Williams, *Loyalties* (London: Chatto & Windus, 1985), p. 307.
60. This point is made most forcefully in 'Welsh Culture' (p. 53), where Williams recounts meeting a 'young bureaucrat, just back from California, describing rural mid-Wales as a 'wilderness area', for the outdoor relief of the English cities... And here was he, with the concept in his flight bag, looking on a map at rural Wales: at fields and hills soaked with labour, at the living places of farming families, and not even seeing them, seeing only a site for his wilderness.'
61. Raymond Williams, *Second Generation* (London: Chatto & Windus, 1964), pp. 321–2.
62. See 'Marxism, Poetry, Wales', p. 170.
63. James Clifford notes that '[i]t is less common today than it once was to speak of "the East", but we still make casual reference to "the West", "Western

culture", and so on. Even theorists of discontinuity and deconstruction such as Foucault and Derrida continue to set their analyses within and against a Western totality'. Clifford, *The Predicament of Culture: Twentieth-Century Ethnography, Literature and Art* (Cambridge, MA: Harvard University Press, 1988), p. 272.

64. Said, *Culture and Imperialism*, p. xi.

65. Said, *Culture and Imperialism*, p. xii.

66. See 'Welsh Culture', p. 56.

67. A useful introduction to the 'revisionist' debate in Ireland is Ciaran Brady (ed.), *Interpreting Irish History: The Debate on Historical Revisionism 1938–1994* (Dublin: Irish Academic Press, 1994).

68. See 'Wales and England', p. 72.

69. The problematic term 'internal colonialism' was applied to the Celtic nations in Michael Hechter's influential *Internal Colonialism: The Celtic Fringe in British National Development, 1536–1966* (London: Routledge, 1975).

70. See 'Region and Class in the Novel', p. 255.

71. See 'A Welsh Companion', p. 279.

72. See 'The Importance of Community', p. 313.

73. Emyr Humphreys, *Conversations and Reflections*, ed. M. Wynn Thomas (Cardiff: University of Wales Press, 2002), p. 189.

74. The quotations come from the revisionist histories of Dai Smith, *Wales! Wales?* (London: Allen and Unwin, 1984), p. 27, revised as *Wales: A Question for History* (Bridgend: Seren, 1999), p. 49. The revisionist case is also made forcefully by Tim Williams in 'The Anglicisation of South Wales', in Raphael Samuel (ed.), *Patriotism: The Making and Unmaking of British National Identity Vol. 2: Minorities and Outsiders* (London: Routledge, 1989). Gwynfor Evans's *Land of My Fathers: 2000 years of Welsh History* (Talybont: Y Lolfa, 1992) is a popular nationalist history of Wales; a more sophisticated history, written from a self-critical nationalist standpoint, is John Davies's *History of Wales* (London: Penguin, 1993).

75. See 'Welsh Culture', p. 54.

76. See 'Boyhood', p. 106.

77. Smith, *Wales: A Question for History*, p. 49.

78. Terry Eagleton makes a similar point in another context, where he supplements a critique of Irish revisionist history with reference to feminism: 'In a similar way, most feminists reject the idea that men are simply creatures resting between rapes, but nonetheless find in that aberrant act something typical of patriarchal sexual relations in general. Hamstrung by his empiricist education, the revisionist historian is sometimes slow to appreciate the symbolic dimension of action, and must accordingly go to school with the cultural critic.' Terry Eagleton, 'Revisionism Revisited', in *Crazy John and the Bishop and other essays on Irish Culture* (Cork: Cork University Press, 1998), p. 319.

79. This is how Emyr Humphreys conceives of the language in 'Taliesin's Children', in Humphreys, *Conversations and Reflections*, p. 28.

80. See especially Gwyn Williams, *When Was Wales?* (London: Black Raven, 1985); Davies, *A History of Wales*; and Smith, *Wales: A Question for History*.
81. See 'Wales and England', p. 68.
82. See 'The Practice of Possibility', p. 62.
83. Williams, *Politics and Letters*, p. 120.
84. Raymond Williams (ed.), *The May Day Manifesto* (1967; Penguin Books, 1968), p. 163.
85. See 'Wales and England', p. 72; 'Boyhood', p. 107.
86. See 'Freedom and a Lack of Confidence', p. 240.
87. Adrian Hastings, *The Construction of Nationhood* (Cambridge: Cambridge University Press, 1997), p. 181.
88. See 'The Shadow of the Dragon', p. 128.
89. See 'The Culture of Nations', p. 343.
90. In this respect, Williams's thought seems to follow the familiar philosophical division between 'the state' and 'civil society' formulated most influentially by Hegel and adapted by Marx. When Williams refers to 'community', he often seems to be referring to what others would call 'civil society'. On the history of these terms, see Shlomo Avineri, *Hegel's Theory of the Modern State* (1972; Cambridge: Cambridge University Press, 1980), pp. 141–54, and the same author's *The Social and Political Thought of Karl Marx* (Cambridge: Cambridge University Press, 1968), pp. 17–22.
91. John Hutchinson, *The Dynamics of Cultural Nationalism* (London: Allen and Unwin, 1987), p. 30. Eric Hobsbawm and John Breuilly are particularly dismissive of cultural nationalisms in general, and of Welsh nationalism in particular. Hobsbawm quotes the notoriously biased 1847 'Blue Books' report on the state of education in Wales as if its denunciation of a primitive and outmoded language was historically accurate, and suggests that 'Welsh language enthusiasts... are even now devising Cymric place names for places which never had any until today' (*Nations and Nationalism*, p. 112). John Breuilly, in discussing the ways in which nationalists construct myths, gives the example of 'the epic Ossian, which has played so important a role in modern Welsh nationalist thought', and notes that '[i]n Scotland and Wales ... the Gadhelic [*sic*] and Welsh languages only survive as language [*sic*] of the community in highland regions: otherwise they are preserved only by minorities of cultural enthusiasts' (Breuilly, 'Approaches to Nationalism', in G. Balakrishnan (ed.), *Mapping the Nation* (London: Verso, 1996), pp. 151, 152–3). To compare Wales, a nation in which around 20 per cent of the population speaks Welsh, with Scotland, in which fewer than two per cent has any knowledge of Scots-Gaelic, is somewhat misleading. The epic Ossian played an 'important role' in Scotland, but not in Wales. Both Hobsbawm and Breuilly attempt to hide their total ignorance of Wales and its history behind the loaded word 'enthusiast' for those who speak a language other than English. A more sympathetic account of cultural nationalism is to be found in Benedict Anderson's *Imagined Communities* (London: Verso, 1983).

92. In this respect, Williams's analysis challenges the views of anti-nationalists such as Hobsbawm, and of pro-nationalists such as Tom Nairn, who bases his defence of Scottish nationalism on a rather simplistic distinction between 'ethnic' and 'civic' forms of nationalism in *After Britain: New Labour and the Return of Scotland* (London: Granta, 2000).

93. See 'Community', p. 78.

94. See 'Remaking Welsh History', p. 135.

95. See 'Community', p. 81.

96. Raymond Williams, *Towards 2000* (London: Chatto & Windus, 1983), p. 174.

97. See 'Are We Becoming More Divided?', p. 321.

98. See 'Wales and England', p. 66.

99. See 'The Culture of Nations', p. 339.

100. Francis Mulhern, 'Towards 2000, or News from You-Know-Where', in Eagleton, *Raymond Williams: Critical Perspectives*, p. 87.

101. Paul Gilroy, *'There Ain't No Black in the Union Jack': The Cultural Politics of Race and Nation* (Chicago: University of Chicago Press, 1987), pp. 49–51.

102. See 'The Culture of Nations', p. 341; quoted by Gilroy, *'There Ain't No Black in the Union Jack'*, p. 49.

103. Gilroy, *'There Ain't No Black in the Union Jack'*, pp. 49–50.

104. See 'The Culture of Nations', p. 341.

105. Gilroy, *'There Ain't No Black in the Union Jack'*, p. 59.

106. Gilroy, *'There Ain't No Black in the Union Jack'*, pp. 49–50.

107. See 'Boyhood', p. 107.

108. See 'The Culture of Nations', p. 340.

109. See 'The Culture of Nations', p. 342.

110. Donald Nonini refers to Williams's 'unfortunate intervention regarding race' in *Towards 2000*, and quotes this passage as evidence that Williams's conception of identity was based on 'the Welsh countryside of his youth'. The passage is quoted as I have it here, except that the phrase 'into which in the nineteenth century there was massive and diverse immigration' is omitted! Donald M. Nonini, 'Race, Land, Nation: A(t)-Tribute to Raymond Williams', *Cultural Critique*, 41 (Winter 1999), 170.

111. Cornel West, 'The Legacy of Raymond Williams', *Prophetic Thought in Postmodern Times* (Monroe MA: Common Courage Press, 1993), p. 173.

112. Williams, *Keywords*, pp. 213–14.

113. See 'Wales and England', p. 66.

114. See 'Wales and England', p. 70.

115. Walter Benn Michaels, 'Race into Culture: A Critical Genealogy of Cultural Identity', in K. Anthony Appiah and Henry Louis Gates, Jr. (eds), *Identities* (Chicago: University of Chicago Press, 1995), p. 60.

116. See 'Marxism, Poetry, Wales', p. 175; 'Wales and England', p. 67.

117. See 'Community', pp. 78, 82.

118. Raymond Williams, *Marxism and Literature* (Oxford: Oxford University Press, 1977), pp. 51–2.

119. See 'Freedom and a Lack of Confidence', p. 239.
120. There are, of course, fairly obvious limitations to Williams's constructed canon. The omission of women writers, notably Margiad Evans in the 1930s, is being rectified by contemporary critics, and the emphasis on realism from 1920 to 1940 inevitably marginalises the disturbing surrealism of writers such as Glyn Jones and Dylan Thomas in the 1930s.
121. Prendergast, *Cultural Materialism: On Raymond Williams*, p. 18.
122. Prendergast, *Cultural Materialism: On Raymond Williams*, p. 18.
123. See 'All Things Betray Thee', p. 285.
124. See 'Dylan Thomas's Play for Voices', p. 163; 'Working-Class, Proletarian, Socialist', p. 274.
125. See 'Remaking Welsh History', p. 134; 'West of Offa's Dyke', p. 88.
126. See 'West of Offa's Dyke', p. 88.
127. See, for instance, Homi Bhabha, *The Location of Culture* (London: Routledge, 1994).
128. I attempted, tentatively, to place Williams within this wider field of debate in an article written in Welsh: 'Cymdeithas a Chenedl yng Ngwaith Raymond Williams' ('Nation and Community in the work of Raymond Williams'), *Taliesin*, 97 (Gwanwyn 1997), 55–76.
129. See 'Decentralism and the Politics of Place', p. 350.
130. See 'Decentralism and the Politics of Place', p. 351.
131. See 'The Practice of Possibility', p. 358; 'The Welsh Industrial Novel', p. 198. Williams's writings of the 1980s seem to share a number of characteristics with the 'post-Marxism' of Ernesto Laclau and Chantal Mouffe in this respect. The basis for their analysis of *Hegemony and Socialist Strategy* was the realisation that '[m]any social antagonisms, many issues which are crucial to the understanding of contemporary societies, belong to fields of discursivity which are external to Marxism'; Ernesto Laclau and Chantal Mouffe, *Hegemony and Socialist Strategy* (1985; London: Verso, 2001), p. ix. Laclau seemed to be reiterating Williams's arguments of the 1980s in more recent observation that '[t]here is no future for the Left if it is unable to create and expansive universal discourse, constructed out of, not against, the proliferation of particularisms of the last few decades'; Judith Butler, Ernesto Laclau and Slavoj Žižek, *Contingency, Hegemony, Universality: Contemporary Dialogues on the Left* (London: Verso, 2000), p. 306. It is this emphasis on the possibility of creating an 'universal discourse' out of a social plurality of interests that differentiates Laclau – and Williams – from postmodernists such as Lyotard.
132. See 'The Welsh Trilogy', p. 228; 'The Culture of Nations', p. 344.
133. See 'Freedom and a Lack of Confidence', p. 240.
134. Gwyn A. Williams, *When Was Wales?* (London: Black Raven Press, 1985), p. 304.
135. See 'Marxism, Poetry, Wales', p. 172.
136. See 'The Shadow of the Dragon', p. 127; 'Are We Becoming More Divided', p. 317; 'West of Offa's Dyke', p. 188.
137. See 'Who Speaks for Wales?', p. 47.

CULTURE

∎ ∎ ∎

WHO SPEAKS FOR WALES?

The Guardian (3 June 1971).
Review of Ned Thomas, *The Welsh
Extremist* (London: Gollancz, 1971).[1]

Who speaks for Wales? Nobody. That is both the problem and the encouragement. Encouragement because the most valuable emphasis in Welsh culture is that everybody should speak and have the right to speak: an idea of an equal-standing and participating democracy which was there in experience before it became theory. Problem because Wales has suffered and is suffering acute economic, political, and cultural strains, and by the fact of history has to try to resolve them in a world of crude power relationships and distant parliaments.

I used to think that born into a Border country at once physical, economic, and cultural, my own relationship to the idea of Wales was especially problematic. But I now see, from Ned Thomas, among others, that it was characteristic. I remember focusing first on the powerful political culture of industrial South Wales: in the first half of this century one of the major centres of socialist consciousness anywhere in the world. But the necessary movement from that kind of centre was into a larger society. Anyone who knows British socialism and British education knows how richly the Welsh have contributed to these much wider movements, and in the majority as exiles. The long crisis of British socialism, now coming to a decisive stage in the condition of the Labour Party, has made many of these people exiles in quite another and more important sense.[2]

But there was always another idea of Wales: the more enclosed, mainly rural, more Welsh-speaking west and north. For me, in the beginning, that was much more remote. It is a commonplace that in consciousness there is often a great distance between what can be called but are not really the two halves of the country. In the last decade especially, and to a large extent because of what had happened to the earlier and wider movements in politics and education, another idea of Wales, drawn from its alternative source, has come through in the campaigns of Plaid Cymru[3] and the Welsh Language Society.[4]

The relation between these two phases has been especially difficult. Many English Socialists, and many Welsh Labour Party people, have seen the later phase as a marginal or romantic irrelevance, or as worse. 'Nationalism means Fascism', somebody said to me angrily. He is especially the kind of man who should read Ned Thomas's book. For the strange thing is this: that through its radical emphasis on identity and community, and in its turn to popular campaigning, to demonstrations and to direct action, this new Welsh movement – at least an important section of it – has come through as part of the new socialism and the new thinking about culture which in many parts of the world has been called the New Left.

There are of course many ambiguities and uncertainties. If the form of the campaign has specific local features it can attract and be corrupted by a falsely inward-looking, regressive, and complacent localism. But then it seems to be true that in late capitalist societies some of the most powerful campaigns begin from specific unabsorbed (and therefore necessarily marginal) experiences and situations. Black Power in the United States, civil rights in Ulster, the language in Wales, are experiences comparable in this respect to the student movement and to women's liberation. In their early stages these campaigns tend to stress as absolutes those local experiences which are of course authentic and yet most important as indices of the crisis of the wider society.

This is the continuing ambivalence in Wales as elsewhere. It is precisely the problem of the border country as I remember experiencing it. Ned Thomas has written a description of his own experience and position relating it to modern Welsh literature and the feel of the language. But from that specific and local idea of Wales he comes to conclusions which I would wholly endorse: that the only thing to do is 'to live out the tension, to try to work it out by changing the situation'. This means challenging, personally and publicly, and from wherever we are, the immense imperatives which are not only flattening but preventing the realities of identity and culture. It is a cause better than national and more than international, for in its varying forms it is a very general human and social movement. And perhaps to young English Socialists Ned Thomas's book should be specially recommended, for it will bring them in touch with people very much like themselves, whom they have often not noticed, beyond the misunderstandings, only a short train journey away.

Notes

1. Ned Thomas (1936–) is a critic and editor. Founder editor of the journal *Planet*. See his autobiography *Bydoedd* (Talybont: Lolfa, 2011). *The Welsh Extremist* sought to explain and justify the struggle to defend the Welsh language in the terms of the New Left.

2. For discussion and analysis of the role of the Welsh in the Labour Party see Duncan Tanner, Chris Williams and Deian Hopkin (eds), *The Labour Party in Wales* (Cardiff: University of Wales Press, 2001), and the broader history offered in Daryl Leeworthy, *Labour Country: Political Radicalism and Social Democracy in South Wales 1831–1985* (Cardigan: Parthian, 2018).

3. Plaid Cymru (lit. and, since 1998, officially 'The Party of Wales') was founded in 1925; it was first known as Plaid Genedlaethol Cymru ('The National Party of Wales'). The party's history can be traced in D. Hywel Davies, *The Welsh Nationalist Party 1925–1945* (Cardiff: University of Wales Press, 1983), Laura McAllister, *Plaid Cymru: The Emergence of a Political Party 1945–2001* (Bridgend: Seren, 2001), and Richard Wyn Jones, *Rhoi Cymru'n Gyntaf: Syniadaeth Plaid Cymru* (Caerdydd: Gwasg Prigysgol Cymru, 2007). Laura McAllister describes Williams, along with Saunders Lewis and D. J. Davies, as one of the 'three key thinkers' in Plaid Cymru's development (pp. 55–9). Richard Wyn Jones draws attention to Williams's centrality in rejuvenating the party's thought after the failed 1979 referendum on devolution (p. 224). Williams himself notes that he joined the party for 'a year or two' in 'Decentralism and the Politics of Place'. The Raymond Williams Papers at Swansea University includes his membership card for 1969, suggesting a longer engagement with Plaid Cymru than was previously thought (Richard Burton Archive Reference: WWE/2/1/12/1).

4. The Welsh Language Society, usually known by its Welsh title, Cymdeithas yr Iaith Gymraeg, was set up in 1962 largely as a response to the attempt by Plaid Cymru to widen its electoral base by moving away from its linguistic, culturalist roots, and to a growing sense of the terminal crisis faced by Welsh-speaking communities as highlighted by Saunders Lewis in his 1962 lecture 'Tynged yr Iaith' ('The fate of the language'). The movement embarked on a continuing programme of civil disobedience. The society's history is traced in Welsh by Dylan Phillips in *Trwy Ddulliau Chwyldro*

(Llandysul: Gomer, 1998), and by Colin H. Williams, 'Non-violence and the development of the Welsh Language Society 1962–1974', in *The Welsh History Review*, 8/4 (1977), 426–55. For further information on Saunders Lewis, see 'Community', n. 8.

WELSH CULTURE

Culture and Politics: *Plaid Cymru's Challenge to Wales* (Cardiff: Plaid Cymru, 1975), pp. 6-10.

Delivered as a talk on BBC Radio 3, 27 September 1975. Collected in Raymond Williams, *Resources of Hope* (London: Verso, 1989), pp. 99-104.

An excerpt appeared as 'Variations on a Welsh Theme: On Aspects of the Welsh "Fixation on the Past"', *The Listener*, 94 (2 October 1975), 429-30.

When we hear the word 'culture', some of us reach for our fancy dress. Real life is home, family and a job; wages and prices; politics and crisis. Culture, then, is for high days and holidays: not an ordinary gear but an overdrive. So if you say 'Welsh culture' what do you think of? Of *bara brith* and the *Eisteddfod*? Of choirs and Cardiff Arms Park? Of love spoons and *englynion*? Of the national costume and the rampant red dragon?[1] All these things are here, if at different levels and in different ways. But over and above them is another culture. Not the alien Saxon, who belongs, in truth, with the fancy dress. Not even, in any simple way, the alien or at least different English. Taking culture in its full sense you would be speaking of something quite different: of a way of life determined by the National Coal Board, the British Steel Corporation, the Milk Marketing Board, the Co-op and Marks and Spencers, the BBC, the Labour Party, the EEC, NATO. But that's not Welsh culture. Maybe, maybe not. It's how and where most people in Wales are living, and in relation to which most meanings and values are in practice found. Depopulation, unemployment, exploitation, poverty: if these are not part of Welsh culture we are denying large parts of our social experience. And if we have shared these things with others, that sharpens the question.

Where is it now, this Wales? Where is the real identity, the real culture? It's worth walking with this question around the Folk Museum at St Fagans.[2] It's a lovely place. Along the paths and under the trees are the re-erected farmhouses and cottages of the periods and regions of Wales. Inside the houses are the old furniture, the old utensils, the old tools. You can touch the handle of a shovel and, closing your eyes, feel a life connecting with you: the lives of men and women whose genes we still carry; the labour now dissolved into what may seem a natural landscape of high field and culvert and lane. And beyond these the tannery and the weaving factory, the chapel and the tollhouse and the cockpit. It is all there, you say, the real Wales. And then you look up at the big house on the mound, in whose park this image, so precisely material, has been rebuilt, reconstructed. It is not that it cancels the decency or the dignity of the farms and the cottages, but it is there all the time, as another part of the culture.

The castles of Wales, most of them the monuments of an invading and occupying political system: are they too part of Welsh culture, to be set down indifferently in the tourist literature? Maybe, again. Anything old enough will do, it can seem at times. Even the steam locomotives, once they stopped running, became a cultural attraction. It's very hard to hold this in balance. The feeling for the past is more than a fancy, but it's how past and present relate that tells in a culture. You go out of the park, your mind still filled with the peace of those farmhouse interiors – of course an unreal peace; there is never any dirt on the tools or on the floors; the attendants have prepared for us a clean homecoming – and there you are, suddenly, in the car park, among the Cortinas and the Allegros, and then the traffic lights and the road signs.

The Welsh Folk Museum: a lovely place. But what happens to a people when it calls itself, even temporarily, a folk? That hard German sound is softened and distanced in English, and it is in the softening and distancing that you select your memories. For it's significant, isn't it, where that Folk Museum stops. Just before, precisely before, the Industrial Revolution. You look among all those places and instruments of work, and you remember, up the road, industrial South Wales: coal and steel and their derivatives; the thickly populated valleys, the terraces, the slagheaps; the place of life and work of the majority of the Welsh.

I had a fancy once, looking across from the oldest of the farm-houses. Give the present generation of industrial bureaucrats their head, stop fighting them, and the Folk Museum could be remarkably expanded. A nostalgic colliery cage would rise beyond the tannery. An out-of-date ironworks would share a stream with the weaving. A depressed and ravaged country, passing quickly through the status of a marginal region, would find its cultural reincarnation in the lovingly preserved material relics of an open-air museum.[3]

It isn't only, when you think of it, the industry. I remember a young bureaucrat, just back from California, describing rural mid-Wales as a 'wilderness area', for the outdoor relief of the English cities. He never understood why I was so unsocially angry. In the North American continent there are still real wildernesses: untouched and some of it untouchable country. And here was he, with the concept in his flight bag, looking on a map at rural Wales: at fields and hills soaked with labour, at the living places of farming families, and not even seeing them, seeing only a site for his wilderness. He had a friend, an economist, who used to prove to me, once a week, that the sheep, by nature, is an uneconomic animal, and that all this marginal farming, with returns on capital that would cause instant suicide in the Barbican, must be simply written off. 'And the people with the sheep?' I ventured to ask. 'Of course, in that capacity', he replied without hesitation.

If you forget the past and think about the future for a minute, you can see this whole model: the uneconomic collieries, the out-of-date heavy industry, the marginal farms. Save a few bright spots – Port Talbot, Milford Haven – where the terms measure up to those plan-ning standards, and what have you got? Poor old Wales. And how will the Welsh live, those at least who haven't followed their fathers down the Black Rock to England? 'The region', they said, 'has obvi-ous tourist and leisure potential.' And that, I suppose, is where the culture comes in again: as a resort and a festival, both meticulously and distinctively Welsh.

But this is the problem: the real problem of cultural identity. I wish I could see it in one of its popular forms: in a kind of emphasis on Welshness against an alien and invading culture; in a consequent emphasis on culture as tradition, and on tradition as preservation. I can feel, very easily, the strength of that position. Here is a language spoken and written since the sixth century, still a native language for a significant minority, and to want to keep it, to insist on keeping it, is then as natural as breathing. With the language goes a literature, and with the literature a history, and with the history a culture.

It is a real enough model, as far as it goes. The language wasn't only driven back by the Industrial Revolution and its movements of people. It was also driven back by conscious repression, by penalty and contempt, and in a late phase by deliberate policy in the schools. You can still see, as carefully preserved as the old tools, the little boards, the 'Welsh Nots', which children caught speaking their mother tongue had to hang round their necks, for shame. It is bound to be wrong to forget or forgive that. It is bound to be right to use and to teach a language still living, after all the attacks on it.

But does the rest follow: the history, the culture? Only part of it, in fact. It is easy to speak of a proud independent people. The rhetoric warms the heart. But you can be proud without being independent; you often have to be. In the older epochs of conquest, and in the modern epoch of industrial capitalism, there hasn't been that much choice. The self-respect, the aspirations, were always real and always difficult. But you don't live for centuries under the power of others and remain the same people. It is this, always, that is so hard to admit, for it can be made to sound like betrayal. And so a genuine identity, a real tradition, a natural self-respect, can be made to stand on their own, as if nothing else had ever happened.

I was late learning this. At school I was never taught any English history. First it was Welsh history, with brave princes and heroes amassing gold and cattle: the English or Saxons (the terms interchangeable) usually slain ('slain' for a child; keep 'killed' for later); slain in great numbers, though there were always, I remember, some young beauties left, for the contracting of noble alliances. That at elementary school; indeed elementary enough. And I went straight on, as it happened, by the form of the School Certificate syllabus, to British Empire and Commonwealth history; more slaying and amassing, though now called the spread of civilization. This left me not only with some understandable confusions about the identity of the enemy, to say nothing of the identity of our own side. It left me also without much clue to this very odd world I started noticing outside school. There was a gap, that is to say: a gap in the Welsh history for the four centuries after the Acts of Union; a gap in the English history, or was it also Welsh, which had brought the tramroad and the railway through our valley, and which was there visible every night, above Brynarw, when they cleared the blast furnace at Blaenavon and the glow hung in the sky. All the complications, all the real difficulties, are there in those gaps, and it is these that not only I, but most of us, find so hard to grasp, to decipher, to connect, as we try to make sense of what is called Welsh Culture.

Where there are real gaps there is not only inquiry; there is also the making of myths. Trying, under pressure, to define our identity, we have invented and tolerated many illusions. That we are physically distinct, for example: a specific race; the last of the old Britons, hanging on in the west. But the physical mix of the people of Wales is essentially that of the whole island, though in different areas, including the different regions of Wales, the proportions in the mix vary. Another form of the illusion is that we are the Celts, whoever they may be. The tall fairhaired warriors who charged the Roman legions, naked except for their ornaments of gold. That doesn't fit very well with the dominant physical image, to say nothing of the rest of the cultural match. Or then the Celtic temperament, in either of its versions. Natural radicals, dissidents, nonconformists, rebels? It depends which period you take. Think of Catholic, royalist Wales, as late as the Civil War. Are these the same people as the radical nonconformists and later the socialists and militants of the nineteenth and twentieth centuries. It was not the race that changed; it was the history.

Or the other incarnation: the dark brooding and magical imagination; the nation of poets and scholars; or in the cut-down English version: the people with that endless gift of the gab. These too are history: Welsh literature with its very marked and very distinct classicist and romantic tendencies, manifesting quite different qualities; Welsh talk, with its range from a fluent, dynamic enlivening articulation to an overbearing, repetitive windiness. Facing ourselves as we are, we know all these possibilities. What comes out, on balance, is indeed distinct and distinctive, but it contains elements too complex, too infolded, to be defined by the simple traditional images. Who has not heard, for example, of the fluent, quicksilver Celt, making rings round the slow dumb English? The energy of the talk is indeed not in doubt, but we have to listen more carefully to what it is really saying. It is often a lively exuberance. It is just as often an unmitigated flow to prevent other things being said. And what those other things are we hear more often among ourselves, an extraordinary sadness, which is indeed not surprising, and at the edges, lately, an implacable bitterness, even a soured cynicism, which can jerk into life – this is what makes it hard to hear – as a fantastic comic edge, or a wild self-deprecation, as a form of pride: a wall of words, anyway, so that we do not have to look, steadily and soberly, at all that has happened to us.

What is it that has happened? It is nothing surprising. It is in general very well known. To the extent that we are a people, we have been defeated, colonized, penetrated, incorporated. Never finally, of course. The living resilience, in many forms, has always been there. But its forms are distinct. They do not normally include, for example, the fighting hatred of some of the Irish. There is a drawing back to some of our own resources. There is a very skilful kind of accommodation, finding a few ways to be recognized as different, which we then actively cultivate, while not noticing, beyond them, the profound resignation. These are some of the signs of a post-colonial culture, conscious all the time of its own real strengths and potentials, longing only to be itself, to become its own world but with so much, too much, on its back to be able, consistently, to face its real future.[4] It has happened in many places.

Real independence is a time of new and active creation: people sure enough of themselves to discard their baggage; knowing the past as past, as a shaping history, but with a new confident sense of the present and the future, where the decisive meanings and values will be made. But at an earlier stage, wanting that but not yet able to get it, there is another spirit: a fixation on the past, part real, part mythicized, because the past, in either form, is one thing they can't take away from us, that might even interest them, get a nod of recognition.

Each of these tendencies is now active in Wales. The complexity is that they are so difficult to separate, because they live, often, in the same bodies, the same minds. There is the proud and dignified withdrawal to Fortress Wales: the old times, the old culture; the still living enclave. There is the moving out from the enclave; the new work, the new teaching, the sense and in places the reality of a modern Welsh culture. But there is also the accommodation, in its different forms. There is the costume past, as a tourist attraction: things never distinctly Welsh, the tall hats and the dressers, presented as local pieties, things invented in the bad scholarship or the romantic fancies of the late eighteenth and nineteenth centuries – versions of bardism and druidism.

And more harmful than either is an evident tendency to play to our weaknesses, for commercial entertainment. If the Welsh, as the English sometimes say, are dark, deceitful, voluble and lustful Puritans, find a scene, find a character, play it on English television; admit and exaggerate your weaknesses before they have time to point them out. Or play the larger-than-life exile, your local colour deepening with every mile to Paddington or across the Severn Bridge and up the M4. Be what they expect you to be, and be it more. Tell the joke against yourself before they do, like Jewish humour in an anti-Semitic time. Show the distinctive bits and pieces they've already cast you for. It's easier and more successful than living with the whole of yourself. It's not me exactly, or you exactly, but by God it's Welsh, and by God it will slay the English.

A last word about these English. They are much more various than the myths allow. Anything really of our life can find alliance there, as well as the evident antipathy and patronage. A friend from the north of England said to me recently that the Welsh and the Scots were lucky to have these available national self-definitions, to help them find their way out of the dominance of English ruling-class minority culture.[5] In the north, he said, we who are English are in the same sense denied; what the world knows as English is not our life and feelings; and yet we don't, like the Welsh or the Scots, have this simple thing, this national difference, to pit against it. Then you might get through, quicker, to the real differences, the real conflicts, I said. No, he said, to get the energy to do that you need the model. I still don't agree, altogether, but it is how we might look at it.

People have to, in the end, direct their own lives, control their own places, live by their own feelings. When this is denied them, in any degree, distortions, compensations, myths, fancy dress can spread and become epidemic. But to define what has denied them, so as to see it and change it: that is something different and difficult; you need all the help you can get, and the doubtful help is the problem.

As Welsh culture changes, and as on the whole it gets stronger, it is this living complexity which we must come, are perhaps coming, to understand, to possess, and to work with.

Notes

1. Williams is listing a series of often stereotypical symbols of Welsh identity. *Bara Brith* is a traditional Welsh bread. The *Eisteddfod* is a cultural festival, with the National Eisteddfod, an annual week-long celebration of Welsh-language culture, being the most significant event of its kind. The stadium generally (if erroneously) known as Cardiff Arms Park preceded the Millennium Stadium as the national rugby stadium. The 'love spoon', a permanent feature of Welsh craft shops, was traditionally handed from boy to girl as a sign of love. The *englyn* is a traditional form of Welsh strict-metre verse.

2. Now known as 'The Museum of Welsh Life', the folk museum opened in 1948 in the grounds of St Fagans Castle, near Cardiff. It was modelled on the folk museums of Sweden.

3. These meditations on the Welsh Folk Museum offer an interesting example of the way in which Williams's cultural criticism informed his fictional writings. Chapter Four of *The Volunteers* (London: Methuen, 1978), pp. 26–30, is essentially a transposition of these meditations into fictional form.

4. The field of post-colonial theory and criticism established itself in the late 1980s and 1990s, and Williams has been widely criticised for ignoring questions of empire and imperialism in his writings. It is therefore striking that Williams used the term 'post-colonial' to describe the Welsh experience in 1975. I discuss this in the 'Introduction'. Postcolonial approaches to Welsh literature and culture have proliferated since the original appearance of *Who Speaks for Wales* in 2003. See Kirsti Bohata, *Postcolonialism Revisited* (Cardiff: University of Wales Press, 2004), which discusses Williams on pp. 24–5; Jane Aaron and Chris Williams (eds), *Postcolonial Wales* (Cardiff: University of Wales Press, 2005). Williams has been a figure of some importance for several postcolonial critics. See especially Edward Said, *The World, the Text and the Critic* (Cambridge MA: Harvard University Press, 1983), pp. 226–37; Aijaz Ahmad, *In Theory: Classes, Nations, Literatures* (London: Verso, 1992), pp. 46–50.

5. This friend is likely to have been the cultural critic Fred Inglis, who recounts a similar conversation in his biography, *Raymond Williams* (London: Routledge, 1995), pp. 258–9.

THE ARTS IN WALES

▦

Introduction to Meic Stephens (ed.), *The Arts in Wales*
1950–1975 (Cardiff: Welsh Arts Council, 1979), pp. 1–4.[1]

▦

W e learn to see by distinguishing shapes, and this is as true of a culture as of the physical world. What we see and hear every day is part of our culture, but just as important are the invisible, intangible shapes we carry around and bring to bear. Thus we see Wales as a small country, but even standing on the Brecon Beacons, looking south to the valleys and the seaboard where most of us live, looking west and north to the pastoral uplands, remembering beyond the far mountains another crowded coast, it is not smallness we see; it is land and distance, familiarity and strangeness. We are, we say, a small people, but in immediate human terms what is small, what is knowable, about twenty-five hundred thousand people: more than we can ever talk to or know? Smallness, then, is a shape we are carrying. Walk across the land and it is not what you feel, but learn a shape in another practice – take the shape of a small country because you have seen and heard of large ones – and it is there as a shaping idea in what you still, at life size, see and hear.

It is necessary to learn some shapes of this kind, yet we should never, by habit, suppose them to be natural. They are conventional ways of seeing and knowing and defining ourselves: some chosen, some inherited, some imposed. It can be said at times that the certainty of these shapes, their undoubtable currency, is a strength in everyday living. But at other times this may not at all be so: some shapes confine us, confuse us, indulging and magnifying or degrading and belittling. All significant shapes move, even if it is only a move to a new confirmation. The shape of Wales, more than most, is in constant movement, and this is of course unsettling. But our experiences have been so dynamic and so shifting that if the shapes had not changed we should now be wholly adrift: adrift of ourselves.

There has perhaps never been a time in which the shape of Wales has been more intensely explored and, in contested ways, affirmed. This process is occurring at so many levels that it is at once exciting and exhausting, clarifying and contradicting. This book is concerned with what can be taken, conventionally, as one of these levels, the arts. Conventionally, because we cannot be sure, until we look, that these arts belong together in any way more substantial than their habitual grouping. Or, if they belong together, as arts, in what sense again, beyond administrative classification, do they belong as the arts in Wales?

The first merit of this book is that it asks these questions in the most ready and useful way, by taking the classifications we are used to and then following through, in different minds, the details and the shaping of details that underlie them. And then we find, before the questions, and as the only kinds of roads to answers, sifted and collected but also crowded information. A small culture? That was always the implied shape. But we know, at life size, as we absorb this information, as we find in this field or in that things we did not know, signposts to places where we have not been, that even the conventionally small culture is bigger, more active, more crowded than our initial inclinations and perceptions suggested. We find details for this shape and for that. We are quite differently engaged. We have been given emphases, and we can consider and reconsider our own emphases. Newly latent shapes are perceptible, new questions of connection and disconnection, new assessments of achievements and of problems.

The book has been sponsored by the Welsh Arts Council, which has been in existence for only just over a decade.[2] The idea of an Arts Council, in its presently known form, is itself only just over three decades old. These are young bodies, still active and controversial. As it now stands an Arts Council is an intervention between two powerful alternatives: on the one hand, that of the market; on the other hand, that of the direct public authority. It is an attempted innovation, to encourage, to support and to extend the arts, beyond the short and indifferent terms of a market of commodities, and at the same time beyond governmental or bureaucratic direction. As that kind of intervention and innovation it gathers, without effort (though it has sometimes, additionally, made efforts), both enemies and sceptical observers. Anyone who has seen it, close up, knows that it can do with the latter. Indeed some of the best of that kind are inside it, trying and often failing to improve it. But past all that it is a shape that we have sketched and are trying to fill in. It is a notion of a need and of a kind of priority. It speaks, tries to speak, to a sense of a culture which is connected with a society and yet which is never merely derivative from its more general political and economic definitions. In Britain as a whole it is having its difficulties. There is the glamorous and aching pull of a metropolis. In its precise area, of culture, there are often crippling class divisions. What is being contested, not always sensibly, is a dark area of ignorance and suspicion. What is being affirmed, through rushed meetings, is sometimes enlightenment, at other times, complacently, the mere gig-lamps of posture and fashion. But it is in process. It is where the arguments can be focused as well as the year-to-year arrangements made. It is a place where shapes are made, very practically, as the money flows or fails to flow, but at its best (a best which needs change and struggle) it is a place where shapes are also glimpsed and questioned, attempted and revised. In the larger process of shaping a culture it is a necessary agency, a necessary kind of agency. The Welsh Arts Council has one special advantage: that it is attempting its difficult work at a time when both levels of its definition – the Welshness and the arts – are in active movement. This makes its work harder but even more necessary. In my independent judgment, having watched comparable work in England, its spirit is quite exceptionally impressive. The very problems of Wales – the two languages of its literature, the deepening cultural crisis – have provoked, here as in other areas of Welsh life, initiatives and kinds of confidence that on their own but especially comparatively are remarkable. And this has to be said before we go back into our more local, confused and often frustrating moments. The present book is an apt example. To try to make a shape out of twenty-five years of diverse activities is difficult, from the start. In a familiar (I almost say English) mood the difficulty becomes improbability and soon a corrosive doubt: the sad hand moving to the resigned mouth. Here, accepting the probability of mistakes and inadequacies, and the certainty of difficulty and unevenness, the thing is done, is issued, and the process continues. It is the first attempt I know of to bring together what has to be brought together, to see how it all looks. In this respect, and beyond all the details, we see one emergent and inspiriting shape: the active culture of a contemporary Wales.

Nobody needs telling that this culture has problems. Most of them come through, in convincing detail, in the particular chapters. And there are other problems, just beyond the terms of this book's definition. The present state of a once-dominant English culture, to which Welsh work was related as a regional variation; the present condition of European and North American culture, to which the English is now increasingly related as a regional variation in its turn: these are formidable dimensions. There are many profound questions in the changing relations between the identity and rootedness of certain kinds of art and the mobilities and extended learning of a more consciously international scope. Such questions are not to be settled by old kinds of labelling. But always one way of approaching them is to see what is happening where you are. Sometimes, when you do this, you find that the most local is also the most general. Thus while all my own imaginative writing moves around the Welsh Black Mountains, I find a movement of very different Black Mountain writers in North America, and I know, in new ways, something of what they mean.[3] There are many cases like this, and there are also the other cases, where it can seem that only the most alienated work, belonging nowhere and thus exportable everywhere, will prevail. Between these two extremes are many thousands of mixed cases.

What this book does is to say what we are doing and what some of us think we are doing. In that learning of shapes and of rhythms which give us our senses of our lives, the arts, in all their diversity, are leading and indispensable elements. In a period of great difficulty and complexity, it is good to pick up so many encouraging signals. There is John Rowlands referring to 'unparalleled opportunity and encouragement for the Welsh writer', or Roland Mathias tracing positive developments from the literary situation of the fifties and early sixties, or Malcolm Boyd writing of transformation in our musical life, or Roy Bohana of the past thirty years as the 'most productive period in the history of music in Wales', or Eric Rowan of the 'remarkable growth of the visual arts'. Of course, other questions push at the edges of these judgments, and this is most clear in Elan Closs Stephens's account of the different ways of seeing developments in Welsh drama and theatre: from one point of view the important expansion represented by the arts centres and the professional companies, from another point of view the supersession or incorporation of a more native or radical activity. All these informed judgments offer opportunities for the sustained and substantial and extending discussion which is now more than ever necessary, and which should come through to determine policies for the arts in Wales.

Notes

1. Meic Stephens (1938–2018) was a literary editor, translator and poet. From 1967–90, he was literature director of the Welsh Arts Council. See his autobiography, *My Shoulder to the Wheel* (Talybont: Y Lolfa, 2015).
2. The Welsh Arts Council (1967–94) was a committee of the Arts Council of Great Britain, and became the autonomous Arts Council of Wales in April 1994. It became accountable to the National Assembly for Wales on 1 July 1999, when responsibility was transferred from the Secretary of State for Wales. See also Williams's article on 'The Arts Council' (1979), in *Resources of Hope* (London: Verso, 1989), pp. 41–55.
3. The Black Mountain Poets were a group of writers centred at Black Mountain College, Asheville, North Carolina, founded in 1933 by dissident faculty and students of Rollins College (Florida) and foundering in 1956. Its major figure was the poet Charles Olson (1910–70), whose important students included Robert Creeley (1926–2005), John Wieners (1934–2002) and the Welsh-identifying Denise Levertov (1923–97).

WALES AND ENGLAND

New Wales, 1 (1983), 34-8.
Collected in John Osmond (ed.), *The National Question Again* (Llandysul: Gomer, 1985), pp. 18-31, and in Raymond Williams, *What I came to Say* (London: Hutchinson Radius, 1989), pp. 64-74.

It can be said that the Welsh people have been oppressed by the English State for some seven centuries. Yet it can then also be said that the English people have been oppressed by the English State for even longer. In any such general statements all the real complications of history are temporarily overridden. Even the names, when they are examined, begin to blur or dissolve. As late as the nineteenth century, radical Englishmen were still identifying oppression as the 'Norman Yoke', which had been clamped on the necks of free Saxons. Down to our own day, some radical Welshmen mutter the comparable curse of the 'English Yoke'. Neither party is mistaken about the facts of oppression and exploitation, but how these are interpreted is a matter for argument. The Norman State; the Anglo-Norman State; the English State; the British State: at different points in this sequence the real complications begin to reveal themselves. Earlier again, how do we understand what the Cymry said of those same free Saxons or English, or what they said and must have said of 'their own' British Princes?

In a period of great tension and of necessary conflict it is especially important to be sure about names. In our own quite exceptional difficulties, it is especially important to be sure of what Welshmen mean by 'English'. I grew up in border country, where the names learned at school were of general and rather vague geographical areas: England to the East, Wales to the West, and where we were, too

small for the maps, a village in Monmouthshire, coloured this way
or that, or dubiously hatched, by what seemed the mapmaker's fancy.
As I learned a little history I saw no border but frontier country: the
decaying Norman castles, quite literally overlooking us. Yet one of
the worst ravagers of our immediate land had been English Harold,
killed by the Normans at Hastings. But then, as we used the castles
for picnics, and looked up the closer history and statistics, there was
a new administrative entity: England-and-Wales. Meanwhile, where
we were, we spoke English but recited Welsh poems at anniversaries
and sang in English or Welsh at the village eisteddfod. It was a place
to find intimations of complexity. As Emyr Humphreys put it, intro-
ducing one of my readings: not *Border Country* by Raymond Williams
but *Raymond Williams* by Border Country.[1]

It is not now the personal history that matters, but the learned
perspective of England. In the politics anxiously watched by a schoolboy in the thirties, there was the British Empire, sedulously taught
but by me sullenly cursed in our Welsh grammar school, and then
somewhere in the pages of the *Daily Herald*, for repulsion more
than attraction but in any case for definition, an England which
was an amalgam of Neville Chamberlain and Sir Samuel Hoare and
Lord Halifax, of Jubilee and Coronation, of London and the Home
Counties (I puzzled for years about those Home Counties: home to
whom or for what?).[2] So potent, indeed, was this offensive amalgam
that it almost obliterated further questions. Anything that was not
it had attractions: the Welsh rugby team, outrucking Chamberlain
and Hoare and Halifax and the young toffs they'd persuaded to stand
in for them; or Konni Zilliacus and the League of Nations and the
Soviet pavilion in Paris, none of these Home Counties; or then,
suddenly, Yorkshire people, who were not Home Counties either
but who vigorously insisted not only that they were English – I had
a go at arguing them out of it – but that they were the real English,
not that lot down there.[3]

This was not just a village boy's perspective. Many years later I
had a difficult argument with a highly educated Belgian friend, who
had just seen the Beatles on television and then, at closer quarters,
some visiting Liverpool football fans, and who asked, with some
insistence, what on earth had happened to the English, who were
well known to be emotionally reserved, quietly behaved, and decently

and soberly dressed. When I tried to say that these English – with a few Liverpool Irish but then there were to be other football fans, from London and Manchester and Birmingham – had been there all the time but he'd only just seen them, I could feel his world trembling. He knew, as we in Wales sometimes *know*, what England is, what the English are. And what was known just happened to exclude both the great majority and most of the diverse minorities of the actual English. England, that for me still awful and sobering name, was for these actual English many quite different things. But for most of the rest of us, England – we can surely see it now – was this dominant English class, these alien figures who ruled us and disposed of us. England – this class, this system; but there all the time, when we went to visit or live among them, all those other incongruous, incompatible English.

Well, that is their problem, though until they solve it there will be not much peace for the rest of us. But it won't help, either side of the border, to mistake the State for the real identity, or the projections for the people. What we can do positively, meanwhile, is explore those regions of habit or argument in which the differentials of Wales, and thus its effective relations with England, are asserted or denied.

We need not stay long in one of the most populated regions, that of race. The ethnic history of what is now Wales is one of extreme complexity, from the earliest times. There seem to be quite basic differences between the Neolithic and Bronze Age settlers and the Iron Age arrivals, though in legend and platitude all tend to be assimilated in terms of the subsequent contrast with 'Saxons' and to be confused as Celts. When this last difficult description is asserted, we have to reply that, on the available evidence, the 'Celts' were the first invading linguistic imperialists. We have also to remember, near the roots of some modern loyalties, that the 'old language' which has been so central to the identity of Wales was the product of an ex-colonial situation in which the native language, British, had been profoundly modified by the imperial language, Latin.

Then in terms of people in the implied racial sense, we have to remember not only the pre-modern immigrations from Ireland and England and even Scotland, but the fact that very large numbers of the Cymry or pre-Cymry went on living in what is now England, and their descendants are among those we now gaze at as the English. Modern movements of population have been even more drastic, and they have occurred both ways and in a multitude of directions, to say nothing of the long complexities of intermarriage. Many wholly identifiable modern Welshmen must, on the record, be third or fourth generation English and Irish and Scottish immigrants. Sometimes the names tell us this, but often not, since females have lost their family names. Beyond this, of course, that devastation of naming systems imposed by English administration has left us with some of the most radical identity confusions of any modern people. We do not even have wholly to deny some possible genetic correlations with personality and culture, or those observable clusters of some physical features – trends and emphases within a most complex map – to continue to insist that the significant differentials are not in this region at all.

The differentials of culture are altogether more serious. Yet I have spent so much of my working life trying to analyse culture that here too, but now more positively, I have to emphasize great complexity. The central problem is that there are, on the one hand, some very significant continuities and, on the other hand, some unusually drastic changes of direction and periods of effective remaking. The central continuity is of course the language, and this remains critical to cultural identity not only in those who have retained or are re-acquiring it, but even in many of those to whom it is now lost or marginal. The Welsh/English language differential is then quite fundamental, and direct or indirect action by English administration and education against the native language is not only unforgivable – that is an old score – but must still lead to the most intense and active resistance.

What then needs also to be said, however, is that there is another kind of significant differential – how that majority of the Welsh who have lost their native language now speak and write English. It is true that within Wales this is not greatly noticed, and also that in certain situations, involving relations with the native language, it can even be resented, as the mongrel mark of the 'Anglo-Welsh'. But in relations between Wales and England it is still a most significant differential, of a kind which fosters some effective cultural identity. We have only to think of other places where something like this has happened (it is most visible, though not really most important, in literary production – the identifiably Irish writers in English; the English Northern poets and entertainers) to realise that it does indeed matter. It is significant both as a cultural dimension of an otherwise merely geographical or administrative area and, against heavy pressures of standardisation, as an unforced and steadily available community.

There is then an area which I find much more intractable. It is clear, to start with, that we can make a significant contrast between the Welsh and English literary traditions. Welsh literature, for quite basic reasons of language and conventions – and even where there has been, as in the later centuries, traceable and important English influence – is in no sense a region of English literature but is at once autonomous and important. What is then difficult, however, is the quite common extrapolation from literary evidence to a more general cultural identity. The idea that the spirit of a people is essentially expressed in its literature obviously speaks to some real situations, but in its ordinary form it speaks to too many, and in the end falsely. Indeed, one of the strongest and least noticed English influences on Welsh thought is just this version of cultural nationalism, in which the continuity and inner essence of a people is discovered in a (selective) version of its 'national' literature.

Of course, writing in any time and space bears the marks and carries the factors of its time and space. The relative (changing) continuity of a language carries many of these marks and factors into a further perceptible space. But to jump from this complex process, which is in fact always being remade and reinterpreted, to such concepts as continuity and essence is to reproduce that ideology which was forged in the composition of nation-states. It is then not only peculiarly inappropriate to Wales. In its false projections it disguises the more substantial and interesting process of certain autonomies hard won within a subordination.

It is this mixed and uneven process which is the true and complex cultural identity of Wales. The ideology which overrides it, compounding Aneirin and Dafydd ap Gwilym and Daniel Owen and distilling ideal qualities from the forced compound, is not just wrong but hostile.[4] For if there is one thing to insist on in analysing Welsh culture it is the complex of forced and acquired discontinuities: a broken series of radical shifts, within which we have to mark not only certain social and linguistic continuities but many acts of self-definition by negation, by alternation and by contrast. Indeed it is this culture of Wales, profoundly and consciously problematic, which is the real as distinct from the ideological difference from a selective, dominant and hegemonic English culture.

It would take a book to trace this whole process, for which we are only now, in the work of a new generation of committed and critical Welsh historians, getting enough of the detail. One central area would be analysis of the cultural impulses towards democratic community, which have been regularly discussed. Now I do indeed believe that these impulses are stronger in Welsh than in majority English culture, though there can be no simple contrast, and the political effect, which is very complicated, needs to be separately discussed. At the broadest cultural level it is possible to see real relations between twentieth-century expressions of these impulses, as in Waldo Williams and those influenced by him, and the popular cultural initiatives of nonconformism and of the revival centred on the modern Eisteddfod.[5] But that is not an essence, it is a history.

Moreover, it is a complicated history. Nonconformism, with its great cultural values of self-organization and common literacy, came in over the English border. At one level, indeed, some of the crucial initiations were specifically English. But then they made their way into a people and a culture which for other reasons, within the general subordination, had a great store of readiness and longing and potential energy, which came to give the movement quite specific passions and intensities. Much the same was to happen, later, with trade unionism. The intensity of the specific Welsh development is a great and continuing modern value. But unless we relate it, at every point, to the long experience of defeat and subordination, we project a quite false essential autonomy. The religious history of Wales is indeed very complicated, and there are some important distinctions to be made between the old Marches, where the interaction with England was most direct, and the old Principality. But we can never exclude from any of its phases the element of seeking an alternative to the current and changing forms of English cultural dominance. An earlier Royalist Wales is not easily included in the projection of a radical and democratic Welsh essence, but it makes more sense that Wales was like that when England was going the other way. The cultural forms in which a subordinated people try to express their distinctive identity can be specifically quite discontinuous, and these discontinuities are better related to the realities of subordination than to the idealizations of a submerged essence. Thus it makes little sense, in my opinion, to connect modern democratic cultural impulses with the customs and beliefs of the old Cymry. It is not that we will fail to find some resemblances, nor that some of the earlier ideals are unavailable, as an idealizing and inspiriting mode, to a later and very different world. But the fixed forms of a retrospective essence can be very deceptive. There is an exact analogy in English culture, in the idea of the 'Norman Yoke' and the earlier free Saxon England. The image of a lost communal freedom could sustain and motivate oppressed and otherwise despairing people, but we all know quite well that no English or Welsh radical, from the seventeenth century onwards, could be content for a moment to live within the archaic tribal and early feudal structures of those past English or Welsh centuries. And yet it cannot be a case of merely deriding the idealization; that, in its turn, would overlook some relevant exemplary communal experiences. The real situation is that in the difficult process of enduring, understanding and then trying to find ways of resisting subordination, there is a very complex creation of images of the past as a way of amending images of the present and of finding images of the future. This very complex creation is, surely evident again in the modern national cultural revival.

Thus the experience of England was obviously a leading factor in the revival of forms of Welsh culture. This is not only in some of the significant sites of the more organized revival, among London exiles or in the border counties. It is also in the consonance of some of its forms (including the familiar admixture of forgery and fantasy) with contemporary English and European forms of the revival of folk culture and the cult of medievalism. It is still extremely difficult to disentangle these modes – in the forms of the modern Eisteddfod or the Gorsedd, or in the attitudes towards early and medieval Welsh literature, and especially the romances – from those elements of continuity and recovery which can properly be seen, and which undoubtedly eventually became, general impulses towards autonomy and, interacting with the intense nonconformist culture, a genuine popular revival.[6] But in any case this revival is the working through of a history, among now radically dislocated as well as subordinated people, rather than the fortunate re-emergence of a subdued essence.

It is in interpreting this history that the real modern relations between Wales and England begin to come into focus. The history of the period of simple subordination is, in its most general outlines, reasonably clear. English law and political administration were ruthlessly imposed, within an increasingly centralized 'British' state. The Welsh language was made the object of systematic discrimination and, where necessary, repression. Succeeding phases of a dominant Welsh landowning class were successfully Anglicized and either physically or politically drawn away to the English centre. Anglicizing institutions, from the boroughs to the grammar schools, were successfully implanted. All these processes can properly be seen as forms of political and cultural colonization.

But then two major and related economic developments changed the shape of these basic relations. English capital and English management penetrated a relatively under-developed economy, inaugurating the major industrial development of iron and coal. At the same time, the rural economy was penetrated in new ways and, even more significantly, was marginalized. Lines of communication, from the turnpike roads to the new railways and canals, were driven through Wales on bearings evidently determined by the shape of the larger economy and trading system (and indeed of the larger political system, in the routes to Ireland). Few of these were ever related to the internal needs of Wales, as a developing country, or (as the Rebecca rioters of 1843 recognized) to the customs and needs of the traditional rural economy.[7] The exploitation of Welsh iron and coal for the expanding British industrial and then imperial system went alongside the ruin, from other parts of the same system, of small Welsh rural industries and, even more generally, alongside the increasing marginalization of Welsh within a marginalized British agriculture.

At many levels, within these complex and devastating processes, Welsh people resisted what was being done to them. Resistance ranged from the Merthyr Rising and militant trade unionism in the industrial areas to Rebecca and the tithe struggles in the rural areas.[8] But, given the complexity of the process as a whole, and especially the radically differential internal responses − of industrial conflict within rapid economic development and of agrarian conflict within impoverishment, depopulation and marginalization − it was and has remained difficult either to confine or to unify these vigorous and diverse struggles within a national Welsh–English perspective. Indeed, on one count, it is surprising that there was as much national feeling as there was: a common perception of identity, within such diverse situations and conflicts. That this identity was primarily cultural – in language, customs, kinship and community – rather than in any modern sense political is, in this situation, not surprising at all.

It is equally not surprising that over and above this cultural identity large numbers of Welsh people found temporarily effective political identity in wider movements which then in new ways incorporated them: the ideology of Empire, in which there was so much direct (though as between coal and farming contradictory) interest; the ideology and organization of Liberalism, at once the expression of local radicalism and, in its wider bounds, the means of its containment and displacement; the ideology and organization of Labourism, at first an expression of local militancy and correctly perceived class conflict but again, in its wider bounds, the eventual means of containment and displacement.[9]

The main point is not that each of these phases was marked by certain specificities of Welshness, as most notably in Liberalism and Labourism, where the quality and quantity of Welsh contribution were significantly proportionately high. It is that in each of these phases – and the third is not yet concluded – the complexity of relations between these successive effective incorporations and the continuing (distinguishing or contradictory) self-identification as the Welsh was bound to be extreme. This complexity can be seen both positively and negatively.

Negatively, it has led not only to division but to self-division, as people have found themselves caught in what are ultimately incompatible interests and loyalties, which they yet have urgent and often desperate need to try to unify, so that their conditions might be improved. At its most negative, this had led, on the one hand, to archaic or residual types of nationalism, in which a received, traditional and unproblematic identity has been asserted as overriding all those modern economic and political relations which are in fact inevitable and determining. It has led, on the other hand, to pseudo-modernist rejections of the specificities of Welshness and the Welsh situation, in which the confident imperatives of the incorporation – a transforming Liberalism, a redeeming and transforming Labourism

– are repeated long after they have practically failed, both at the centre and in Wales itself. The pseudo-modernist rejections have typically included, also, a particular spitefulness against all or any countervailing Welsh specificities; a distinguishing Welsh form of anti-Welshness, finding only partial and insufficient excuse in the excesses of romantic nationalism. It is within these negative forms of the central complexities that much of the surface politics of contemporary Wales is still conducted, and the negative effects have to be reckoned as still predominant (as the 1979 Referendum on devolution so damagingly showed).

But the complexity can also be seen positively. As earlier, in certain phases of the culture, the painful recognition of real dislocations, discontinuities, problematic identities has led not only to division and confusion but to new and higher forms of consciousness. It is true that these are very difficult to disentangle from the available forms of description and statement, as is clear in the latest phase of nationalism. But it is, for example, very significant that one tendency in contemporary Welsh nationalism is, so to say, an anti-nationalist nationalism. This has important cultural precedents, in suspicion of any centralized state. But it is also a correct and far-reaching response to certain dominating contemporary political and economic developments, which are outdistancing all earlier forms.

Perception of the relations between Wales and England is then radically affected. New insights are forming beyond the old perspectives of England as the conqueror, the colonizer, the exploiter and even the big neighbour. It is not only a matter of the visible weakening of England, in the aftermath of the weakening and dissolution of the British Imperial order. It is also a matter of the visible weakening of centralized nation-states and economies of just that English size: their inability to maintain political and economic autonomies and sovereignties of the traditional kind; their further inability, as they are themselves increasingly economically and politically penetrated, to maintain their old kinds of singular relation with their peripheral and dependent areas. Many of the things that happened, over centuries, to the Welsh are now happening, in decades, to the English. The consequent confusion and struggle for identity, the search for new modes of effective autonomy within a powerfully extended and profoundly interacting para-national political and economic system, are now in many parts of the world the central issues of social consciousness, struggling to come through against still powerful but residual ideas and institutions.

Of course, the surviving power of England – the specific power of its ruling political and economic class – still presses heavily on Wales as on other marginalized communities, including many of the regions of England itself. But at many levels, from the new communal nationalisms and regionalisms to the new militant particularisms of contemporary industrial conflict, the flow of contemporary politics is going beyond the modes of all the incorporated ideologies and institutions. The Welsh, of course, have been inside these cross-pressures for much longer than the English. And as a result we have had to learn that we need to solve the real contradictions between nationality and class, and between local well-being and the imperatives of a large-scale system. Consequently, we may be further along the road to a relevant if inevitably painful contemporary social consciousness. But in any case the ideological defences of the old and now disintegrating system are less powerful, though they are still powerful enough to be more damaging, in confused and peripheral Wales, than in bewildered and ex-central England. What seemed a sectoral problem and impetus, to be dressed or dissolved in mere local colour, is now more and more evidently a focal problem and impetus: not particular to but to a significant extent particularized in Wales.

It is not possible to see any quick or easy way out of the present confusions and complexities. The euphoria of first insights, and of the energy and comradeship they have generated, is likely to have to endure more delay, more quarrelling, more frustration than is ordinarily at all allowed for. Even the authentically differential radicalism of the Welsh, as analysed by Hechter* and still residually widely celebrated, will be put to many new tests.[10] For if radicalism is merely the Liberal Establishment and Labour Loyalism – both demonstrably stronger in Wales than in England – it could quickly rot, indeed already is rotting from the inside. Again the authentically differential communalism of the Welsh, product of a specific history rather than of some racial or cultural essence, could become residual if it does

* Michael Hechter, *Internal Colonialism: The Celtic Fringe in British National Development, 1536–1960* (London: Routledge & Kegan Paul, 1975).

not grow beyond its current elements of false consciousness. The ideological notion, for example, that Wales is classless, because we do indeed have easier immediate ways of speaking to each other, could become a powerful barrier to that practical communalism which requires difficult transformations of political and economic institutions and relations, rather than friendly and informal accommodations to them. The differentials that still matter will have to be taken very much further, and in new and contemporary terms, if they are not to decline into accommodating illusions. Radical and communal Wales, that is to say, will be real to the extent that it develops, in plan and practice, new forms of co-operative work and communal socialism, new kinds of educational and cultural collectives, rather than by what happens to the Labour or even the Nationalist vote.

These are hard things to say, but then the general situation, between Wales and England, has been and remains hard and complex. Indeed the harder we now are, especially with ourselves, the better we shall be, including better, beyond 'England', with the English.

Notes

1. Emyr Humphreys (1919–2020) was a leading Welsh novelist, whose novels – despite having been written from a more overtly nationalist position – share a number of thematic and formal concerns with those of Williams, most notably in their commitment to realism and their concern with the transmission of beliefs, values and cultural practices across several generations. A useful introduction to Humphreys's life, thought and writings, is M. Wynn Thomas (ed.), *Emyr Humphreys: Conversations and Reflections* (Cardiff: University of Wales Press, 2002), and also M. Wynn Thomas, *Emyr Humphreys* (Cardiff: University of Wales Press, 2018).

2. Neville Chamberlain (1869–1940) was British prime minister (1937–40), famous for advocating a policy of appeasement with Nazi Germany. Samuel Hoare (1880–1959) was Home Secretary 1937–39, famous for surrendering large parts of Ethiopia to Mussolini as foreign secretary in 1935. Edward Wood, Lord Halifax (1881–1959), was foreign secretary (1938–40) and supported Chamberlain's policy of appeasement toward Nazi Germany.

3. Konni Zilliacus (1894–1967) influenced Labour Party policy from a position in the League of Nations in the 1930s. He became a Labour MP in 1945, but was expelled from the party in 1949, charged with being a communist sympathiser due to his persistent opposition to the Labour government's foreign policy. Reinstated in 1952, he was an MP from 1955 until his death.

4. Aneirin is one of the earliest Welsh-language poets – the 'Cynfeirdd' – writing in the latter part of the sixth century. He is believed to be the

author of 'Y Gododdin', a long poem which commemorates a battle fought at Catraeth (Catterick) about the year 600. Dafydd ap Gwilym (fl.?1320–?70) was the most important and innovative of Wales's medieval poets. His poems have been widely translated. Daniel Owen (1836–95) was the first major Welsh-language novelist, whose works mount a powerful critique of the hypocrisy and repressions of late Victorian society. An introduction to the novelist's work in English is Robert Rhys's essay 'Daniel Owen', in Hywel Teifi Edwards (ed.), *A Guide to Welsh Literature c. 1800–1900* (Cardiff: University of Wales Press, 2000), pp. 146–65.

5. Waldo Williams (1904–71), was a school teacher, nationalist, pacifist and one of the most original poets of modern Welsh-language literature. A brief introduction to the poet's life and work is James Nicholas, *Waldo Williams* (Cardiff: University of Wales Press, 1975). Tony Conran has translated Williams's poems in *The Peacemakers: Selected Poems* (Llandysul: Gomer, 1997), and a sense of the author's cultural thought can be gleaned from Damian Walford Davies (ed.), *Waldo Williams: Rhyddiaith* (Caerdydd: Gwasg Prifysgol Cymru, 2001), which contains several articles in English. On the 'eisteddfod', see 'Welsh Culture', n. 1.

6. 'Gorsedd' refers to Gorsedd Beirdd Ynys Prydain (lit. 'The Throne or Assembly of Bards of the Isle of Britain'), a society of poets, musicians and other representatives of Welsh culture founded by the greatest Welsh 'inventor of traditions' Iolo Morganwg (Edward Williams) in 1792. Since 2019, it has been known as 'Gorsedd Cymru', with its activities largely confined to the key literature ceremonies of the National Eisteddfod.

7. The Rebecca Riots were a major disturbance in south-west Wales between 1839 and 1843. The main target of the rioters were the toll-gates, which were attacked by men disguised in women's clothing. The root cause of the protest lay in the imposition of a money economy upon a society dominated by a small caste of landowners. See David Williams, *The Rebecca Riots: A Study in Agrarian Discontent* (Cardiff: University of Wales Press, 1955); Rhian E. Jones, *Petticoat Heroes: Gender, Culture and Protest in the Rebecca Riots* (Cardiff: University of Wales Press, 2015).

8. The Merthyr Rising (1831) was a popular rebellion amongst the workers of Merthyr Tydfil, which developed into an armed insurrection. It resulted in the hanging of Dic Penderyn (Richard Lewis), in Cardiff on 13 August 1831. Penderyn is widely regarded as the first martyr of the Welsh working class. Raymond Williams refers to the event several times in his writings on Wales, and this volume contains his *Guardian* review of the most significant history of the rising, Gwyn A. Williams's *The Merthyr Rising* (London: Croom Helm, 1978). The 'Tithe War' was led by nonconformist farmers in the 1880s who refused to pay tithes to the Established Church. See David W. Howell, *Land and People in Nineteenth-Century Wales* (London: Routledge and Kegan Paul, 1978).

9. On the ways in which the allegedly 'universalist' ideologies of Liberalism and Labourism functioned to 'contain' and 'displace' particularistic 'local' forms of

Welsh radicalism and nationalism, see Simon Brooks, *Why Wales Never Was: The Failure of Welsh Nationalism* (Cardiff: University of Wales Press, 2017).

10. Richard Wyn Jones argues that 'one of the weaknesses of modern Welsh studies is an aversion to big-picture thinking, witnessed, for example, in the hysterically hostile reception afforded Michael Hechter's *Internal Colonialism*' ('The Colonial Legacy in Welsh Politics', in Aaron and Williams (eds), *Postcolonial Wales*, p. 25). The reception of Hechter's work would be a valuable project. His influence is here acknowledged by Raymond Williams.

COMMUNITY

The London Review of Books (24 January 1985), 14-15.

Collected in Raymond Williams, What I Came to
Say (London: Hutchinson Radius, 1989), pp. 57-63.

Review of Emyr Humphreys, The Taliesin Tradition:
A Quest for the Welsh Identity (London: Black Raven
Press, 1984) and Jones (London: Dent, 1984); Dai Smith,
Wales! Wales? (London: George Allen and Unwin, 1984);
and Jan Morris, The Matter of Wales: Epic Views of a
Small Country (Oxford: Oxford University Press, 1984).[1]

Two truths are told, as alternative prologues to the action of modern Wales. The first draws on the continuity of Welsh language and literature: from the sixth century, it is said, and thus perhaps the oldest surviving poetic tradition in Europe. The second draws on the turbulent experience of industrial South Wales, over the last two centuries, and its powerful political and communal formations.

It would be possible, within an English perspective, to see these truths as of different kinds, literary and political: one or other to be emphasized or reduced to background. Yet the distinctive Welsh character of each offered truth is that it is simultaneously political and cultural. This is a mode of argument, but perhaps even more of assumption, which has often seemed alien and unacceptable east of Offa's Dyke, though its relevance to the English experience can be shown to be just as direct. Within Wales, the two truths, or those versions of them which are reciprocally dismissed as inadequate, are matters of intense and often bitter controversy. Indeed, perhaps the least known fact, by others, about contemporary Welsh culture and politics is that there are harsh and persistent quarrels within a dimension which is seen from outside as unusually singular. The nearest analogy I can find is with what is known in England, more properly in London, as the Hard Left, where a confidently named sector, marked off from all others, is often riven by controversies more bitter than anything in a more established politics.

Yet there is, after all, a distinguishable Hard Left, and in the same sense a distinguishable Welsh culture. Each can be tracked in its general affiliations, but the more profound community is its area of discourse: the very specific issues which it selects for argument. For myself, when I say 'two truths', it is not from some sense of detachment or balance but because, seeing the matter in my own living conditions from both inside and outside, I am especially aware of the common elements of authenticity in each apparently alternative case.

The argument for an essential cultural continuity, informing a people long threatened by suppression, is well made in Emyr Humphreys's *The Taliesin Tradition*. At one level the book can be usefully read as a history of Welsh literature, by one of the finest of modern Welsh writers. Indeed I am tempted to a review which would simply insist that English students of literature should read it, since it remains a scandal that a body of writing of this substance, composed on this island, should be so largely unknown to readers of strict literary interests. A general impression from Matthew Arnold will not do.[2] The major verse of Dafydd ap Gwilym and the romances of *Pedair Cainc y Mabinogi* (in English the *Mabinogion*) are evident classics in the writing of this island.[3] Moreover the interest of several Welsh verse forms is considerable. Even polemically, one must wonder at the students of Hopkins who do not know *cynghanedd* (a set of techniques still practised).[4]

> Fy ing enfawr, fy ngwynfyd – fy mhryder
> Fy mhradwys hyfryd;
> Ei charu'r wyf yn chwerw hefyd
> A'i chasau'n serchus o hyd.
>
> Alan Llwyd[5]

This *englyn,* as so often, is dependent on particular Welsh assonances, but in at least some cases, and certainly in Dafydd ap Gwilym and the *Mabinogi,* the achievements are accessible in translation. Consider only this brief extract from the technique of a rapid sequence of metaphors and comparisons, the *dyfalu*, in Dafydd's poem on the seagull as love messenger: 'a piece of the sun, a steel glove at sea, and yet swift and proud and light on the wave, fish fed, foam footed, lily of the sea, contemplative of the wave, like a written page, speak for me.'[6]

Yet Emyr Humphreys has written much more than a literary story. He argues that the continuous poetic tradition, named from the first Taliesin, the sixth-century poet of the British kingdom of Rheged (now south-west Scotland), has 'contrived to be a major factor in the maintenance, stability and continuity of the Welsh identity and the fragile concept of Welsh nationhood'. The difficulties attending this argument are almost too obvious. The land now known as Wales, the people now known as Welsh, have experienced over those long centuries so many major changes of use and condition that continuity, except in the language, and even there in eventual decline, seems a merely mythical construct. Indeed, in an earlier phase of what appears to be the same argument, in a dominant tendency within a revived Welsh nationalism between the wars, the construct was plainly ideological. Against all the modern political experience of Wales, this tendency was on the cultural Right then influential throughout Europe. Wales was offered by some as the last noble fragment of a classical and catholic world. Welshness had the function of 'Englishness' in Leavis or of 'timeless' in Eliot: a stand of old values against a destructive industrial civilization.[7] Its most memorable expression was a poem 'The Deluge', by the nationalist leader Saunders Lewis, which began:

> The tramway climbs from Merthyr to Dowlais,
> Slime of a snail on a heap of slag.[8]

That industrial landscape or wasteland was accurately observed, but the sting was the judgement: 'here once was Wales.' It is then unsurprising that the inhabitants of that landscape, now the great majority of the Welsh, and with English as their main or only language, rejected a sense of Wales and of Welshness which seemed designed to exclude them.

Emyr Humphreys's argument is different, or partly different (he quotes the Saunders Lewis poem with apparent approval, or at least

80

without dissent). He sees the myth-making that is at work in any construction of a 'timeless identity', but then argues: 'The manufacture and proliferation of myth must always be a major creative activity among people with unnaturally high expectations reduced by historic necessity, or at least history, forced into what is often described as a marginal condition. In fact this marginal condition is now the essence of the human condition, with or without material security: we can bear even less than a little reality when it hovers over our heads in the shape of a nuclear missile.' Part of this connects with an argument which I have used myself: that the long Welsh experience of a precarious and threatened identity has informed Welsh thought with problems now coming through to once dominant and assertive peoples: most evidently, in our own time, the English. Yet the argument can then move in several ways. The most common, as in much Modernist writing and very strongly in serious North American culture, is an attachment to the dynamics of mobility. Old and dissolving identities are at best raw material for an exchange of new and deliberately provisional universals, on which settled identity is the past from which there must be escape to the precarious and invigorating excitement of the new. In Wales, among otherwise different tendencies, the argument has not gone this way. This is what makes its writers and thinkers – traditionally based in a social status and obligation wholly different from the idea of the isolated artist or intellectual – a centre of opposition to the dominant literary and intellectual modes of Western Europe and North America. For the major Welsh response to the dissolutions of community and identity, which have been so repeatedly and directly experienced, has been to make, or to try to remake, communities and identities which will hold.

Emyr Humphreys finds these in a cultural tradition. Dai Smith, as a vigorous exponent of the second truth, finds them in the communal struggles and loyalties of a Welsh industrial proletariat. Yet even within this contrast there are shared assumptions. In a recent radio report on the people of the mining valleys during the present bitter coal strike, Dai Smith said that the three words he kept hearing were 'culture', 'community' and 'jobs'. The first two are not the classical words of an industrial proletariat, as universally theorized. Indeed they are words which I have been so whacked for using in England, as if they were my private inventions or deviations, that this reminder of a genuine area of shared discourse was especially welcome. Among some English Marxists this strain has been tagged as 'culturalist'. It is to be hoped that some of them at least will notice that this is the language of what has been, in the worst days so far of the strike, the most solid working class of the British coalfields.

Dai Smith, in *Wales! Wales?*, a book based on his recent television series, attacks Emyr Humphreys's argument directly. He accuses him of confusing the 'functional role of myths' with a 'deliberate mytholo-gising'. The risk is undoubtedly there. To accommodate the evident changes in Welsh life, which as one of its most distinguished modern recorders Emyr Humphreys knows very well, there is a shift within the concept of continuity. This is expressed with reference to one of the themes of the literature: Taliesin the shape-shifter. At a simple level this is merely suggestive, but it is potentially indicative of an observable historical process: at its weakest, the endless fantasies of a subjected people, magnifying past greatness or present uniqueness as forms of disguise not only from others but from hard-pressed selves; at its strongest, however, a capacity for active and flexible survival, in which powers of a certain kind – hope, fidelity, eloquence – are repeatedly distilled from defeat. The test of the strongest sense would then be the welcoming admission of the latest shift: not as the aban-donment of 'Welshness', in some singular and unitary form, but as the positive creation of a still distinctively Welsh, English-speaking working-class culture.

It is here, on the ground, that the schools and parties divide, though in adversity they are now speaking with each other in some new ways. An economic analyst said recently that there is no Welsh economy: there are two city regions, Cardiff and Swansea; there is upland pastoral Wales; and there is Greater Liverpool. This is a famil-iar type of identification of 'regions' within what we call the Yookay. What has then to be asked, though, is why there is such pressure, from many different positions, to hold to some version of a unifying identity, within and across some of the most radical differences of condition that can be found anywhere in Europe. Whether any of its processes are 'functional myths' or 'deliberate mythologising' is being very sharply tested, all the time, in practice. The recent tenta-tive emergence of a new kind of National Left is the most significant current attempt, but then its mood is decidedly not mythical, in either sense.[9] The shift-shape it is attempting is material to the core: the remaking of a land and a people. One of the most striking facts about the second truth, in industrial South Wales, is that the remarkable school of modern historians of which Gwyn A. Williams is the leading member and to which Dai Smith is a vigorous contributor, had no sooner got their work into print, in what was consciously described as a restoration of memory, than events as dramatic as they had described, and in some cases uncannily of the same kind, began to occur in the very valleys which they had recorded and mapped.[10] The months from spring 1984 have been in many ways like a fast re-run of what was being researched and studied as labour history. In one sense, the repetitions are dislocating, since so much has so clearly changed; the miners themselves, for example, have been pressed back over the years, in apparently endless pit closures, to a small minority. Yet there is another, primary sense of an affirmed location. I have stood with easy and friendly men and women, organizing communally donated food for the two hundred babies born in Gwent mining families during the strike, packing their thousand plastic bags a day of basic adult food, and heard the precise words of the histories: the closeness with each other, the intense determination and anger against those who are now so clearly and exultantly their enemies. As so often in Welsh history, there is a special strength in the situation of having been driven down so far that there is at once everything and nothing to lose, and in which all that can be found and affirmed is each other.

It needs only a small shift of position, beyond the crowded closeness of the valleys, to see this communal spiritual energy as tragic. But then this is another paradox of the second prologue. The story of Welsh labour is shot through with suffering, and militant formations are repeatedly on the record. Yet a major strain of the culture of the valleys, well brought out by Dai Smith, is a high-spirited, mocking, even brash style: best exemplified, perhaps, in a literary sense, in the development of that remarkable novelist Gwyn Thomas.[11] His first, unpublished novel was *Sorrow for Thy Sons*, bitter and angry in the suffering of 1935. By the 1950s he was producing those hilarious novels and stories, the most agonizingly funny writing in English in his time, which were not only his but a quite general response to a devastation which had forced many into a hopeless and ironic laughter. The tone is very far from the grave voices of the major Welsh tradition; the alternatives of the prologues are stark in this. Yet his late work is consonant with a quite different kind of energy, in which the industrial Welsh were bypassing the muted tones of English culture for their version of the brash expansiveness of North Americans. Something like this happened also, more generally, in the English working class, as they used cinema and then television, but until recently there was this difference: that these popular and studied popular styles extended, without break of connection, to some of the most gifted writers and poets. From Welsh-language Wales this was often seen, as earlier in the case of Dylan Thomas's *Under Milk Wood,* as a vulgar, Anglicized betrayal of 'Welshness'.[12] Yet Anglicized, at least, it was not. The work of the English-language writers of industrial South Wales is unmistakably indigenous; its English in tone and rhythm is not an English literary style. There seems good justification, in these writers and in the everyday speech of the valleys, for the recent significant assertion, from within what has been the 'nationalist' tendency, that English is a Welsh language. A distinctive culture is using that diverse and flexible language for its own unmistakably native writing and speech.

There remain problems inside both truths. There are moments in Dai Smith's engagingly exuberant presentation when the gesture towards North America, the intellectually and emotionally sophisticated movement outwards from the confines of a narrow inherited tradition, sits uneasily beside the simple and heartfelt proletarian continuities. This is especially so at a time when many of the same external forces are directly allied, in their presentation of a desirable social world, with the forces which are working to break up not only a restricted working-class culture but all the values which have gathered, under long pressure, around both class and place. Yet again, in the other kind of account, there is the problem of relating Emyr Humphreys's new novel *Jones* to the thesis of *The Taliesin Tradition.* At one level, the smart, empty, fashionable Jones – the Welsh émigré on the make – is precisely caught. It takes one back, though more explicitly, to the experiences of his very fine early novel, *Hear and Forgive*, where the structures of dislocated mobility are more deeply explored than in that later run of English novels of the fifties which made the theme fashionable. Yet back where Jones came from, in that hill farm which is so often seen as the homeland of Welshness, there is shown so deep a native failure that quite new questions are raised. Is this, after all, an old way of life which not only from outside pressures but from something in itself could not shape and hold and inform its own people? It is the last bitter question about Wales: the nature of the Welsh who have turned their backs on it, within and outside the country, or who have settled for some portable, export-style facsimile.

It is probable, taking it all in all, that we can as yet engage few English readers in the intricate internal culture and politics of Wales, though its themes, so intensively explored, are close and coming closer to the English condition. It is possible to strike out on a quite different path, as Jan Morris has done in *The Matter of Wales*. The book is engagingly inward with Welsh landscape and history, though whenever it came very close (as in my case on the Black Mountains) I heard a different, informed and sympathetic but observing, voice. In its presentation, however, it is outward: a long open journey through the diversity of Wales, more accessible and I would expect more persuasive than those internal voices of which the interested reader from elsewhere must always wish that he or she had come in at the beginning, to get the shape of the discourse and to understand all the references back. Here, for a certainty, is a book to make other readers want to see and know more of Wales: that interest which has in fact been growing so strongly in England but which in parts of Wales, in ways that can eventually be explained, is treated as a sort of final insult.

This then may be the paradox. The English reader who wants to be better-informed about Wales itself can go to Jan Morris. The same reader who wants to know what, locked in with themselves, the Welsh have contributed and are contributing to European politics and letters can go to Emyr Humphreys and Dai Smith and that whole vigorous school of contemporary Welsh writers and historians.

Notes

1. On Emyr Humphreys, see 'Wales and England', n. 1. Dai Smith (1945–) is a historian, critic and author of several books including the biography *Raymond Williams: A Warrior's Tale* (Cardigan: Parthian, 2008). Jan (formerly

James) Morris (1926–2020) was a travel writer whose *The Matter of Wales* is part subjective history, part travel narrative. Paul Clements offers a useful commentary on her writings in *Jan Morris* (Cardiff: University of Wales Press, 1998).

2. Williams is referring to the 1866 lectures of Matthew Arnold (1822–88), collected as *On the Study of Celtic Literature* in 1867. See R. H. Super (ed.), *The Complete Works of Matthew Arnold Vol. III: Lectures and Essays in Criticism* (Ann Arbor: University of Michigan Press, 1962). For a Welsh-inflected discussion of Arnold, see Daniel G. Williams, *Ethnicity and Cultural Authority: From Matthew Arnold to W. E. B. Du Bois* (Edinburgh: Edinburgh University Press, 2006).

3. On Dafydd ap Gwilym, see 'Wales and England', n. 4. *Pedair Cainc y Mabinogi* is the collective name given to four Welsh legends of the Middle Ages. The term 'Mabinogion' was introduced by Lady Charlotte Guest, whose translations of these tales appeared in three instalments between 1838 and 1849. Proinsias Mac Cana (1926–2004) offers a useful brief introduction in *The Mabinogi* (Cardiff: University of Wales Press, 1977), as more recently does Mark Williams in 'Magic and Marvels', in Geraint Evans and Helen Fulton (eds), *The Cambridge History of Welsh Literature* (Cambridge: Cambridge University Press, 2019), pp. 52–72.

4. The influence of Welsh poetic forms on the writings of Gerard Manley Hopkins (1844–89) is discussed by Tony Conran in *Frontiers in Anglo-Welsh Poetry* (Cardiff: University of Wales Press, 1997), pp. 74–91.

5. Alan Llwyd (1948–) is a leading Welsh-language poet. The *englyn* quoted here is 'Cymru 1976' (Wales 1976), which is reproduced with a translation in Jan Morris's *The Matter of Wales*, p. 154. The poet meditates upon his ambivalent feelings towards the Welsh nation. Morris's translation reads: 'My great agony, my bliss, – my anxiety / My lovely paradise; / I love her bitterly too / And hate her affectionately always.'

6. The translation appears in Humphreys's *The Taliesin Tradition*, p. 19. The original 'Yr Wylan' (The Seagull) appears in Dafydd Johnson et al. (eds), *Cerddi Dafydd ap Gwilym* (Caerdydd: Gwasg Prifysgol Cymru, 2010). 'Dyfalu' refers to the medieval Welsh literary practice of multiplying comparisons by using tropes such as metaphors and personifications.

7. Frank Raymond Leavis (1895–1978), was a Cambridge born, bred and educated critic who taught Raymond Williams and influenced his method of literary criticism, whilst also being a major intellectual adversary. On Williams's relationship with Leavis, see Fred Inglis, *Raymond Williams* (London: Routledge, 1995), pp. 162–95. T. S. Eliot (1888–1965), the leading modernist poet, is discussed by Williams in *Culture and Society* (London: Chatto & Windus, 1958), pp. 227–43, and in *Drama from Ibsen to Brecht* (1968; London: Hogarth Press, 1993), pp. 174–98.

8. Saunders Lewis (1893–1985) was both a playwright and poet, and in 1925 co-founder of Plaid Cymru (see 'Who Speaks for Wales?', n. 3). It is not clear from Williams's analysis here that 'The Deluge' was written in Welsh

as 'Y Dilyw 1939'. See Saunders Lewis, *Cerddi*, ed. R. Geraint Gruffydd (Caerdydd: Gwasg Prifysgol Cymru, 1992), pp. 10–11. Excerpts of the poem are quoted both by Dai Smith in *Wales! Wales?* (London: George Allen & Unwin, 1984), pp. 60–1, and by Emyr Humphreys in *The Taliesin Tradition*, p. 223. A translation appears in Alun R. Jones and Gwyn Thomas (eds), *Presenting Saunders Lewis* (Cardiff: University of Wales Press, 1973), pp. 177–9.

9. The National Left, set up at a fringe meeting in Plaid Cymru's 1980 conference in Porthcawl, was an attempt by left-leaning nationalists such as Dafydd Elis-Thomas (1946–) to fuse the strands of leftist opinion in Wales into a coherent movement, following the disappointing result of the 1979 referendum on devolution.

10. Gwyn A. Williams (1925–95) was a historian and broadcaster. A member of the Communist Party, he became a key figure in Plaid Cymru, which he joined following the devolution referendum of 1979. For further details, see Gwyn A. Williams's own autobiographical volume *Fishers of Men* (Llandysul: Gomer, 1996), and the obituary by Dai Smith in *History Workshop Journal*, 41 (1996), 306–12. *The Welsh in their History* (London: Croom Helm, 1982) is an excellent collection of his writings.

11. Gwyn Thomas (1913–81) was a novelist and dramatist whose fictional depictions of industrial south Wales are characterised by a mordant wit and a sense of solidarity with the values and aspirations of the working class. Raymond Williams's introduction to his novel *All Things Betray Thee* (1949; London: Lawrence & Wishart, 1986) is included in this volume. For an account of Thomas's literary and historical significance, see Dai Smith, *Wales: A Question of History* (Bridgend: Seren, 1999), pp. 163–90. Victor Golightly places Thomas within the context of the transatlantic Left in '"We who speak for the workers": The Correspondence of Gwyn Thomas and Howard Fast', in Tony Brown (ed.), *Welsh Writing in English: A Yearbook of Critical Essays Vol. 6* (Cardiff: New Welsh Review, 2000), pp. 67–88. Laura Wainwright reads Thomas as a 'grotesque modernist' in *New Territories in Modernism: Anglophone Welsh Writing 1930–1949* (Cardiff: University of Wales Press, 2018), and Barbara Prys-Williams begins to trace the sources of both his humour and intolerance of the Welsh language in *Twentieth-Century Autobiography* (Cardiff: University of Wales Press, 2004).

12. Dylan Thomas (1914–53) is the most internationally recognised Welsh poet. His radio play *Under Milk Wood* (1954) is discussed by Williams in 'Dylan Thomas's Play for Voices' (1959), included in this volume, and in *Drama from Ibsen to Brecht* (1968; London: Hogarth Press, 1993), pp. 211–19.

WEST OF OFFA'S DYKE

New Society (4 July 1986), 28-9.
Review of Tony Curtis (ed.), *Wales: The Imagined
Nation* (Bridgend: Poetry Wales Press, 1986).[1]

The imagined nation, or the nation imagined? The intensity of Welsh arguments about identity is such that virtually any formulation becomes a challenge. In recent years the books and television programmes have kept coming, but we have only to look at the titles of some of the best of them – *When Was Wales?*, *Wales! Wales?* – to pick up the tone.[2] Ironically, in the same period, there have also been many books which, to the non-Welsh reader, seem to confirm a clearer and stronger image of the country and its people than at any earlier time.

There is a paradox here. East of Offa's Dyke there seems to be more acceptance of Welshness – and on the whole a respecting acceptance – than at any time since the Act of Union. This is so even when the requirement to speak Welsh as a qualification for a social services appointment in a Welsh-speaking area is referred to the Commission for Racial Equality, while calling Kinnock 'a Welsh windbag' is not.[3] Yet, west of the Dyke, if this more general acceptance is mentioned, you are quite likely to hear that it is all simplification, romanticism or patronage: 'rugby, miners and male voice choirs' or, more simply, 'Dylan Thomas'.

There is ground for some specific arguments, but the difficulty for the non-Welsh reader is to know where to start, or indeed why one should. I have been an active participant in the internal Welsh argument but, living so much in England, I have thought from an early stage that the issues being explored are of much more general significance. It is not only that in a world of paranational economics, militarism and mobility the confidence of much larger peoples, and perhaps especially now the English, is being questioned or shaken. It is also that the effective images of identity can be seen, under pressure, to have been concealing, all along, radical differences of conditions and values.

What then are these images, and how do the simpler and more persistent symbols relate to them?

Lacking a state, the Welsh have been primarily identified by their culture. Yet among the English, and increasingly after the end of empire, a cultural tradition has also been offered as the essential identification: whether in F. R. Leavis's proposition of an 'Englishness' based in its literature, or in the current 'English Heritage' campaigns.[4] But we do not have to look very far into these actual offerings to realize how profoundly and even explicitly selective they are. 'Natural idiomatic language and realism'; but that was why Milton had to go into the corner. 'Castles, country houses and green pastures'; but that was why the industrial towns and inner cities were not on the posters.

And meanwhile the Welsh? The thrust of this collection of essays, by a relatively young generation, is a questioning of an accepted cultural version of Welshness. On the one hand, it challenges a recently powerful tradition in which an essential identity is still defined by the Welsh language, even when four out of five Welsh people no longer speak it. On the other hand, and more closely and sharply, it challenges the version composed primarily from Dylan Thomas and from novels like *How Green Was My Valley*.[5]

The main value of the collection is in the second challenge. The first is in any case more complex. There has, of course, been mythmaking about the significance of the remarkable continuity of literature in the Welsh language from perhaps the seventh century, but there has as yet been no significant study of that cultural phenomenon which has been so marked in Europe in this century, especially in modernism, and in Wales as clearly as anywhere: the specific kinds of writing which come from linguistic borderlands even where, and often because, dominant languages have been practically adopted.

It will be in this work, by its nature comparative, that the tensions between Welsh-language writers and thinkers and Welsh writers and thinkers in English will be properly understood and at least in part resolved.[6] Moreover, this work should replace the long-range sniping (much of which misses) and the occasional easy (and mutual) sneers which the lack of a strict intellectual context permits.

There are important signs in some of these essays that new disciplines are being applied. Historical analysis, as in Prys Morgan's 'Keeping the legends alive', is already relatively very strong in Wales, but there is substantial innovation in, for example, Tony Bianchi's essay on 'R. S. Thomas and his readers'. Bianchi argues that 'more than any other English-language writer in Wales, R. S. Thomas has been reconstructed in the image of his own audience'.[7] Drawing on several kinds of contemporary analysis of cultural formations and the construction of works and ideologies by specific social groups, Bianchi concludes that this most widely respected living poet in Wales 'has provided the means of acknowledging a national literature in English which yet derives its legitimacy from its subordination to the older literature'. The addendum to this argument is that there can be no effective Welsh intelligentsia 'within the terms of the dominant literary discourse', though Bianchi sees the beginnings of change in 'history, sociology and, to a degree, nationalist politics'.

James A. Davies's essay, 'A picnic in the orchard: Dylan Thomas's Wales', is similarly deconstructive in effect, though its method is quite different. The central and, at first sight, surprising argument is that 'a sense of Wales as a bourgeois bastion in the west was fundamental to Thomas's career'. The poet related less to any actual Wales – a country of which he knew relatively little, beyond his Swansea suburb, and which he often disparaged – than to the tension of a bourgeois upbringing: his verse then a rhetoric of 'the imaginative potential of suburban man'.

Or again, Dai Smith, in 'A novel history', finds the significant Welsh novels of the 1930s in a mode made clearer by contrast with the best-known of them, *How Green Was My Valley*: 'Llewellyn utilised the mythology of a Fall-from-Grace to explain the bewildering pattern of Welsh industrial history, since it was only by reference to the past that the dog-days of the thirties could be understood and only by a distortion of that past's meaning that the decade could be consigned to meaninglessness ... Its vacuousness lies in its attempt to make political fantasy the cause of the desolation.'

These are samples from this lively collection, which also includes essays on recent poetry, film, television, painting, theatre and images of Welsh women. It is often, in practice, a sign of vigorous identity that there is this kind of roughing-up of the ancestors, but the more substantial point is that this is a generation questioning who its real ancestors are.

The recurrent mocking of cultural and literary stereotypes of Welshness is not at any point, in my judgment, a move away from Wales. On the contrary, it is the accompaniment of a very urgent contemporary concern. And this is why the book deserves to be widely read, for it is, in our time, not only the Welsh who have to discover and affirm an identity by overcoming a selective tradition.[8]

Notes

1. Tony Curtis (1946–) is a Welsh poet and critic. See his *From the Fortunate Isles: New & Selected Poems 1966–2016* (Bridgend: Seren, 2016).

2. Gwyn A. Williams, *When Was Wales?* (London: Black Raven Press, 1985) and Dai Smith, *Wales! Wales?* (London: Allen & Unwin, 1984) are both reviewed by Raymond Williams in this volume, pp. 127–30, pp 78–87.

3. Neil Kinnock (1942–). Leader of the Labour Party 1983–92. Richard Jones discusses the representation of Kinnock by the English press in 'The Kebabbing of Neil Kinnock', *New Welsh Review*, 17/5 (Summer 1992), 4–10.

4. On Leavis, see 'Community', n. 7.

5. *How Green Was My Valley* (London: Joseph, 1939) is a novel by Richard Llewellyn (1906–83). A best-seller, which also became an Oscar-award-winning film directed by John Ford, the novel's depiction of life in a mining community has been widely criticised for its sentimentalism and nostalgic yearning for a pastoral, pre-industrial, Wales. See Ian Bell, 'How Green was my Valley', in Janet Davies (ed.), *Compass Points: Jan Morris Introduces a Selection from the First Hundred Issues of Planet* (Cardiff: University of Wales Press, 1993), pp. 257–64.

6. The most notable examples of the kind of comparative analyses of the two literatures of Wales called for by Williams are the works of M. Wynn Thomas, *Internal Difference* (Cardiff: University of Wales Press, 1991), and *Corresponding Cultures* (Cardiff: University of Wales Press, 1999).

7. Ronald Stuart Thomas (1913–2000) was a nationalist and religious poet. A useful introduction to the man and his work is Tony Brown, *R. S. Thomas* (Cardiff: University of Wales Press, 2009), and Damian Walford Davies (ed.), *Echoes to the Amen: Essays After R. S. Thomas* (Cardiff: University of Wales Press, 2003).

8. Williams elaborates on what he means when he speaks of 'selective traditions' in *Marxism and Literature* (Oxford: Oxford University Press, 1977), pp. 51–4.

HISTORY

THE SOCIAL
SIGNIFICANCE OF 1926

Llafur: Journal of Welsh Labour History, 2/2 (1977), 5–8.

Collected in Raymond Williams, *Resources of Hope* (London: Verso, 1992), pp. 105–10.

An address to the commemorative conference, 'The General Strike and the Miners' Lockout of 1926' organised jointly by *Llafur* and the National Union of Mineworkers at Pontypridd, 9–11 April 1976.

I came down this morning from a village above Abergavenny: travelling the quite short distance to this centre of the mining valleys, and travelling also, in memories, the connections and the distance between one kind of country and another. In 1926, in that village, my father was one of three signalmen in the old Great Western Railway box. He was an ardent participant in the General Strike; so was one of the other two signalmen, and the stationmaster, who was subsequently victimized; so too were the platelayers.[1] One of the signalmen was not. In the discussions and arguments that took place during those critical days, among a small group of men in a very specific social situation, some of the most important themes of the general social significance of 1926 became apparent. They were often recalled, in later years. I heard them throughout my childhood, and I went through them again, consciously, with my father, when I was preparing to write the General Strike sequence in *Border Country*.[2] In a way it can seem marginal to rehearse them here, in places where the direct causes, the central actions and the long consequences of the strike are so close and evident. But while joining in paying homage to that central action, I see a need to consider the complex social action, and the complex problems of consciousness, which occurred, precisely, at a relative distance and in a more mixed situation. These seem to me to raise issues which have become more rather than less important in the subsequent history of British industry and the subsequent development of the working class.

Consider first that specific situation. These men at that country station were industrial workers, trade unionists, in a small group within a primarily rural and agricultural economy. All of them, like my father, still had close connections with that agricultural life. One of them ran a smallholding in addition to his job on the railway. Most of them had relatives in farm work. All of them had gardens and pigs or bees or ponies which were an important part of their work and income. At the same time, by the very fact of the railway, with the trains passing through, from the cities, from the factories, from the ports, from the collieries, and by the fact of the telephone and the telegraph, which was especially important for the signalmen, who through it had a community with other signalmen over a wide social network, talking beyond their work with men they might never actually meet but whom they knew very well through voice and opinion and story, they were part of a modern industrial working class. It is a special case, of course, but a significant one in the context of the General Strike, which is still too loosely assimilated to strikes of a different kind, with which it of course has connections but from which, in crucial ways, it has extensions – extensions that raise quite central problems of consciousness.

Think only, to begin with, of our traditional virtue of solidarity. This begins – and how could we expect it to be otherwise? – in very local, even physical ways. It is the ethic of a group which has already been decisively established, often it is true by the initial action of others – the capitalist employers who have offered work and who have drawn men, as to these valleys, to take it – but then, in shared immediate working experience, in the developing experience of a local community, in growing ties of family and kinship, a group which has the potential of solidarity already physically present within it. This is not to under-estimate the long struggle that then must occur: the organizing, the raising of consciousness, the hard experience of recovering from disappointments or betrayals, the equally hard learning of collective disciplines, as when action against blacklegs is sometimes required, that especially difficult action, against members of the known group. And then there is variation, obviously, between places and kinds of work, written everywhere in the history of trade unionism: the relative ease or difficulty of organizing and of sustaining organization. Along these lines, with a necessary unevenness and variation, the labour movement builds itself. One of the decisive extensions is, to unionization of one whole industry, across wide physical distances. Both the miners, relatively concentrated, and the railwaymen, relatively dispersed, had achieved this extension, and of course it was crucial. But there is then the problem of another kind of extension: from the workplace, from the industry, to the class.

Now of course, theoretically, this had been achieved again and again. It is the history of socialism as distinct from (though always connected with) the history of industrial unionism. But nobody close to that history, at any point, can fail to recognize the difficulty of that particular extension of organization and consciousness: an extension which indeed when it is complete – and it is still not complete – must transform the whole social order and allow existing social relationships. It is hard enough to sustain organization and consciousness when they are directly centred on an immediate and local material interest: the struggle to improve conditions and wages, within a systematically or blatantly exploiting workplace, or, as in 1926, not to improve or even maintain but to fight against actual worsening. And then think what is being attempted when other men, in another situation, perhaps just emerging, bruised and depleted, from some struggle of their own, or perhaps in some temporary lull, are asked, urged, to act in solidarity, now in a different sense: not by place or work or by physical connection, but in essence by an idea, an idea that may even contradict their immediate and local material interest: an idea of the class, of the solidarity of the class, and of this, often – as notably in 1926 – in contradiction of the idea of a larger loyalty to which we have all been trained: to what is called the nation, the national interest, and expressing this the significant formalities of contract and of law.

What remains of decisive importance from the events of 1926 is the achievement of that consciousness. It is still a tangled story; all I can offer you is this immediate and local experience, with a sense of its wider significance. The theory of the General Strike was already important in certain socialist tendencies. There had been successes and failures in its practical application, in different countries. There had been the difficult history, in Britain, of the attempts at conscious alliances between major unions, the miners and the railwaymen prominent among them. But always, when it comes to the point, in an action of this kind, which is at the far end of the scale from some bureaucratic or representative collective action, individual men and groups of men have to cross a line in their minds. All history and all theory may be there, but real men, under difficulty have to struggle to make their own effective choices.

Now of course, there in that country station, there were real connections – of neighbourhood, of kinship, of trade – with the mining valleys. It was not a struggle from a blank, though another social reality – the small firms, the mixed rural villages – was of course physically much closer. 'To help the miners'; 'to stand by the miners': these were there from the beginning, in most conscious men, as effective impulses. And then, working in the same direction, there was loyalty to their own union and to the general trade union movement: the instruction to join – what? The National Stoppage. It is an extraordinary phrase: deliberately limited and negative, but of course, even at that, a challenge sufficient to bring out all the power and anger of the state and the ruling class. And as it turned out, as we all now know, these had made their preparations more effectively than our own people. From patriotic ideology to the OMS, they were ready.[3] Also, as it happened, they were more in touch with modern social communications. Our side relied on print, and even in that were under grave difficulties with distribution on a national scale; the local strike papers were always more significant. The ruling class had the wireless, and this was indeed a portent. By now we all know these and other reasons for the eventual defeat.

But what has also to be registered is the element of victory: nothing to be idealized, for it is important to draw lessons from the general defeat, but certain advances, certain clarifications, which as a matter of fact are still resonant in consciousness, as this anniversary, which is much more than formal, reminds us. At the level of national history, big-time politics, the General Strike is written off as anything from a disaster to a mistake: a consequent moderation and reformism is ideologically deduced from it. But the part of the history that most needs emphasis, and that was actually very evident in that country station and in thousands of other places up and down the country, was the growth of consciousness during the action itself. What began with relative formality, within a representative dimension, became, in its experience, the confidence, the vigour, the practical self-reliance, of which there is so much local evidence, and this was not just the spirit of a fight; it was the steady and remarkable self-realization of the capacity of a class, in its own sufficient social relations and in its potentially positive social and economic power. The detailed discussion, on the railways, about priority traffic and exception traffic, was an experience of decision-making of a quite new kind: not just instrumental, within an imposed system, but from the bottom up, as a way of deciding what came first in the society, what mattered in it, what needs and values we live by and want to live by. Certainly, in that station, the positive confidence grew, slowly, during those days, though of course in a small station, and with their other rural work always there for them, there were limits to what they could do, and there were marginal alternatives, which had much to do with their sense of confident independence. There, as elsewhere, when the stoppage was called off, the response was one of amazement and then of bitterness. The support had been growing not declining. The mood was very positive. And then the extraordinary and wretched business of the railway company's counter-action, its demand for signatures to an impossible document, its selective victimization, and through this the confusion of the misleading telegrams from union headquarters: all this raised the level of the action. Nationally, as you know, there were more men out on the day after the action was called off than during it. This, indeed, was the high point, and the national failure was a failure to go on from that: the very opposite lesson from that which we are usually asked to draw.

But there are also other lessons. In the half-century since 1926 the physical locations, the types of community and the social distribution of the British working class have changed very significantly. In 1926 the mining villages were modern communities; our village, even with the railway through it, an older type. Today we have to deal with a social and physical distribution in which mixed communities, not centred on single industries, are much more characteristic. The special struggle for class consciousness has now to be waged on this more open, more socially neutral ground. I still find it impossible, whenever I come to the mining valleys, to understand, at first, why there is not yet socialism in Britain: the need and the spirit have been evidenced so often, in these hard, proud places. But then I remember all the other places, so hard to understand from this more singular experience, although the actual development of industrial South Wales in the intervening half-century has been in that other direction, with a complex intersection with the older type of community. In the local studies of 1926, which are now so usefully being extended, we need to look for the differentials between different types of community: differentials in action and support for the strike, which are quite marked but which should not be exaggerated. For the significance of 1926, in so short a time, is still the rise and extension of consciousness, during those days, to an effective national and class presence; differentials also, though these are less heroic and more distasteful studies, in recruitment against the strike, in the OMS and in other ways. The legendary figure of 1926, on the ruling-class side, is the undergraduate driving the train, the middle-class housewife shifting supplies. They were there, of course, but also – and differentially, in different parts of the country and in different types of community – there were working men, wage-earners, indeterminate class figures, whom the ruling class hired; but that is only one way of putting it, for there were also volunteers. In our village, the signalman who opposed the strike had his own place to go to: his smallholding. In the cities and towns it was and is different, and money is money, as we start by knowing. But it is also more than that. During the General Strike itself, and in the long months after it, when the miners held out, it mattered, in our village, that we had a physical and communal and not an abstract connection: at a distance, it is true, but one that did not cancel the sense of neighbourhood, a district, perhaps a country. The collection and transport of food, from where it was available to where it was needed, followed the strike along some of the same paths of social connection. It was not so everywhere. Then, as now, the hungry can be simultaneously recognized and neglected, at an effective social distance.

These differentials are crucial, because they connect 1926 and 1976, in old ways and in new. A child of five, as I was then, can gain from a father who had experienced that complex struggle for consciousness – a spirit and a perspective that have lasted, often under pressure, in the radically different places, where I have since lived and worked. But part of the perspective is the sense of complexity and difficulty, in the differential social and industrial and communal history and geography which was then and is now, increasingly, our world. My brief and inadequate contribution to this historic anniversary is offered as a reminder that necessarily alongside the central, concentrated and heroic actions are the smaller, the marginal, the mixed, the diffused scenes in which the effective struggle for a new consciousness also occurs.

Notes

1. The General Strike (4–12 May 1926) resulted from the rejection by the Miners' Federation of Great Britain of an ultimatum by the coal-owners. The Trades Union Congress capitulated to Stanley Baldwin's government and the miners were left to struggle alone in the seven-month lock-out. By the following December the miners had been starved back to work on worse terms than had existed before the strike. The sense of disillusion and defeat is captured by the poet Idris Davies (1905–53) in his long poem of 1943, *The Angry Summer*. See Dai Smith and Hywel Francis, *The Fed: A History of the South Wales Miners in the Twentieth Century* (1980; Cardiff: University of Wales, 1998), pp. 52–73; Daryl Leeworthy, *Labour Country: Political Radicalism and Social Democracy in South Wales 1831–1985* (Cardigan: Parthian, 2018), chapter 4.

2. *Border Country* (London: Chatto & Windus, 1960) was Raymond Williams's first published novel.

3. The OMS – Organisation for the Maintenance of Supplies – was created by the government during the General Strike.

BOYHOOD

Raymond Williams, *Politics and Letters:
Interviews with the* New Left Review
(London: Verso, 1979), pp. 21–38.[1]

What was the character of your family and its immediate community?
I come from Pandy, which is a predominantly farming village with
a characteristic Welsh rural structure: the farms are small family
units. My father began work when he was a boy as a farm labourer.
But through this valley had come the railway, and at fifteen he
got a job as a boy porter on the railway, in which he remained
until he went into the army during the First World War. When
he came back he became an assistant signalman and then a signalman. So I grew up within a very particular situation – a distinctly
rural social pattern of small farms, interlocked with another kind
of social structure to which the railway workers belonged. They
were unionized wage-workers, with a perception of a much wider
social system beyond the village to which they were linked. Yet
at the same time they were tied to the immediate locality, with its
particular family farms.

There was all the time a certain pressure from the East, as we
would say – from England – because we were right on the border of
a different kind of rural residential life, with larger country-houses
and retired Anglo-Indian proprietors. But that remained very marginal and external.

How large was the community?
It is a classic example of a dispersed, rather than nucleated, settlement – the characteristic pattern not only for rural Wales but for

much of Western Britain generally. The immediate parish was three miles one way and four miles the other. About three to four hundred people lived in it. So the farms were about a quarter of a mile apart, although there were small clumps like the house in which I grew up which was one of a group of six. The contrast is very sharp with the typical Eastern English rural settlement nucleated around the church. The village was served by one school which was under the control of the Church of Wales, a church, a Baptist Chapel and a Presbyterian Chapel. It had four pubs.

From what you say it sounds as if it was in many ways a very untypical region, in any case unusual for the English countryside proper, in that what you are describing is really smallholder agriculture without any major exploiting group. It was certainly nothing like the triad system of landowner–farmer–agricultural labourer which was the dominant pattern in England.
That's right.

At the same time, while your father worked in a classical working-class occupation, it was nevertheless very abstracted from the normal environment of the modern urban proletariat.
I think this is the point. It took me a long time to realize that my situation was not typical. More than half the population of the village were small farmers. The farmers were not on the whole involved in exploitation in their immediate activities (except within the family, where there was indeed a good deal of exploitation: but within the family, not outside it). They were not characteristically employers of labour. The average size of a farm would be no more than 60–100 acres, about half of which would be rough grazing land on the hillsides, and half pasture in the valley. Nevertheless, the farmers were so clearly the real solid stratum of this community that other people did feel themselves to be, as it were, less established in the place than they. The others would be the usual mix. There was the railway, which would account for 15–20 families, the jobbing builders, a few people beginning to travel to work in town, ordinary rural craftsmen.

These farmers may have seemed very solid, but actually smallholding can be relatively insecure economically: you get good and bad years.
Yes, it was the depression then and small farming is still chronically undercapitalized today. Also, as I said, the labour within the family is exploitative, there is no question about that. There is pressure to delay marriage. You get great injustices between brothers and sisters according to the chance of what age the parents die, what happens in the disposition of the inheritance and, of course, the children are working from a very early age. They do not see this as exploitation but it is very hard work. But the strange thing is that when such a family sold up, it suddenly seemed as if they must have been very substantial property holders. One can get a very peculiar double vision, seeing the amount of value realized then. For in such families there is virtually never any disposable capital, it is all sunk in buildings or animals: the availability of a few pounds in cash at any given time is often less than many people have on a really low wage. Of course, selling up is a disaster, because it means the family has ended in some way.

All the time the process of engrossing which had been going on throughout the nineteenth century was still advancing. It is sometimes difficult to believe even now that there are so many small farms. But if you go back a hundred years there were two or three times that many. Since then there has been almost continuous emigration from this kind of area, so that even the surviving smallholdings are engrossments of two or three farms of an earlier time.

The community as a whole was shrinking between the wars?
The population was diminishing because at all times there was a group which had got no obvious work waiting for them. They were the landless families like my own. My grandfather, for instance, had been a farm labourer and then he had a row with his boss – this was about twenty miles away. He then became a roadman. But other people I know of in the same situation went off to the mines – there was a lot of movement into the mining valleys – or into the towns to work. In the twentieth century there was a big migration to Birmingham, where many of my family had gone. So people were constantly moving out. There had always been a huge exodus of women, which actually preceded that of men. The girls moved out into domestic

service; the biggest loss of rural population in Wales was first of all among women. Then the men began to leave for alternative jobs. That is why the railway was so important: the job of a railwayman was incredibly highly valued, because it was regarded as secure. It sounds ironic now, but in the twenties and thirties the one thing that was always said about the railway was that it was steady well-paid work.

What were relations like between the railwaymen and the farmers?
There seemed to be absolutely no social barrier at all between them. Typically, my father's closest friend was a farmer. He was a lifelong friend whom he would help in the harvest, in whose field he would plant his rows of potatoes which were an important part of our food. If you moved towards a few of the larger farmers you would begin to be aware of some social distance, in the sense that you would notice when somebody had a car, which two or three were beginning to acquire. The schoolmaster would also have a car.

The interesting thing is that the political leaders in the village were the railwaymen. Of the three signalmen in my father's box, one became the clerk of the parish council, one the district councillor, while my father was on the parish council. They were much more active than anyone else in the village. All of the railwaymen voted Labour. Most of the farmers, by contrast, voted Liberal. Within the village, there would be local divisions of interest between the two – typically over expenditure. The railwaymen were a modernizing element who, for example, wanted to introduce piped water and other amenities. They read a lot. They also talked endlessly. This is where their other social dimension, quite outside this locality, was decisive. Characteristically, because signalmen had long times of inactivity between trains, they talked for hours to each other on the telephone – to boxes as far away as Swindon or Crewe. They weren't supposed to, of course, but they did it all the time. So they were getting news directly from industrial South Wales, for example. They were in touch with a much wider social network, and were bringing modern politics into the village. That meant raising the rates, which the farmers opposed, since they literally did not have much disposable money. If the farmers counter-organized, they would tend to win. But apart from these conflicts, the regular personal relations between the two groups were very close: it would be typical to go to the signal box and find one or two small farmers sitting in the box, especially on a wet day, talking to the railwaymen. All of which had consequences, I think, for my initial perception of the shape of society.

What was the role of religious denominations in the area?
The farmers were overwhelmingly Nonconformist, Baptist more than Presbyterian (Calvinistic Methodist). In my case, my father's and my mother's family were mixed Church and Chapel. My father was very hostile to religion. When my grandmother came to live with us and was strongly Chapel, I was sent to Chapel; when I was older I went to Church. Chapel was very much more consciously Welsh. Later, I refused to be confirmed, but my decision caused no crisis in the family.

Did you know Welsh?
We were not Welsh speaking. Ours was an area that had been Anglicized in the 1840s – the classic moment usually described as when 'the mothers stopping teaching their children Welsh'. In fact, of course, there was an intense and conscious pressure through the schools to eliminate the language, which included punishment for children who spoke Welsh. The result was to leave a minority of families who were bilingual and a majority who spoke only English. However, a certain number of Welsh expressions survived and also affected the speaking of English. Characteristically, these were every-day greetings and swearing. But for the majority of the population Welsh was now an unknown language.

At the same time, Welsh poems and songs were learnt by heart for special occasions. For this was one of the areas where the Welsh cultural revival started in the early nineteenth century.[2] This often happens in border districts, which produce a conscious nationalism. In the elementary school, Welsh songs and poems were taught to the children.[3]

What was your attitude to learning these songs? Did you at any time feel that they were an embarrassing archaism?
I felt that very strongly when I was at grammar school. My reaction then was associated with a general revulsion against what I saw and

still see as the extreme narrowness of Welsh Nonconformism. Its attitude to drink, for example, was very difficult for an adolescent to accept. What I did not perceive at the time but I now understand is that the grammar schools were implanted in the towns of Wales for the purpose of Anglicization. They imposed a completely English orientation, which cut one off thoroughly from Welshness. You can imagine how this combined with my hostility to the norms of Welsh Nonconformist community. The result was a rejection of my Welshness which I did not work through until well into my thirties, when I began to read the history and understand it.

You've spoken of Welsh language and religion. But what about national identity as such? Would the people in your village, your father and your grandparents, if asked what they were, say they were Welsh? Or would they not use such a category at all?
They were very puzzled by this. I heard them talking about it. I think the sense of a specific local identity was much stronger. There were good historical reasons for that. For Wales had never been a nation: it had always had a cultural rather than a national existence. It was precisely incorporated into 'Britain' before it developed a really separate national identity. So people would always ask what Wales actually was. This is how I in the end understood the question myself, because I found that virtually all Welshmen ask themselves what it is to be Welsh. The problematic element is characteristic. Of course on the border, it was more problematic than in North or West Wales, in the still Welsh-speaking communities. They are that much further away from England. There was a curious sense in which we could speak of both Welsh and English as foreigners, as 'not us'. That may seem strange, but historically it reflects the fact that this was a frontier zone which had been the location of fighting for centuries.

Did you consider yourself as British?
No, the term was not used much, except by people one distrusted. 'British' was hardly ever used without 'Empire' following and for that nobody had any use at all, including the small farmers.

Could you say something about your father's political views and activities?
He had been very conscious as a boy of his father's political change, from Liberal to Labour. It was provoked by the traumatic moment when his father was sacked and turned out of his home – the classic case of the tied cottage – to become a roadman. When you are the victim of a farmer who is a Liberal, your class interest declares itself: at that point he went over to Labour. So this was already my father's orientation. Then he was very unwillingly conscripted into the First World War. He came out of the army in the mood of so many soldiers, by this time totally radicalized. Coming back to the railway, it happened that his first job was right down in the mining valleys which were very politicized, with a fairly advanced Socialist culture. By the time he moved home to the border again, he had acquired its perspectives.

So you grew up in a Socialist family and from your very earliest you were aware of that as such.
Absolutely. I was five at the time of the General Strike which was very bitterly fought out on a small scale in the village. The stationmaster was victimized by demotion for his role in it because he was a conscious Socialist. There was a very big conflict inside the second signal box when two of the men struck and the other did not. The chapter in *Border Country* which describes the Strike is very close to the facts. Then in 1929 I remember a euphoric atmosphere in the home when Labour won the elections. My father was running the Labour Party branch in the village, and we greeted the results with jubilation.

So the politics came mainly through your father and your mother accepted them? Was she active?
It was the classic situation of a Labour Party woman. She makes the tea, she addresses the envelopes, she takes them round – she does not have very many political activities in her own right. But my mother had her own opinions. She actually felt much more hostile to the farmers than did my father, who was mixing with them all the time. She still makes very hostile remarks about farmers as a class, whom

she conceives as the ultimate in exploiters! But then these were about the only social relations she ever directly experienced. Her mother had been a dairy maid on a larger farm, and she had worked on one as a girl, so there was a sense of farmers as employers.

What about your own reading, your intellectual development as a boy?
I read extraordinarily little except school books. That was still so after grammar school. I think it probably had to do with the availability of books. We had very few in the house, hardly any apart from the *Bible*, the *Beekeeper's Manual* (which was my father's craze), and the usual things for children like *The Wonder Book of Why and What*. So where did you get books? You got them at school. Therefore I was strongly directed by the curriculum, at least until sixteen or seventeen when I began to get access to the Left Book Club. But it took me twenty to thirty years, if it ever changed, to get used to the idea that books were something to be bought. Mind you, this is a habit I share with a majority of the British people.

What about your pattern of choice within the school curriculum? Your eventual specialization at grammar school level was literary and linguistic – English, French and Latin. The absence of history from your adolescent intellectual interests seems very striking.
The explanation lies in the culture I received, not in my character. What history we were taught in the elementary school was a poisonous brand of romantic and medieval Welsh chauvinism given us by the school-master. The reading was dreadful – nothing but how such and such a medieval Welsh prince defeated the Saxons, and took from them great quantities of cattle and gold. I threw up on that. It wasn't only that it didn't connect. It was absolutely contradicted by how we now were. The irony was that when I entered the grammar school we started to do the history of the British Empire. We plunged somewhere straight into the middle of the 18th century, with the conquest of Canada and then went through India and South Africa and the whole imperial expansion. That kind of history did not interest me very much either. The curious result was that I later had to reconstruct for myself the main lines of the history, not just

of England, but even of my own region. I did not feel any loss at that time. But I felt it enormously later, when I had to settle down and read the main body of British history – including, of course, the history of Wales. The highest marks I got at school certificate were languages and English and so that is what I did, when I went to the sixth form.

Was it quite a big step to go from the elementary school in the village to the grammar school in Abergavenny?
It happened that the village had its golden year when I sat for the scholarship – seven pupils won County scholarships. There was a group photograph taken because it was such an exceptional event: six girls and me. But the girls – several of them were farmers' daughters – would usually go only as far as the fifth form and would then leave. The other boys from the village also went to the fifth form, where they then often had difficulties in passing the matric. So by the time I got to the sixth form I was the only one from Pandy.

But there was no sense of isolation from the village. The grammar school was intellectually deracinating, as I can see now. But I was not conscious of it at the time, because in everything that was not schoolwork there was no sense of separation.

The grammar school was seen from within the village, and by your family, as a completely natural extension of your life?
Oh, totally. Indeed, I used to blame my father – although I do not now – for pushing me too hard. It happened that I passed top of the County exam, so he assumed that when I went to the grammar school, I was automatically going to be top of the form. When I came second at the end of the first year, it was inexplicable to him. I felt extremely resentful that he could think that coming second was bad. I think that I probably started to feel then that shameful academic competitiveness which I finally got rid of only at my last examination.

But there was absolutely no sense in which education was felt as something curious in the community. Years later I talked to Hoggart about his sense in childhood of being described as 'bright', with the implication of something odd.[4] My experience was quite the opposite.

There was absolutely nothing wrong with being bright, winning a scholarship or writing a book. I think that this has something to do with what was still a Welsh cultural tradition within an Anglicized border area. Historically, Welsh intellectuals have come in very much larger numbers from poor families than have English intellectuals, so the movement is not regarded as abnormal or eccentric. The typical Welsh intellectual is – as we say – only one generation away from shirt sleeves. There was, after all, no establishment in Wales to maintain a class-dependent intelligentsia. Class-dependent intellectuals by definition emigrated. It is important to remember that the Welsh University Colleges were built by popular subscription in the 1880s, which would have been a difficult project in England at the time. Education was, of course, also regarded as one way out of frustrating employment. I remember once, when I protested to my father: 'What is it for, anyway?', he said: 'Well, for example, you can get a job as a booking clerk.' That would mean a pound or two up a week.

Was that your perspective at the time?
No. But I wasn't thinking of further education either. The idea of a university came as a surprise to me. Indeed, it was done over my head. When I sat for the Higher School Certificate, the 'A' level equivalent, which I took very early because I had got through the course quickly, the headmaster decided to approach my father about my going to Cambridge. My father said afterwards: 'We didn't tell you in case you'd be disappointed if they'd not taken you.' The headmaster wrote to Trinity asking them to accept me; and they took me, without the ordinary admission or any examination. I had never been to Cambridge before, I arrived there as an undergraduate. It was just presented to me. By that time, however, I had a definite view of what I wanted to be, in which the university was not primary but which it did not contradict.

What was that?
I think I can honestly say that it was very much what I am now. Not what I am as a university professor – I have to keep reminding myself that I am that – but as a writer. By the time I was sixteen, I was

111

writing plays which were performed in the village, together with my closest friend, who was the son of the Baptist minister. We produced them together in the village hall, and everybody came. I also wrote a novel which nobody is ever going to see, called *Mountain Sunset*. It was about the revolution in Britain – one of whose critical battles took place on the border – I am afraid there was some infection from that despised Welsh history! I sent it to Gollancz, of whom I knew at this time because of the Left Book Club. They sent it back, of course, but with a kind note that they wanted to see more. Within six months I couldn't bear to reread it.

What was the character of the plays you wrote?
We did two full-length ones. The most ambitious took the form of a detective play which yet uncovers a social villain. I would now know that this was fairly characteristic of radical melodrama. We were by this time regarded very differently from somebody like my father, because we were campaigning around in politics. Nevertheless everybody came, the village hall was packed.

Did you have village references within these plays?
Yes, some, but we had to be careful. When I was at Cambridge, I wrote a short story called *Mother Chapel* which was a criticism of a narrow Nonconformist community radically reproving sexual error and deviance, in which the minister's daughter herself becomes pregnant before marriage – hence the title. Somehow, I still don't know how, the magazine in which it appeared got back home and all hell broke loose. A son of the village had gone away to slander it. Actually, the fictional episode was a fairly typical one. I had become very contemptuous of the hypocrisies involved. The earlier plays we did were much more respectful of local constraints.

What was the political campaigning which made you so differently regarded from your father?
In the 1935 elections the local Labour candidate was Michael Foot, straight from Oxford, for whom my father organized a meeting. We

thought this very boring. We decided to go out to the Tory candidate. The constituency was Monmouth: the solid east-of-the-county vote always makes it Conservative. We had prepared figures for what black labourers in South Africa earned and we got up and asked him how he could justify them. He completely put us down, with a lot of support from the audience, saying that this was not a matter of great importance in the current county campaign, as he was sure the electors would agree – making fools of us, in effect. But this sort of question was a different political language from anything that was familiar in the village.

What was the local branch of the Left Book Club like, and the general impact of the Club on your development?
The Club in Abergavenny, which had about fifteen to twenty members, was run by Labour Party activists. They used to organize discussions and meetings and invite speakers. We weren't subscribers; I used to borrow books from whoever subscribed, so I didn't see them all. But it was from the Club that I read about imperialism and colonialism. This was the time of the war in Abyssinia. We were also very conscious of the Chinese Revolution, since we read Edgar Snow's *Red Star over China*, and of course the Spanish Civil War.[5] Among the visiting speakers, I remember being especially impressed by Konni Zilliacus, who at that time was still working for the League of Nations; he seemed the first wholly cosmopolitan man I had met.[6]

Your father's politics grew in a very direct sense out of his immediate work experience and family situation. Yet from what you have been saying it seems that much of the pressure and focus of your teenage politics was international, rather than local or even national?
Yes, to a fault – our interest was almost too much the other way. The traditional politics of locality and parliament in the Labour movement was seen as part of a boring, narrow world with which we were right out of sympathy. To us international actions were much more involving and interesting. This was where the crucial issues were being decided. The Left Book Club essentially represented the insertion of those larger perspectives and conflicts into the Labour movement. Older people went along with it but I think that their

sense was of a benevolent association rather than of international solidarity. We made the leap to international solidarity without having
to go through the other experiences, of local and national struggles
– although it always seemed to me, even then, that the great problem
of the Labour movement was how the two interests spoke to each
other. But the times were changing and the issues actually were much
more internationalist then.

Did you join the Labour Party and think of yourself as a Labour man?
No, I didn't join the Labour Party. My father, who was the branch
secretary, asked me to in 1936. But I actually rather disliked Michael
Foot – something that is easier to say now. He was a new phenomenon, straight out of the Oxford Union, who did sound a bit odd
in Pandy village hall. I said to my father: 'What has this to do with
the Labour Party?' He thought my attitude was quite wrong and that
Foot was a very clever young man. But I did not particularly want to
join. In fact, the only time I have ever been a member of the Labour
Party was from 1961 to 1966, when I actually had a card – a very
peculiar period to do so, of course.

Otherwise I would work for Labour in the elections because
there was no other choice. But I always had a very reserved attitude
to the Labour Party.

*Did you have arguments with your father about this? Did he think that
you would in the course of time join the Labour Party?*
Yes, to the extent that after the War, he wrote to me and said that the
whole group of which he was part, I suppose the survivors of the Left
Book Club, wanted to propose me as the local candidate to fight the
1945 election. I think that he was hurt that I was not interested. Not
that I think if they had proposed me, I would have been nominated:
the Labour Party by that time was being run by a quite different sort
of people in the constituency.

*The milieu of the Left Book Club was much closer to the CP than the
Labour Party. The whole field of its political culture was the Popular*

Front. When you were at Abergavenny didn't this present a conflict or choice for you? What was your attitude towards the Communist Party?
The really extraordinary fact – it might have been just accidental to that region – is that there was no awareness of a British Communist Party. You only had to go thirty miles to find some of the most solid Communist bastions in the country, in the Rhondda.[7] Yet I was not conscious of any Labour–Communist antagonism, as positions between which you had to choose. You must understand that this had never been an issue with my father. He did not think of Communists as another or different force within the Labour movement: it was a matter of course to him that there were Communists in the leadership of the railway unions. Then these were now the days of the Popular Front, which rejected the whole idea of a division: our attitude was very much 'no enemies on the left'.

What you say is still slightly astonishing. After all, your father must have been aware of the Zinoviev letter. The Bolshevik menace, the un-English nature of Communism, were relentless themes of bourgeois propaganda in the inter-war period. These matters were national political issues.[8]
That is what the bosses said. You did not believe it. Equally, these questions were not the terms in which your own struggle was formulated. I think that this is true of many of my father's generation and perhaps even of the succeeding one of Labour Party militants who joined before the Cold War and the conscious splits and proscriptions which followed it. Of course in the big industrial centres, there were organized and conscious ideological battles. But for many Socialists, Communism was a branch of the Labour movement, and certainly if the press and the government attacked it, then it must be generally all right. There was a combination of acceptance and distance towards it.

Reconstructing your vision of the world up to the time of the university, what would have been your most representative image of the ruling or exploiting class?
The first one to come to mind would actually have been a very antique figure – the rural magnate or landlord, whom we mocked. The immediate cultural image was that of a Tory squire.

Did they really exist within the compass of your experience?
You could not go and see them. You could see a park wall, not beyond it. After that, we would characteristically have thought of bankers. I remember long discussions with my father about the ownership of industry by banks. Then, of course, there were the railway-owners and the mine-owners. But the rather archaic agrarian stereotype was still dominant. I don't think that it was just because I lived in a rural area. This displacement away from the decisive class enemy of the last hundred and fifty years, the industrial employer, to older antagonists has been surprisingly persistent in the perception of the ruling class on the British Left. In my case, I also had the natural adolescent reaction that the ruling class was not just wrong but out-of-date – the characteristic conviction of the young that the rulers are old, irrelevant and not of our world. I thought all Tories were stupid by definition. This was a very common rhetoric in the thirties. It carried certain real feelings. On the other hand, it disarmed people, including me and a lot of my friends, from understanding the intelligence and capacity of the ruling class, and its contemporary implantation.

In my case, distance from London probably did have some importance. I never saw any of the central metropolitan power definitions. Of course, I knew of what the troops had done in the mining valleys – we were constantly told of it. But that was second-hand. We were in no doubt at all about the character of the employers, but the ruling class still did not seem very formidable. The result was to build up a sense, which was very characteristic of wide sectors of the Labour movement at the time, that the working class was the competent class that did the work and so could run society. That was said so much after the General Strike. It was disabling ultimately. But as an adolescent I remember looking at these men even with a certain resentment – they seemed so absolutely confident. I have never seen such self-confident people since.

One might say, then, that in your boyhood there was an absence of the typical town–country relation, absence of direct confrontation between privileged exploiters and working people, and absence of antagonism between manual and mental labour. Your early experience appears to have

been exempt from a whole series of typical conflicts and tensions which
most people of your generation from working-class families would have felt
at some point. Your own history seems to have escaped nearly all of them.
Firstly, which is in a way the most remarkable fact, there is the absence
of any deep division between town and country. If you were from a major
urban concentration, you would have inevitably been largely alienated from
the natural world. This is something which was not true of you. Secondly,
you came from a working-class family with a strong class consciousness, yet
in an area which lacked any centrally important sector of the ruling class.
Factory workers would have a different experience in large towns or in the
capital. There the capitalists, the rulers, embody an unmistakable power:
they are not comic, they are oppressive and they instil fear. That seems
to have been absent from your environment in a real way. Thirdly, there
does not seem to have been any real tension between manual and mental
labour – something that can be very important in many working-class
areas. You never encountered distrust or resentment of intellectual pursuits,
or a difficult ambiguity of feeling about education, for instance – not
uncommon patterns in other working-class cultural regions. Then there
seems to have been no problem about religion. Your father was actually
opposed to religion, and when you refused to be confirmed, it caused no
crisis in the family. It was not a disturbance in your childhood – whereas
in many areas of English working-class life the transition would not have
been such a smooth process at all. Finally and most importantly, you did
not have to effect a break to enter politics, in the way that even in core
working-class districts it is possible to be a union man or to vote Labour,
but actually to be politically active is a change beyond that – which can
lead to tension in a family if somebody does so. But this was not the
case in your family. Then beyond that again, there was a kind of generic
unity or amity between what could be called left Labour or Communist
positions – no sense of hardened divisions or barriers, and consequently of
conflicts or crises in passing from one to the other. One gets the cumulative
impression that by the time you reached the university, all your energies
as a person must have been to an exceptional degree whole and available
to you – that is, unimpaired by the sort of intense early conflicts that
mark so many biographies. The passage through boyhood would typically
be a more divisive, sometimes depleting struggle – whatever its long-term
consequences. Your trajectory seems unusually free of direct strain, up to
Cambridge. Would you say that was true?

I think it is true. It is never easy to talk about one's own personality in that sense, but for what it is worth my own estimate is that I arrived at the university with about as full an availability of energy as anyone could reasonably have. Indeed my expression of energy was unproblematic to a fault. All the problems came later. At the time, it was very much a sense of hitting Cambridge, being extraordinarily unafraid of it. I got relatively afraid of it afterwards. I measure myself against it today, with a kind of calm hostility, but then the notion that there were deep blocking forces to contend with never occurred to me. There are only about three or four people who really knew me as I was then: they would give a totally different account of my personality from those who reckon they know me now – the fraught, balancing, tense creature of some people's caricature. Anyway I was absolutely unlike that then.

In your essay Culture is Ordinary, *you remark that on getting to Cambridge you quite liked the Tudor courts and chapels: Cambridge in no way oppressed or daunted you, because you felt that your own culture and history predated it.*[9]
Was much older, yes. There is the joke that someone says his family came over with the Normans and we reply: 'Are you liking it here?' But that was playing the game.

A schoolboy or schoolgirl coming from a working-class urban background to Oxford or Cambridge would have been unlikely to have had that historical self-confidence. It is partly a question of Welshness, but also, within it, the fact that you came from a much denser school situation. If you go to a grammar school and a lot of working-class people living around you are not going to grammar school, then the social cleavages which are later represented and intensified by Oxford and Cambridge are much more difficult to handle in childhood, as your working-class friends no longer wear the same clothes, or do the same things.
That is right. Those classic contradictions were to some extent not there. But in a way they were saved up to take their maximum effect later. Why didn't my headmaster send me to a university in Wales? That would have been an orientation which would have suited my

life much better. It is no use going back over it, but it would have. But this is what he was there for – to find boys like me and send them to Cambridge. I don't say this in any spirit of hostility to him; he thought he was doing the best thing for me. But it was partly because of the devices of the English implantation in Wales that blockages were not there for me in a way that they typically were in British culture as a whole.

On the other hand, once I was sent to Cambridge, I had a very strong sense, which was revived briefly again in '45, of having my own people behind me in the enterprise. So that the characteristic experience of isolation or rejection of the institution did not occur. It was not till later that I saw that this was not something to be negotiated only at the emotional level – in the end you have to negotiate it in real relations, which are much harder things. But at the time I felt mainly the confidence of having people behind me. Even my brashness in writing *Mother Chapel* reflected it. When there was a problem with my grant coming through after the War, that supportive area was still close enough – despite the row the story had caused – for the local pub to make a collection for me straight away. There was no question about it: this was something that had to be done. My father, typically, paid the money back. So there was no sense of being cut off.

You went to Geneva for a youth Conference organized by the League of Nations, just before Cambridge?
Yes, it was my first journey abroad: I gave the report on the current international situation – there is an account of it in one of the League memoirs written by a thirties' journalist. On the way back, we stopped in Paris and I crept out of the hotel and went straight to the Soviet pavilion at the international Exhibition. I remember it very clearly. There was a peculiarly contemptible British pavilion with a large cardboard cut-out of Chamberlain and a fishing rod. The Soviet one had a massive sculpture of a man and woman with a hammer and sickle on top of it. I kept saying: 'What is a sickle?' – I had used the damned thing and we called it a hook. It was there that I bought a copy of the *Communist Manifesto*, and read Marx for the first time.

Notes

1. The *New Left Review* editorial team that interviewed Williams were Perry Anderson, Francis Mulhern and Anthony Barnett. On the making of *Politics and Letters*, see Fred Inglis, *Raymond Williams*, pp. 259–65.

2. The Welsh cultural revival that occurred in south-east Wales in the early nineteenth century centred on the ideas and example of two individuals: Thomas Price, 'Carnhuanawc' (1787–1848), and Augusta Hall, known as both 'Lady Llanofer' and 'Gwenynen Gwent' (1802–96). Price was an antiquarian and promoter of the Welsh language and its culture, establishing influential Welsh societies such as 'Y Cymreigyddion', in Brecon (Aberhonddu) in 1823 and Abergavenny (Y Fenni) in 1833, in an attempt at halting the process of Anglicisation in those areas. Hall was a patron and promoter of Welsh folk music and dance, and was an early member of Price's 'Cymreigyddion' society in Abergavenny. See Simon Brooks on 'Herder's comrades in Wales', in *Why Wales Never Was* (Cardiff: University of Wales Press, 2017), pp. 39–44.

3. The learning of Welsh songs is dramatised by Williams in *Border Country* (1960; Cardigan: Parthian, 2006), p. 145. On the significance of linguistic difference on Williams's realism, see Daniel G. Williams, 'Writing Against the Grain: Raymond Williams's *Border Country* and the Defence of Realism', in Katie Gramich (ed.), *Mapping the Territory: Critical Approaches to Welsh Fiction in English* (Cardigan: Parthian, 2010), pp. 217–43.

4. Richard Hoggart (1918–2014) was a cultural critic and author of *The Uses of Literacy* (London: Chatto & Windus, 1957). The lives and careers of Williams and Hoggart are compared by Stefan Collini in *English Pasts* (Oxford: Oxford University Press, 1999), pp. 210–30. See also Dai Smith, *A Warrior's Tale*, pp. 436–40.

5. Edgar Snow, *Red Star Over China* (New York: Random House, 1937) recounted the months that the author spent with the Chinese Red Army in 1936, and is seen to have engendered sympathy for Chinese Communism in the West.

6. On Zilliacus, see 'Wales and England', n. 3.

7. See Chris Williams, *Democratic Rhondda: Politics and Society 1855–1951* (Cardiff: University of Wales Press, 1996); Douglas Jones, *The Communist Party of Great Britain and the National Question in Wales 1920–1991* (Cardiff: University of Wales Press, 2017).

8. The Zinoviev letter was allegedly sent in 1924 by Gregory Zinoviev, chairman of the Comintern, to Christian Rakovsky, a member of the Communist Party in the Soviet Union, encouraging British communists to promote revolution through acts of sedition. The letter was intercepted by MI5. Ramsay MacDonald, the British prime minister, then in the midst of the 1924 election, told MI5 to keep the letter a secret, but it was leaked and appeared in *The Times* and *Daily Mail* four days before the 1924 election, contributing to the defeat of MacDonald and the Labour Party. It is now widely assumed that the letter was a forgery, and that Joseph Ball, an MI5 agent, leaked it to

the press. In 1927, Ball went on to work for Conservative Central Office, where he pioneered the idea of spin-doctoring.

9. 'Culture is Ordinary' first appeared in Norman Mackenzie (ed.), *Conviction* (London: MacGibbon and Gee, 1958). It is collected in Raymond Williams, *Resources of Hope* (London: Verso, 1989), pp. 3–18.

ON GWYN A. WILLIAMS: THREE REVIEWS

THE BLACK DOMAIN

The Guardian (8 June 1978).
Review of Gwyn A. Williams, *The Merthyr
Rising* (London: Croom Helm, 1978).[1]

We refer to the industrial *revolution*, but the noun is no longer very active, and its implicit metaphor or analogy is usually dead. In many places in Britain, but especially on Dowlais top looking down into Merthyr Tydfil, the need for a really active description can seem overwhelming.

My own first word, whenever I stand there, is *convulsion*. What Gwyn Williams calls those 'lacerated hills' seem quite literally to have heaved, writhed, fallen back into a livid debris. But of course, as in most landscapes, what we are seeing is the work of men. And it is only when you get to know the facts of that labour and that history that the need for an active description is quite overwhelming, yet you know that *convulsion* is not enough.

What Government Commissioners in the early nineteenth century called 'the black domain' – that complex of iron and coal working running from Hirwaun to Blaenavon, on the borders of Gwent, Brecon and Glamorgan – produced a culture as well as a disorder, just as in its industrial production it produced both wealth and poverty, in a single complex process.

Gwyn Williams's title, taken from a single remarkable event, is then especially appropriate. What happened in Merthyr in 1831 is of quite outstanding importance in British working-class history.[2] And it is significant that while it is deeply remembered in Wales it is relatively little known in England, though more people were killed there by the military than in the Peterloo massacre, and the succeeding events are almost certainly of more historical importance in British trade unionism than even the Tolpuddle martyrdom.[3]

It is not, of course, a matter of competitive assessment; all these events are directly related. Yet it is instructive to see why Merthyr in 1831 is less widely remembered and respected. At Peterloo the soldiers rode, killing and wounding, into a peaceful crowd asking for Parliamentary reform. At Tolpuddle six men trying to organize a trade union were transported. These events now find a place within a liberal as well as a Socialist perspective.

Merthyr is different and harder. Beginning in the agitation for parliamentary reform, it became an insurrection against a whole social order. Thousands of working men and women took direct action against the existing property structure, and when troops were brought in to repress them drove them out and took military possession of the district for four days. Twenty-five or more people were killed by the soldiers.

In the subsequent trials, a young miner, Richard Lewis, was sentenced to death for stabbing a soldier in the thigh (an act he almost certainly did not commit). He was hanged at Cardiff and passed into Welsh legend as Dic Penderyn. His widely reported last words – O Arglwydd, dyma gamwedd; O Lord this is wrongdoing – express one major and persistent response.

But there was another major response, in which his memory also served: the organization of a new kind of militancy: the hard and active unions of the Welsh working class.

We can see, then, why Gwyn Williams is right to call the events a rising: in the local sense, that though the events had their victims, including their innocent victims, it was indeed an insurrection, against a social order not to be cured by liberal reforms; and in the general sense, that the events were a transition – a rising transition – from the prehistory to the conscious history of a working class.

This profoundly accurate theoretical interpretation is only one of the virtues of this valuable book. It is remarkable in the detail of its

sociology of Merthyr: the complexities of the new industrial enterprises; the differences between particular working-class communities;
the complex connections and the conflicts between middle-class political radicals and the militant workers.

Again the social and economic significance of Merthyr is unfor-
gettably established: in 1831 the largest inhabited place in Wales; the
leading edge, in that period, of the whole British industrial revolution, producing 40 per cent of all its pig iron; the 'frontier town'
where a predominantly Welsh population crowding into a small area
went through a double crisis of culture and economic identity, under
mainly English masters and within the English state and economy: a
crisis that is still, in new forms, very active.

It is a book to read and re-read, written, as it had to be, by
a professor of history whose initial and substantial qualification is
that he was born and grew up in Dowlais, and thus knows how it
is necessary in the view from that top, to bow the head in mourn-
ing and respect, but necessary also, as the history connects, to raise
it again.

PUTTING THE WELSH IN THEIR PLACE

■

The *Guardian* (9 September 1982).
Review of Gwyn A. Williams, *The Welsh in
their History* (London: Croom Helm, 1982).

■

Why as so often this year, do the English sing Rule Britannia?
Why do they count King Arthur, who defeated the English
invaders of this island, among their legendary heroes? Why do they
call the most identifiably British people in the island by the old
English name for foreigners: Welsh?

These are no longer plaintive Welsh questions. They strike through to the general questions of identity and ideology. The recent remarkable revival of Welsh history is important for the Welsh but may have even more to contribute to an understanding of the urgent general problem of the relations between nationality and patriotism, and between both and the current crisis of the nation-state.

Certain historical ironies may provoke this. It was a Welshman who christened English colonial expansion the *British* Empire, and indeed provided title to parts of North America through the legendary voyages of a Welsh prince.[4] Earlier, it was a Welshman of Breton descent who popularized the Arthurian mythology and forged an effective ideology of Britain which was heavily used in the making of a newly centralised nation-state.[5]

Some Welsh people claim these precedents with pride, as giving them an even higher title to sing Rule Britannia! But when the political problem is to stop singing it, and to look instead at our actual condition, we need all the real history we can get, and through it an understanding – for exposure alone is insufficient – of the forms of ideological history which have been set in place to confuse it.

Professor Gwyn Williams has collected a number of his essays and lectures to offer aspects of the real history and to confront, polemically, some of the most damaging ideology. His earlier books, *The Merthyr Rising*, *Madoc: the making of a myth*, and *The Search for Beulah Land*, were solid and lively studies of phases of the history. In his new book he brings the issues together, over a wide range, culminating in the remarkable lecture 'When Was Wales?' His central argument is that the Welsh people have survived, so far, by anchoring themselves in various forms of Britishness. It is those various forms that have a substantial interest outside Wales.

Sometimes a definition of Britishness, as the heritage of the old Romano–British imperium, has worked very well for the most powerful English and for a few client Welsh, but has been almost wholly irrelevant or damaging to everyone else. At other times a different definition of Britishness, as an old culture hostile and alternative to an English aristocratic or bourgeois state, has produced quite opposite results.

The most sympathetic characters in Gwyn Williams's wide cast are the radicals and democrats of the 1770s, who combined an intense attachment to what they took to be the old British culture, now the fruitful inheritance of the Welsh, with active support of the American and French revolutions. It is interesting that in these two opposite cases there was a substantial admixture of historical fantasy and of effective or actual forgery of evidence. These need to be traced, but not only exposed. It was how a marginal and disorientated people found new active alignments, and any account has to include what they were aligned for and against.[6]

The same is true of more recent alignments. Who ever heard of a prosperous Wales, boomtown sector of the British export trade, predominantly imperial and Atlanticist in its outlook? That existed, in the steel and coal of South Wales, in the late nineteenth and early twentieth centuries. On it was built a new liberal hegemony: what has been called the rebirth of a nation.

The devastating collapse of that export sector, after the First World War, produced another Wales: depressed, depopulating, proletarian; a time of labourist hegemony and yet another version of Britishness: a soon-to-be-Socialist Britain.

As all these versions have weakened or collapsed, the problems of Welsh identity have remained acute. Yet this is not only what most English people see as a 'regional' or 'minority' problem. There is a case for saying that the long crisis of the Welsh has prefigured the crisis which is now hitting the English, and within which the same kinds of confusion of historical fact and fantasy, the same overriding bursts of displaced patriotic enthusiasm, are painfully clear.

Gwyn Williams draws attention, in several periods, to groups of intellectuals who sensed this kind of crisis early and who tried to define the interests of their people in new ways, even against the grain of received national beliefs. He respects, as I do, the more rooted figures, but he emphasizes the value of those more mobile and distanced figures, European in range and outlook, who worked against the received history, in any of its versions, so that their people might be free to understand and then to make their own actual history. This spirit of the new contemporary Welsh historians is of substantial importance in a changing Britain and Europe.

THE SHADOW OF THE DRAGON

※

The Guardian (24 January 1985).
Review of Gwyn A. Williams, *When Was Wales?* (London:
Black Raven Press, 1985); Wynford Vaughan-Thomas,
Wales: A History (London: Michael Joseph, 1985).

※

Before we can be sure that the dragon has two tongues, we have to be sure that it is the same dragon. We had better also, while we are about it, look into the natural history of dragons.

Something like this may be happening in the current television series on the history of the Welsh, with which these two books, by the joint presenters, are associated. Its *Dragon Has Two Tongues* title is borrowed from a useful book by Glyn Jones, which explored the complexities of a national literature written in two languages.[7]

Much more is at stake in any general history. What we have so far seen, in the early programmes and now in the books, is an adversarial kind of history, by two Welshmen as different from each other, in detail and in general, as could reasonably be hoped. This could be a useful Welsh riposte to the smothering monotones of more assured, more dominating and more complacent traditions.

Yet the dragon itself is still in question. There it is, with its forked or arrowed tongue, on the jacket of Vaughan-Thomas's book. The cover-note reassures us that 'Wales is a Principality close to England geographically and politically, but it is also very diverse.'

This is smoke, not flame. The use of 'Principality' for the whole country begs the key question of the long division and contrast between Principality and Marches. Yet in its framework for a Prince, already provided from elsewhere, it interlocks neatly with the significant name-change to 'United Kingdom' now being naturalized by officials and businessmen. Who knows what is Welsh or Wales when all is UK or Yookay? Will there be Yookayans yet?

One of the central advantages of being born and bred among the presumed Welsh is the profusion of official identities. Wales and Monmouthshire, as it was for me at school, with special force since we lived in the appendage. England-and-Wales: that administrative, legal and even weather-forecasting area. Wales for rugby but All-England for cricket. Welsh Wales and English Wales. Wales and Cymru. To anyone looking for an official status it was a nightmare. To anyone trying to think about communities and societies a blessing: a native gift.

These alternative responses inform these two books. For Vaughan-Thomas there is an assured Welsh identity and continuity, strong enough to include the pre-Celts and pre-pre-Celts. For Gwyn Williams there is a long process of dislocation and remaking and dislocation again. The necessary distinction is between a story and a history.

Vaughan-Thomas is a skilful raconteur, with strong feelings for the physical land of Wales. The warm phrases and anecdotes, some of which, I have to say, maddened me even in elementary school, come through with the geniality which most others have found persuasive. And then there is the balance of the book: fourteen concluding pages, from two hundred and sixty-one, on the extraordinary and shattering events since the 1920s. No reader should be in any doubt about what kind of book, and what kind of historical preference, this is.

On the other hand a one-volume general history, by the leading historian of industrial Wales, bristles with problems and questions. Some of these are semantic: that is, central. Wales, in Gwyn Williams's argument, and as its Old English name for the land of foreigners suggests, came into existence in the ninth and tenth centuries 'as a junior partner in a Britain run by England'.

The British and other peoples – the others almost certainly a majority – who had previously lived in that land went through a long and still unfinished process of naming and being renamed; at times pulling back into an internally contested Cymric unity; at times, as around the Tudor Court, believing that they had recovered England for Britain and the British, and actually naming the British Empire.

Then, in the Industrial Revolution, an actual British nation, a working unitary social order, emerged and for two centuries succeeded, leaving the Welsh – again redefining themselves – as at worst a region, at best a cultural 'nation'. Even in this brief summary, the question 'when was Wales?' is a question about definitions well before events and dates.

I find this the best general history of the Welsh now available. It is especially strong from the medieval period onwards, and in the modern period, with one possible reservation, remarkable. Where I wanted most to ask further questions was in the earlier periods, where a professional historian is most limited by the extreme scarcity of evidence.

There is a reasonable scepticism about the simplest versions of 'the Celts', but there are important structural similarities between their kind of military invasion and domination and the three much better recorded later cases of what many Welshmen are reluctant to admit is the same kind of event: Roman, English and Norman. Within a perspective of 'the Welsh' or indeed of 'Wales', this is obviously difficult to handle. Much of the surviving Welsh identity has been in a Celtic language. Yet there is apparent physical and material evidence that the real history of this people, so confused by shifting names, begins in that relatively early period, beyond all the current ideologies.

The bravest chapter of *When Was Wales?* is the exploration of the realities of the long Roman and post-Roman periods. Social and economic analysis, on admittedly scarce evidence, begins to undercut the simple tales of kings and saints. The opening to Europe, as again in the epoch of the Marches, is Gwyn Williams's basic perspective on our own time. It is a perspective that can be shared by all those who in loyalty to their own actual people refuse to assimilate to singular and romantic national traditions.

The possible reservation? That we are invited to agree that we are 'now nothing but a naked people under an acid rain'. This is a condition being offered, indeed worked at, but the strength of this book, and other difficult but real kinds of strength, are evidence that it is being refused and can be surpassed.

Notes

1. On Gwyn Alfred Williams, see 'Community', n. 10.
2. On the Merthyr Rising, see 'Wales and England' n. 8.
3. The Peterloo Massacre, 1819. On 16 August 1819, a crowd of over 50,000 gathered in St Peter's Fields in Manchester to hear a speech on parliamentary reform by Henry Hunt. The crowds were well behaved, but the local

authorities panicked and attempted to arrest Hunt and disperse the crowd. Eleven people were killed, and around 400 injured. The Tolpuddle Martyrs were six Dorset farmworkers who were transported in 1834 to the colonies for seven years, because they had taken an illegal oath to a labourers' union.

4. John Dee (1527–1608 or 1609) was court astronomer for, and adviser to, Queen Elizabeth I, but spent much of his time on alchemy, divination and Hermetic philosophy.

5. Geoffrey of Monmouth, Latin Galfridus Monemutensis, Galfridus Arturus. Welsh: Gruffudd ap Arthur, Sieffre o Fynwy; *c.*1095–*c.*1155. Best known for his chronicle *The History of the Kings of Britain* (Latin: De gestis Britonum or Historia Regum Britanniae).

6. 'The radicals and democrats of the 1770s' were largely a group of expatriate Welshmen who, influenced by the American and French revolutions, began (in Gwyn Williams's words) 'to manufacture' a Welsh nation in London. Their influential society, the 'Gwyneddigion', organised its first Eisteddfod in 1789. Amongst the key figures were Richard Price (1723–91) – whose defence of the French Revolution in *A Discourse on the Love of our Country* (1789) provoked Edmund Burke (1729–97) into writing his *Reflections on the Revolution in France* (1790) – and the most prolific of Welsh 'inventors of tradition', Iolo Morganwg (Edward Williams) (1747–1826). In addition to Gwyn Williams's essays, see Prys Morgan, 'From Death to a View: the hunt for the Welsh past in the Romantic period', in Eric Hobsbawm and Terence Ranger (eds), *The Invention of Tradition* (Cambridge: Cambridge University Press, 1983), pp. 43–100.

7. *The Dragon Has Two Tongues* was the title of a book on Welsh writing in English by the novelist and poet Glyn Jones (1905–95), published in 1968. It was reprinted by the University of Wales Press, with an introduction by Tony Brown, in 2001. The title was adopted in 1985 for a series on the history of Wales on Channel 4, which was co-presented and written by Wynford Vaughan-Thomas and Gwyn A. Williams.

REMAKING WELSH HISTORY

Arcade: Wales Fortnightly, 4 (12 December 1980), 18–19.
Review of David Smith (ed.), *A People and a Proletariat:
Essays in the History of Wales 1780–1980* (London: Pluto
Press, 1980); Hywel Francis and David Smith, *The Fed:
A History of the South Wales Miners in the Twentieth
Century* (London: Lawrence & Wishart, 1980).[1]

In 1939 Saunders Lewis wrote, in a poem that we should all read and think about:[2]

> The tramway climbs from Merthyr to Dowlais,
> Slime of a snail on a heap of slag;
> Here once was Wales, and now
> Derelict cinemas and rain on the barren tips.

The familiar imagery of industrial devastation and economic dereliction slips easily into the mind. The material evidence has been so open to our eyes. Yet within this resonant familiarity something else is being said.

Here once was **Wales**. That must mean it is not Wales now. Between Merthyr and Dowlais? What then can 'Wales' mean? Something different, evidently, from the lives and struggles of actual Welsh people. And so the rhetorical observation, protected within the common sense of devastation and dereliction, becomes an outline of history.

It is a familiar outline. It has been sketched, in much the same form, across Offa's Dyke, where an idea of 'England' has been radically separated from the actual lives and identities of most English people. But there at least, in its most influential form, it was 'Old

England'. As an explicit version of history, it could be challenged as history.

But still what gave it resonance, what moved very different people to accept or adopt or acquiesce in it, was a specific Welsh history, in which loss and disturbance were actual, and in which powerful experiences and impulses were, so to say, looking for an idea. What was arrived at, however, in its simplest form, was a Wales, that, as a matter of principle, was not contemporary Wales, and Welsh people who were not most Welsh people.

The eventual collision between that form of thought and the ineradicable actual existence of so many places and people was then in its turn a loss, a disturbance, a sadness. It was also, more importantly, an impulse to new thought, new effort, new actual work.

This is the underlying significance of the new work in Welsh history of which these two books are such excellent examples. It is true that the collision came in different places at different times; it is not a single moment. But it was in the 1970s that the effective new work began to appear, on a sufficient scale to influence the more general conflict and confusion of ideas. What it began with, unheroically, was an admission of ignorance.

Yet the central impulse is different. What is identified as ignorance is at once interpreted as a challenge to research. But then, even more important, there is a vigorous inquiry into the causes of ignorance; indeed in the end an explanation of the ignorance as structural.

Thus Gwyn A. Williams:[3]

Industrial capitalism seems to destroy the popular memory; perhaps it needs to.

Or again, tracing a complicated historical process from the 1840s to the 1980s:

In this process, the Welsh working class lost its memory. This is very different from the conventional gap between interpretation and evidence which is the historian's professional concern and challenge. What is being traced and indicated is not only a loss but a suppression of memory. This is then

132

much more than a historical question. It is a central question about the continuing processes of culture and politics.

It is what leads David Smith to write:

These historians are ... utterly convinced that only a people with a tingling memory can ever catch the omnibus to a meaningful future.

Tingling this new history certainly is. Alive and exciting, but often also painful. We all have in our minds what we take to be memories: of the proud, independent, marginal culture of rural Wales in the 19th century; of the grey misery and hopelessness of South Wales between the wars; and so on in a hundred particulars.

The work of these new historians will have most effect on the received memories of industrial South Wales. There is the crucial description of the nineteenth-century 'Imperial' and 'Atlantic' economy, in iron and then coal, which is the true historical matrix. That wealth and power, that scale of world-economic significance, is as much to be remembered as the subsequent depression, for it is from the political interactions and effects, in each period, that the complexity of culture derives.

This in turn determines the new accounts of the militancy which had been so often excluded from versions of the 'waste and hopelessness' of the inter-war years, but what is then restored (as most remarkably in *The Fed*) is not a simple militancy, but one full dispute and faction and struggle, and this not only internally but in its interaction with a 'respectable' culture (a Welsh culture?) of another and often very different kind.

This is industrial South Wales recovering its actual history, beyond the simplifying images, but there may be just as much effect in, for example, the essay by Merfyn Jones on 'Class and Society in 19th-Century Gwynedd', in which the image of a backward but proud, organic and unified culture dissolves, or in David Jenkins's 'Rural Society Inside Outside', which in its fine evidence of language and practice explores what was and was not a 'natural community' and an 'organic folk'.

Every reader of this new history will find, at some point, a moment when his own memory stirs and becomes that new thing, a historical memory, a new sense of identity and relationships. I can record my own moment. I have always remembered my father, a railwayman, growing potatoes along the edge of a neighbouring farmer's field, and then helping his farmer friend with the harvest. But I just did not know the complex history of potato-setting, and its formal and informal labour obligations as traced by David Jenkins.

The personal memory, local and specific, is then suddenly connected with the history of thousands of people, through several generations. As the particular and the general, the personal and the social, are at last brought together, each kind of memory and sense of identity is clarified and strengthened. The relations between people and 'a people' begin to move in the mind.

By definition this will happen in different ways. For some it will be the moments of 'the secret world' of the South Wales miner, patiently recorded as oral history by Hywel Francis, or of the inside story of victimization, accidents and disease, clearly and honestly explored by Kim Howells. But then what is starting to move, through these and similar moments of recognition and connection, is a new kind of common sense: incomplete as it must still be, but founded from the beginning on people's actual lives and experiences, as distinct from the short cuts and the phrasemaking which seek to persuade us that we already know who we all are, and what we have all been.

That is the moment of crisis, of course. It isn't a comfortable experience. 'Who is now for Wales?' That cry and challenge has never been more urgent. Is there time, really, to go into all these details of the past? Isn't there a tumble of live issues on which we must come together, to defend, to rescue Wales?

But of course it is the coming together that is the deep point and problem. 'Wales', David Smith writes, 'has been a plurality of cultures.' Once this is clearly said, we realize that we have always known it. It has been the true historical source of all those problems of definition and self-definition of Welshness.

It is still the historical ground on which we divide or can be divided, not only at the extremes of material interest, but in places and among people whose objective common interest is quite evident.

It is then from recognizing the plurality, instead of insisting on the authority of any chosen (but then competitive) singularity, that we can learn to be open to each other and to make the effort to move through to effective new common ground.

The main thrust of the new history has come from the industrial valleys. Part of it, necessarily, is a factual polemic against the ideas of community which came from an older rural base. What can then again be polarized is an idea of the proletariat against an idea of the community, and the residual scrapping will persist.

Yet what is now clear, both from history and from current development, is that each has been changed in its real base and has then to be changed as an idea. There can be no easy resolutions. The old simple forms are still resonant, in the emptying spaces that have been left and are being extended in the cruel history of both industrial and rural decline and penetration. New impulses will come only from a constructive, connecting present.

Yet one of the curious things about real historical writing, concerned as it must be with the evidence of the past, is that it can take the weight of the old off us, by letting us see it clearly as it was.

It can then indeed often inspire us, but necessarily to be different. It is what any loving father will say to his son: 'Your turn. Your life. Remember what I've told you but find your own real way.'

Notes

1. On David Smith, see 'Community', n. 1. Hywel Francis (1946–2021) was a Welsh historian, adult educator and Labour politician. Author of *Miners Against Fascism: Wales and the Spanish Civil War* (London: Lawrence & Wishart, 1984). Member of Parliament for Aberavon from 2001 to 2015.
2. On Saunders Lewis and his poem 'Y Dilyw, 1939', see 'Community', n. 8.
3. On Gwyn A. Williams, see 'Community', n. 10.

'FOR BRITAIN, SEE WALES'

Times Higher Education Supplement (15 May 1981), 14.

Review of Kenneth O. Morgan, *Rebirth of a Nation:*
Wales 1880–1980 (Oxford: Oxford University Press, 1981).[1]

What if the veterans of a century ago were permitted to
see … the transformation of the Rhondda valley from a
sleepy hollow in to the most active and thriving community
in Great Britain or the world?

That little exercise in time travel was printed in the *Western Mail* on
the first day of the twentieth century. If it reads now like a malign
joke, it is still, in its chosen terms, no fantasy. By the standards of
capitalist production and export which are now being so vigorously
revived as the criteria of an 'active and thriving community', the
Rhondda and the other Welsh coal valleys were then success stories to gladden the heart. In Dr Morgan's estimate, the products of
South Wales then constituted 'about a third of the coal exports
of the world'. Indeed his prose at that point captures the authentic lilt:

The domestic heating of eastern and western Europe, the
railways of France, Italy, Brazil and Argentina, above all the
oceanic steam-driven carrying fleet of the world, all rested to
a great degree on the expanding production and aggressive
marketing of Welsh coal.

An oceanic moment indeed. And if the Rhondda, since then, has
been widely used in alternative images – of a devastated, derelict
and depressed economy, or of an intransigent and educated militancy – still the connections must predominate. All three are more

than images; they are readings and interpretations of a complex and volatile history.

The remarkable revival of Welsh historical studies in recent years is too little known in England. Even where it is known it is easily pigeon-holed as 'regional': that word the English still use for everything beyond their confidently named Home Counties. Yet 'regional' begs all the questions. Industrial South Wales – built on iron, coal, steel and exports – is a central case of that selective version of the production and creation of wealth as the essential ground of a society, which is now – to be sure with different products, but that is the selectivity – being revived from almost every political position. Virtually every model of the growth of a society can be tested there, on historical and contemporary grounds.

Is national revival 'expanding production and aggressive marketing', after which, but only after which, we get our social relations right and start providing 'the things we all want'? The answer comes not only in the driven labour, the industrial illnesses, the mortality of those valleys, but, as decisively, in the liberal nonconformist culture which those who were appropriating the surplus so solidly created. It is now often said that England never had a fully bourgeois culture; that it turned aside into empire and gentrification.[2] Liberal Wales, at the turn of the century, described at once admirably and in general admiringly by Dr Morgan, will serve as this alternative cultural universe. We can see the sort of world fashioned by the coal owners, shippers, merchants, academics, bankers, lawyers , ministers and bureaucrats of that 'affluent region'; even follow it to London with Lloyd George.

It is full of solid building and cultural establishment; confident and self-respecting; in its own ways socially progressive. It is worth a very long look, because it is an excellent example of an administered culture, of the kind that came through also in English Fabianism: doing good on the profits of an expanding capitalist economy. Its loyal agents, still ideologically powerful in a residual liberalism and social democracy, have never understood what they see as a betrayal by the very people they were administering and civilizing: the self-organizing and differently oriented working people on whom the equation of administered culture and capitalist progress depended. They explain and explain and explain again what a desirable world this could be. The people seem to listen attentively, in the institutions built for the explanations, but then – the buggers – they mitch and demarcate, go to the pub and the football or (fatally for the equation) go on strike. This kind of struggle between chapel and union, and within both, in industrial South Wales, is one of the key cultural struggles, for all its local specificities, in modern industrial society anywhere.

But then is growth to be found in the alternative perspective: the building of a labour movement: the organized working class coming through to its destiny? There is rich Welsh material for that also. The Welsh working-class movement of the interwar years is as conscious, as heroic and as intelligent as can be found anywhere. Is not this then a model? In thought and feeling it still often is, but there are two qualifications. First that though it had its roots in the turbulent period of industrial expansion, it came to flower only in the succeeding period of economic depression, with coal exports declining and nearly half a million Welsh people having to leave their country. It was nevertheless still supposed that planned production – planned socialist production – would *as such* bring back prosperity as still in a residual Labourism. But this, in its usual form, was a gross misunderstanding of the nature of industrial production *for trade*: the precise form which had been inherited and which was now, by a necessary logic, beginning to abandon the valleys it had disembowelled, grown respectable on, could now leave its slagheaps and crowded terraces for more profitable trade elsewhere. Nothing could renew that extractable wealth, and industrial production for trade, in developing and overtaking world market, could in its pursuit of a successful economy only abandon large sections of the society this was supposed to support. What happened in South Wales is now happening widely in England, and Labourism – the attempted parliamentary direction of a capitalist mode of production – has as little of practical use to say in the one country as in the other. Moreover, though unheroically, we have to add the second qualification: the character of the culture that came through as Labour gained political power in Wales: a test case, in all its light and shade, of the orthodox notions of the public interest and representation of the people.

There is then a third mode, for which Wales and Dr Morgan provide abundant evidence. This is the idea of growth through a culture and a community, supported but not directed by an economy. Of course all the periods overlap, but if the peak of Liberalism – an enlightened bourgeois society – comes around 1900, and the peak of the labour movement in the twenties and thirties, the peak of this third movement was in the late sixties and seventies. It had learned much from previous experiences, of both Liberalism and Labourism, but it drew also, as each of those in different ways had drawn, on older Welsh resources of social thought and feeling. Were not the Welsh, in their own language, the Cymry, the fellow countrymen or comrades, the sons and daughters of cultural community? Was not Welsh social feeling audibly different from the repressed, anxious, class-ridden culture of England? Indeed, as some of the Liberals had been saying, was not Wales already classless, all its gentry and social climbers having conveniently emigrated? This persuasive, generous and encouraging sentiment, which bore some fruit in social thought and imaginative writing, encountered a dreadful reality on several occasions but most humiliatingly in the campaign and result of the devolution referendum. What the sentiment could not admit was now there in cold figures: that at the very root of these ideas, that of a common and distinctive Welshness, too much had happened or had always been wrongly assumed. What was taken as a grounding reality had to be seen as at best (though none the worse for that) an aspiration. The historic divisions of North and South Wales; the less noticed divisions of the 'Principality' and the Marches; the dramatic contrast between industrial and pastoral Wales; the changing fortunes, now reaching crisis, of the native and the adopted dominant language: all these but also the quite evident class division, of an orthodox kind, among the Welsh and the increasingly numerous immigrant English, revealed what had long been there: not an inheritance but a crisis of Welsh identity, not a unifying but a dividing issue. As the identity of the English, or Englishness, moves now into comparable crisis, as in so many old nationalisms within a dominant and reckless international economy, the case of Wales and of Welshness, again for all its specificities, is a study conveniently close to hand. The old joke of the encyclopedia entry – 'For Wales, see England' – can now be put the other way: 'For Britain, see Wales'.

Dr Morgan's most useful history, the first of six planned volumes of the history of Wales, can then be especially recommended to

English readers and as much more than a regional study. It is admirably detailed and explanatory over a sufficiently long period, and thus quickly takes the reader beyond the selected images of Welshness which have become common currency in England and which some Welsh cultural exports have done much to encourage. The dominant perception has been organized around certain powerful identifying elements: miners, choral singing, chapels, rugby, rhetoric, radicalism. These have all been active in modern Wales, but it is interesting to go through the history and see how many of them are, at least in origin, English implantations. The supposed national character is not entirely myth, but much of it, in its best-known forms, has been shaped and reshaped by the long pressures of a more powerful neighbouring economy and culture.

Indeed, that was what was wrong with some early phases of nationalism: that it supposed Welshness to be in effect genetic or, more plausibly, linguistic, when the actual cultural formation had been a prolonged interaction between always diverse native elements and the both dominant and alternative effects of an occupying power. By Dr Morgan's period this long and intricate history had diverse potentials: for a liberal bourgeoise; for a militant working class; for new kinds of clerisy; and, still under the greatest pressure, for a popular culture based in the old language and its remarkable literature. All four, in his century, have developed but also confronted each other. Neither relative prosperity nor absolute economic depression brought them more than temporarily together.

This is not a complaint. The mode of threnody, still active in Wales as in England, is becoming increasingly irrelevant. But at the same time there can be no simple celebration of the birth or rebirth of anything so coherent as a nation. The contemporary importance of Wales, for the Welsh but also for its neighbours now encountering comparable problems and internal struggles, is that because its phases of dislocation were at once early and dramatic, there has been some genuinely contemporary reflection and thinking – often resilient and constructive: as often baffled and bitter – of a kind which is becoming necessary in peoples once much prouder, more confident and more settled. The central problem is the realistic discovery of a working, non-mythical identity and community against and beyond the pressures of an international economy which has no real use for either, and which is even having to renege on its only positive proposition – that all people are producers and consumers – the 'all' now drastically revised to 'some' or even 'a few', with the rest, in that now decisive term, 'redundant'.

This is the real force behind the contemporary revival of Welsh historical studies. It is a remarkable enough history to attract both professional and general attention, but the distinguishing quality of some of the best recent work is that the full historical detail is being sought as a contribution to understanding a contemporary impasse. This is especially true of Gwyn A. Williams and his colleagues: the essays *A People and a Proletariat*, edited by David Smith (1980) are an excellent introduction to this.[3] Dr Morgan's perspective, but also evidently his brief, is rather different. He has given us the one-volume history of a decisive century, from which the general reader can start and to which all students of the history and the culture will need, for its scope and fullness, to refer. It is in some ways a very Welsh history, in its quite integral inclusion of poetry and novels with the politics and economics. But he does not need to be told that it is around his central concept, that of 'nation' in the sense of national identity and rebirth, that the current Welsh argument in history and in politics moves and at times rages. One obvious centre of this argument will now be his evaluation of that Liberal Wales which underlies his perspective. I have indicated my own different evaluation of it, but like thousands of other readers I shall remain in his debt for the clarity of its exposition.

What alternative general concepts are there? Two can be briefly mentioned. The first, which made an impression but is now (perhaps unjustly) fading, is that of the 'internal colony' (as in M. Hechter, *Internal Colonialism*, 1975).[4] In some respects this is still illuminating, as an indicator of the character of cultural and marginally political nationalism within external dominance. It is in any case notably better than the orthodox English concept of 'region'. But the second concept, of 'uneven development', is now more to the point.[5] To stand in the Brecon Beacons and look south and then north is to see, on the ground and then very readily in the history, the reality of this apparent abstraction. To the south, now, are the dwindling remains of that explosive development of the iron and coal trade. To the north are the depopulated but marginally surviving pastoral hills. But the reality now is that both are old, and both marginal.[6]

141

I looked these two ways as a boy, growing up in that country, and that sense of an uneasy border – an internal border, even more important than the political border with England – has since shaped most of my work. While the nation was being reborn, in Welsh national liberalism, or the proletariat being formed, in those valleys to the south, I saw Welshness after Welshness, and neither was quite mine nor that of my own people: we were held and pulled between them. It seemed a very local experience, but the sense I now get of much of Wales, and of region after region of what was once England, is clearer in these terms than in any others I know. It is an internal division generated by a quite objective dislocation. It is the pressure of an imposed, confident, reckless unevenness: the capitalist version of the nature of human production. Its consequences in Wales can now connect us to others, in a common history that simply has to be changed.

Notes

1. Kenneth O. Morgan (1934–) is a Welsh historian and Labour peer; his memoir titled *My Histories* was published by the University of Wales Press in 2015.
2. Williams seems to be referring here to the 'Nairn-Anderson' thesis, developed in *New Left Review* by Perry Anderson and Tom Nairn. The key essays appear in Perry Anderson, *English Questions* (London: Verso, 1992), and in Tom Nairn, *The Break-up of Britain* (London: New Left Books, 1977).
3. David Smith (ed.), *A People and a Proletariat*, is reviewed by Williams in 'Remaking Welsh History', included in this volume.
4. Michael Hechter, *Internal Colonialism: The Celtic Fringe in British National Development, 1536–1966* (London: Routledge, 1975). See 'Wales and England', n. 10.
5. Williams is making a distinction between 'internal colonialism' and 'uneven development'. The economic dimension of Hechter's 'internal colonialism' thesis is based on a theory of uneven development and draws explicitly on Immanuel Wallerstein's *The Modern World-System: Capitalist Agriculture and the Origins of the European World-Economy in the Sixteenth Century* (New York: Academic Press, 1974). Williams seeks to emphasise the unevenness of capitalist development within Wales itself. Hechter is not unaware of this unevenness, but the internal colonial model tends to see the distinction as that between a developed English 'core' and an underdeveloped Celtic 'periphery'. In the post-devolution age, 'internal colonialism' seems to have become a metaphorical description of 'uneven development', such as when Simon Brooks sees north Wales as having become an 'internal colony' of Cardiff, in *Why Wales Never Was*, p. 126.
6. The same point, that 'both were old', is made at the end of Williams's novel *The Fight for Manod* (1979; London: Hogarth Press, 1988), p. 206.

BLACK MOUNTAINS

Ronald Blythe (ed.), *Places: An Anthology of Britain*
(Oxford: Oxford University Press, 1981), pp. 215-22.

1

See this layered sandstone among the short mountain grass. Place
your right hand on it, palm downward. See where the sun rises and
where it stands at noon. Direct your middle finger midway between
them. Spread your fingers, not widely. You now hold this place in
your hand.[1]

The six rivers rise in the plateau of the back of your hand. The
first river, now called Mynwy or Monnow, flows at the outside edge
of your thumb. The second river, now called Olchon, flows between
your thumb and the first finger, to join the Mynwy at the top
of your thumb. The third river, now called Honddu, flows between
your first and second fingers and then curves to join the Mynwy,
away from your hand. The fourth river, now called Grwyne Fawr,
flows between your second and third fingers, and then curves the
other way, joining the fifth river, now called Grwyne Fechan, that
has been flowing between your third and your little finger. The sixth
river, now called Rhiangoll, flows at the outside edge of your little
finger. Beyond your hand are the two rivers to the sea. Mynwy carrying Olchon and Honddu flows into the circling Wye. Grwyne and
Rhiangoll flow into the Usk. Wye and Usk, divided by the Forest of
Gwent, flow to the Severn Sea.

It was by Wye and Usk, from the Severn Sea and beyond it, that
men first came to this place.

The ridges of your five fingers, and the plateau of the back of
your hand, are now called the Black Mountains. Your thumb is Crib
y Gath or Cat's Back.[2] Your first finger is Haterall. Your second finger is Ffawyddog, with Bal Mawr at the knuckle. Your third finger
is Gader, with Gader Fawr at the knuckle. Your little finger is Allt

Mawr, and its nail is Crug Hywel, giving its name to Crickhowell below it. On the back of your hand are Twyn y Llech and Twmpa and Rhos Dirion and Waun Fach. Mynwy and Olchon flow from Twyn y Llech. Honddu flows from Twyn y Llech and Twmpa. Grwyne Fawr flows from Rhos Dirion. Grwyne Fechan and Rhiangoll flow from Waun Fach.

You hold the shapes and the names in your hand.

2

It was by Wye and Usk, from the Severn Sea and beyond it, that men first came to this place.

We have no ready way to explain ourselves to you. Our language has gone utterly, except for the place name which you now say as Ewyas. The names by which we knew ourselves are entirely unknown to you. We left many marks on the land but the only marks that you can easily recognize are the long stone graves of our dead. If you wish to know us you must learn to read the whole land.

3

The long barrows of the first Black Mountain shepherds are clustered on flat grasslands between the steep northern scarp, at your wrist, and on one side the wide valley of the Wye, on the other the valley of the Usk and the basin of Llyn Syvadon, now called Llangorse Lake.

When the first shepherds came there was thick oak forest from the rivers to the level of these grasslands. Then the forest thinned, and there was good pasture among the scattered trees. On the ridges above them, in the climate of that time, there were great winter bogs in the peat above the deep sandstone, but there was some summer grazing on the slopes. They lived at that chosen level, at first only in the summers, going back to the rivers in the winters, but later yearthrough.

These are still flat grasslands, grazed by thousands of sheep and hundreds of ponies. Below them and above them the land has changed and been changed.

4

We can count in generations. Say two hundred and twenty generations from the first shepherds to us. Then a new people came. Say one hundred and sixty generations from them to us. They came when the climate was changing. Winters were much colder and summers hotter and drier. While elsewhere in the island men were moving down from chalk uplands, because the springs were failing, here the sandstone ridges and the plateau were drying, and there was new summer grazing. Surviving tracks show the change. To every ridge, now, there are long transverse, sometimes zigzag, tracks from the middle heights to the crests. They are often sunken, making a characteristic notch where they break the ridge. The local name for such a track is rhiw. Along these tracks, sheep and cattle were driven for the summer grazing. Meanwhile, below the old grasslands, the forest was changing. The damp oak forest fell back, and new clearings were made among the more diverse woods. And this people felled along the slopes of the ridges. There was then more grass but also the heather began to spread. They lived and worked in these ways for sixty generations.

5

New peoples came. Say a hundred generations from them to us. And again the climate was changing. Winters were milder, summers cooler and wetter. They settled a little higher than the first shepherds, and in new ways. They built folds and camps at the ends of ridges: at Pentwyn, Y Gaer, Crug Hywel, Castell Dinas. There were summer pastures behind them, along the lower ridges, for their sheep and cattle and horses. And still they cleared towards the valleys, in small square fields. There were peaceful generations, but increasingly, now, more peoples were coming from the east. The folds and steadings became armed camps. The names of history begin with the Silures. But then a different arrival: an imperial people: Romans. These said of the Silures: 'non atrocitate, non clementia mutabatur': changed neither by cruelty nor by mercy. Literate history, imperial history, after more than a hundred generations of history.

6

In literate history the Black Mountains are marginal. They are still classified today as marginal or as waste land. After the Silures no new people settled them. The tides of conquest or lordship lapped to their edges and their foothills, leaving castles facing them – Ewyas Harold,

Ewyas Lacy, Grosmont, Skenfrith, White Castle, Abergavenny, Crickhowell, Bronllys, Hay, Clifford – to command their peoples. Romans drove military roads at their edges. Normans pushed closer, but had no use for land above seven hundred feet. In the mountains and their valleys the people were still there, with their animals. They were the children of the first shepherds and of the upland people and of the camp-builders. Roman governors wanted them to come down and live in new towns. Some went, some stayed. When the Romans left the island, some came back to the mountains. By at latest the sixth century, in modern reckoning, the Black Mountains were a kingdom, which lasted, precariously, until the twelfth century. Twenty generations of Roman rule and its aftermath. Twenty-five generations of a small native kingdom. They called the kingdom by a very old name: Ewyas.

7

Where then are the Black Mountains? The physical answer is direct. The literate and administrative answer is more difficult.

At a certain point on the narrow and winding road which we drive in summer for shopping – past Pentwyn and Parc y Meirch, below the source of the Mynwy and over the brooks of Dulas and Esgyrn – at a certain point on this secluded road between high banks and hedges of hazel and holly and thorn, at this indistinguishable point there is a ridged bump in the roadway, where the roadmen of Brecon (now Powys) and the roadmen of Hereford (now Hereford and Worcester) have failed to see eye to eye. It is a trivial unevenness, deep within this specific region. It is the modern border between England and Wales.

And this is how it has gone, in literate and administrative history. The small kingdom of Ewyas – not small if you try to walk it, but politically small – was often, while it still had identity, redrawn or annexed or married into the neighbouring kingdoms of Brycheiniog or Gwent or Erging (Archenfield). Its modern political history is differently arbitrary. A dispute between the London court and a local landowning family, at the time of the Act of Union between England and Wales, led to a border which follows no natural feature or, rather, several in an incomprehensible series. In the twentieth century, three counties had lines drawn across and through the Black Mountains:

lines on maps and in a few overgrown and lichened stones. Brecon pushed one way, Monmouthshire another, Hereford a third. The first was part of Wales, the third part of England; Monmouthshire, until it became Gwent, anomalous between them. A national park boundary followed these amazing administrative lines. Then Brecon was incorporated into the new Powys. Monmouthshire in name became the old Gwent. Hereford and Worcester, unwillingly joined, considered and rejected the name of West Mercia. It was almost, even in name, a very old situation: this marginal, this waste land, taken in at the very edges of other, more powerful, units.

Within the Black Mountains, these lines on the map mean nothing. You have only to stand there to see an unusually distinct and specific region. Or go on that midsummer Sunday – Shepherds' Sunday – when they drive the tups from above the Usk to above the Monnow and track down unmarked sheep. An old internal organization, in the region's old activity, still visibly holds. Later, of course, the externally drawn lines and their consequences arrive, administratively, in the post. They are usually bills.

8

How to see it, physically? At first it is so strange. You need your hand on the stone to discern its extraordinary structure. Within the steep valleys, or from any of the ridges, this basic shape of the hand is not visible. And of course at every point there are minor features: cross valleys, glaciated cwms, rockfalls (darens), steeply gouged watercourses. It is so specific a country, yet its details take years to learn.

Black mountains? From a distance, like others, they are blue. From very close they are many colours: olive-green under sunlight; darker green with the patches of summer bracken; green with a reddish tinge when there are young leaves on the whinberries; dark with the heather out of flower, purple briefly in late summer; russet in the late autumn bracken; a pale gold, often, in the dead winter bracken, against the white of snow. Black? Entirely so, under heavy storm clouds. Very dark and suddenly solid under any thick cloud. The long whaleback ridges can be suddenly awesome.

But then their valleys are so different. Now Mynwy and Olchon and Honddu and Rhiangoll are farmed; Grwyne Fawr is forested and dammed; Grwyne Fechan is farm, a little forest and then upland pasture. The oldest modern farms are half-way up each slope from the valley beds, where the springs mostly rise. The old valley roads are at this level. But there are now roads and farms right down by the rivers, where there can be some flat fields. Then from these and the others the cleared fields climb the slopes, to uneven heights. Ash and thorn and rowan and cherry are still felled, bracken ploughed, to enclose a new field from the mountain. Others, once cleared, have gone back to scrub and bracken. At the farthest points, often surprisingly close, are old ruined stone farms, thick now with the nettles marking human occupation. In the Napoleonic wars there was this high and intensive settlement. It fell back with the decline of the Welsh woollen industry. The fields have been taken in to other farms. The rest of the story is what is called depopulation.

But the valleys are bright green, under the different colours of the mountains. Trees flourish in them. From some ridges the valleys still look like woodland, with the farms in clearings. But there is always a sharp contrast between the bleak open tops, with their heather and whinberry and cotton sedge and peat pools, their tracks which dissolve into innumerable sheep tracks, their sudden danger, in bad weather, in low cloud and mist with few landmarks, and the green settled valleys, with the fine trimmed farm hedges, the layered sandstone houses – colours from grey and brown towards pink or green, the patchwork of fields. At midsummer the valleys are remarkable, for on the trimmed hedges of thorn and holly and hazel and ash and field maple there is an amazing efflorescence of stands of honeysuckle and pink or white wild roses, and on the banks under them innumerable foxgloves. It is so close to look up from these flowers to the steep ridges. By one of the ruined farms there was once a whole field of foxgloves. It is now back to bracken and thistle. But in the next field they are felling and clearing again, and the ploughed earth above the sandstone goes through a range of colours from wet dark red to dried pink among the bright grass.

So this extraordinarily settled and that extraordinarily open wild country are very close to each other and intricately involved. Either, with some strictness, can be called pastoral, but then with very different implications. As the eye follows them, in this unusually defining land, the generations are distinct but all suddenly present.

9

It is a place where you can stand and look out. From Haterall there is the vast patchwork of fields of the Herefordshire plain, across to the Malverns and the Clees. From Twmpa there is distance after distance of upland Wales, from Radnor and Eppynt to Plynlimmon and Cader Idris and the neighbouring Beacons. From Allt Mawr there is the limestone scarp, on the other side of the Usk, where the iron industry came, and in the valleys behind it, Rhymney and Taff and Rhondda, the mining for coal.

Land, labour, and history. It can be cold standing there. The winds sweep those ridges. You go back down, into the settled valleys, with their medley of map names.

Different views, different lives. But occasionally, laying your right hand, palm downward, on the deep layered sandstone, you know a whole, intricate, distinct place. The Black Mountains. Ewyas.

Notes

1. Published in 1981, these passages, in slightly amended form, reappear as the opening section of Williams's final fictional project, *People of the Black Mountains I: The Beginning* (London: Chatto & Windus, 1989), p. 1.

2. The Welsh name for the mountain known in English as 'Cat's Back' is in fact 'Crib y Garth'. The 'Gath' used by Raymond Williams here is the mutated form of *cath*, which is 'cat' in Welsh. *Garth* means 'mountain ridge' or 'promontory'. *Crib* is 'crest' or 'summit'. It would seem that the aural similarity between 'Garth' and 'Cath' resulted in the Anglicised name, which has been translated back into Welsh, erroneously, by Raymond Williams. The version of this passage that forms the opening of *People of the Black Mountains* (see n. 1 above) omits the English version, but keeps the erroneous Welsh form. Williams's etymological method, as evidenced famously in *Keywords* (London: Fontana, 1976), may have its roots in the convoluted, multi-lingual, etymologies of his native Black Mountains / Y Mynyddoedd Duon.

LITERATURE

DYLAN THOMAS'S
PLAY FOR VOICES

Critical Quarterly, 1 (1959), 18-26.
Collected in C. B. Cox (ed.), *Dylan Thomas: A Collection
of Critical Essays* (Englewood Cliffs, NJ;
Prentice-Hall Inc., 1966), pp. 89-98.

I

Under Milk Wood, in approximately its published form, was first
played in New York only a few weeks before Dylan Thomas died
there. His work on it, during the last months of his life, was work
against time and breakdown, yet in essence we can regard it as complete. The marks of the history of the play are, nevertheless, quite
evident, and in particular the many revisions which the plan of the
play underwent remain as separable layers, if not in the total effect
of the work, at least in its formal construction. The play grew from
a broadcast talk, 'Quite Early One Morning', which described the
dreams and waking of a small Welsh seaside town. Daniel Jones, in
his preface to *Under Milk Wood*, describes the stages through which
this developed towards the work as we now have it. There was the
insertion, and subsequent abandonment, of a plot, in which the
town was to be declared an insane area, and the blind Captain Cat,
at a trial of sanity, was to call the inhabitants in their own defence.
The defence was to be abandoned, finally, after the prosecution's
description of a sane town, the inhabitants of Llaregyb at once peti-
tioning to be cordoned off from such sanity.[1] Thomas worked on
this scheme, under the title 'The Town was Mad', but later changed
the action back to a simple time-sequence description of Llaregyb
itself. This was published, as far as it had been written – up to the

delivery of letters by the postman Willy Nilly – as *Llaregyb, a Piece for Radio Perhaps*, in 1952. Then this was again revised, the title changed to 'Under Milk Wood', and performed, again incomplete, in May 1953. John Malcolm Brinnin has described the last-minute writing and revision for this performance, which was part of Thomas's American reading tour.[2] By the following October, having left aside certain things he had planned to include, Thomas had finished the play as we now have it.

This confused and racing history seems not to have affected the spirit of *Under Milk Wood*, though the loss of 'The Town was Mad' is a thing to regret. It is in construction that the different intentions are evident, and in particular in the multiplication of narrators. The original narrator, the blind Captain Cat, was an obvious device for radio. Then, in the scheme of 'The Town was Mad', Captain Cat became a central character, so that eventually another narrator was necessary. With his public readings in mind, and following also the habits of this kind of radio play, Thomas moved steadily back towards emphasis on the narrative voice. In the final version there are two narrators, First Voice and Second Voice, and there is also narration by Captain Cat and the Voice of a Guidebook. Formally, this is confusing, though part of the difficulty lies in the whole concept of a play for voices.

A primary complaint against the majority drama of this century has been the thinness, the single dimension, of its language. The development of domestic drama, and the emergence of the theory of naturalism, had brought themes and situations nearer to ordinary everyday life at the sacrifice of the older intensity of dramatic language. The words to be spoken by ordinary people in ordinary situations must be a facsimile of their ordinary conversation, rather than a literary expression of their whole experience. But then the paradox is that the very method chosen to authenticate the reality of the experience – that the play sounds like actual people talking – turns, in its overall effect, to a deep conviction that, after all, important elements of reality have been excluded. And this is, indeed, not difficult to understand, when we consider the nature of speech and experience, and ask ourselves to what extent our own sense of personal reality, the full actuality of our experience, can in fact be adequately communicated in the terms of ordinary conversation.

Many of our deepest and richest experiences are unlikely to be reducible to conversational terms, and it is precisely, the faculty we honour in poets that, by means of art, such experiences can find public expression.

However, in the case of drama, it is not easy to accommodate this kind of communication within the framework of an action limited to observed external probability. The revolt against naturalism, which has distinguished the drama of this century, is a many-sided attempt to get beyond the limitations imposed by a criterion of reality which is essentially external. The difficulty has been, throughout, that in certain respects drama is inescapably explicit, has inescapably to be shown. The idea of the play for voices, primarily developed in terms of sound broadcasting, is one of many attempts to make a new convention in which the necessary explicitness is preserved, yet without limitation to a single dimension of reality. It is a very difficult undertaking, and it is not surprising that the device of narration should have gained such a crucial importance. In terms of recent stage drama, narrative can be called undramatic, but in fact, on a longer view, it can be seen that in some of the most satisfactory dramatic forms ever achieved – in Athenian tragic drama in particular – narrative has had an important place. The rehabilitation of narrative, in broadcast drama, was a sound instinct, and *Under Milk Wood*, in spite of the crudity of its narrative structure, is the most successful example we have of its dramatic usefulness.

There is another reason for the emphasis on narrative. The craft of dialogue, in modern drama, has been ordinarily so much practised in terms of naturalism, that to a poet, or a writer with similar intentions, it has come to seem the hardest and most baffling part of drama: not only because it is in any case difficult, but because to lapse into the dialogue of a single dimension is so easy and so frustrating. Narrative, in comparison, is free, and in a way is turned to in relief. There is a similar turning, wherever possible, to such devices as chorus and song, because these again follow relatively directly from kinds of writing practised elsewhere. In the case of *Under Milk Wood*, the narrative structure must be seen, finally, as in part a successful convention for a particular kind of play, in part a residue of weakness following from both general and personal inexperience in this kind of dramatic attempt.

II

I have distinguished three elements – three kinds of writing – in *Under Milk Wood*: narrative, dialogue, song. If we look at examples of each, we can make certain important judgments of value. The narrative of the first and second voices is, in my opinion, relatively unsuccessful – perhaps, indeed, because it was too well-known, too easy a manner. This sinuous, decorated, atmospheric writing has become commonplace in broadcast drama, and I think it is ordinarily unsatisfactory, and particularly so in Dylan Thomas, where it opens the gate to certain observable weaknesses of his poetry. Near the beginning, for instance, we find

> the hunched, courters'-and-rabbits' wood limping invisible down to the sloeblack, slow, black, crowblack, fishingboat-bobbing sea.

The 'sloeblack, slow, black, crowblack' device seems a nervous habit rather than actual description; a facile assonance rather than a true dramatic rhythm. This can be seen more clearly by contrast with a piece of successful narration, where significantly Thomas is involved with action and character rather than with suggestion of an atmosphere:

> The Reverend Eli Jenkins, in Bethesda House, gropes out of bed into his preacher's black, combs back his bard's white hair, forgets to wash, pads barefoot downstairs, opens the front door, stands in the doorway and, looking out at the day and up at the eternal hill, and hearing the sea break and the gab of birds, remembers his own verses...

The suggestiveness of the former piece is strictly casual, a simply verbal device, whereas in the latter piece the rhythms point and make the action, and the verbal order plays its part in character. 'His bard's white hair' is not merely decorative, like 'sloeblack'; it contains both relevant meanings, the man's appearance and the sense, in the word order, of the bard's part he is acting. The rhythmic stop and surprise, so casually placed, of 'forgets to wash', is again serving the whole situation being presented. It is the difference between dramatic writing and unattached tremolo.

There is some significance in this distinction, when extended to Thomas's work as a whole. *Under Milk Wood* is important because it seems to break a personal deadlock, a long imprisonment in a particular kind of practised effect, in much the same way that Yeats's plays mark the development from the imprisoning 'wan, pale, languishing' world of his early poetry to the fine hardness and clarity of his later work. It is a movement out of a self-regarding personal rhythm into a more mature and more varied world. Whenever Thomas touches the action of his town and its people, there is a sudden sharpening and deepening, very different in effect from the posing rhythms of the anxious, word-locked, suggestive observer.

The actual voices are very different from the atmospheric voices of the narrators:

2W. And look at Ocky Milkman's wife that nobody's ever seen.
1W. He keeps her in the cupboard with the empties
3W. And think of Dai Bread with two wives
2W. One for the daytime one for the night.
4W. Men are brutes on the quiet.

It is ordinarily this one sharp comic lilt, but it is markedly better than

The lust and lilt and lather and emerald breeze and crackle
of the bird-praise and body of Spring ...

The imprisoning rhythm is broken whenever the drama is actual, and it is interesting to notice that it is also broken for the songs, which are not set romantic pieces, but ballads in the mood of the successful dialogue:

In Pembroke City when I was young
I lived by the Castle Keep
Sixpence a week was my wages
For working for the chimbley sweep.

Those of us who were most critical of Dylan Thomas's earlier method, though recognizing that it had produced three of four remarkable poems, welcomed *Under Milk Wood* because it was the beginning of a break-out from a fixed, affected manner, which he seems to have recognized, in his last years, as increasingly unable to express all the varied life that was actually his experience, and that at last broke through in this play.

III

The main literary source of *Under Milk Wood* is the similar 'play for voices' in the Circe episode (Part Two, section twelve) of Joyce's *Ulysses*.[3] The parallels are remarkable, and some of them should be cited. I will put what in *Ulysses* is printed as stage-direction (though of course it is not this) into the narrative-voice form which Thomas adopted:

> *N.* Ellen Bloom, in pantomime dame's stringed mobcap, crinoline and bustle, widow Twankey's blouse with mutton-leg sleeves buttoned behind, grey mittens and cameo brooch, her hair plaited in a crispine net, appears over the staircase banisters, a slanted candlestick in her hand and cries out in shrill alarm
> *EB.* O blessed Redeemer – what have they done to him! My smelling salts!
> *N.* She hauls up a reef of skirt and ransacks the pouch of her striped blay petticoat. A phial, an Agnus Dei, a shrivelled potato and a celluloid doll fall out.
> *EB.* Sacred Heart of Mary, where were you at all, at all?
> *N.* Bloom, mumbling, his eyes downcast, begins to bestow his parcels in his filled pockets but desists, muttering. A voice, sharply
> *V.* Poldy!
> *B.* Who?
> *N.* He ducks and wards off a blow clumsily.
> *B.* At your service.
> *N.* He looks up. Beside her mirage of datepalms a handsome woman in Turkish costume stands before him …

If we compare this with the ordinary method of *Under Milk Wood*, the technical continuity is obvious:

N. Mr. Pugh reads, as he forks the shroud meat in, from *Lives
of the Great Poisoners.* He has bound a plain brown-paper
cover round the book. Slyly, between slow mouthfuls, he
sidespies up at Mrs. Pugh, poisons her with his eye, then
goes on reading. He underlines certain passages and smiles
in secret.
Mrs. P. Persons with manners do not read at table,
N. says Mrs. Pugh. She swallows a digestive tablet as big as
a horse-pill, washing it down with clouded peasoup water.
Mrs. P. Some persons were brought up in pigsties.
P. Pigs don't read at table, dear.
N. Bitterly she flicks dust from the broken cruet. It settles on
the pie in a thin gnat-rain.

The continuity, moreover, is in more than technique. Compare:

Mr. Pugh minces among bad vats and jeroboams, tiptoes
through spinneys of murdering herbs, agony dancing in his
crucibles, and mixes especially for Mrs. Pugh a venomous
porridge unknown to toxicologists which will scald and viper
through her until her ears fall off like figs (Thomas)

I shall have you slaughtered and skewered in my stables and
enjoy a slice of you with crisp crackling from the baking tin
basted and baked like sucking pig with rice and lemon or
currant sauce. It will hurt you. (Joyce)

Soon it will be time to get up.
Tell me your tasks, in order.
I must put my pyjamas in the drawer marked pyjamas.
I must take my cold bath which is good for me. (Thomas)

You will make the beds, get my tub ready, empty the pisspots
in the different rooms. You'll be taught the error of your
ways. (Joyce)

There is an evident similarity between *Under Milk Wood* and *Ulysses*
(each covering the life of an ordinary day), not only in kinds of
imagination, but also in certain marked rhythms. I do not make the

comparison to show Thomas unoriginal, though that he learned from Joyce is obvious. The interest is rather in the kinds of speech both are able to develop, as alternatives to one-dimensional 'public' conversation. Thomas is writing for speaking, rather than writing speech (conversation) in the ordinary sense. The ordinary poetic alternative to conversation has been rhetoric, but this is by no means the only variant. There is the chorus of cries:

> Try your luck on spinning Jenny! Ten to one bar one! Sell the monkey, boys! Sell the monkey! I'll give ten to one! Ten to one bar one! (Joyce)

> How's it above? Is there rum and laverbread? Bosoms and robins?
> Concertinas? Ebenezer's bell? Fighting and onions? (Thomas)

Or the simple, hard chanting:

> I gave it to Molly
> Because she was jolly
> The leg of the duck
> The leg of the duck. (Joyce)

> Boys boys boys
> Kiss Gwennie where she says
> Or give her a penny.
> Go on, Gwennie. (Thomas)

By weaving a pattern of voices, rather than an ordinary conversational sequence, the reach of the drama is significantly enlarged. It can include not only things said, but things left unsaid, the interpenetration of things seen and imagined, the images of memory and dream, the sharp rhythmic contrasts of this voice and that, this tone and that, this convention and others. When we first read *Ulysses*, it seems that we are reading actual conversation, hearing our own full voices, spoken and unspoken, for the first time. The ordinary dialogue of a naturalist play seems, by comparison, artificial and theatrical. *Under Milk Wood* is slighter than *Ulysses*, but there is the same achievement of a living convention: the voices, in their strange patterns, are among the most real we have heard. This success raises interesting possibilities for the drama as a whole, when we remember that, in England at any rate, the ordinary modern alternative to naturalism has been, not a pattern of voices, but the single general-purpose poetic rhythm of Eliot or Fry. It is significant that the varied pattern of voices has been achieved only in the context of an abandonment of ordinary naturalistic action. The Circe scene in *Ulysses*, and *Under Milk Wood*, follow the methods of expressionist drama, which similarly aims not at representation but at a pattern of experience. Yet it is not only in modern expressionism that we find this intention; we find it also in Ibsen's *Peer Gynt*, in the *Walpurgisnacht* scene of Goethe's *Faust*, and, interestingly, in the storm-scenes in *Lear*. The pattern of voices of Lear, the Fool, and Edgar as Poor Tom seems to me basically similar, in method and intention, to this writing by Joyce and Thomas. Lear is an obviously greater work, and the storm-writing is only one element in it, but the resemblance matters, and the authority of *Lear* is important, if we are not to confine our conception of drama to a single-level, tidy, public representation.

IV

I have emphasized technical points, in the foregoing analysis, because we are still searching for a satisfactory contemporary dramatic form, and the partial success of *Under Milk Wood* is particularly instructive. It was not written for the stage, yet in fact, after some rearrangement, it was staged very successfully. It remains true, in the drama and the theatre, that we do not know what we can do until we have tried; our ordinary conceptions of what is theatrically possible, what is properly dramatic, remain timid and custom-bound, though constant experiment is essential. *Under Milk Wood* justifies itself, if only as this.

Yet in substance, also, it is not inconsiderable. It is true that it is very much a boy's-eye-view, like most of Thomas's writing of this kind. Yet there is a warmth of acceptance in the experience, a willing return to the absorbed absolutes of boyhood, which deserve recognition in a period soured by a continual, prematurely-aged rejection. It is not a mature work, but the retained extravagance of an adolescent's imaginings. Yet it moves, at its best, into a genuine involvement, an actual sharing of experience, which is not the least of the dramatic virtues.

161

Is it an expressionist play, dramatising a mind, or a poetic documentary, dramatising a way of life? In the main, of course, it is the latter, but through the medley of voices, through the diverse experiences, a single voice and a recognisable experience emerge. The play can be seen in three parts:

(a) *Night and Dreams*: 'you can hear their dreams'; pp. 1–22
(b) *Waking and Morning*: 'rising and raising ... the shops squeak open'; pp. 22–61.
(c) *Afternoon, Dusk and Night*: 'the sunny slow lolling afternoon ... down in the dusking town ... dusk is drowning for ever. It is all at once night now'; pp. 61–86*

The distribution of interest is characteristic. The strong feelings are of dream, hiding, the effort of waking to the pretences of the day. Single feeling, in these modes, flows through the many voices. At near the beginning and near the end are the drowning memories of the blind Captain Cat – the private poetry; and again, by contrast, the morning and evening verses of Eli Jenkins – the public poetry of woken self-conscious sentiment. The neighbours' chorus (pp. 9–13) clacks through the day with its hard, waking judgments. The three fullest portraits – of Mog Edwards and his Myfanwy, of Mrs. Ogmore-Pritchard and her dead husbands, of Pugh obsequiously hiding his hatreds – have a clear family likeness: the rejection of love, in whatever terms – money, house-pride, cold self-sufficiency. These are the hated, woken world, set in relief by the exceptions – the loving, fighting Cherry Owens; the dreamers of love – Lily, Gossamer, Bessie, Waldo and Sinbad; Dai Bread and his two wives; Polly Garter. The town is mad because the exceptions are so many, but only because we hear their dreams. Only, at the climax of the day, another world breaks through, and 'the morning is all singing' – the three songs, two of the children, one by Polly Garter, between morning and night.

It is not a formal structure, but the shape of the experience is clear. The little town is observed, but in a curve of feeling familiar from Thomas's poems: a short curve from darkness to darkness,

* *Under Milk Wood*, London: J. M. Dent and Sons, 1954.

with the songs and dreams of the day cut through by the hard, mask-ridden, uproariously laughed-at world. This, in the end, is the experience, in a single voice, and the chosen technique, which we have discussed formally, must now be seen as necessary to the experience. The language of dream, of song, of unexpressed feeling is the primary experience, and counter-pointed with it is the public language of chorus and rhetoric. The people, in the end, hardly talk to each other; each is locked in a world of dream or a convention of public behaviour. In the storm-scenes in Lear, Edgar and Lear are like this; the technique follows from the kind of experience. The play for voices has many uses, but for experience of this kind it is the only adequate form. In at last bringing these feelings through to his triumphantly actual dramatic world, Dylan Thomas wrote his adequate epilogue, his uproarious and singing lament.

Notes

1. Raymond Williams is working from an early published version of *Under Milk Wood*, which rendered the fictional name 'Llareggub' (derived by reversing the phrase 'bugger all') as 'Llaregyb'. Dylan Thomas preferred Llareggub, which first appears in his short story 'The Burning Baby' (1936), *Collected Stories* (London: Weidenfeld & Nicolson, 2014), p. 39.

2. John Malcolm Brinnin, *Dylan Thomas in America* (Boston: Little Brown, 1955).

3. James Joyce is a significant figure in Williams's life and criticism. Speaking of his initial period as a student in Cambridge, Williams noted that 'Joyce was without question the most important author for us. *Ulysses* and *Finnegans Wake* – which had just appeared in 1939 – were the texts we most admired.' *Politics and Letters* (London: Verso, 1979), p. 45. The analysis of Joyce in *The Country and the City* (London: Chatto & Windus, 1973), pp. 244–7) reiterates some of the observations made here; 'the most deeply known human community' notes Williams 'is language itself' (p. 245).

MARXISM, POETRY, WALES

Poetry Wales, 13/3 (Winter 1977), 16-34.[1]

*Can I begin by joining two questions together; the often-asked question
'Will poetry survive?' and the question of why your own writing doesn't
deal directly with poetry very often. Is poetry now less useful in some sense?*
I don't feel that. I'm quite sure the short poem, which is what we're
really talking about, will survive, because in a way it has less problems
than the other major forms. I have never written exclusively about it,
although actually I've written more about it than is sometimes said,
and I've written a good deal about poetry and drama, where for a
long time I was interested in the use of verse in drama rather than
other kinds of writing; and a fair amount about the earlier poetry
from the point of view of particular themes. But the forms I've
written about have tended to be the ones I've written in or tried to
write in myself. I always have a feeling that serious practice of the
short poem is another kind of writing. I remember Donald Davie
saying that after – I can't remember the age he said, 30 or 35 – you
can't be seriously both a poetry man and a novel man, you've got
to be one or the other, though there can also be exceptions to this.[2]
That's how it's been; I've always taken a great interest in it and read
a lot but I don't write about it.

*So what do you think the short poem does now, or should do now, in the
light of all you have written about the 'social', and the centrality of the
social reality in our time?*
Well, the word that suggests itself and is often used, is voice. It more
specifically is a voice as I read it, respond to it, hear it, than the novel,
or even drama which is after all writing for voices. I mean in each
of those cases something else begins to happen; people start moving,

even though only through these words. In the novel a story takes over, and an action comes, a place, and so on. Well of course these things can happen in poems too. There's often very much sharper observation of place, action, character in some short poems, but characteristically rather singly seen, not in this sustained and complicated way. But then what it can do so strongly, and what I value it for, is that it has this much stronger sense of voice. I think of it in that way as a more personal art although people always talk about its impersonality. The short poem has a voice which has got into words, and I've found sometimes that in certain passages of a novel I've wanted to write what is in effect a short poem just for one passage, although actually it's very difficult to integrate. People find it surprising in the form.

You wrote somewhere that most people now see more drama in one week than people in earlier times would see in their whole lives. Does this militate against the natural acceptance of the single-voiced poem, or could that very difference be an advantage, making the contrast all the stronger?
I think that given the real frequency of what you've got to call exposure to drama, it's almost not functioning as an art. The hardest thing I think for people to realize is that all the drama they see, as well as the apparently photographed real event, is all being 'produced'. By comparison this very sharp sense of the poem, an unambiguous sense of something that has been produced and made on paper and which isn't making that kind of offer – this is very important because it's a qualitatively different experience. I do think that given the whole direction of the culture poetry is bound to recover this aural and spoken dimension, which after all needn't always be face-to-face now, because of recording. But I think this would be very good, because a lot of the qualities I value in it at least remain the same in those conditions or may even actually be strengthened.

From another angle; if we think of the poem as the form particularly concerned with the quality of the single word, you seem to have an interest (as in Keywords *and at the start of* Culture and Society*) in words perhaps non poetically; as though what more matters to you there is that* *we have a network of certain important words through which we are conscious of ourselves and society. Could this again militate against a poetic feeling for words?*

This kind of analysis I do now, in things like *Keywords* – which in fact began as an appendix to *Culture and Society* all that time ago and then got cut out because of length, and then developed over the years until someone suggested I make a book out of it again – this of course is a kind of interest, for which there isn't much precedent, in the historical variation of words; and from that point of view is an interest in a specific kind of history, history inside language. Now if I am asked where I got on to that kind of thinking about language, which on the whole doesn't exist in any of the ordinary disciplines of language teaching, it *was* from the process of reading the earlier poetry and being aware both of changed meanings of words, from earlier poetry, *and* of this thing which everyone was discussing when I was a student; of ambiguity precisely. It's odd to say 'ambiguity precisely' but that was the way it was done. And almost if a word was not ambiguous – this was the sense when I was a student – it wasn't a poetic use. Now, I don't know whether this militates against one kind of attention to the poem. I notice now that the historical awareness of changed meanings has so declined – I mean among students who I think are otherwise better informed than my generation of students were – that a word with a perfectly good seventeenth- or eighteenth-century meaning in a seventeenth- or eighteenth-century poem but which is not wholly understood by a twentieth-century reader is instantly diagnosed as ambiguous. I mean that there is a kind of reading which has become standard for reading 'the poem'. If you think of Johnson's Epitaph on Levet, you know, where Levet is described among other things as 'officious', it's very curious that reading a couple of hundred clever and informed undergraduates writing about that, you've got five or six who both noticed the word and knew it had a different eighteenth-century meaning even if they weren't quite sure what that was, about half the rest didn't notice the word as being curious (which indeed it's bound to be if you're responding to the poem) and the others said that this was an interesting 'ambiguity' because Levet had been both officious and kind, and this showed that he had contrasting sides of his character! Now if you say the poetic use is an interest in ambiguity and that this is more significant than the historical meanings which for instance I looked at in *Keywords* then I would disagree with that, because I think one has to know what Johnson meant by 'officious'. But of course it does happen, and this is a rich source for a certain kind of poem. The thing that is technically called 'multiaccentuality' in a word, the fact that there really is more than one proper meaning, all the associations and root qualities and so on – this then becomes crucial, and one begins to see that use of words as almost material. But then this is after all how I increasingly see words, as really quite material. And this sense, of the best poetry actually *handling* these words like handling physical material, this I think is very important. It is very mysterious. And of course it does also happen in drama and fiction, but so many other things are happening there at the time which also have to be forwarded.

Does your emphasis there on the materiality of the poem imply a resolution now, in your own work, of what has apparently been an internal argument about the base–superstructure distinction in Marxism?
It means that I can now state, I think in much more satisfactory terms, what I was trying to state really from the '50s on, and worrying every Marxist in sight by saying that I believed that language and communication were primary activities. Not 'primary' implying that labour and production were secondary, but that language and communication were also primary. This worried every Marxist, and enraged some, because they said we just won't own *that*; labour comes first and everything else is superstructure to that base. I didn't then know how to describe it. I mean, I knew that it was so, I had every historical and observational grounds for knowing that it was so, but I think I do now know how to express the fact that it is so. And this is precisely the question of the materiality of language, of language use as *literally* a form of production – the movement from the first kinds of language in which we're using only the resources of our own bodies, producing our sociality really, and our practical consciousness, in an articulate way out of our own resources, and then learning this extraordinary means of production which is writing. It is one of the great transformations of productive technique. And people tend not to think of it in that way because they cut out the process, they go straight from the thing in the head to the thing in somebody else's

head. Whereas I think most people who work with this material are very aware that this is a productive process. And this is not meant to downgrade all the other productive processes, but it is meant to say that this is among the primary processes. And this means that what I originally just had to assert, is an integral condition of literature. It seemed to me very important to rescue this from the implicit downgrading it had received from other kinds of social and political theory and from reactions to them in aesthetic theory. I think I have now resolved this theoretically.[3]

If then writing is a primary form of production, can we get round the criticism of Marxism one hears, that it is itself an ideology and part of the superstructure, by saying that Marxism, that is Marx's writings, have a poesis in them? That they are a kind of 'Word' with a capital W, like Homer or the Bible? Is that just fanciful?

I think this is very difficult. I find I want to say yes and then to put in a couple of qualifications. I think the analysis that Stephen Marcus did of Engels's writing, for instance, was very interesting, because it was quite clear it wasn't just a matter of seeing what was happening in Manchester, a new kind of relationship between people; it was a looking for ways to write it. And once you start to read, say, Engels's *Condition of the Working Class in 1844*, as a piece of writing, you do see that finding images, finding ways of organizing the words, so that this new experience can be described, is a crucial part, it is composition in that sense. And I think there are moments when you feel this with Marx. The real difficulty is this, with certain kinds of writing, say history, where there's a mass of fact to be got into some kind of order, or some very difficult theoretical argument, where to pursue a theoretical argument you have got to tie something down to some very sharp definition, and you've then got to go on making relations between these abstractions; these are forms of writing in which I don't think the activity of composition, in the sense in which it's talked about in literature, can really happen. Because if they did I don't think the other things could happen. What is depended on – and it's always a matter of conventions then – is whether there is available a form of conventional writing or a form of direct analysis. Now this is a great difficulty where you've got some very original theoretician like Marx. He writes marvellously when his imagination is touched historically or when he becomes indignant or moved, and the whole thing comes to life and you can feel him writing. But if you are going to conduct a theoretical argument you've got to say, this means this, this means that. You can't allow yourself to 'compose', you've got to fix those things almost unnaturally, and then it doesn't feel like writing. It still is, but it doesn't feel like it.

But do you think many people have been gripped by Marx's writing – not simply bowled over by rhetoric, but gripped by its poetry?
I think that in historical passages and in certain things, yes, I'm sure it's true. They've been moved in exactly the same way as if they were reading Tolstoy or Balzac, for example.[4]

If we can now bring in certain attitudes obviously concerned with Wales? Are Marxism and nationalism compatible, for instance?
It used to be thought not, and it depends what kind of nationalism it's going to be. Originally the Marxist challenge was precisely that the proletariat has no country. Whereas any good Marxist who has to preserve practice in history, even if he proposes to transcend it, has had to notice ever since that one of the most tenacious holds of the proletariat is to a country. I think the point about nationalism really is this, that we're dealing with an entirely different phenomenon when it is a case of the marginal or absorbed or oppressed nationality, the sense of difference from some particular dominant large nation-state or of course empire. In the twentieth century we've seen so many examples of people breaking free from that kind of sense of domination, and I don't see how any serious socialist in the Marxist tradition could be other than with them. You see it's all right when it's the heroic examples like the North Vietnamese, or the Africans, which actually raises the problem of nationality in the most acute sense; they were not nations but they were peoples. When it comes back to Europe, there's been such a lot of impatience among traditional Marxists that I found that Sartre writing about the Basques had for me a lot of the right sense of this, that people should determine, since it is the crucial thing for them, the conditions of their own social

being.[5] And this is the Marxist project. It is extraordinarily difficult to rule out on abstract grounds some particular project which describes itself as nationalist. I often think that is not what it is, but it is the obvious thing to call it, when it comes up in Wales or Ireland, or Scotland or Brittany.

You've mentioned the materiality of words, and the mystery too. Can't both these terms be transferred to a particular nation also, a patch of land which is 'ours', not as an example of 'nationalism' in the abstract? Whereas the Marxist may well see himself as an instance of something more universal?

I think we can put it in this way. There was the phenomenon, in the very large empires, where you find that many of the effective Marxists had, often not through their own choice, lost their own little country, or their own big country. If you think of the conditions of exile within which most of the Marxist tradition was formed, it is inevitable that the perspective should be different – and still to this extent this is right, that it is impossible to think about Wales, or what they call Great Britain, or even what they call the EEC, without thinking about a very much larger reality within which what happens in any of those pieces is going to be determined. But this does not mean, I think, that there should be a kind of ritual cleansing of anybody's real relations to a place or a country if he has them, if he's not been forced into exile, if he's not had to escape with his life, or from jail. If he has these relations, he not only does not have to be ritually cleansed of them in order to become a Marxist, I think it's more than that . This is going to be very important in different kinds of Marxism, because what is quite clear is another dimension. The negative power of Marxism is very great in present circumstances, and yet its one great positive is now operating only at the periphery of the world system. The revolutionary breakthrough which is now operating, at extraordinary speed really historically, is at the periphery. At the centre of the system there is every kind of frustration and stagnation; yet certain affirmatives – never, I think, 'my country as against my class', but ways of seeing a country and a class and the future as connected – these will be necessary if within these old nation-states we're to have a significant kind of change.

Can we now make the question of 'nation' quite different perhaps, and more personal? A lot of your writing, even in clearly critical or theoretical passages, is noticeably autobiographical. Has this any connection with Wales? What do you personally feel about this country?

It's always rather puzzled me! You must remember I was born on the border, and we talked about 'the English' who were not us, and also 'the Welsh' who were not us. Actually if you look at it historically, our region as far back as you can trace – sixth century or so – was always some ambiguous state, you know, Erging or Ewyas and so on, little Welsh-speaking kingdoms being absorbed from one direction or another. But then I found to my surprise that many things I had thought were rather local to that border area, which was now Anglicized Wales, were really only problems that existed in much of the rest of Wales, once I really started to talk to people who had come from other parts. And particularly this transforming experience of industrial South Wales, but also in the general tensions about the language in so much of the rest of Wales. So I was interested, but if I was asked where I was from, I would be rather precise about that area, that particular border area. I have got more and more interested because the ways in which what I think is the genuine Welsh revival have been going are ways which are very congenial to me. When it was Wales as simply another nationality – well, you know it seems to me that the mix-up in these islands has been so great that this soon becomes a kind of myth-making, and I was tired of endlessly meeting a certain kind of very upper-middle-class Englishman (and there was nothing else you could call him) who would disclose at some point that he was really a Highlander or an Ulsterman or a Manxman, and it was clear he was nothing of the kind. Well, I didn't want to identify myself like that. And also some of the early phases of Welsh nationalism, I mean when we were the last bit of Christian Europe against the democratic and industrial tide and so on; it's powerful when anyone feels it, but there again Wales would be a very odd specimen in that one would have to abolish so much of the actual Wales for it to be plausibly that. But then when people started saying there are specific experiences of democratic communities, specific moral concerns within the religious tradition, specific attachments through language and the literature to values which are under pressure nearer the centre; and that out of this there are the materials for an alternative direction – all that positive emphasis, as well as the understandable but more negative emphasis that this is a neglected country (which I felt, because after all the area I came from was being depopulated through every generation of my family I can trace back, and I could see in my own family that this was still happening) – when these feelings came together to identify themselves with Wales, I began to feel I could relate, and not just to my own area but to an entity one was then calling Wales. Although I still find it problematic; and whenever I have a really satisfactory conversation it is always when people raise these questions in the same way. Because I then find we're exploring reality rather than asserting a version of it which may be protecting us against it.

Can one talk of an Anglo-Welsh poetry, as opposed to Welsh poetry or on the other hand a kind of regional poetry, or is this just an invention?
I wish I knew more about this; I see it asserted that the Welsh poet writing in English is doing something different from the English poet, and I can see in an amateur way some of this. Whether this is in his craft or in a set of feelings and references is often difficult to separate I think. I remember the ferocity of the attack of the Movement poets of the '50s on Dylan Thomas, as against that drunken, lurching, word-gas poetry, you know, and what was being pushed in its place was this certainly quite attractive verse of its kind, light social verse – a sort of shrug, polite, carefully not going beyond the emotions of what was probable, in almost a conversational prose which occasionally just to shape itself lurched into a kind of resonance.[6] And they had ruled out the emotional intensity and the kind of writing that goes with it. I remember being very hostile, and it's the only time in my life since about 12 or 13 that I sat down after reading it and wrote in their manner, a poem called 'On First Looking Into "New Lines"' which was a piece of doggerel! Picking up from remarks like 'a neutral tone is nowadays preferred' and this sense of limitation. I mean it seemed to me then that Dylan Thomas was not just another English poet.

Is there something of an English–Welsh comparison there in the sense we mentioned earlier? Do writers like Pinter, for instance, use the language as a kind of voice only, with a lot of the words as 'solid objects' taken out,

whereas with Dylan Thomas the word as a little gold nugget is being used all the time? I wonder what you think of R. S. Thomas's poetry, for example, with its very material and natural references in single words.[7]
Of course I respond very strongly to R. S. Thomas's poems because they are so very much of the same landscape, although a very different part of Wales, and this materiality of the country and the words is actually very difficult to separate in that kind of writing. And I don't feel that it's regional either, because 'regional' as a description suggests that the predominant characteristics are still national but with some slight local variation – I don't think this is slight. But it's difficult to trace out because I find that some northern poets, for example, are radically different from some southern English. I think the whole problem is not whether one can feel Welsh, although God knows that has problems enough, but I think that's a relatively simple thing next to the problems the English have about feeling English, because of the different parts of England, the real difference between the West Country and East Anglia for example – and it seems to me huge – and the constant sense of difference I get from the North, especially since one has only the one term 'England' to describe all this. And given the dominant mode in this century in England, which has been very much South-East England, and a limited social part of that, then Wales is very sharply distinct, not in a regional way but in a way that is better called national.

Doesn't one notice that the leading English poets of the time, Bunting, Larkin, Ted Hughes, Hill, are not from South-East England, in contrast to most Movement poets?[8]
I do think that is an uncreative culture, of the South-East, that very effective administrative urban culture of the South-East; I mean I think they can do most things except these central matters of thinking and creating; although of course they control the conditions in which almost everybody else has to do them.

You make the distinction in The Country and the City *between not so much urban and rural but 'forms of settlement' and 'forms of exploitation'. Is a small nation a form of settlement in that sense?*

I think it is, and I think it can become so. What I enjoyed as a change of generation in nationalism, for instance, was when people started talking about 'this Wales we're going to make'. The feeling I have now, although sharing all the difficulties which I suppose every European shares, is that there is actually more of a sense, despite all the disagreements, of a future here, than there is in the parts of England where I work. For instance the South-East, which has this incredibly narrow and selective way of living, this turn-over on hire purchase, and that was all you really had in common. Now the jolt that it got, from 1973 and the depression then, and the further jolt it's going to have when it is realized that that isn't temporary – I think it really dis-orientated people, because at that point, theoretically anyway, socialism takes over, and yet there was no movement that way at all; none. People aren't reacting towards socialism from this crisis.

Should they?
I think socialism has lost so much of its meaning, within the various political adaptations and suppressions that have gone on, that it is the problem of finding some positive content that people could identify with, and I think that that is only likely to happen if you've got something more than a critique of capitalism. You've got to have some sense of what genuinely would be a different way to live, because it would be hard enough to get; and if you've got merely a name, or the repetition of various heroic events elsewhere, then people will try to put something together which is visibly breaking to pieces, and this is very frustrating. You've got to have something much stronger and more positive if you're going to have a socialist movement which is a popular socialist movement.

In The Country and the City *you warn against the danger of looking back for a communal, rural England that once was, finding that each century saw that in the one before, not in itself. Yet you say very little there about the earlier Celtic societies which some people in Wales in a sense look back to. The suggestion may not be that these should be revived, but certainly that they have been overlaid by the industrial and capitalist*

174

culture, whereas perhaps they could be rediscovered in some way as a basis to build on. Is this possible?

I think it's the right question to ask, and this is something I'm now working on although I've never had much occasion to talk about it. I have become very preoccupied by the prehistory and early history of this part of the world, particularly in my own specific part. And the problem about it is that I find I'm thinking not only of the Celtic past but the pre-Celtic past, and I find I'm having to do this in very physical ways because of all the physical problems about a Celtic and pre-Celtic population. I've been spending my time this summer going round the relevant places which are very thick in the area where I grew up, precisely on the border between the Celtic and pre-Celtic populations, and I find the history of that stage is very curious. Now I find when I do this that I'm not sure which is this 'past' that could be recovered. If I think of the radical, egalitarian, rural Wales, I think that is a creation of a long experience of domination and neglect, quite late, and I'm not sure it is much like the Celtic society which preceded it. Indeed I'm not sure about the relations between the Celtic society and the one it overlaid in Wales. So I think that what you can have very strongly in Wales because there's the great continuity of the language and the awareness of the difference in the past, is just the sense, which I think is very important at this stage in the twentieth century, that it is possible to *be* a different people. There isn't just one model. But I have a strong sense also that it will be much more made than recovered. Much harder than making the institutions that are required is having the feelings that make the institutions work, and I think there is a very rich resource for that in Wales. And I think that when I look at the literature – slowly learning to read it in Welsh as well as English writing from Wales – I see something of this, although again not all, because an important part of early Welsh literature comes from a very different and very hierarchical society quite understandably, and is a very different kind of world.

On a different point: all through from Culture and Society *and* The Long Revolution *to* The Country and the City *you have an emphasis on a social totality, a shared, collaborative culture, and this comes over in a very sane and indeed 'English pragmatist' way. You seem not to*

175

need a dimension of the mysterious or unknown, perhaps religious. What do you say to that?

Well, it surprises me you put it that way although I think it could be perfectly fair. I must say that the things which have most surprised my own contemporaries, although it's been different with the younger generation, but certainly 'surprised' would be a mild word for my elders is that I have said things that seemed to me the simplest common sense, but which have been taken as this very odd way of thinking about society. And I have since been told, by people more thoroughly Welsh than I am, that I took this way of thinking with me out of rural Wales, however Anglicized. I am not sure it is entirely that. On the point of other dimensions; of course the whole international socialist and Marxist movement is crucial, and in a sense I feel very European that way. I feel as close now to people battling it out at the edges, at the Left edges of the Italian communist party, I feel much more involved now in what they're doing than I do in English politics and that is crucial. But in the other thing you mention − I do in fact now have an attitude to land, to physical land, which is in one way very material, because what always interests me is how it was made. I have a very strong sense of people making landscape, and this is even after growing up in an area in which an important part is clearly not man-made although man-affected. And I do find that when I think about this, tracing these old hollow roads for example or looking at old barrows or even simply old fields, it feels like an experience or interest that other people call mystical or religious. It doesn't feel like common-sense although at another level I feel it is the most immediate common-sense. I know what happens when you cut a ditch, and I know the really extraordinary thing which still absolutely amazes me, that a man cutting a ditch four thousand years ago − his mark is still there; and I've seen it described, when it appears in other people's thinking, as a religious feeling. But it is a very strong feeling, that's all I can say.[9]

Is that kind of feeling at the centre of poetry, in the way that a social concern might be at the heart of many novels?

I think it's an incredibly important experience to express. I don't say it is impossible in a novel, in fact I'm going to attempt it. But with poetry, yes; I find a very strong tradition of writing which has that sense. This is the sense in which Hardy, for instance, is very important to me, and Clare and so on, and much modern Welsh writing is of great interest to me for that reason, the strong sense of the land.[10]

When one is cutting a ditch or reading a compelling poem, is the experience, if not timeless, certainly at a different dimension from social concern, so that that withers away? Not the actual suffering of people, but the arrangements, the social structures – do they fade away in the presence of this very direct, compelling experience?

I think it's a matter of attention. I think that if at the moment of attention one is having to say that other things don't matter, then the attention hasn't succeeded. There are moments when the attention is so intense, the writing or physical activity, that the other is not there; however, this is different from negating it. Because if you negate it – and this is the system that some people have moved into – if you put this over against social concern, so that you have to choose between the two, then I'm not with that. But there are moments of attention which are absolutely crucial, and moreover I think the awareness of those ought to inform any social concern which is going to be good and human. Because otherwise social concern can become a very frustrating and shallow-based thing. But I find I move from such moments of attention to thinking inevitably about the social order in this quite different sense, that out of something as absorbing and practical and obvious as it often is, as digging the ditch, building the wall, clearing the field – that out of such things the social order actually happens. And this is the interest of Marxism, which at its best is the one social philosophy that insists on this. It is from digging ditches and building walls, and not from kings and constitutions and so on, that history happens. And so I find you can move from these moments which for the time being are so important that only they are there, to this kind of thinking about the social order which can then go all the way. But if you start from the abstractions – and I notice this so much now about politics – it's not only that that's thinner than this other kind of attention, but that in the end it can't deal with what it's supposed to deal with.

A final question. Should poetry, if it's not economically viable, be subsidized?
I have no doubt that it should be; and we have to call it 'subsidized' because that's the only term we can put to the sort of institutions that are going to give it. I've always taken a very simple view on this, that literature like all the other arts more than pays for itself, but it has a very complicated system of collecting its dues. If you look at any art in the world over sufficient time it has more than paid for itself in quite simple financial terms, not just that it has created other kinds of wealth. And really all a body giving money to a contemporary writer or magazine or company is doing, is arranging some credit, or realizing some already created value which it is advancing, so that this kind of work can continue. I don't regard it as taking money from something else to do this. I'm glad there is the pressure for this, and it's as crucial as that.

Notes
1. The interview was conducted by the poet and critic John Powell Ward (1937–). Ward was editor of *Poetry Wales* from 1975 to 1980, and is the author of *Raymond Williams* (Cardiff: University of Wales Press, 1981).
2. Donald Davie (1922–95) was an English Movement poet, and literary critic.
3. See Raymond Williams, 'Base and Superstructure in Marxist Cultural Theory', in *Problems of Materialism and Culture* (London: Verso, 1980), pp. 31–49.
4. Count Lev Nikolayevich Tolstoy (1828–1910), usually referred to in English as Leo Tolstoy, was a Russian novelist, discussed by Williams in 'Lawrence and Tolstoy', *Critical Quarterly*, 2 (1960), 33–9. Honoré de Balzac (1799–1850), was a French realist novelist and author of the series of interconnected novels known collectively as *Comédie humaine*.
5. Jean-Paul Sartre's essay on 'The Burgos Trials' was translated from the French into English by the Welsh poet Harri Webb (1920–94), and published in *Planet: The Welsh Internationalist*, 9 (December 1971/January 1972), 3–20. It is also collected in Janet Davies (ed.), *Compass Points: Jan Morris Introduces a Selection from the First Hundred Issues of Planet* (Cardiff: University of Wales Press, 1993), pp. 23–41.
6. 'The Movement' was a term coined by J. D. Scott, literary editor of *The Spectator*, in 1954, to describe an emerging group of writers including Kingsley Amis (1922–95), Philip Larkin (1922–85), Donald Davie (1922–95) and D. J. Enright (1920–2002). On the reaction against Dylan Thomas, see James Keery, '"If we are going to call peots bda ...": Kingsley Amis and Dylan Thomas', in Kieron Smith and Rhian Barfoot (eds), *New Theoretical*

Perspectives on Dylan Thomas (Cardiff: University of Wales Press, 2020), pp. 133–57.

7. Harold Pinter (1930–2008). The playwright famous for his exploration of the layers of meaning in language, pause, silence and speech, is discussed by Williams in *Drama from Ibsen to Brecht* (1952; London: Hogarth Press, 1996), pp. 322–5. On R. S. Thomas, see 'West of Offa's Dyke', n.7.

8. Basil Bunting (1900–85) was from Northumbria, Philip Larkin (1922–85) was born in Coventry, Ted Hughes (1930–98) in West Yorkshire, and Geoffrey Hill (1932–2016) in Bromsgrove.

9. For a reading of the presence of the 'mysterious' in Williams, see Clare Davies, 'Fathers and Phantoms: Revealing the Unconscious Residues in Raymond Williams's *Border Country*', *International Journal of Welsh Writing in English*, 4 (2017), 1, DOI: 10.16995/ijwwe.4.2.

10. Thomas Hardy (1840–1928) was an English novelist and poet. Williams viewed Hardy as having been unjustly omitted from F. R. Leavis's 'great tradition', and considered his development of a narrator who was a 'participant' but 'also an observer' as offering a model for his own novelistic practice. See Williams, *The English Novel from Dickens to Lawrence* (1970; London: The Hogarth Press, 1984), p. 110. John Clare (1793–1864) was an English poet known for depictions of the joys and sorrows of the English countryside; discussed by Williams in *The Country and the City*, pp. 132–41.

THE WELSH INDUSTRIAL NOVEL

Raymond Williams, *The Welsh Industrial Novel*
(Cardiff: University College Press, 1979).
Collected in Raymond Williams, *Problems in Materialism and Culture* (London: Verso, 1980), pp. 213-29.
The inaugural Gwyn Jones Lecture
given in Cardiff, April 1978.

Walking from Swansea to Neath on a 'dull and gloomy afternoon' in November 1854, George Borrow[1] had 'surmounted a hill' when

> an extraordinary scene presented itself to my eyes. Somewhat to the south rose immense stacks of chimneys surrounded by grimy diabolical-looking buildings, in the neighbourhood of which were huge heaps of cinders and black rubbish. From the chimneys, notwithstanding it was Sunday, smoke was proceeding in volumes, choking the atmosphere all around. From this pandemonium, at the distance of about a quarter of a mile to the south-west, upon a green meadow, stood, looking darkly grey, a ruin of vast size with window holes, towers, spires and arches. Between it and the accursed pandemonium, lay a horrid filthy place, part of which was swamp and part pool: the pool black as soot, and the swamp of a disgusting leaden colour. Across this place of filth stretched a tramway leading seemingly from the abominable mansions to the ruin. So strange a scene I had never beheld in nature. Had it been on canvas, with the addition of a number of diabolical

figures, proceeding along the tramway, it might have stood for Sabbath in Hell – devils proceeding to afternoon worship, and would have formed a picture worthy of the powerful but insane painter Jerome Bos.*

The painter, presumably, is Old Hieronymo.[2] Borrow turned to him again when he arrived at Merthyr, which

> can show several remarkable edifices though of a gloomy horrid Satanic character. There is the hall of the Iron, with its arches, from whence proceeds incessantly a thundering noise of hammers. Then there is an edifice at the foot of a mountain, halfway up the side of which is a blasted forest and on the top an enormous crag. A truly wonderful edifice it is, such as Bos would have imagined had he wanted to paint the palace of Satan.**

That is one way of seeing what is now, more politely, called industrial development. So conscious a view of a sketch for Hell is one of the ways of seeing which led to the industrial novel. It was not confined to vagrant, romantic, literary men. Consider this from the inventor of the steam hammer, James Nasmyth, in his autobiography as edited by Samuel Smiles:[3]

> The Black Country is anything but picturesque. The earth seems to have been turned inside out. Its entrails are strewn about; nearly the entire surface of the ground is covered with cinder-heaps and mounds of scoriae. The coal, which has been drawn from below ground, is blazing on the surface. The district is crowded with iron furnaces, puddling furnaces, and coal-pit engine furnaces. By day and by night the country is glowing with fire, and the smoke of the iron-works hovers over it. There is a rumbling and blanking of iron forges and rolling mills. Workmen covered with smut,

---

* *Wild Wales*, 1862, ch. 102.
** Ibid., ch. 104.

and with fierce white eyes, are seen moving about amongst the glowing iron and the dull thud of forge-hammers.

Amidst these flaming, smoky, clanging works, I beheld the remains of what had once been happy farmhouses, now ruined and deserted. The ground underneath them had sunk by the working out of the coal, and they were falling to pieces. They had in former times been surrounded by clumps of trees; but only the skeletons of them remained, dilapidated, black, and lifeless. The grass had been parched and killed by the vapours of sulphureous acid thrown out by the chimneys; and every herbaceous object was of a ghastly gray – the emblem of vegetable death in its saddest aspect. Vulcan had driven out Ceres.*

What we can observe, in each case, is an authentic sense of shock at the unaccustomed sight of an industrial landscape, and the mediation of this shock through received conventional images: the panorama of Hell, as painted by Bosch, or the irruption of the classical Vulcan. There is much writing of this kind in the nineteenth century, but it is only a step towards a new kind of novel. For within the panorama there are as yet no men, or men are there only as figures attendant on this landscape. The apparent chaos of their labour has within this perspective obliterated or incorporated them. The movement towards the industrial novel is then, in this phase, a movement towards describing what it is like to live in hell, and slowly, as the disorder becomes an habitual order, what it is like to get used to it, to grow up in it, to see it as home.

But that full movement is not yet. The first phase of the industrial novel is a particular crystallization within English culture, from the mid-1840s to the mid-1850s, when a group of middle-class novelists, for the most part not themselves living in the industrial areas, began to explore this turbulent human world. Charles Dickens visited Preston, and his first response to it, in the Coketown of *Hard Times*, is in the panoramic manner:

---

* James Nasmyth, *An Autobiography*, ed. Samuel Smiles, 1883.

a town of red brick, or of brick that would have been red if
the smoke and ashes had allowed it; but as matters stood it
was a town of unnatural red and black, like the painted face
of a savage.*

In this first general view Coketown

contained several large streets all very like one another, and
many small streets still more like one another;

an accurate enough observation, but then

inhabited by people equally like one another;

the external, incorporating perspective, which, characteristically, Dickens did not sustain or try to sustain for a moment, once
he touched other springs and made his always variable people –
Dickensian people very unlike one another – move and relate. And
that second look is the significant transition. Not only are you not a
devil if you live in this new sketch of Hell; you are not an automaton
if you are a secular Vulcan; you are not a savage if you live in this
savage-looking landscape. But you are still, perhaps, a labouring man
and only a labouring man. Certainly that external, representative and
as a matter of fact highly class-conscious perspective is the method
of other novelists in this group; of Disraeli, in *Sybil*; of Kingsley, in
Alton Locke; even of Dickens among the workers in *Hard Times*. But
the true second look came from the one novelist who lived in her
landscape; Elizabeth Gaskell, especially in *Mary Barton*, and even
more, if we could get back to it, in the abandoned first version of
that novel, *John Barton*, when the crisis was not to be observed but
experienced, internalized; the world of industrial conflict seen from
the point of view of a militant who is at the same time

my hero, *the* person with whom all my sympathies went.

---

* London, 1854, Book I, ch. 5.

Under pressure she drew back from that transforming identification, but still what she wrote was the best of these early English industrial novels: a story of these changes happening to people who were, are and remain individual human beings through all the fierce and dynamic trajectories of social and economic transformation and conflict. All these English middle-class novelists observed the industrial landscape under the pressure of industrial and political crisis: specifically the crisis of Chartism. All shaped what they saw and show with images and narratives of the reconciliation of conflict. That part of their ideology is easily recognized. But all to some extent, and Elizabeth Gaskell to a remarkable extent, succeeded in peopling this strange, fierce world; succeeded, that is, in the crucial transition from the industrial panorama to the industrial novel.[4]

It was a remarkable crystallization, but what is also remarkable is that it did not last. As the social crisis faded, as it assumed new forms, other forms of fiction succeeded it. There is a brief and altered example in the 1860s, in George Eliot's *Felix Holt*, shaped by the crisis of the suffrage.[5] There is a specific new form, in the 1880s, in the novels of George Gissing, *The Nether World* and *Demos*, but these, as more simply in the Cockney School of the 1890s, are primarily novels of the crisis of the city – of course the industrial city which London's East End had become, but also that East End against a West End; an area of darkness – 'Darkest London' – physically contiguous but socially in another world from the luxurious and powerful Imperial capital.[6] These novels again coincide with a period of open crisis: the new class struggles of London's East End. There is also a new ideology: not now of reconciliation, and not only of shattered hopelessness; rather a sour distancing, as between East and West, and specifically, as Gissing goes on, a distancing between the lives of working people and the values of literature: a distance which has become institutional in that dominant fraction of English writing. Lawrence, of course, was to come, but we can understand some of his difficulties as well as part of his development if we remember that characteristic comment by Katherine Mansfield, on one of his plays, that it was 'black with miners'.[7]

Black with miners, meanwhile, were the valleys of South Wales. There, indeed, was to be a new crystallization, a new form of the industrial novel. But knowing what we do of the history, this coming of the Welsh industrial novel is, at first sight, surprisingly late. It is the lateness as well as the significant emergence that we have now to try to understand.

In certain respects, and notably in ironworking and in mining, the Industrial Revolution came almost as early to Wales as to England. By the middle of the nineteenth century three workers out of five in Wales were in jobs not connected with farming. One in three were in mines, quarries and industrial enterprises. But then in the second half of the nineteenth century there was a further major transformation: the intense development of valleys like the Rhondda, in the independent coal trade; the very rapid expansion of Cardiff as a coal port. But still, through almost the whole of the nineteenth century, the Welsh industrial novels did not come. There is perhaps one quite general reason for this, which would be relevant also in England. The English industrial novelists, when you look more closely, touched mainly the textile districts, the new mills, or as in Kingsley the sweatshops of London. George Eliot, in the next generation, is in touch mainly with craftsmen, though she is aware, as in *Felix Holt*, of a mining district, of which she is clearly imaginatively (and perhaps otherwise) nervous. There may be complex differentials, here, in the kinds of working-class life and community which are accessible to this kind of observing fiction. It may be significant that the first internal English working-class novel – Tressell's *Ragged Trousered Philanthropists* – is set in the small-scale provincial building trade: a social location which has important effects on its tone; the small, relatively unorganized group as distinct from the major collectives of large-scale industry.[8] Thus it is not, even in English, until the second decade of the twentieth century, with Lawrence, that fiction effectively touches the kinds of industry and community which have been most important in Wales. So in that sense, for these kinds of work, there is perhaps no specifically Welsh delay. But there is nevertheless, I believe, a distinguishably Welsh reason for lateness, and this has to do, above all, with the central problems of language and the literary tradition. These are still very difficult to analyse, but you have only to look at the English-language and Welsh-language literary traditions, at any point in the nineteenth century, to see how much more central, in English, was the tradition of prose fiction. Moreover, in just that century, and closely involved with the social and economic consequences of industrialism, the relations between Welsh and English, within the country, were decisively changing. It is difficult to be certain, but one might risk the hypothesis that Welsh industrial working-class life was relatively inaccessible to the new kind of fiction because of the combined influence of the types of working-class community (which were also still inaccessible in English), of the relative lack of motivated and competent middle-class observers, and, perhaps prepotently, because of the problems of the two languages and the relative unfamiliarity, in Welsh, of the appropriate realist form.

Those may be the reasons for delay, but they are also, in the twentieth century, reasons for the special character of the Welsh industrial novels when they at last appear. For, unlike the English nineteenth-century examples, when they come they are, in majority, written from inside the industrial communities; they are working-class novels in the new and distinctive twentieth-century sense. Thus, for all their problems – and these, as we shall see, are many – they compose, when they come, a distinctive and special contribution.

The decisive decade was to be the 1930s, but it is necessary to pick up a few scattered earlier examples. In Welsh there is John Thomas's *Arthur Llwyd* (1879; 1892), which includes an account of the opening of a mine in farming country, but this is really a scene within different kind of fiction: a temperance novel.[9] T. Gwynn Jones's *Gwilym Bevan* (1900) has the life of a quarryman.[10] Then, in writing in English, there is one significant moment of emergence or perhaps, more strictly, pre-emergence. It can be traced to 1871, in what the writer concerned described as the 'charming, pastoral village' of Mountain Ash.

Joseph Keating was the son of an immigrant Irish Catholic, and grew up in The Barracks, the Catholic settlement, very aware of his family's difference from the West Country immigrants in Newtown and of course from the native Welsh, in just the years when the pits there were opening.[11] He went down the pit at the age of twelve and worked there until he was sixteen. Then he moved out to clerical work and eventually to journalism, on the *Western Mail* in Cardiff and then to London. He was writing novels – among them *Gwen Lloyd*, *Maurice*, and *Son of Judith* – from the late 1890s, and he published an interesting autobiography, *My Struggle for Life*, in 1916.

Keating – Kating as he liked it to be pronounced – is significant as an example of a much wider cultural history. From the beginning of the formation of the industrial working class – as indeed earlier among rural labourers, craftsmen and shepherds – there were always individuals with the zeal and capacity to write, but their characteristic problem was the relation of their intentions and experience to the dominant literary forms, shaped primarily as these were by another and dominant class. Within a relatively coherent religious culture, the difficulties were less formidable; the modes of witness, confession and praise were more generally accessible. But within a culture and especially a literature in which contemporary social experience had become important and even central, as is clearly the case in English after the bourgeois consolidation of the eighteenth century, the situation of the working-class writer is exceptionally difficult. In verse he may have the support of traditional popular forms, and these produced, in fact, an important body of street ballads and work songs. But in prose the forms which are nearest to him are the autobiography and the novel, and it is significant that for several generations it was the autobiography that proved most accessible. These writers, after all, although very conscious of their class situations, were at the same time, within it, exceptional men, and there are central formal features of the autobiography which correspond to this situation: at once the representative and the exceptional account. The formal features of the novel, on the other hand, had no such correspondence. The received conventional plots – the propertied marriage and settlement; the intricacies of inheritance; the exotic adventure; the abstracted romance – are all, for obvious reasons, at a distance from working-class life. It is then hardly surprising that for several generations the most powerful writing of working-class experience is in autobiographies. Indeed this situation has lasted so long that one might still say that the most effective writing about mining life in South Wales is in the autobiographical work of B. L. Coombes, and especially in *These Poor Hands*.[12]

But there is of course another and at first sight plausible tactic: to accept one of the dominant forms and to insert, to graft on to it, these other experiences, of work and struggle. There is a considerable history of such attempts, but Keating is significant because he illustrates the consequent problems so graphically. I will take as an example *The Flower of the Dark*, published in 1917: a novel which contains, in separation, several remarkable elements, but which taken as it comes, as it essentially presents itself, has quite specific significant difficulties.

The first difficulty is to get past the second page:

> The mountains under her small feet had made her a rich young woman, owing to the fact that dark workings of collieries, in which she held the largest share of proprietorship, ran beneath her lawn and increased her wealth while she amused herself or slept in gentle happiness. Whether she had ten thousand or twenty thousand pounds a year she had never tried to discover. Before she had come into the world, Richard Parry, her father, had bought a few fields, knowing that there was coal under them. Her mother had died while her father was struggling to get rich. Mr Parry had become rich. Then he died, and the fruit of the golden tree he had planted dropped into his daughter's red mouth.

It is so high a romantic strain, not to know whether you have ten or twenty thousand a year, that even the 'orange aigrette' in Aeronwy's hair and her 'brocaded shoes with emerald heels and buckles of emeralds' may not quite pull you through.

Yet this is the real problem, for in less than thirty pages you are in another world:

> Tomos, in his stall far down and in under the mountains, with his lamp swinging at his belt, was testing the coal with his mandrel. He had stripped himself to the waist, as the place was warm. A forest of posts held up the roof, which was so low that he was bent almost in double beneath it. He had worked in the Cragwyn mine since he was a boy of seven and knew every subtle characteristic of coal, as far as getting it out of its bed was concerned. Each swing of his pick was the stroke of a master craftsman. His mandrel was the inspired tool of an artist achieving the complete expression of an idea. He cut skilfully. Yet when the big slip came down, it crumbled as if it were only black flour. Tomos, coughing

in the cloud of dust, swore at the heap of rottenness. He wanted big lumps for his tram, but could only see two or three bits like pickled walnuts in the dust on the ground. He tried again at another slip. His task was troublesome, owing to the impossibility of cutting out any large pieces, and he frequently paused to gaze in sorrow at the seam, with his lamp held close to it. The face did not shine under the rays as good coal would have done. It looked dull and dismal. It had all the jointures and sections of coal formation. But when the sharp points of the mandrel touched it, it shuddered and broke as if it were nothing but solidified mud veined with slag and bast that stretched across it like rows of old wounds on a black man's cheek.

'Is it worth while trying to earn a living in the Cragwyn pit?' Tomos was asking himself seriously, as all pay for his work depended on the number of tons of solid coal he sent out.

What Keating is writing here, of work in which he had shared, is an unusually early and an exceptionally strong realization of the shift that most mattered: the shift to work as a primary kind of consciousness: that shift which is still so rare even in the most social, most industrial of novels, and which is held at a fictive distance in the overwhelming majority of fictions. Here, but of course only fragmentarily – as I said, inserted, temporarily allowed – is a working man's consciousness: his consciousness as working man.

Yet no such consciousness determines the form of the novel. In its place, corresponding no doubt to Keating's own trajectory but also and more decisively to his period and its dominant ideology, interfused as it was with a dominant and popular fictional form, the shaping element is that of the romantic heroine's choice between a good and a bad man, and the good man, significantly, is a hard-working manager, while the bad man – but there the ideology and the date are decisive – the bad man, Cragwen, is selling his coal to the German Navy, while all the good people are producing it for the British Navy. Within this direct presentation of the patriotic romance, the other elements – all potential elements of a quite different kind of novel; realistic accounts of strikes, of blackleg colliers, of conscription, of a slide of a slagtip – are not only diluted; they are fundamentally displaced; incidentally substantial, like the account of Tomos at the coalface, but then formally instrumental to the structure which overrides them, of which the only real outcome, after all, is that Aeronwy marries her Osla.

That is as late as 1917, just a few years before the decisive events that shaped a new phase of Welsh history and culture, and with it a new generation of writers. What we can now see, from those years between the wars – years of profound depression and of intense struggle – is the emergence of what is, I believe, within the general category of the industrial novel, a specifically Welsh structure of feeling, but a structure still facing quite radical problems of form.

What basically informs the industrial novel, as distinct from other kinds of fiction? Both the realist and the naturalist novel, more generally, had been predicated on the distinctive assumption – I say assumption, though if I were not being academic I would say, more shortly, the distinctive truth – that the lives of individuals, however intensely and personally realized, are not just influenced but in certain crucial ways formed by general social relations. Thus industrial work, and its characteristic places and communities, are not just a new background: a new 'setting' for a story. In the true industrial novel they are seen as formative. Social relations are not assumed, are not static, are not conventions within which the tale of a marriage or an inheritance or an adventure can go its own way. The working society – actual work, actual relations, an actual and visibly altered place – is in the industrial novel central: not because, or not necessarily because, the writer is 'more interested in sociology than in people' – which is what a degraded establishment criticism would have us believe – but because in these working communities it is a trivial fantasy to suppose that these general and pressing conditions are for long or even at all separable from the immediate and the personal. The abstracted categories of 'social' and 'personal' are here, in these specific human conditions – the conditions, moreover, of the great majority of human beings – inter-fused and inextricable though not always indistinguishable. The privileged distances of another kind of fiction, where people can 'live simply as human beings', beyond the pressures and interruptions and accidents of society, are in another world or more specifically in another class. Here, in the world of the industrial novel – as indeed in the best rural fiction; in Hardy for example – work is pressing and formative, and the most general social relations are directly experienced within the most personal.

So then, if we have learned to look in this way, it is no surprise to find at the centre of so many of the Welsh industrial novels of this period one decisive experience: the General Strike of 1926 in its specifically Welsh form; that is to say the General Strike followed by the long months of the miners' lockout, by the long years of depression, and, very deeply, by the pervasive sense of defeat. The defeat becomes fused with the more general sadness of a ravaged, subordinated and depressed Wales, but also, and from both these sources, there is the intense consciousness of struggle – of militancy and fidelity and of the real human costs these exact; the conflicts within the conflict; the losses and frustrations; the ache of depression and that more local and acute pain which comes only to those who have known the exhilaration of struggle and who also come to know, having given everything, that they have still not given enough; not enough in the terms of this world, which has not been changed, which has even, in the Depression, got worse.

But then also, beyond this, and very specific to this particular community, there is a structure of feeling which has one of its origins in the very distinctive physical character of the Welsh industrial areas, and beyond that in the distinctive physical character of Wales as a whole. The immediate landscape, the physical presence of industrial development, in the era of steam and coal, is almost invariably dark, smoke-ridden, huddled. These are its true physical bearings. In the mines these general qualities are intensified: the sense of darkness, of running grime, of a huddled enclosure. Yet not only in coming back up from the pit, to a general daylight, but also at any time in any Welsh mining valley, there is the profoundly different yet immediately accessible landscape of open hills and the sky above them, of a rising light and of a clear expansion, into which it is possible, both physically and figuratively, to move. These familiar experiences of the hills above us are profoundly effective, even when they are commonplaces, in so much Welsh feeling and thought. But in this specific environment they have a further particular effect. There are sheep on the hills, often straying down into the streets of the settlements. The pastoral life, which had been Welsh history, is still another Welsh present, and in its visible presence – not as an ideal contrast but as the slope, the skyline, to be seen immediately from the streets and from the pit-tops – it is a shape which manifests not only a consciousness of history but a consciousness of alternatives, and then, in a modern form, a consciousness of aspirations and possibilities. The traditional basic contrasts of darkness and light, of being trapped and of getting clear, are here on the ground in the most specific ways, and are the deepest basic movement of all this writing. Yet there are problems in interlocking this basic rhythm – the adequate basis of so many poems – with the close and absorbing human relations of any industrial novel. As imagery it can run, but there are still acute compositional difficulties between these essentially general feelings and any access-ible human formations. I want now to look briefly at some of the local forms through which these shared general feelings were in fact articulated, and at this level, inevitably, it is a story of some losses as well as some gains, of limitations as well as of achievements.

The most accessible immediate form, in this kind of novel, is the story of a family. This gives the writer his focus on primary rela-tionships but of course with the difficulty that what is really being written, through it, is the story of a class; indeed effectively, given the local historical circumstances, of a people. The family has then to be typical, carrying the central common experiences, but in rela-tionships, in a bonding, which are in the whole experience much wider. And there is then a further problem. The immediate family can be seen, from much attested experience, as the local bonding, of love and care, against the general hardship. But then, in one powerful form, what happens to this family, as not only industrial develop-ment, and not only industrial conflict, but now industrial depression, at once unites it in a common condition and then pulls it this way and that, dividing or even breaking it, in the struggle for survival. Gwyn Jones's *Times Like These*, published in 1936, is a memorable example of this form.[13] Its deliberately general social and historical placing, signalled by its title, interacts with this at once real and formal emphasis on a family: the immediate nuclear relationships but within them the spread of alternatives, the pressures to go different ways, including going away altogether, solving their problems differently. There is then a characteristic tension of this generation of Welsh writing: that the family is being pulled in one direction after another and yet that the family persists, but persists in a sense of defeat and loss. The bitter experience of that period – of the massive emigrations to England and yet of the intense and persistent family feeling of those who stay and those who remember – are then powerfully but always temporarily articulated: the moment of a very local sadness:

> Do without – that's what we always been doing, Luke told himself, back in his old bed. Always doing without something or other. What did Olive ever have out of life? Or mam? Mary was a lucky un, she was. Poor old Olive! I do miss that bad, look, Olive. His eyes filled with tears, and he was very conscious that the bed was unshared. 'Never mind,' he could hear his father saying: 'We can manage, ay. We'll manage, mam.' P'raps they would.
>
> At last he slept, not lonely in sleep, until towards morning he awoke to hear the clatter and tramp of the depleted night shift returning over the hill to Camden. That was life, that was: sleeping and waking to one empty day after another. No need to get up yet, for there was nothing a fellow could do. It passed a bit of time to stay in bed. 'Indeed to God,' he said quietly, and without profanity, 'what are we in the world for? Everything do seem useless, somehow.'
>
> THE END

Another memorable example of this same basic form – of the immediate family but of that family under pressure – is the later *Chwalfa* (1946) of T. Rowland Hughes: in the different environment of the North Wales slate quarries, and in the earlier historical crisis of the struggle over the contract system, the long strike and its repression, and then what happened to a community but now in formal immediacy to a family: the dispersal (*Chwalfa*) – to the waterworks at Rhayader, to the Liverpool docks, to America, to coal and copper mining.[14] The old simple nucleus, in which there are organically extending links between family, village, place and class – and in and through all these, of course, the specific link of Welshness – is at once affirmed and seen in dispersal. The very form of the affirmation, of the family carrying these general meanings, is then in effect an elegy: what is affirmed is also lost. Or, as more generally in this period of Welsh writing, loss and dispersal are what are most closely affirmed.

Of course this is not the only way in which the family can be used as an immediate compositional form. In Lewis Jones's novels – *Cwmardy* (1937) and *We Live* (1939) – a related but different general orientation is evident.[15] The family, now, is an epitome of political struggle, and the conflicting versions and affiliations of that struggle are represented not only generally – in the events of the lockout and the struggles in the Miners' Federation and between parties – but inside the family, between Len and Mary and Ezra – and the movement in the end, for all the loss that is attested, is beyond the family, in a kind of willing break: the transfer of affiliation to a cause and to a party.

We can now easily see the problems, in this as in the earlier form. The deep and unmediated dispersal, breaking, of the family can end in a sense of enclosed loss. The political projection of a family can move out from this, but the move only retains its validity – a validity of substance – while the form of the affiliation remains unproblematic. Yet how problematic it was – in a serious sense, beyond the details of immediate and divisive controversies – we can see if we turn to a quite different form, that of Jack Jones's *Rhondda Roundabout* (1934), which some people say is not really a novel at all.[16] The difficulty with the insertion of a complex political struggle into a local family form is that it can quickly become too selectively exemplary, and then too early limited by exemplary consonances of personal quality and political correctness. The episodic randomness which the very title of *Rhondda Roundabout* so directly signals is indeed a kind of loss; an affective loss. But it is an attempt, very similar in some ways to *The Ragged Trousered Philanthropists*, which it partly resembles also in tone, to write to the variety, the complexity and – crucially – the disconnections of a wide political and cultural life. Certainly Tressell found a unity, at another thematic level, which Jack Jones did not, but the point is really how this episodic form moves, if jerkily and unrelatedly, towards the wider shape of the actual society, a shape which characteristically the family form had compressed. Moves towards but does not arrive. What comes through, as so often in working-class writers, when for understandable reasons the received forms are unavailable or are refused, is a series of sketches, at most a panorama.

It is not a new whole form, but it can include elements which older whole forms could not.

In his later work Jack Jones moved, with others, to a particular form which is one of the available extensions of the family novel: the family as history, not the years of one generation but of several generations. *Black Parade* (1935) was originally three times as long as its published version, and this raises a general point.[17] There are many internal problems of form in the twentieth-century novel, but there are some outstanding external problems, and notable among them this problem of length. By our own day the commercially preferred, and often imposed, length of a novel is some eighty thousand words; and indeed that is long enough for some kinds of fiction. But for one important kind of fiction, and especially for the extending realist novel, it is absurdly restrictive. A dominant mode in English fiction has in any case moved away from these themes as well as this form. But for Welsh writers, less willing than those English to restrict or cancel their sense of community and of history, it is a special kind of obstacle. A contemporary writer, in this extended realist mode, is expected or required to make a whole work at a length which is less than a quarter or a sixth of earlier works of this kind. Every writer can cut, and almost always with advantage, but this basic pressure on length remains a major limitation of this otherwise attractive and experienced form.

Black Parade, nevertheless, shows what can be gained by a sense of historical movement. The black despair of locality can, paradoxically, be surpassed in the run of the years. In the run from the rough years of immigration into the coalfield, down to the thirties and emigration, there is a strong perspective, and it is interesting that increasingly it is this historical perspective, as a formal element, that novelists have sought. But historical perspective is not the only sense of history, even in *Black Parade*. Waiting seductively for this form is another, the historical romance.

It is always difficult to make any categorical distinction between the historical novel and the historical romance. Except at the extremes of the simpler form, which are really not even romance but costume fiction, the same apparent elements enter the composition, and, in the case of Welsh industrial fiction, it could even be said that more history – both the wider process and the critical details – can be found in the romances than in the novels. Actually one of the possible distinctions is closely related to this fact, since the mode of realist fiction both allows and requires its characters to exist at moments other than those of manifest and colourful historical crisis, whereas the mode of romance enacts a kind of absolute convergence between selected familiar persons and the best known events. It is indeed in this respect that we must remind ourselves that there is no necessary generic superiority of the realist mode: some kinds of convergence enact a deeper movement than the more bystanding and incidental versions of realism.

Black Parade is strong because, in its earliest periods at least, it includes the many-sided turbulence, the incoherence and contradic- tions, which the more available stereotypes of the history exclude. It can be properly contrasted with Richard Llewellyn's *How Green Was My Valley* (1939) on just this point, and the contrast indicates one of the terms in which the more general contrast of forms can be described.[18] It is not that the realist mode excludes either senti- ment or rhetoric. It is rather that the romance is wholly organized by a single, central, sentimental or rhetorical figuration, which is at once its simple and particular coherence, its readily indeed instantly communicable potency, and of course, at any second look, its form of excluding limitation or reduction. But *How Green Was My Valley*, widely and properly seen as the export version of the Welsh industrial experience, is not the most difficult case to understand. Its senti- mental figuration is of its period, but perhaps that is not its only difference from the rhetorical figurations of Alexander Cordell.[19] For what remains remarkable in Cordell is the scale of the admission, to be sure within this mode, of a history at once wide and intense: a history that writers closer to its specific consequences, less able to stand back and read the general history of a place and a people, had not, at least at first, been eager or even willing to include. At the same time this work can be no more than transitional. Its rhetorical figuration, boldly announced and resolutely executed in *The Rape of the Fair Country* (1959) and similar so-to-say headline novels, was perhaps understandably inaccessible, from deep inside the culture, in a period of close-up contemporary depression and militancy. The will to a wider perspective, always more readily accessible to a fascinated observer than to the sons and daughters of the history who had its defeats, its settlements, its local rhythms and local fractures in their bones, has now increasingly more pull, more weight, in a different phase of the national culture. It is at any rate in this direction that much contemporary writing is moving.

Yet in fact, at a turning point from the one period to the other, and from inside the culture, there was one major achievement which in effect stands quite alone, although its general connections with the underlying structure of feeling, and with the more particular elements so far described, are very close. Gwyn Thomas's *All Things Betray Thee* (1949) is a remarkable creative achievement.[20] Its mode is surprising, in retrospect, both in its deliberate distance from the close identifications of the realist manner, and in its effective distance from the simple figurations of romance. It has evident historical origins, not too far from the crises of nineteenth-century Merthyr. But it is not only that in place names and in style it is deliberately distanced—moving, indeed, in character and action, to an effectively legendary distance. It is also that in mode it is less representation – the common currency of fiction – than rehearsal and performance: a composition primarily governed by the rhythms of speech and song, in an action centred, at once traditionally and with a significant contemporary emphasis, on the harpist. Its inner movement is then the possibility of writing – singing, playing – this general experience: the first movement of art away from a turbulent involvement; the succeeding movement towards its deepest and most inevitable fidelities and commitments. There is then at once a wariness about the literary and ideological small change of the history, and yet the passion of discovery of what really lies beyond this and is more profoundly general. The deep structure of the novel is indeed very general: that awareness of light, of song, of human liberty, which are there close enough to grasp, yet seemingly always just out of reach, in the harsh close-up world of deprivation and struggle. It is for a people and not for a separated observer that one of its characters declares:

> Some of us are cursed with the urge to be making assertions that are either too big or too deep to fit into the box of current relations.

'Cursed', you notice; that deep ambiguity of a subordinated people, a subordinated class, whose visions are larger not only than those of the alien system by which they are dominated but larger also than is tolerable, when you are that far down and still seeing that far up. It is an extraordinarily difficult feeling to sustain. Follow the movement in this passage:

'Men like John Simon Adams and myself, we are not much more than leaves in the wind, bits of painful feeling that gripe the guts of the masses. From the cottages, the hovels, the drink-shops and sweat-mills, anger rises and we are moved. No choice, Mr Connor, save perhaps the last-minute privilege of adjusting the key of the scream we utter.'

The voices are indeed of that kind: anger rising, painfully, fragmentarily, as the decisive alternative to 'a replete and sodden silence'. But the movement is so precarious that the voice literally hesitates in the throat. Just beyond that consciousness is another tone: the relieving irrelevance, the bitter displacing joke, the distracting or reductive idiosyncrasy which not only keeps the pain at a distance but in time can be sure of its on-cue and relieving, exportable, laugh. Not here, however. Against every difficulty – and the weight is shown to be crushing – the accents of a fidelity at once visionary and historical are precisely achieved. It is a novel of voices and of a voice, and that voice is not only the history, it is the contemporary consciousness of the history.

At a point of transition; and every element of the transition is still, we do not need reminding, very bitterly contested. What is happening now, in a new kind of crisis, is a wider movement than that of the industrial experience alone, and if that movement ('nationalism') is sometimes evasive – for the body of the industrial experience is still here and still decisive – it is also, at its best, a reaching for new perspectives and new forms.

Meanwhile it is right to look back and to honour – honour because we know the difficulties; indeed know them too well, having so closely inherited them – that effective generation, that brotherhood of fiction writers; adapting, as we can, these words from *All Things Betray Thee*:

'We state the facts,' said Jameson. 'We state them now softly, now loudly. The next time it will be softly for our best

voices will have ceased to speak. The silence and the soft-
ness will ripen. The lost blood will be made again. The
chorus will shuffle out of its filthy aching corners and return.
The world is full of voices, harpist, practising for the great
anthem but hardly ever heard. We've been privileged. We've
had our ears full of the singing. Silence will never be absolute for us again.'

Notes

1. George Borrow (1803–81) was the English author of *Wild Wales* (1862). A
   useful analysis of the man and his work is David Williams, *A World of His
   Own: The Double Life of George Borrow* (Oxford: Oxford University Press,
   1982).
2. Hieronymus Bosch (?1450–1516) was the most distinctive and idiosyncratic
   of fifteenth-century Netherlandish artists, who produced a body of work
   remarkable for its depiction of fantastic, often diabolic, creatures.
3. James Nasmyth (1808–90) was one of the great inventors of the Industrial
   Revolution. Samuel Smiles (1812–1904) was an author of a number of
   biographies of industrial leaders, and is principally remembered for his 'guide
   book' on morality and ethics for the mid-nineteenth-century bourgeoisie,
   Self-help (1859).
4. Charles Dickens (1812–70), Benjamin Disraeli (1804–81), Charles Kingsley
   (1819–75) and Elizabeth Gaskell (1810–65) were all nineteenth-century
   English novelists whose works were influentially grouped as 'The Industrial
   Novels' by Raymond Williams in *Culture and Society* (London: Chatto &
   Windus, 1958), pp. 87–109.
5. Williams also discussed *Felix Holt* (1866) by George Eliot (1819–80) as one
   of the 'Industrial Novels' in *Culture and Society* (see n. 4 above).
6. The best-known work by George Gissing (1857–1903) is *New Grub Street*
   (1891). Gissing is discussed by Williams in *Culture and Society*, pp. 172–80.
7. D. H. Lawrence (1885–1930) is one of the key subjects of Williams's literary criticism. See especially, *Culture and Society*, pp. 199–215; *The English
   Novel from Dickens to Lawrence* (1970), pp. 169–84; *The Country and the City*
   (1973), pp. 264–8. Katherine Mansfield (1888–1923) was the pseudonym of
   Kathleen Mansfield Beauchamp, a modernist short-story writer.
8. Robert Tressell, the pen-name of Robert Noonan (?1870–1911), is remembered for his posthumously published novel about the lives of skilled and
   unskilled men in the decorating and undertaking business, *The Ragged
   Trousered Philanthropists* (1914; London: Flamingo, 1993). The ironically
   named 'Philanthropists' of the title are the workers who contribute their
   labour to the masters for pitiful wages.
9. John Thomas (1821–92) was a preacher and writer, mainly known for his
   Temperance novel, *Arthur Llwyd y Felin* (1879).

10. Thomas Gwynn Jones (1871–1949) was a leading Welsh-language poet, whose novel *Gwilym Bevan* is rarely discussed. See M Wynn Thomas, *The Nations of Wales 1890–1914* (Cardiff: University of Wales Press, 2016), pp. 185–213; and Robert Rhys, 'T. Gwynn Jones and the Renaissance of Welsh Poetry', in G. Evans and H. Fulton (eds), *The Cambridge History of Welsh Literature* (Cambridge: Cambridge University Press), pp. 365–87.

11. Joseph Keating (1871–1934) is a neglected author, mainly known for the novels mentioned – *Maurice* (London: G. Allen, 1905), and *Son of Judith* (London: G. Allen, 1900). The son of Irish immigrants, Keating was a supporter of the Irish Nationalist Movement.

12. Bert Lewis Coombes (1894–1974), whose first book, *These Poor Hands: The Autobiography of a Miner Working in South Wales* (1939; 2nd edn, Cardiff: University of Wales Press, 2002), was widely acclaimed. On Coombes's life and work, see Bill Jones and Chris Williams, *B. L. Coombes* (Cardiff: University of Wales Press, 1999). Jones and Williams have also published a useful collection of writings, *With Dust Still in his Throat* (Cardiff: University of Wales Press, 1999).

13. Gwyn Jones (1907–99) was a major figure in the field of Welsh writing in English, and a widely acclaimed scholar in the field of Scandinavian studies. Founder of the journal *The Welsh Review* in 1939, and, perhaps most famously, translator with Thomas Jones of *The Mabinogion* published by the Golden Cockerel Press in 1948, and by Everyman's Library in 1949. A brief introduction to the man and his work is Cecil Price, *Gwyn Jones* (Cardiff: University of Wales Press, 1976).

14. Thomas Rowland Hughes (1903–49) was a Welsh-language poet, novelist and playwright best known for a series of novels largely based on his memories of life in the slate quarries of north Wales: *O Law i Law* (Llundain: Gwasg Gymraeg Foyle, 1943); *William Jones* (Aberystwyth: Gwasg Aberystwyth, 1944); *Chwalfa* (Aberystwyth: Gwasg Aberystwyth, 1946); *Y Cychwyn* (Aberystwyth: Gwasg Aberystwyth, 1947). *Chwalfa* is famous for its depiction of the plight of working-class families during the Penrhyn Lockouts of 1896–7, 1900–3. All novels have been translated by Richard Ruck. A useful introduction is John Rowlands, *T. Rowland Hughes* (Cardiff: University of Wales Press, 1975).

15. Lewis Jones (1897–1939) was a miner, novelist and (from 1936 until 1939) one of two Communist members of Glamorgan County Council. He is best known for his two novels mentioned by Williams – *Cwmardy* (1937; London: Lawrence & Wishart, 1978), and *We Live* (1939; London: Lawrence & Wishart, 1978). Both works attempt, in Jones's words, to 'novelise a phase of working-class history'. Jones died in the week Barcelona fell, having addressed over thirty street-meetings in south Wales in support of the Spanish Republic. Further information can be found in David Smith, *Lewis Jones* (Cardiff: University of Wales Press, 1982). See also Emma Smith, '"He was a queer lad for his age": The Crisis of Masculinity in Lewis Jones's *Cwmardy*', *Welsh Writing in English: A Journal of Critical Essays*, 8 (2003), 29–45.

16. *Rhondda Roundabout* (London: Faber, 1934) was the first novel published by the popular novelist Jack Jones (1884–1970). Jones was known for thoroughly researching his novels, and was an admirer of the realist and naturalist writers of America in the 1920s and 1930s, notably Sinclair Lewis (1885–1951) and James T. Farrell (1904–79). He was a member in turn of the Communist, Labour and Liberal parties, and joined Oswald Mosley's New Party for a period in the early 1930s. He is one of the writers discussed with some sympathy by Glyn Jones in *The Dragon Has Two Tongues* (1968; Cardiff: University of Wales Press, 2001).

17. *Black Parade* (1935; Cardigan, Parthian, 2009) was Jack Jones's second novel, which he had worked on from the mid-1920s onwards under the title *Saran*, a much longer novel that was never published.

18. On Richard Llewellyn's *How Green Was My Valley*, see 'West of Offa's Dyke', n. 5.

19. Alexander Cordell (1914–97), the pseudonym of George Alexander Graber, was born in Colombo, Ceylon (now Sri Lanka), and settled in Wales in 1950. Cordell was a productive popular novelist, who is best known for a trilogy of novels set in the industrialising Wales of the nineteenth century: *Rape of the Fair Country* (London: Gollancz, 1959); *The Hosts of Rebecca* (London: Gollancz, 1960); and *Song of the Earth* (London: Gollancz, 1969). A case for the importance of Cordell's writings is made by Chris Williams in *Planet: The Welsh Internationalist*, 121 (1997), 12–18.

20. On Gwyn Thomas, see 'Community', n. 11.

THE WELSH TRILOGY
AND *THE VOLUNTEERS*

Raymond Williams, *Politics and Letters: Interviews with
the New Left Review* (London: Verso, 1979), pp. 271–302.[1]

*Can we start by asking you something about the position of your novels
within your work as a whole? From your own account, there seems to
be a discrepancy between the proportion of fiction in your publicly visible
work — so far four novels out of a total of twenty books published — and
the amount of moral and intellectual energy you must have invested in
your work as a novelist. Looking at your biographical dates, it seems
that between 1947 and 1960 you wrote something like seven successive
versions of* Border Country *alone, together with three other unpublished
novels. The same pattern seems to recur in the later sixties and seventies:*
The Fight for Manod *going through five versions over twelve years from
1956 to 1977, and* The Volunteers *taking six years to complete. Is
there a major difference for you between discursive and fictional works in
your practice as a writer?*

It's certainly true that I have given relatively far more time, in comparison with what became visible and valued, to fiction than to any
other form of writing.[2] In the late forties, I regarded the novels as
the work which I most wanted to do. Now I feel differently about
them. All along there have been certain things pressing on me, which
I could simply find no alternative way of writing; today, however,
fiction is something I'm prepared to work on a long time without
feeling any urgency to finish quickly.

But the reasons for the peculiar chronology of my writing involve
more than that. I've been aware since *Border Country* that I've been
living in a time where, for my kind of interest anyway, the basic

forms of fiction are against any simple connection of a writing intention and a relatively rapid or available completion. To this extent I
have been conscious of writing against the grain of the forms. The
nineteenth-century forms of the novel were shaped within a bourgeois world. So the first modes of access to working-class experience
in fiction were often those of some distanced observer. Then between
the wars writers emerged who had grown up inside a working-
class community and sought to re-create its world – typically the
world of childhood or of the family – while cancelling their present
selves from this original situation. The result was the separated novel
about the working-class community, which became a kind of regional
form – the enclosed class as a regional zone of experience. It was
very characteristic of all these novels that they were retrospective – a
recapturing of an early experience from another social world. The
early versions of *Border Country* were continuous with these kinds
of writing. But I was dissatisfied with that form, initially without
quite knowing why. Then I gradually realized that with the degree
of change after 1945 the problem was to find a fictional form that
would allow the description both of the internally seen working-class
community and of a movement of people, still feeling their family
and political connections, out of it. That change of experience was
exemplified in so many individual lives that it seemed to have a
certain social importance. But the forms for it weren't easily accessible. The new forms of the fifties, to which many writers quickly
turned, were usually versions of the novel of escape, which one part
of Lawrence had prepared. Their theme was really escape from the
working class – moving to the room at the top, or the experience of
flight. They lacked any sense of the continuity of working-class life,
which does not cease just because one individual moves out of it, but
which also itself changes internally. Often these novels would display
very rude attitudes towards the world where they were arriving, and
sometimes sentimental recollections of the world which they were
leaving. But they were not about what interested me most, which was
a continuing tension, with very complicated emotions and relationships running through it, between two different worlds that needed
to be rejoined. There was no form for this. I found that what I was
writing was an experience of uncertainty and contradiction, which
was duplicated in the problem of discovering a form for it. So I learnt

the hard way the theoretical lesson that if a writer in a certain mode does not have social forms available to him for development, then his writing experience is likely to be prolonged and difficult, and the work very much more problematic. The actual process of composition was never so halting: the problem has always been in the form, of finding some shape with which I can be satisfied.

Of course, there were probably all sorts of other reasons in myself for certain of the delays – when I got blocked on one work I would move on to another, and so on. There was a long alternation between *The Country and the City* and what became *The Fight for Manod*. In fact *The Country and the City* went through much the same process in that it was laid aside for three or four years while I worked on something else. But in general I have found in the last ten or fifteen years that I can plan a theoretical book and execute it fairly straight-forwardly, whereas the novels have always been written this other way – even if someone could once say to me, meaning it to be kind and complimentary, that he had sat down of an evening and read *Border Country* straight through, as if it had just flowed from the pen, which was so very different from the experience of writing it.

Did you have any literary reference-points or previous models in looking for appropriate fictional forms?

I was aware of the Welsh writers about the working class of the inter-war period, who produced a distinct body of work which is very varied, although not much read now. They too had been try-ing to find a form. But the problem was always that those writers who stayed in the working class had great difficulties with the novel as such, tending to move towards the autobiography or political pamphlet or a curious panoramic genre like Jack Jones's *Rhondda Roundabout*; while those who moved out of it, like Gwyn Jones who was a university teacher when he wrote *Times Like These*, produced novels of an enclosed working-class world in which the movement outwards was not made part of the fiction – people continually have to get away for economic reasons, but the experience of combined continuity and discontinuity didn't enter as a theme.[3] Of course, where it did enter was in Lawrence, but to an excess of discontinuity, as his later work developed away from full social relationships. I only really felt easy when I could establish the difference between the two worlds and explore the problem of rejoining them; crucially, when I could get the sense of the tension inside that working-class life by splitting one of the central characters to illustrate diverging roads.

In the nineteenth century, as a matter of fact, I found some important precedents for what I was trying to do – successful studies of one kind of mobility, the uncertainty of moving between two kinds of life. But what I then noticed was the almost embarrassingly practical point, that the simple physical space enjoyed by nineteenth-century novelists was so much greater than that available within post-war fiction. If you are trying to depict two different kinds of social life and people moving between them, the scale of the canvas on which writers of the last century could work was about five times that which any post-war British novelist could realistically expect. The economics of commercial publishing now impose extraordinary restrictions on writers. The first reaction of a publisher to a novelist these days is: 'Fine, but not more than 80,000 words.' This was a major problem for me. I kept building up something which I thought was the right pace, and then found that what was intended to be one movement in the novel was already longer than anything a publisher would accept. So much of the work was then looking for condensations or formal solutions to knit the materials together in some more economical way. This was another sense in which I felt I was writing right against the grain.

One way round the diminution of scale in contemporary fiction which has been taken by many twentieth-century writers is the serial novel, which can re-create a comparable space across a number of books. Did you ever entertain this solution yourself?
The series has been the most significant response to this difficulty, but it has its own internal problems. First, you can never guarantee that people will read the novels either in any particular sequence or as a whole. You therefore have to establish elements in each individual novel to stand on their own, which you wouldn't in a longer single work. Then you tend to be forced into a kind of recapitulation of the past of your characters in summary form, unless you adopt the convention which is quite common now of presenting people

unexplained, without a history. The nearest I've come to the serial form are certain character continuities between *Border Country*, *Second Generation* and *The Fight for Manod*. I kept finding that I wanted to assume that the reader would know these characters, yet of course I realize that this usually won't be so. But I think the series is the only technical solution which is open to a contemporary novelist who is interested in a broad band of social experience. I should add, however, that I am not convinced that the economic problems of a long novel are as difficult as publishers make them out to be. When long novels arrive from America or Russia people say how wonderful it is that at least somewhere writers still have the necessary breadth and depth of imagination. When you've been compressed, that's hard to hear. The situation may be unique in Britain, because of the peculiar dependence of fiction on the public library system.

Economic constraints have certainly led to a contraction in the scale of the novel in England. But surely there are social and ideological reasons for the difficulties of the realist form as well?
Of course. To begin with, there is the problem of narrative location. You can move very much faster, more economically, if you adopt a single unproblematic narrator. But the single unproblematic narrator is precisely in question today, especially in the sort of novels that I have tried to write. The conditions of movement between different worlds are much more complex than in the large-scale realist novels of the past century, while the space for realizing them has conversely diminished. That is one difficulty. Another is much more directly ideological. In most modern fiction a character appears without much explanation. He or she is given a name, usually presented saying or doing something; not much is learnt about their social or personal identity beyond what is made evident in the subsequent action of the novel. By contrast if you look at a nineteenth-century realist novel, when people are introduced, they are given a whole network of history – all sorts of minor technical variations are used to ensure this. In the same way when a place is introduced, it is not just the site of an event as is typical of contemporary fiction, but the materialization of a history which is often quite extensively retraced. This is precisely the kind of thing for which there is ordinarily no

room today, and which seems easiest to cut. But the omission is actually a crucial change. For what these formal devices corresponded to was the highest moment of bourgeois cultural engagement: a moment from which historical materialism is itself a development. In the dominant pattern today, there is no longer any effective history. At any moment a person is a free-floating individual who makes his life through a series of encounters, which are really quite undetermined by any larger forces. If you're interested in those, they say, you should write sociology or history, not novels. The dropping of these principles of presentation has an ideological effect. The result is a late bourgeois fictional form, which maybe we cannot escape anyway. But at least it should not be taken as unproblematic.

These modifications within contemporary conventions are clearly inimical to the writing of socialist fiction. But there is another and deeper question. Are there any inherent difficulties in reproducing the achievement of classical bourgeois realism in the nineteenth century from a working-class standpoint in the twentieth century? That in turn breaks down into a number of interconnected issues. Firstly, does such a shift in actual social stance itself involve in certain crucial respects a different compositional way of looking at society? To what extent are the accomplishments of the nineteenth-century novel directly continuous or germane to the problems posed for another social class in the twentieth century? Secondly, there is the question of the change in the structural dimensions of capitalist society – not only within each national framework but perhaps especially in the internationalization of so many of the determinant processes of common life. Could the canons of nineteenth-century realism hypothetically cope with the increased complexity of twentieth-century industrial capitalism, whose much greater anonymity and impersonality – it is often argued – preclude the kind of totalizing imagination classically to be found in Balzac or even Dickens?[4] Then thirdly, it may be wondered whether the confidence of bourgeois realism in the nineteenth century was not inseparable from its theoretical innocence of the analytic discourses which eventually developed into the social sciences in the twentieth century. Did you feel any of these problems acutely yourself?
The general problem, which has exercised many producers – perhaps more often in plays than in novels – is whether to break with the

realist tradition altogether or to try and extend it. I think there is a case for seeing how far certain areas which the bourgeois form typically excluded could now be integrated in the novel. The experience of work is a good example. Before Hardy the work of the majority of people never got into fiction as an important experience at all. Of course, the work of the bourgeois world is sometimes rendered as in Balzac's fiction, but not that of the labourer, the industrial worker. Their experience still offers the possibility, with all sorts of difficulties, of seeing whether the realist form is capable of extension and transformation. I myself think the project is worth attempting, and I've tried to explore it in my novels.[5]

The question of internationalization raises an absolutely crucial issue here. For some of the most faithful documentary novels of working-class life did become, as I said earlier, in effect regional novels. Although this in a way expressed what was happening to certain important parts of the working class, it's not possible to underwrite that form. The rural novel became regional not because the Lake District is less important than Central London but because you cannot conceivably write a realist novel about the Lake District in which the much broader economy outside it is absent. That has produced extreme complications for the traditional form because it did depend, in my view, on the idea of a knowable community, and now we are faced with the fact that this cannot be called a community and is not knowable in the former ways.[6] The result is an extreme crisis of the form. I find it interesting that so many writers, of course for other reasons as well, have turned to the essentially different form of drama to write this experience, rather than to fiction.

So far as the development of separate discourses is concerned, if you look at the classic example of George Eliot, she was the reverse of innocent of them. She was not only aware of other kinds of discourse, but in a very interesting way used some of them in fictional form.[7] There are very strong presuppositions in English culture that the writer should not think too much, because ideas cannot be accommodated in fiction. But by no means all English novelists have respected them. There are obviously difficulties in incongruity of idiom: I find that when I am revising a novel I often cut out phrases which quite clearly come from a different consciousness. But I think that a much more extensive theoretical discussion of the possibilities in all the available forms is necessary, because I don't think that in the end the ready move to a certain kind of television drama, which on the whole is the most interesting option recently made by socialist writers, can do more than a certain small part of the job which has to be done. Alongside this theoretical debate we need a lot of examples of practice, so that people can see how far a particular form can be taken. We must be very experimental about it.

How did your own experiments in writing novels develop? It was a decade before Border Country *was completed and published. In the same period you wrote three unpublished novels. What sort of books were they?*
The first, which I wrote in 1948, was called *Ridyear*. It was a curious attempt, which I can now see was greatly mistaken, to get across certain ideas about contemporary social and political experience by taking a fairly rare account I had found of an Englishman who had gone to Klondike. It described his journey there and his experience in the gold-fields – where he made a strike but eventually ended up with nothing. The form I chose was an adventure story, but I was trying to make the novel a sort of parable as well. *Adamson*, written two years later, was again an attempt to use an available convention – this time of the man who reaches a crisis of identity and disappears from his old life, re-emerging elsewhere with a new identity.[8] The third experiment with a simple form was called *Grasshoppers*. Today, I'm glad it wasn't published, although at the time I wanted to see it out. The novel isolated a group of people unable to reconcile their feeling for the urgency of change with the rather inert society around them, who set themselves up as a comic commando travelling around to institute certain changes. If a town was trying to reorganize its public transport system and was bogged down in the usual bureaucratic delays, they would simply go out one night and move the road signs. The title suggested both their mode of intervention in local political deadlocks and also what I felt about that kind of activity. Looking back, I can now see that if it had been published people might have said it was a fairly characteristic novel of the fifties, or an anticipation of the sixties, and so it was. It was the only one of these early novels I tried hard to publish.[9]

*You've said that as a young man you very much wanted to write fiction,
and not to be a university lecturer or a critic. Talking of your literary
formation in the thirties, you remarked that the work which most interested
and attracted you was* Finnegans Wake *– the farthest shore of inter-war
modernism. Yet the texture of the first novel you published is not at all
what one would imagine from an admirer of Joyce.*[10] *At a purely verbal
level* Border Country *is quite austere, making very little use of either
metaphor or simile. The style of the book is extraordinarily sparing.
Intensity is nearly always achieved through the rhythms of spoken dialogue,
without any recourse to rhetorical figures. Was there some major change
in your literary sensibility after the war? How deliberate was your writing
strategy in* Border Country*?*

I can remember, like most of my contemporaries, producing exercises
in the manner of Joyce, which was an incredibly impressive method
of writing for us in the forties. At that age, you have an ambition to
write which is very generic and unlocalized – it's not yet the case
that, as I would now put it theoretically, what you write is in a very
wide sense of identity and social relationship what you are. Nearly
all socialist writers of the time were excited by Joyce, but I would
think that few were later influenced by him, unless the impact went
a long way – not their own way. Joyce's personality is too strong;
you can be influenced by other writers but the danger is of being
overwhelmed by him. I discovered in the end that what excited me
in Joyce belonged to a very specific and very relevant kind of consciousness which happened not to be my own. So that once you have
worked past the formal fascination you realize that your own projects
can coexist with admiration for another kind of writing which you
don't want to do yourself.

In writing *Border Country*, on the other hand, I was conscious of
wanting to be very careful not to write in what had become identified in England as a 'Welsh style'. This was a general reaction among
most of my contemporaries. The Welsh style that got established in
England as a popular mode did, in fact, have certain relations to Joyce,
in its extreme verbal exuberance – everything from free-association
to extraordinarily vivid metaphor. Dylan Thomas was the most notable example of this period of Welsh writing, which had the effect of
making Welsh people into the characters which the style demanded
– garrulous eccentrics. The fact that it represented a development of

observable forms of Welsh social habit made it all the more necessary to draw back. It is not that I don't admire it. But when Welsh writing became fashionable between the late thirties and the early fifties, I shared with a lot of my contemporaries the feeling that it was necessary to get away from the perception of the Welsh that it seemed to project to the outside world. Many people now say – some much more strongly than I would – that its language was a form of cultural subordination, the only – slightly degraded if subtle – way the Welsh could present themselves to a London audience.[11] At all events, I was certainly determined to avoid that.

If you were in partial reaction to a traditional Welsh style, was your writing practice in Border Country *fairly deliberate?*
Writing fiction is a quite different experience from any other forms of composition. You do not really know what you are going to say. To give this a more secular explanation than the usual way in which it is presented, I think that what probably happens is that writers commit themselves to certain rhythms – in my case the rhythms of certain kinds of ordinary Welsh speech. At the same time I was very aware of the problem of the distance between the language of narrative and analysis and any language of speech which is other than the most tidied up standard English. I didn't want there to be a contradiction between the two in the novel. But in general the process of composition was much more unpredictable than with other kinds of writing, where I find that I have in front of me on a piece of paper the outline of what I am going to write – unexpected things may happen, but broadly you know where you're going.

Did you revise successive drafts of Border Country, *or rewrite it largely afresh each time?*
No, it was never quite starting afresh although in fact in the last unpublished version, I put the lot away, but by then I knew most of it from memory. It was more a case of revising drafts – a very complicated business in the last stages of *Border Country*, when I remember adopting the undignified procedure of walking between piles of paper on the floor, arranging and rearranging them to get the right shape.

Once I'd done that, then I rewrote them to get the proper sense of flow into the novel.

The central figure of Border Country *is the railwayman Harry Price. The portrait of him is a very powerful one. Its effect is achieved partly by the contrast with his friend Morgan Rosser, who becomes a small manufacturer, and his son Will, who becomes a university lecturer. Morgan and Will are in quite different ways more restless and uncertain personalities. Harry is presented as someone with a wholeness of character that commands an absolute respect: his life appears the dominant centre of value in the book. Now although the characterization of him is credible and moving, the thematic significance attached to it seems more problematic. In effect, Harry is seen as a figure virtually without contradiction; even the physical descriptions of him emphasize a singleness of being which appears to have a normative force in the novel. In the key scene where Morgan attempts to persuade Will to join him in running his new factory, Harry is asked for his opinion on the matter and says: 'You set yourself a job, you finish it; agreed the job may be wrong, you might have done better. But get the habit when it's difficult of stopping and going off somewhere else, then it's not the job's useless, that may not matter, but you, yourself. Nobody sets himself what he doesn't want. What you set yourself you wanted, or seemed to want it. And now it isn't the chance you'd be missing, I don't care so much about that. Only once turn aside from what you've set yourself, once keep back just a bit of your strength, then whatever happens, succeeding or whatever it is, whatever the others say, still it don't matter what you get, you're finished with yourself.'* What is surely wrong with this is that after all people have very conflicting desires, impulses and aspirations; they do set themselves aims they later don't want; they are always liable to crises and change. The very possibility of areas of acute strain, which seems to be the normal condition, is discounted in Harry's credo. Such a moral integrism – character either given as one bloc, or if not, fissure seen as a flaw – is not persuasive novelistically or in real life.*
I agree with your criticism of that way of seeing things. My intention in the novel was to show that it produces both an undoubted strength and an illusion. For the idea that nobody sets himself what he doesn't

---

* Raymond Williams, *Border Country* (London: Chatto & Windus), p. 240.

want is untrue about him as well as about most other people. Harry Price has not set himself a life, he was set into a situation where he goes through a process of adaptation and integration as well as clearing a certain space for living in which he can feel that more of himself is there. The central thrust of the novel is actually that the kind of strength which that apparently integrated view of moral value gives is insufficient. In Harry's case, it fails in the end when death approaches, which sets a term to any perspective. There is a sense of total bewilderment in this otherwise very strong and confident man, when he becomes ill, when he can no longer work, when he's dying. What had seemed like a connection between an integrated view of life and a force of character falters once the conditions which were carrying it really go, his own physical strength, health, and the place to which he's got used. The effect of the scene where his mind is almost disintegrating is that the meanings which had seemed so powerful are losing their power. His son sees not only the physical nearness of death, but also the confusion and withdrawal of interest as it approaches. This is the reason for the son's great difficulty – he is bound to respect his father's example, and yet he is bound to feel that it isn't complete. That is the crisis in his response.

You've explained your purpose very clearly. But does it come through so definitely in the novel? Death, and the fatigue and bewilderment that precede it, is a general biological limit which can cancel any project. Can the reader easily construe the specific significance of it of which you've just spoken?

Will's final comment is meant to convey his experience. He says: 'It was as if I stared straight at the sun. A sun that was blinding me, as I was learning to see.'* The image is of a light that is literally a source of life, something acknowledged to be extremely powerful, but which can also blind the beholder. The normal sense of a son getting his notion of identity and life from a father is here intensified by the sight of an unusual kind of self-sufficiency which in the end had proved insufficient. The decision to treat the character of Harry Price in this way was one I took after several rewritings, and was not based on my

---

* *Border Country*, p. 351.

own experiences. Harry is not my own father, because a lot of him went into Morgan too. It would have been possible to combine his contradictory impulses in the same character; I tried that but in the end decided to separate them out by creating another figure who represented the much more restless, critical and self-critical side of my father's nature. I realized the danger that if I took away those characteristics I might be left with too single a character. You may be right that, as often happens, the strengths of one particular way of looking at the world are so communicated in the novel that the qualifications or limits set to it aren't fully noticed.

One of the overt exchanges between people in Border Country *which seems to run against your intention is a conversation between Morgan and Will after Harry has fallen ill. Morgan says: 'Harry's different. He changes a thing because he wants the new thing and he settles to it because he wants it right through, not because the rejection is driving him', Will answers, 'It comes to the same thing' – to which Morgan replies: 'No, Will, it's coming to a different thing. Take a look.' Then Will says: 'Yet in the end he's lying up there, on the edge … If it was right, he'd be right, that's why I get so impatient … We take good care not to live like him, we take good care of ourselves.'* Now the suggestion here is that Morgan is making a self-criticism of his own equivocal compromises, as someone who was moved by dissatisfaction, who did negatively reject his circumstances, and whose desire for change took him from work in the signal-box to ownership of a jam factory – a shift of class position that is certainly presented in a critical light. On the other hand, when Will takes his distance from his father's position, the sense of his reply is that it represents an unobtainable standard of value, that will break anyone who tries to match it – but the force of the ironic 'We take good care of ourselves' is surely that to renounce it is a form of self-protection. In other words, the suggestion here seems to be not that Harry's way of living is insufficient, but rather that it is too demanding. Would that be a misreading of it?*
The idea of settling to do the new thing because you want the new thing rather than because you don't like the old thing is underwritten. It is a difference. But when the son says, 'If it was right, he'd be

---

* *Border Country*, p. 288.

right', the sense is not only that the father is dying, but that if it was right then it would be a good way for us all to follow. Saying 'we don't usually put ourselves that much at risk' is also a way of asking: if we did put ourselves that much at risk, would it be right? Would it be something which could sustain itself against all the forces which are inevitably much larger than the strongest possible kind of man? That's what I had in mind.

A small biographical question – did you take the dual naming of the son, Will and Matthew, from your own experience?
Yes. All the people who knew me till I was eighteen called me Jim. I adopted my legal name Raymond at university. The two names in the novel, and in my own experience, point up the problem of being two persons to know, and of negotiating between two different worlds. Yet I always find it strange how quickly one adjusts to being called a certain name in a certain place.

Border Country *is in the widest sense a novel about class relations in Britain. One of its major episodes occurs in the vortex of the General Strike. The representation of class struggle, however, poses a particular problem once the class position from which the realist novel is written changes. For in the nineteenth century, an inclusive movement of the fictional imagination could be achieved by certain authors – Eliot, Zola or Hardy would be examples – looking downwards from a familiar bourgeois or bourgeois-assimilated world in which they were living and working, towards the world of the exploited and oppressed.*[12] *Impulses of social sympathy – most evident in Zola, very clear in Hardy, not to be underestimated in Eliot – permitted a comprehensive exploration of the social hierarchy in their novels. The world of manual work, which you mentioned, is emphatically present in Zola as much as in Hardy, but political revolt as well. At the same time these writers had no difficulty in representing the possessing classes. The question arises, however, whether that inclusiveness is ever likely to be reproduced in reverse in the twentieth century. Isn't it improbable that working-class writers, attempting to connect the experience of their own social class with the totality of the structures that determine it, would be able to extend their imagination with anything like the same degree of sympathy, for very good reasons, to the oppressor world? In that sense, one could conjecture that the span of concrete re-created life – to use* Scrutiny *terminology – is likely to be much more uneven in a twentieth-century realist novel written from a proletarian stance than in certain nineteenth-century novels, although it was very uneven in most of them too, of course.*[13] *In* Border Country, *the bourgeois world is very remote – scarcely impinging at all on the village of workers and farmers. But this is a very special case, since the community which the novel describes is one without a major local exploiting stratum, for the biographical reasons we have discussed. But had there been a powerfully entrenched local ruling class, wouldn't the movement to capture it in the novel have posed severe problems for you?*

Yes. The class relations in *Border Country* come through literally at the end of the line, in the way the railway company tries to treat the workers after the General Strike through its remote telegrams and notices. The capitalist world is not a presence, it is never directly introduced in the novel. If it had been, I would have felt in a quandary. If you read the sympathetic nineteenth-century novels, which go down from the mill owner's house to the mill-hands and then back to the house, what you notice is a certain sense – however fraught it may be as in George Eliot – of being able to settle in that house and treat the people in it familiarly and fairly. That would now be extremely difficult. For one thing, the mill owner's house and the mill below were more characteristic of the nineteenth-century form of close and immediate class oppression. Where would capitalist power be exercised now? In offices, through structures whose description would need something other than physical observation. To follow the processes of an accountant's decision to close a particular works would involve a very different problem from the imaginative seizure of a more local kind of capitalism. In *Border Country* I was writing about a social situation which could be described in smaller scale because it was more visible. I am aware that the different kinds of relationship had not so wholly separated out as more characteristically in a modern industrial community. I found when I was writing *The Fight for Manod* that I had to go back up to Whitehall, where ministry meetings make long-distance decisions. It is a world I now know better, but it still may not be adequately realized.

Second Generation *appears to have been an exception among your novels, in that it seems to have been written in one burst between 1960 and 1962. Does that mean that you found in* Border Country *the impetus for its successor?*
It did go fairly consecutively, although it started out as a quite different novel. My original idea was to take a group of students in Oxford and follow their different paths for five years or so afterwards. The son of the car worker, who eventually became the central character of *Second Generation*, was simply one of the group. I then found the familiar problem that if I was to pursue this project with enough people, the result would be an impossibly long novel. So I got more and more interested in this character, as a way of contrasting worlds within a single city. Once I'd fixed on that, I wrote the book fairly quickly.

Did the conception of Second Generation *develop out of your completion of* Border Country*, or was it entirely subsequent?*
I had some idea of the theme at the time of writing the earlier book. I wanted to set the next novel away from Wales and to bring in the experience of the university. But the actual shape of *Second Generation* only emerged after *Border Country* was finished.

Did you feel the same kinds of difficulty of form or not?
Some. The basic problems were different, however, because the notion of the intermediary figure moving between one kind of life and another was now more complex. In *Border Country* the movement was a physical one, in the journeys of Matthew Price from London to Wales, and so in that sense was simpler. In *Second Generation* I found I wanted more room. The novel in the end came out much too long. The helpful suggestion was then made that it might be difficult for me to shorten it but one of the publishers' editors would be very glad to have a try. The editor turned out to be C. Day Lewis. He did produce a masterly condensation, which succeeded in reversing the whole meaning of the novel. I couldn't bear to read it after the first ten pages, but my wife did: every time there was an argument between the car worker's son Peter Owen and his academic

217

supervisor Robert Lane, in which Lane pointed out the need for a balanced view of English society and Owen made a radical criticism of it, Lane's cautious speeches would be left in and Owen's replies taken out. The result was that I had to take the manuscript back and shorten it myself. The episode is worth noting because the editor was Day Lewis: the irony of this continuity from the thirties didn't escape me.

Second Generation *is a much more directly political – one might say intransigently militant – book than* Border Country. *It is not surprising that it was attacked nearly as widely as the earlier novel was praised, given its portrait of class struggle in the motor industry and of compromise and corruption in the academy. There is, however, one pattern that seems to be common to the two books, which could be questioned from the Left. This is the opposition that they appear to suggest between personal and social integrity on the one hand, and intellectuality on the other. In* Border Country *Morgan Rosser initially demands more urgent and sweeping political change than Harry Price; but when his hopes are disappointed with the defeat of the General Strike, his restless and outgoing energies end in pursuit of a somewhat dubious commercial advancement. In* Second Generation, *two working-class couples, Kate and Harold, Gwyn and Myra, represent very much the same contrast. The stress is again on the personal costs of a wider commitment to politics or ideas, taking the different forms of a kind of deadened fatigue in the case of the shop-steward Harold, and of inconstancy and incipient disregard for other people in the case of Kate. Whereas Gwyn and Myra, the other couple of the same generation, exemplify a more limited range of hopes and interests, in the case of Myra with some elements of prejudice, and a relative immobility and refusal to engage in wider issues, except in times of common crisis; but it is they who are undivided and preserve the values of immediate feeling in their home. Do you think this is a typical or necessary tension within the working-class experience?*

I thought so then and didn't change my mind. *Second Generation* was written at a time when I felt there was a profound crisis inside the class. There was a widespread settling for a narrow area of private experience – certainly not with any anti-union attitudes, but essentially living outside that world of work altogether. The kinds

218

of engagement which can operate at different levels, whether it's the hard work of a shop-steward, or a more intellectual horizon, were beginning to come apart from that. An internal division in the working class was occurring, separating the politically and industrially active sectors of it from the rest of the class, which had not withdrawn its general and rather occasional sympathy, but was not living in those ways and was therefore recruitable into quite different social perspectives. I suppose I may have taken that as a general situation more than perhaps I should have done, though it has since greatly strengthened. But it was a process of which I was very conscious from watching a number of people I knew. There was also the special dimension in the novel of the different kind of politics in the university. Perhaps I was over-influenced by the experience of seeing people burnt out after active involvement in politics in that period. However, the emphasis on the costs of engagement was not intended to indicate that some other choice would be preferable. For withdrawal from that world to make an even safer enclosed area, where you can concentrate entirely on private life, doesn't work. But the implication of the contrast in *Second Generation* is not, any more than I intended it to be in *Border Country*, that if you keep to that which within certain constraints you can get under your control, you can live a more integrated kind of life. The form of *Second Generation* should make that clearer than *Border Country*, because there are more differing characters and situations in it – there is no one central or dominant character. The meanings and values of the novel are more distributed.

Counterposed to the different working-class families in the novel are two figures from the university milieu – Robert Lane, a sociologist who is Peter Owen's thesis supervisor, and Arthur Dean, a lecturer in politics who has an affair with Kate Owen. Each represents, with a contrasted tonality, a combination of political conformism and moral corruption. Lane counsels his students towards a wise academic moderation, and exploits his long-suffering wife. Dean enters a manipulative relationship with Kate Owen, while cynically denying any working-class ability to struggle or change society. One in effect preaches a resigned quietism, the other an active nihilism. Now the pairing of qualities in these two characters arouses some misgivings. The direct equation of political reaction and personal hollowness or corruption seems empirically doubtful. There are surely upholders of the bourgeois order, whether in the economic, political or cultural domain, whose private lives are of reasonable rectitude – say, the Keith Josephs of this world? To identify the presence of social reaction with the absence of sexual integrity appears to be a dangerous aesthetic simplification.

As a generalization, yes, but I had watched one particular highly educated socialist, who was 'liberal' in these deliberately identified senses. There was a very characteristic kind of left figure (you know what sort of a left it turned out to be) who was intellectually active in the Labour Party, representing a type of political affiliation which had nothing to do with the militant working class, indeed was objectively using and betraying it. Now, I didn't feel that about Lane, who many people have said to me they find unsympathetic as a character. I did mean him to be a smoother-over of conflicts – this was the whole sense of his relation with Peter. But I didn't intend him to be corrupt, but only to be that again fairly familiar figure of the man who so much wishes everything were better than it is. In that respect you could say that I took a lot of his reactions from elements I could feel in my own personality. There is a contrast with Peter, of course, where I wanted to get the sense of a different and I hoped unidealized kind of commitment coming through – of someone who experiences various kinds of dreadful confusion, but ultimately makes another kind of choice, not an option that is sustainable where it ends, but at least one that is symbolically correct. But he also represents a radically different generation.

On the more general problem of the connections between personal and social corruption, I think I felt in the late fifties and early sixties that what had happened to the Left and to the working class involved a deeper kind of disturbance than was generally admitted. The rhetoric of the time was of breakthrough and liberation, which seemed to me much too simple. Just watching a fair number of people, I got a sense of considerable danger – of the costs of different ways of trying to live under the pressure of an order that systematically frustrated them. More than any other novel I've written, *Second Generation* was based on direct observation. In that respect it is an impressionistic account, which I wouldn't say however seems wrong when I look back. But I hoped that by taking something as basic as the division between intellectual life and manual life, coexisting within one city, I could at least show the real theatre in which these confusions were occurring.

The compositional integration of the conflicts within the intellectual and the industrial worlds is very effective. But there is one significant absence, which perhaps leads to a serious displacement of emphasis. It is noticeable that the struggle of the car workers within the factory never encounters the capitalist enemy itself. The real centres of industrial power remain entirely abstract in the novel: the highest figure ever shown in the company hierarchy is the local personnel manager, whom Harold sees in one memorable but fleeting scene, in which he reflects on the possibility that the man opposite him might have come from a working-class background himself. In general the factory is presented exclusively through the experience of the workers on the assembly line – the reader never sees the controllers of the order against which they are struggling. On the other hand, what is powerfully materialized in the novel is the university. The two lecturers, Lane and Dean, thus tend to function unduly as structural substitutes for a depiction of the employers. The result is a kind of over-signification of them as epitomes of bourgeois Britain. In a climactic scene near the end, Peter denounces Dean publicly with the resounding phrase: 'You rule England.'* But actually, although the universities certainly serve the dominant social order, they are by no means the seat of real political or economic rule, and moreover – partly for that very reason – possess a relative intellectual autonomy as centres of teaching and research. To displace industrial to cultural targets involves an element of false consciousness, surely?

I agree with this. The problem is related to a more general limitation in my own social formation and within working-class experience as a whole. The farthest outer scale of social power with which the working class normally comes into direct contact is the level it encounters in a local confrontation. Now clearly one move that a fiction committed to a political perspective is going to make is to look at the higher levels of decision-making in the economy and society. How far up do you then go? Suppose I had gone to – what? – the

---

* Raymond Williams, *Second Generation* (London: Chatto & Windus), p. 318.

board of the motor company, to the whole interlocking between it, the banks and the state machine. This would have been better, but it is precisely what fictionally is not easy to do. I still mainly know the actual ruling class only by reading about it. But it's incredibly difficult to create characters who you don't feel in the gut; at some level if you don't know who they are you perhaps don't have sufficient energy to project them. It is then that the university often functions as a displaced perception of the ruling social order. It seems to me that at least in that period, and it may still be true, the organized working class tended to see academic figures as preeminent examples of the ruling class precisely because they are at somewhat closer range to it – especially given the typical British characterization of class by external traits of accent, appearance, minor habits, rather than by the exercise of social and economic power. So in a way *Second Generation* has some of the faults of the working-class perspective, which however are not only mine but are part of the way the system operates – that the farthest the ordinary perception of power can reach is some middle functionary. I have been continually struck by this limitation of horizon in working-class experience, as if that whole world of big corporations and banks is too remote to be really registered. I share in that. Not that I don't know the realities of power intellectually, but when it comes to writing about them imaginatively, it's a problem.

It should be said that there are very few novels which attempt to range through a complete social and political scale of power. One work that can certainly be admired in this respect is The First Circle, *which does explore a dramatically hierarchical regime from top to bottom. But of course the USSR is very different in nature from a capitalist society, its social order is at once more uniform and its structure of power more transparent – in that sense it may be imaginatively more accessible. It is probably also of some significance that Solzhenitsyn seems to have been a convinced Stalinist in his youth, so that the problems of projection would be less in his case.*[14] What seems to me extraordinary in *The First Circle* is the perception of a system running right through all the relationships of the novel: finally when you arrive at the summit of the system with Stalin, he is still seen as part of it himself. That is an incredibly impressive achievement. One wishes for a similar integration in British terms, but the world of rather elegantly concealed power which is characteristic of ruling-class relations in this country is much more difficult to get at.

The Cecil King Diaries give a pretty startling impression of what the upper reaches of this world are like.[15] *The two most striking features of it, as they emerge from King's account, are the direct and unmediated personal relations between newspaper magnates, top civil servants, cabinet ministers, big businessmen and service chiefs; and the shedding of polite hypocrisies for brutally explicit discussions of the day-to-day realities of class struggle. Of course, King was something of a rogue elephant in this world, which is normally concealed.*

These are the equivalent of the sort of documents which Disraeli read to find out about the working class in the nineteenth century – novelists like him didn't know about workers from having broken bread with them.[16] King's *Diaries* aren't the only such revelations. Thomson recounted travelling back from a banquet in a limousine with Wilson during the crisis over the old cooperative paper, the *Citizen*, and Wilson trying to persuade him to buy the paper.[17] His comment was: 'Harold, I can't get it through the Monopolies Commission' – to which Wilson replied: 'I'll give you a written guarantee'. Such exchanges are probably typical. When these people move outside their own circles, they are more careful – the shutters are put up. In fiction, I suppose that to some extent you've got to enjoy even wicked people to be able to write about them – to make them more than the cut-out of who we are against. It would be necessary to see the function of the pleasures of food, drink and company in the tone of their arrogant decisions about how to dispose of everything from a factory to an army. If you can't convey how their relish in these generates the good feeling with which they are on occasion capable of conducting their affairs, you won't create credible characters. That ought to be compatible with seeing quite clearly what they do – but it is very difficult in practice.

The Fight for Manod took you over a decade to complete – longer than Border Country, *in fact, although by the mid-sixties you were already an experienced novelist. Why was its composition so protracted?*

Well, to begin with it went very quickly. What are now the second to the seventh chapters seemed just to flow. And I had got not only the village and the valley but the prepared lines through to Birmingham and Coventry, as well as to the Ministry in London, so it was all shaping in that form. Then I did a count. I had done six out of a projected thirty chapters, moving at the only pace at which I judged it could be properly done. It would be well over two hundred thousand words. And then it wasn't only the problem of publishing length; it was that on top of the reaction to *Second Generation*. I tried compressing, but that didn't seem to work. I left it for some time, and then so much else started happening: the decisive political break in '66 and the beginning of that very absorbing work on the Manifesto.[18] Also a television producer who had read *Second Generation* came and asked me to do a play. I found the form interesting, though ironically the first play, *Letter from the Country*, eventually got acted in thirty rather than the original seventy-five minutes, but the second, *Public Inquiry*, was produced at the normal length. I welcomed the form because an action could be isolated, but I still felt, and feel, that the connecting composition of the kind of novel I had planned had more of what I wanted to say. So whenever I had a clear month I would go back to the chapters and try again; and it kept expanding. I had now a couple of additional chapters in Brussels, where one of the main characters goes to track down the source of the corporate initiative to create a new urban settlement in a Welsh valley. All these were ordinary writing difficulties – well ordinary nowadays, though the constraints of length are historically extraordinary – but by the late sixties I became increasingly aware that there was another set of problems, which amounted to a shift in perspective, though there seemed no discontinuity at the time. I saw the whole country and city relation, which from the beginning had been the general theme, as for me the crucial relation in contemporary social analysis. I'd also started, remember, *The Country and the City*, but that had been foreseen as a smaller and more specifically literary book. Now it seemed to run through everything. I expanded its scheme and started a whole new programme of reading. For some time it was my only large-scale project, but then in turn I dropped it, feeling blocked. I did some smaller things, and then suddenly wrote the whole of *The Country and the City*, in its new form, very quickly. And that was all right, but still I would go back and look at those novel chapters. I didn't want to abandon them, but now much of the wider project of the novel had gone into the other book. I kept thinking it through and then I thought I saw an alternative shape. I let it lie a few years but as it continued to make sense I eventually took it up again and completed it without difficulty. Except that it's not, of course, for better or worse, the novel I originally set out to write.

Did you conceive the novel as closing a trilogy from the outset? What were your aims in drawing on the first two, technically unconnected, books to create a related trio?

Yes, I had a trilogy in mind from the beginning. The first two were locally unconnected, but the links between Glynmawr and Trawsfynydd – a few miles apart – had been put ready for use. And thematically the shape of the trilogy was clear. They were interconnecting versions of a specific kind of change, across borders. *Border Country* was the present, including and trying to focus an immediate past; *Second Generation* a true present; *The Fight for Manod* a present trying to include and focus a future. There was even a linkage through the successive means of mobility: *Border Country's* railway; *Second Generation's* car traffic and factory; *Manod's* potential electronic technology. And in each, through these different situations, the decisive problem of the relation of learning to labour, taking different class and political aspects. All this, of course, as the infrastructure of the trilogy; the human specificities had to be dominant at each stage. Incidentally that was another reason for the special difficulties of *Manod*. Much of it is about projecting and imagining a future, but deliberately not as futurism, rather as a future that has in some way to come through from a rooted present. This made a more difficult balance than usual between the lived experiences and the projected – in fact thwarted – historical movement. The novel ends with the sense of a possible direction – I think the main good direction – but only just held on to, beside the heavy certainties of present and past. That precise feeling, of course, was the shape I eventually saw for the novel, as distinct from the larger interactions of the original project.

Much of The Fight for Manod *is constructed around the contrast
between a character from* Border Country, *Matthew Price, and a younger
character from* Second Generation, *Peter Owen — whose different
reactions to the discovery of corruption and speculation in land-use in a
projected new city-development in Wales, largely determine the resolution
of the action. But there is a persistent asymmetry in the treatment of the
two. Matthew is unquestionably the central figure in the novel; the portrait
of him has a depth and inward quality which is not really granted to Peter,
who — for all his structural importance — is nowhere given the personal
consciousness of even some of the secondary characters among the local
country people, who are very finely realized. He is mostly seen from the
outside, through his wife or others. Do you think this is a criticism of
the novel?*

Yes, it could be. Though he is also, in *Second Generation*, presented
mainly like that. I wanted a character whose deep internal life is in
a way inaccessible to him, though of course all the time he thinks
and reasons and acts. I wanted someone whose inner life is in a way
only sensed by others and who then continually disconcerts them.
I think I have known him but of course I can't say whether I've
realized him. I feel sorry I had to let the Brussels chapters go: his
combined flight and productive knowledge were there. But as I saw
the eventual shape they were in too different a dimension. I might,
though, sometime put them back. More generally, of course, there's
a constant problem of asymmetry in these kinds of internal access: a
very difficult problem of conventions because in one sense, as Gogol
observed, there is always asymmetry in the persons of a fiction, and
it is always from one point of view indefensible, though on the other
hand if you go for full symmetry you break the bounds of possible
fictions.[19] The Matthew–Peter contrast is important, of course, and
Peter is absolutely not intended to be shown as in any way, including comparatively, wrong. On the Manod people, it was crucial
that they should be full subjects; Gwen Vaughan particularly, and
Modlen Jenkins, and Trevor and Gethin, even Dance; their autonomies are vital.

*The title of the book has an element of paradox. The present straits of
the valley community at Manod are etched very sharply, and the fate*

that will probably overtake it should Anglo-Belgian corporations move in is also vividly conjured up. But there is surprisingly little actual fight demonstrated in the narrative itself. The press exposure of the governmental plan and its interlock with corporate interests, and the potential aid of Welsh radical groups – these occur so to speak putatively, off-stage. No force is really presented within the action proper that seems capable of resisting or changing the overall course of events. Compared with either Border Country *or* Second Generation*, the absence of collective scenes is striking. There is no equivalent of the solidarity of the railway-line or the car factory. A wedding is the only occasion where a significant group of characters comes together. Was this thinning-out deliberate? It seems to give an undercurrent of sadness to the book that is unlike its predecessors.*

Well, I've given part of the answer to this. The eventual shape has indeed a certain sadness: not the retrospective sadness of so much rural fiction, but a specific contemporary sadness: the relation between a wholly possible future and the contradictions and blockages of the present. There's no term for it, as with nostalgia in the case of retrospect. It's the opposite of that, and of course it's distinctively different from the kind of confidence in the future many of us have had, and that I've often written to try to restore, because it is crucial, and yet to get it again means passing through the shadows of the devastating experiences of war and what happened to the best revolutionary societies and then, here, the terrible disintegration of what was once a labour movement with apparently unproblematic perspectives: all the sadness that came when we began to understand reproduction and incorporation, not just as concepts but as the wearying and displacement of flesh and blood. I wanted to seize that moment, when the common actions are latent, indeed quite precisely latent, but through a whole set of contradictions are not actualizing. The original shape, by the way, had the inner-city and Welsh protest actions which in broader terms are relevant and even decisive, though as we know, the broader you go, the more they don't yet link. Two other elements decide the later shape. First, the quite specific sadness of rural Wales today – the Welsh writers I most respect, Emyr Humphreys especially, have this much more strongly.[20] Then second, the experience of ageing. I don't so much mean in myself, though I've felt it at times, but in a few people I know very well and deeply respect, who have fought and fought and quite clearly had expected that in their lifetime, their active lifetime even, there would be decisive breaks to the future. I have seen one or two of these men actually crying, from some interfused depth of social and personal sadness, and knowing why and knowing the arguments to be set against such a feeling and still in some physical sense absolutely subject to it. I have known this, as a matter of fact, in two of the finest militant intellectuals in Europe; for obvious reasons I'm not going to name them, but they've shown it to me, of their own generation, where they've often publicly overridden it. My writing of Matthew Price, who of course in *Border Country* was quite close to me, was an attempt to understand this in someone who in *The Fight for Manod* has become very unlike me; indeed I feel a coarse hard bastard beside him, but more able, I think or hope, to work and push through.

The Fight for Manod is your most strongly and directly Welsh piece of writing to date. Your feelings about Wales, including your own sense of identity, have obviously undergone important changes since you first left Pandy. Could you tell us what has been the history of your relationship to Wales?

Yes, a big change started to happen from the late sixties. There was a continuity in a quite overwhelming feeling about the land of Wales; as feeling and writing that stays through. But then I began having many more contacts with Welsh writers and intellectuals, all highly political in the best tradition of the culture, and I found this curious effect. Suddenly England, bourgeois England, wasn't my point of reference any more. I was a Welsh European, and both levels felt different. There's still a lot to work through from that, but I can hardly describe the difference of talking and relating now in Wales, with writers and political comrades who are all hard up against it – what's seen from outside is a remarkable vitality, and so it objectively is, but there it's a hard, fierce, internally contending yet bitterly communal feeling, which is also where I happen to be and now in the truest sense to be from. Through the intricacies of the politics, and they are very intricate indeed, I want the Welsh people – still a radical and cultured people – to defeat, override or bypass bourgeois England; the alternatives follow from the intricacies. That connects, for me, with the sense in my work that I am now necessarily European; that the people to the left and on the left of the French and Italian communist parties, the German and Scandinavian comrades, the communist dissidents from the East like Bahro, are my kind of people; the people I come from and belong to, and my more conscious Welshness is, as I feel it, my way of learning those connections.[21] I mean that over a whole range, from when Welsh-speaking nationalists tell me, as if I needed to be assured, how thoroughly Welsh *Border Country* and the social thinking are – which I used not to realize – to when highly cosmopolitan Welsh intellectuals offer recognition of the whole range of my work, which literally none of my English official colleagues has seen a chance of making sense of, then I am in a culture where I can breathe. Or at least take breaths to go back and contend with capitalist Europe, capitalist England and – blast it, but it was there and had to be shown in Manod – capitalist Wales.

How did you come to write The Volunteers *– a very different sort of novel from the Welsh trilogy?*
I wanted to write a political novel set in the 1980s. My original idea was to centre it on the obscure connections between a Labour Minister or ex-Minister and an underground organization involved in subversive actions against the State, against the background of army repression of a strike. There then occurred a ludicrous complication. The Labour politician in the initial version disappears one day, leaving his clothes on a beach, and is later tracked down by a journalist to a hide-out in Switzerland. Shortly after this part of the novel was written Stonehouse more or less acted it out.[22] From that point on I knew that, while my friends would believe me, nobody else would – everyone would regard me as simply cashing in on the Stonehouse affair after the event. So I had to recast the book. I then had in mind a three-part novel in which there would be different narrative positions that would successively intervene. One of these would be the reporter. But to my surprise I found that as I proceeded, it seemed to be just possible to write the whole action in one viable and economical form from his perspective. This decision meant leaving out a lot, which was what most worried me. But at the same time I got taken up with the formal possibilities of this solution and then wrote the novel very quickly.

To what extent were you deliberately taking the popular form of the thriller and using it for political purposes – much as Costa-Gavras' films like Z *or* State of Siege *have done?*[23] *Such a strategy transforms the genre in the process, of course. Were you aiming at a wider reading public with* The Volunteers?

No. It was always much more an option for a convention that would allow me to write my material than a decision to use a convention to get a different kind of reader. When I got sent the jacket of the book and saw it described as a political thriller, I was surprised. But when I said so to the publisher, he replied: 'Years ago, you remarked to me that it would be perfectly possible to take a popular format like the thriller and put it to good use.' So who knows? All I'm saying is that during the actual process of writing I was looking for a formal solution. Of course, what appear to be local decisions can often have a structural effect. But at the time I regretted every bit of the quite different novel that I had dropped to get within the reportorial convention. For example, in the first version the man who is killed in the military attack on the power depot was given a pre-history of the sort we were talking about earlier. In the final version, he just appears as a representative victim of class confrontation, not as the man I had wanted to describe, who entirely regarded his job as a source of income for his family and for his scrambling, and suddenly found himself in an industrial conflict playing a role he had never foreseen.

The novel in its completed form still contains heterogeneous materials which defy what is generally prized as fictional unity. There is even a typographical shift to mark the insertion of the Gwent Writers' Group account of the assault on the power depot. You have been criticized for this mixture of tonalities in The Volunteers. *How far was it intended?*

I wanted it to be that way. In fact if I had been more conscious of writing a political thriller, there would have been more heterogeneity of voices. I meant the novel to be bumpy. The very first page is a signal of that. The reporter makes a sharp take-off after his story, after the news of an assassination attempt has been received. There then immediately follows the transliteration of the brief electronic message into the rounded phrases of news-writing. That was meant to pose the question of language with a jolt straight away. Some people have complained about the insertion of the Gwent Writers' pamphlet, although I reduced it greatly for reasons of overall length. But the bumpiness as you move from one convention to another was a deliberate way of stressing the disjuncture of consciousness between an old idea of industrial conflict and the experience of the workers involved. The character of the journalist himself, Lewis Redfern, is designed to be a plausible centre of different kinds of perception and consciousness. He is a person who because of his left-wing past could have critical reflections on a folk museum, for example, although these are entirely incompatible with the way he talks to his professional colleagues – partly too because he has a reputation for deviousness.

The account of the attack on the power depot by the Writers' Group, and the excursus on folk museums, seem in different ways successful changes of gear within the novel. The first is one of the most powerful stretches in it. However, there are other elements of heterogeneity in The Volunteers *which look less controlled, and more liable to an objection of incoherence. The first sentence of virtually every chapter is a laconic utterance, about six or seven words long. An invariable pattern is laid down, in keeping with the reportorial convention. But at crucial points in the narrative, the whole syntactical rhythm of Redfern's account changes without warning, becoming much more complex, meditative and delicate. An example is the long passage reconstructing the scene of the shooting of the government minister, in reprisal for the seizure of the power depot. The break from it back to the clipped diction of the investigator in a formula-thriller seems unintentionally jarring. One might dismiss discrepancies of this sort as relatively unimportant on the grounds that the narrator is a formal device for presenting a variety of experiences and actions, to which he is himself extrinsic. But at the end of the novel, he becomes the narrative pivot of the whole action itself. So in a sense the cogency of the novel is at stake in his credibility as a character. In the final scenes, the journalist who has been pursuing the underground group responsible for the armed retaliation is converted to a provisional solidarity with them, and himself leaves for an uncertain political destination. The possibility of that change really depends on the prior establishment of a capacity in him to respond to events with a subjective depth and nuance which is radically eliminated from the*

reportorial style. The problem is that by the end of the book the reader
may feel Redfern's conversion is not fully motivated, because it rests on the
narrator's movement to a different kind of feeling or perception which the
bulk of the diction doesn't give one an adequate reason to credit.

I was aware of this difficulty, and I can't judge the extent to which
his change can be felt to be motivated. There is an exchange towards
the end which is intended to give an indication of what the narrator
thinks of his own flip idiom, when he turns on another character
and says 'I know someone who talks like that' – suggesting that the
hard-boiled getting-through-the-world style had always involved at
least a public control of certain other possibilities of expression. The
narrative convention is more his report to someone else than an
internal reflection. But it's also relevant, and I thought a lot about
this, that the conclusion is not really a conversion. The sentence
is meant to have some weight at the end, when it's said, you don't
have any identity outside the process. Objective relations are sharply
administered to him by the end of the novel. Now sure, he could have
gone the other way at any point in these last episodes, because he's
got a story which would make him successful in his own world, and
he could sell out all the people involved in it – he's obviously got the
potential for that, which is why it was necessary to indicate at various
points earlier on that he is also capable of other kinds of feelings. But
I still don't regard him as having in the ordinary sense chosen his way
at the end. Hence the play on the notion of volunteers – he doesn't
really volunteer to throw up his job and give evidence to serve other
people but not himself. He is administered into a situation, where he
finds – and it is often so – that commitment is not always as voluntary
as tends to be thought. In a more integrated person, the change could
have been internal and voluntary. With him, some potential for it is
there, and some blocks. Hence the scene which I wrote and rewrote
in which the underground group comes to exert pressure on him –
he is in a certain amount of danger, he would incur risks if he didn't
make the choice, which can also be taken simply as a reversion to
a previous political loyalty. I didn't want to make a hero of him but
to look at his action in this other way, which is not on the whole
the usual way I've tended to present this sort of situation. Whereas
the actions of the others really are socially delivered in an important
sense, never separated from their individuality, to an important extent

he is a product of these actions, rather than being a voluntary agent who decides to leave one side and join another. His final movement is the term of a whole series of adjustments which come from these divisions and unresolved earlier loyalties and opportunisms.

It may be that what look like contradictions in the narrative stance of the book are partly due to the elements of compression in it. One wonders if certain themes or developments had to be left out for reasons of space. For instance, the very important figure of Mark Evans, the former MP, remains somewhat shadowy, because it never becomes clear whether his entire career was a deliberate construction of a cover, or whether at some stage his political views changed dramatically, if silently. The fact that his half-brother is a unionist active in the struggle over the power depot is presented, but not much is made of it. Were cuts imposed on you? For obviously modulation of different ranges of diction is easier if you have more room, whereas in a confined space shifts of stance will be more abruptly evident.

The final version was 100,000 words. But I was still asked to cut out 20,000 words. Perhaps I should have held out for the extra room for manoeuvre, I don't know. It's interesting that you mention the cases of Mark Evans and of his half-brother. One scene I had to omit was a meeting between the two which explained the relationship. Another is the visit of the narrator to Evans's mother, and a longer exchange with his first wife. I also cut quite heavily the final conversations between Evans and the narrator, where Evans talks about himself. But if I'd included these and other scenes, I would have been driven back to more conventional or received forms, with their greater amplitude.

Can 20,000 words really be a decisive publishing consideration – it can't add more than 50p. to the price of a book, surely?

The publishers are now in a different world, they have standard formats for novels. The price of £4.95 is now a fixed ceiling for a lot of fiction.

In the political future depicted by The Volunteers, *the Labour Party has disappeared altogether: a National Government presides over a Britain where there is no organized working-class resistance to capitalism on a major scale. Local strikes and occupations persist, but the premise of the whole action of the novel is that there is no longer any mass politics on the Left. The operative choices are thus fined down, in the arguments between Redfern and David Evans, the leader of the main underground group, to different modalities of clandestine or subversive action inside or outside the State machine. How realistic did you intend this projection to be? Even granted a political resignation of the working class, couldn't the range of options presented in the novel be taxed with an exaggerated, even adventurist, narrowness?*

The future imagined in the novel is not a desirable one, but it is a perfectly possible one. Projected forward to about 1987–8, the working class remains capable of militant actions, but its militancy is regional in scope and particularist in aims. Where it functions as a political movement, it is betrayed in the usual ways. In such a situation you would inevitably get these other adventures. The novel tries to understand that kind of initiative, but it also suggests an internal critique of it as a charade. There was a much longer argument between Redfern and the group about it, which I had to omit: a few sentences are left, but there was originally a lengthy passage in which he accuses them of adventurism and substitutionism. *The Volunteers* plays out one set of consequences, if the British working class were contained into a local militancy, managed and by-passed and pretty thoroughly defeated by a repressive right-wing government. Then I think you would probably get violent clandestine actions. I wouldn't want them. But I have endless arguments with Italian friends who are in a situation where these options are being taken by increasingly significant if very small sections of the young. I didn't want to underwrite that model – call it terrorist, if you will. But neither did I simply want to oppose it with the old pieties, because I don't think we can rely on them. The prospects, of course, could change.

Are you projecting further novels?

Yes, I want to write two more. One is called *The Brothers*: somewhere between *Border Country* and *Second Generation*. The other would be more ambitious – an attempt to write a historical novel of a different kind.[24] Most or even all such novels are really about one period, rather than about history as such, in a more active sense. From a socialist philosophical standpoint, writing a novel about history ought to be a possible form. But I don't know yet whether it can in practice be done. The great problem is obviously to find the necessary unity. I thought of trying to achieve it through continuity of place rather than of people – taking the same place as it is inhabited in different periods (I would be very selective about these) by different kinds of people, manifesting different social relations, and exercising different ways of using the land. It happens that the district I know best in Wales would be suitable for this kind of continuity, because of its very long agricultural and industrial tradition, going back to communities of neolithic shepherds. I could begin there and end in the twentieth century, or a bit ahead. One of the interesting problems of such a novel would be that the people themselves would usually not be aware of these connections. In one of the episodes I've planned, for example, a wartime American aircraft crashes and the local people go up and get the crew out, one of whom has a Welsh family name. To them this is simply a dead airman, but the reader would know from earlier parts of the novel that this was a descendant of a family which had emigrated to the USA in the nineteenth century. People can be very blank about their own history; the physical stones, ruins, landmarks, names which represent the continuity of it are quite often incomprehensible to them. The point of the novel would be to show that these connections had been broken, but hopefully one would be showing that in this process of disconnection certain things can be reconnected.

Notes

1. Williams's 'Welsh Trilogy' are the novels *Border Country* (London: Chatto & Windus, 1960), *Second Generation* (London: Chatto & Windus, 1964), and *The Fight for Manod* (London: Chatto & Windus, 1979). *The Volunteers* (London: Eyre Methuen, 1978) is another of Williams's novels set in Wales. *On Politics and Letters* and the *New Left Review* editorial team, see 'Boyhood', n. 1.
2. Dai Smith quotes extensively from Williams's incomplete works and drafts in *Raymond Williams: A Warrior's Tale* (Cardigan: Parthian, 2008). See also Dai Smith, 'From "Black Water" to *Border Country*: Sourcing the Textual Odyssey of Raymond Williams', *Almanac: A Yearbook of Welsh Writing in English*, 12 (2007–8), 169–91.
3. On Jack Jones, see 'The Welsh Industrial Novel', n. 16. On Gwyn Jones, see 'The Welsh Industrial Novel', n. 13.

4. On Dickens, see 'The Welsh Industrial Novel', n. 4. On Balzac, see 'Marxism, Poetry, Wales', n. 4.

5. The discussion regarding realism draws both on the debate between Georg Lukács (1885–1971) and Bertolt Brecht (1898–1956) in the 1930s, and the poststructuralist critique of realism, drawing on the work of Roland Barthes (1915–80), and mounted influentially in the journal *Screen*. For a discussion of the ideas, see Daniel G. Williams, 'Writing Against the Grain: Raymond Williams's *Border Country* and the Defence of Realism', in Katie Gramich (ed.), *Mapping the Territory: Critical Approaches to Welsh Fiction in English* (Cardigan: Parthian, 2010), pp. 217–43. Raymond Williams offers a succinct account of his position in 'A Defence of Realism' (1976), in Francis Mulhern et al. (eds), *What I Came to Say* (London: Hutchinson Radius, 1989), pp. 226–39.

6. Williams develops his idea of the 'knowable community' in *The Country and the City* (London: Chatto & Windus, 1973), pp. 165–81.

7. Williams discussed George Eliot's writings in these terms in *The Country and the City*, pp. 166–81.

8. On *Adamson*, see Dai Smith, *Raymond Williams: A Warrior's Tale*, pp. 318–22; Nicholas Royle, *Veering: A Theory of Literature* (Edinburgh: Edinburgh University Press, 2011), pp. 142–3.

9. See Smith, 'From "Black Water" to *Border Country*', 169–91; Clare Davies, 'Fathers and Phantoms: Revealing the Unconscious Residues in Raymond Williams's Border Country', *International Journal of Welsh Writing in English*, 4 (2017), 1, DOI: 10.16995/ijwwe.4.2.

10. On Williams and Joyce, see 'Dylan Thomas's Play for Voices', n. 2.

11. This case is made forcefully by Stephen Knight in *A Hundred Years of Fiction* (Cardiff: University of Wales Press, 2004). For a critique of Knight's approach as it relates to Dylan Thomas, see John Goodby, *The Poetry of Dylan Thomas: Under the Spelling Wall* (Liverpool: Liverpool University Press, 2013), pp. 29–30.

12. On George Eliot, see n. 7 above. Émile Zola (1840–1902) was the central figure in the French school of 'naturalist' writers, who were profoundly influenced by contemporary theories of heredity and experimental science. On Thomas Hardy, see 'Marxism, Poetry, Wales', n. 10.

13. *Scrutiny* was a Cambridge periodical, which ran for 19 volumes from 1932 to 1953. It had a number of editors during this period, but there is no doubt that the periodical's tone and tenor was dominated by F. R. Leavis. See 'Community', n. 7.

14. Alexander Isayevich Solzhenitsyn (1918–2008) was arrested in 1945 for criticising Stalin. He caused a sensation with his first novel depicting the conditions within a Russian labour camp, *One Day in the Life of Ivan Denisovich* (1962; London: Gollancz, 1963), trans. Ralph Parke. His second novel was *The First Circle* (London: Collins, Harrill Press, 1968), trans. Michael Gaylon. Solzhenitsyn won the Nobel prize for literature in 1970.

15. Cecil King (1901–87) was a British media magnate, who owned newspapers and television stations on three continents. See Cecil King, *With Malice Toward None: A War Diary* (London: Sidgwick & Jackson, 1970).

16. Benjamin Disraeli (1804–81) was a novelist and politician, discussed by Williams as one of the industrial novelists in *Culture and Society* (see 'The Welsh Industrial Novel', n. 4). Disraeli was twice Conservative prime minister, in 1868 and from 1874 to 1880.

17. Harold Wilson (1916–95) was Labour prime minister from 1964 to 1970 and from 1974 to 1976.

18. Williams is referring to the 1967 *New Left May Day Manifesto* (London: May Day Manifesto Committee, 1967), which he edited with Stuart Hall and E. P. Thompson. A consolidated version edited by Raymond Williams was published as *May Day Manifesto 1968* (Harmondsworth: Penguin, 1968). Verso published a fiftieth anniversary edition in 2018.

19. Nikolai Vasilevich Gogol (1809–52) was a Russian prose writer and dramatist.

20. For Emyr Humphreys, see 'Wales and England', n. 1.

21. Rudolf Bahro (1935–97). A jailed GDR dissident who attempted to fuse Marxism and environmental ideas in his thinking. After being exiled to the West, he became a major theoretician and leader of the German Green Party.

22. John Stonehouse (1925–88) was a British politician in Harold Wilson's Cabinet in 1970, serving as Postmaster General. In 1974, he faked his suicide by leaving his clothes on a Miami beach, and fled to Australia in disguise and with a false passport. He was caught by the Australian police in Denmark, and after the longest fraud trial in UK legal history was found guilty on eighteen charges of fraud and theft, and served five years of a seven-year sentence.

23. Konstantinos Gavras (1933–). Greek political film maker. In *Z* (1969), he used thriller techniques to tell an explicitly political tale condemning the Greek junta system, thus making his mark on the international film-making community. The picture won an Oscar as Best Foreign Language Film. His *State of Siege* (1973) is based in Uruguay and offers a critique of American foreign policy in Latin America; it was denounced for allegedly endorsing political terrorism.

24. This historical novel would remain incomplete, but two parts were published as *People of the Black Mountains I: The Beginning* (London: Chatto & Windus, 1989), and *People of the Black Mountains II: The Eggs of the Eagle* (London: Chatto & Windus, 1990).

FREEDOM AND A LACK
OF CONFIDENCE

Arcade, 12 (17 April 1981), 16-17.

There are no rules about the novel as a form. It has made them up as it has gone along. From collections of letters to impersonal narratives, from what look like private diaries to what read like tape-recordings of others, from past and present to a variety of futures, it has made its own ways.

But this doesn't mean there aren't effective traditions, in particular times and places. For a run of years and writers the novel can seem, temporarily, to be stable: all the deep choices made by the effective form, leaving writers to their particularities inside that.

This isn't really so anywhere now. A number of forms are internationally current: from thrillers to myth-making fantasies, from science fiction to accounts of enclosed personal relations – this last still claiming a unique authenticity. There are still what are called historical novels, meaning usually stories set in some particular period of the past rather than stories involving the movements of history. There are also still some social novels: presenting people in a crisis of their own place and time.

In this general and international diversity, it is not to be expected that the novel in Wales has any single operative direction or form. The effect, in Wales as elsewhere, is double-edged. It gives us freedom: we can do it our own ways. But this kind of freedom is often, in practice, a disabling lack of confidence. It is one of the paradoxes of artistic freedom that it often flourishes best when there is some deep agreement about purposes and methods.

Moreover, when you put that kind of negative freedom alongside market conditions in which there is more supply than effective demand, and in which novel-writing, in particular, with its long investment of time, can seem quixotic by comparison with journalism, broadcasting, short plays, essays, you are likely to get more than the usual amount of self-doubt, complaint, critical irritability, conspiracy theory and cynical resignation.

These attitudes are not exactly unknown in contemporary Wales, or among its writers in either language. There are some specific reasons, though for the most part the reasons are general and can be found, with much the same effects, almost everywhere. But take the specific reasons. There is a genuine problem between the two languages, exacerbated, in the case of the novel, by the fact that the prose fictional tradition is very much shorter in Welsh than in English.

There is also, nevertheless, the problem of past success, though we seem very reluctant to acknowledge this. From the 1920s, through to the 1940s there was an effective tradition of novels in English about the industrial crisis: Jack Jones, Gwyn Jones, Lewis Jones, Richard Llewellyn.[1] Limited as this was, it is still remarkable in Europe as a form of writing largely by, about and for a conscious working class. But from some of its weaker examples, and from commercial projection and stereotyping, it had an opposite effect, in the end, stabilizing a type of writing about Wales which persisted after the major crisis that had given the original validity.

Moreover this internationally known stereotype obscured different and sometimes more complex writing about a wider and changing Wales, of the kind that was necessary from the 1950s onwards. Being poor and militant and poor and pathetic, or in the end poor and funny, stabilized but then suddenly found itself alone, in an altered country. In fact, all the time, other work had been there or was still coming – in Rhys Davies[2] and Glyn Jones[3] and then in Gwyn Thomas and Emyr Humphreys, and there was a growing body of fiction in Welsh, most of it not translated, but with T. Rowland Hughes as a fine example.[4] We were not failing to produce, but one dominant image seemed to fix and transfix our public presence.

What then, in these circumstances, can we see ourselves as going to do? I think one thing needs to be got clear. We are arguing at every other level about whether Wales – or, put it the other way, the Welsh – is a nation or a people or, as seen from elsewhere, a region. Most of that argument will take place outside the novel, for good reasons. But it touches the novel, or some novels, at one very sensitive point. For there is indeed a place for us – a bit of a place – as 'regional novelists', and it's worth looking hard at what that means.

A region used to mean a kingdom or realm; it eventually came to mean a district, often an administered district. The 'regional novel' is in the latter dimension. The phrase is used to describe novels 'set in' or 'about' the Lake District or Cornwall or the Scottish Highlands or Wessex or ... Wales. And then the first thing to notice is that the phrase is not used to describe novels 'set in' or 'about' London or New York – even Chelsea or Stepney or Manhattan – or, which is even more interesting, 'set in' or 'about' Oxford or Cambridge or what they call the 'Home Counties'. Well, that can be diagnosed and rejected. One place is as real and as potentially interesting as another. Only metropolitan centralization and cultural imperialism would have it otherwise.

But what then follows? That we say we are not regional, but national novelists? That we assert our own place and identity, or, more probably, places and identities. But the fact is that, concealed behind that metropolitan and imperialist patronage of the 'regional' novel, there is a more fundamental distinction, which they couldn't make but which we can't afford to miss.

There is a valid sense of the 'regional' in describing some novels, when a particular life is written about as if no other existed. That makes many London and New York and Home Counties novels as regional as any in our places. And indeed there are times when it works, in fiction, giving the absorbing interest of locality in ways similar to the absorbing interest in a few individuals in one kind of personal novel. But the strain mounts when you are living in any country or region in which it is a fact of everyday experience, at every level from politics and economics to what happens to people and families, that interconnection, interaction, penetration, mobility are normal and often decisive. The novel which decides to ignore these, for love of its place and its own people, can end, paradoxically, by leaving out the most urgent particularities of its place and its people.

This gets truer with every passing year. The inevitably general process breaks down all the operative myths and fictions, until even assertion of a new working identity – a real place, of and for ourselves – has to be restated in terms beyond rather than behind these powerful effects.

So in Wales, anyway, many of us have to write in the full consciousness that other places and their pressures exist. Just as the working-class novel, after its early stages, has to include the real existence of capitalists and the state, so the novel of a place or of a country has to find ways of showing that it is not isolated, however lovely then the local colour. At this point, of course, some writers pull back to a few people, who might be anywhere, or to a past period, or to generalities beyond place and time. Others project to an un-differentiated life, or, under pressure, to those dominant places and lifestyles and preoccupations which are so widely distributed in the very markets they control.

I trust all will not take these paths. The novel, for all its difficulties, is still better able than any other kind of writing to unite the particular and the general, whether in the decisive dimension of individuals and a society – the personal and the social in their quite indissoluble unity – or in the crucial dimension, as now for Welsh writers, of this real country and people and yet both pressured, shot through by – also actively responding to – a much wider world.

Of course it's very difficult. Why should we expect it to be otherwise? We are not next in some line of reputations or monuments. We are, while we keep writing, next in line to an always difficult, usually precarious, at its best always searching effort.

Notes

1. On Jack Jones, see 'The Welsh Industrial Novel', n. 16. On Gwyn Jones, see 'The Welsh Industrial Novel', n. 13. On Lewis Jones, see 'The Welsh Industrial Novel', n. 15. On Richard Llewellyn, see 'West of Offa's Dyke', n. 5.
2. Rhys Davies (1901–78) was a novelist and short-story writer. A key figure in the field of Welsh writing in English, and a presence in London literary circles in the 1930s, his life, work, and friendship with D. H. Lawrence are explored in Meic Stephens (ed.), *Rhys Davies: Decoding the Hare* (Cardiff: University of Wales Press, 2001).
3. Glyn Jones (1905–95) was a poet, novelist and short-story writer, whose surrealistic short stories published in *The Blue Bed* (London: Cape, 1937) are

(like those of the early Dylan Thomas) strikingly different to the dominant realism of that era. His study *The Dragon Has Two Tongues* (1968) began the process of creating a literary canon for Welsh writing in English.

4. On Gwyn Thomas, see 'Community', n. 11. On Emyr Humphreys, see 'Wales and England', n. 1. On T. Rowland Hughes, see 'The Welsh Industrial Novel', n. 14.

THE TENSES OF IMAGINATION

Raymond Williams, *Writing in Society*
(London: Verso, 1984), pp. 259-68.
Based on lectures delivered at the University
of Wales, Aberystwyth, in 1978.[1]

I magination has a history. There are changing and conflicting interpretations of what it is and of its value. Imagination also has a
structure, at once grammatical and historical, in the tenses of past,
present and future.

Commonsense appears to predicate that it is bad to lack imagination but almost as bad to have or use it too much. This follows from
the complex history of the idea. The negative senses are strong and
early in English: 'full of imagination, of dreads' (1390); 'conjecture
and ymaginacion' (1460). This is the idea of a mental conception of
something not present to the senses, but there was always uncertainty
whether this should be valued as vision or dismissed as fantasy. The
Latin root word had at first a simple physical sense, the making of
images or likenesses; it is linguistically related to the idea of 'imitating'. It developed a later sense of picturing things to oneself, and it
is there that the double judgment starts. As in English in 1576: 'they
accounted his undoubted divinations madde imaginations'. Or as in
the lines of *Midsummer Night's Dream*:

> The lunatic, the lover, and the poet
> Are of imagination all compact.[2]

One sees devils, the next sees beauty where there is none, the next
'gives to airy nothing a local habitation and a name'. This last sense
of 'creative imagination' has come through very strongly. It is now

one of the two main positive senses, the other being connected with a capacity for sympathy and understanding in the ability to 'imagine', to 'realize', someone else's situation. Yet in context the 'strong imagination' has 'tricks', summoning but often mistaking the objects of joy or fear.

The ambiguous valuation has persisted, in spite of attempts on the one hand to distinguish and distance 'imagination' from mere 'fancy' and on the other hand to distinguish both from 'reality' and 'facts'. 'Fabricating images without any foundation in reality is distinguished by the name of imagination', Kames wrote in 1762.[3] 'Imagination', Darwin wrote in 1871, 'is one of the highest prerogatives of Man. By this faculty he unites, independently of the will, former images and ideas, and thus creates brilliant and novel results'.[4] But 'facts and not imagination', almost everyone seemed to say, if the occasion suited.

It is not surprising that so powerful and universal a process should have been so variously interpreted. Moreover, there is no simple way of resolving the ambiguity: much that is valuable has been imagined, and much that is worthless and dangerous. Yet at a different level it may be possible to make some different distinctions. In the course of my own work I have often been struck by the varying tenses of imagination. The sense of imagination as working on the past to create some new present is familiar in Darwin's concept and more widely, over a range from associationist psychology to psychoanalysis. The apparently opposite grammatical sense, rooted in ideas of divination but also given different and more rational bases, turns imagination towards the future, towards foreseeing what will or could happen. At the same time one of the strong current positive senses is essentially involved with the present: having enough imagination to understand what it is like to be in some other contemporary condition: bereaved, unemployed, insane.

These are everyday uses and are all important. But in the processes of writing, the considerations and then the actual practices seem to me to be different, and they are different also according to whether the directive tense of the writing is past, present or future. Writers have related in varying ways to the everyday definitions: to the processes of combining images and ideas to create something brilliant and novel; to the process of imagining, down to fine detail, what

244

could happen, given this selection of characters and circumstances; and to the processes of empathy, to be able to write of a condition not directly experienced. All these are involved in different kinds of writing, but there is also a major conflict of ideas, in the long argument about whether imagination, in any of these kinds, produces or can produce things more real than what is ordinarily observable, or whether these are specific processes for 'realizing' – embodying in communicable form – what is already, at other levels, undoubtedly real. There is also the popular bypassing of this problem in the idea that imagination creates autonomous objects of art, which have their own rather than some other reality.

I have thought about these problems, in theory and in practice, but the problems of actual work seem to me quite different. I can give examples only from my own writing, though I think – or imagine – that I notice them also in the work of others. They would not be problems of the same kind if I could believe, like most of my contemporaries, that I am sitting here alone doing the work. I am in fact physically alone when I am writing, and I do not believe, taking it all in all, that my work has been less individual, in that defining and valuing sense, than that of others. Yet whenever I write I am aware of a society and of a language which I know are vastly larger than myself: not simply 'out there', in a world of others, but here, in what I am engaged in doing: composing and relating. And if this is so at what can be seen as one end of the process, it seems to be equally true at the other: what is usually defined as what we are 'writing about'. Many writers talk of researching their fiction, not only for historical novels but for contemporary stories and plays. Even tax inspectors will sometimes make an allowance for travel to get what they nicely call 'copy'. I can't be sure, but while I have often visited places and people and asked questions, and also looked things up, this has usually seemed quite separate from writing. Even the ideas and experiences you think you are taking to the blank page come out differently, again and again, as you go through the actual practice, which is one of intense and locally isolated concentration and yet, at the same time, as I have experienced it, a condition of active presence – assisting and resisting – of the wider forces of a language and a society.

I have tried to understand this after the work has been done. For example my 'Welsh Trilogy' – *Border Country, Second Generation* and *The Fight for Manod* – has a simple structure of past, present and future. This covers the actual periods of the action; a succession of fathers and sons; even the forms of transport that are among the most evident social relations. Yet I could not get *Border Country* right until it was more than the past – the period of *my* childhood. I had to make that past present in the fully independent and contemporary figure of a father: in fact, as it turned out, two fathers, to make an inherited choice of directions actual. But then this was eventually accessible because it was a lived past. For the sequence during the General Strike I could go to my father's direct memories and to the documents he had kept. Yet I had then to invent episodes which activated the sequence, as distinct from what can happen in memories – especially prepared memories, *memoirs* – when what is there is the summary product. There is then also the process – obvious but quite hard in practice – of seeing this happening to a young man rather than to the old man who is telling you about it. Yet still, while the voice is there, the past has this living connection.

It is proving very different in the trilogy I am now writing, on a vastly greater timescale, following a place and its peoples through very long changes: what I think of as historical rather than as period novel-writing.[5] Its only living connections are the physical presence of the mountains in which and under which so many different kinds of life have been lived, and the physical inheritors of all these lives, who are however *not* historically aware of them, whose memories are recent and whose projections, beyond those memories, are usually (not through their fault; it is what has passed for education) vague and wrong. My wife and I have done long research for these novels: research in archaeology and history and in exploration. It has often proved possible to find a real and surprising base: a different physical landscape, different and yet precise kinds of work and living.

Yet what is then involved in making people move and speak on that base – people 'like ourselves' when the point is so often that they are at once very like and very unlike, and differently so as the real history of the place develops: is that imagination? I suppose it must be; it certainly feels like it, not least in its practical surprises, in what has actually got onto the page. Yet much of the time it is as if prolonged thinking about what I have called the base, especially when this is done, far away from books, on the actual ground, however altered, where it all happened, is not imagination in that inventive sense at all, though of course one is literally inventing. It feels, rather, like some kind of contact, and not irrationally so; like some authentic information, stressing every syllable of that word. Then later of course you have to check up and see if you got the discoverable facts right or at least not wrong: facts that are the condition but only the condition of these other lives that you think you have begun to feel move.

I was recently trying to compare this with what at first sight seems most different from it: the experience of writing a consciously contemporary novel, begun in Oxford on a city much like Oxford, with its places and kinds of work and kinds of people all around me. 'Kinds of people': that was where I hesitated and then took the experience across. For if you read the novel *Second Generation* back, from the finished product – and this is the normal procedure for most people who write about what they call imaginative works – you can see a fairly clear set of social relationships, positive and negative, between the car factory and the university in a single city, and these relationships as embodied in people who, however sharply individualized, are social figures of that set of relationships: liberal don and working-class graduate student; shop steward and his politically and intellectually ambitious wife; the non-political home-centred worker and his family-centred wife. I am forcing myself to describe them in these abstract ways, as a way of facing the problem that this is how they might or even should be construed when in conscious practice nothing of that kind of thinking happened at all. Of course I was strongly aware of what I have been calling the base: the strong social, economic and cultural contrasts between the people around the car factory and the people around the university. At an important level I sought to inform myself more fully about the kinds of life being lived: visiting the car factory and talking to people who worked there as well as more consciously observing the university and political circles in which I had a more connected presence. But still there, in an actual city and in an immediate present, this base was only fully relevant at an early and then at a late stage of the writing: preparation and checking, one might say, though each process is more complicated than that. Indeed it was not so very different, in that available actuality, from the later situation in a much more distant, relatively unknown past. But then how can this be so?

I can say only that what seems to happen is the emergence of a structure of feeling. This is a phrase I have used in analysing works written by others, when I know little or nothing of their making but only what has been made. It is a difficult phrase and idea, but it comes much nearer the experience than any other I know. For I remember being preoccupied, before either the car factory or the university was there as material for writing, with that extension of the father-son relationship which comes through as a movement of generations. I was engaged by the experience which I once tried to describe as having, simultaneously, a loved physical father and a quite different 'social father', who in a time of exceptional social an especially educational mobility was taking on many of a real father's functions: passing on knowledge and experience and judgments and values in this differently constituted and discontinuous social situ-ation. Father and son, tutor and student: the relationships are in different dimensions but both, in these circumstances, are real and can become confused.

The simpler structure of feeling of *Border Country*, within a rela-tively more stable world which had nevertheless been brought to a point of radical choice of values and ways to live, was at once con-nected and suddenly much more complicated, and the complication soon settled in the figure of the mother: intellectually ambitious but without her sons apparently defined place and role. That mother, necessarily, invoked another mother, so that Kate and Myra were there with Harold and Robert Lane and Arthur Dean. And then what happened was what writers often describe, that certain charac-ters and situations were being strongly felt, and the base which was there both before and after them was where they lived rather than where they were lived from.

Perhaps that has to happen, if the people are to come through, but I am not persuaded by some reductive accounts of the process, in which persons, 'individuals', simply materialize, in a creative alchemy, any more than I am persuaded by the theoretically opposite reductive accounts, in which the writer reads the real structure of the society and then sets figures to it: types who are then personalized. What I have called the structure of feeling seems to me different from either kind of account. It is strongly felt from the beginning, in the way that important actual relationships are felt, but also it is a structure and this, I believe, is a particular kind of response to the real shape of a social order: not so much as it can be documented – though it ought never, I think, to contradict the documentation – but as it is in some integrated way apprehended, without any prior separation of private and public or individual and social experience.

Moreover, so far as I can understand it, this process is not distillation or novel association; it is a formation, an active formation, that you feel your way into, feel informing you, so that in general and in detail it is not very like the usual idea of imagination – 'imagine if...', 'imagine that...' – but seems more like a kind of recognition, a connection with something fully knowable but not yet known.

There must, all the same, be a radical difference in how this happens as it relates on the one hand to societies in which you are living and then to other societies which are at some significant difference in time. I have known this difference, in obvious ways, in trying to approach a kind of life in which, for example, the land was not known and named but was being explored, or in which very different kinds of primary relationship were decisive: the kind of hunting group or family, for example, in which people were close and loving but where the need to abandon a crippled boy or to be pressed, by custom and scarcity, to female infanticide had to be felt not only as alien and distant but as *recognized* in actual people and situations. Perhaps across such distances it is not possible, yet I have not so far found it so. I know that I am getting beyond my own life, as those structures of feeling form, but in a lesser degree that was also what was happening even when writing about contemporary life in a known place. Either past or present, in their ordinary and reasonable temporal senses, seems to have to go through this other process before, as we say, people begin to move and speak. There may be a very general idea of what one is doing, but all the active and detailed formation seems to happen somewhere else. People may call the results 'imagination', and if the connection really happens 'imaginative', but this is where the matter of tense comes in again, for something very different is involved if a writer tries to 'imagine' the future: to 'project' a future, as it is often put.

I am fascinated by the forms of 'future fiction', just as much as by that other large area of 'science fiction' – the very best of it anyway – in which what I see happening is a structure of feeling formed as some alien life and environment. Often this stands out more sharply than the structure of feeling, even a very similar structure, which in the course of writing has been saturated in known and recognizable and connecting detail: our everyday, which can seem and some-times be the whole object, and is then so different from that distant and surprising and discontinuous 'science fiction' world. I have no direct experience of making that kind of work, though I respect its obviously 'imaginative' reach. But I have now twice – in *The Fight for Manod* and in *The Volunteers* – set novels ahead of their time of writing: in one case more as a plan, in the other case – deliberately and discontinuously – as an action.

I may be wrong but I found in these two very different cases that something much nearer the ordinary idea of imagination was directly involved. I mean that at some important stage, in work with the future tense, a writer sits and *thinks*; assembles and deploys vari-ables; even constructs what in secular planning are called 'scenarios', in the interplay of this and that projected factor, when even the factors are only partly known – their degree of development can be variably estimated – and when their interaction – bringing this factor up, fading that down – is quite radically uncertain. It can of course be argued, and in many cases demonstrated from actual works, that the structures which are projected and realized are usually no more than reproductions of existing structures in externally altered circumstances – the trivial case of those American stories in which Planet Earth encounters aliens through a President and corporations in Washington and New York is only an example of hundreds of more serious cases. Even some of the more surprising futures, in Huxley and Orwell for example, can be shown to rest on striking *interpretations* of the present, from which countervailing or mitigating factors are simply excluded: a negative present, you might say, rather than a positive future.[6]

But beyond reproduction and interpretation there do seem to he cases – Le Guin's *The Dispossessed* is an example – in which there is evidence both of deliberate and sustained thought about possible futures and then, probably both preceding and succeeding this, the discovery of a structure of feeling which, within the parameters of that thought, is in its turn a form of recognition.[7] In *The Fight for Manod* I tried to include some of the relevant thinking and argument about a possible future, but without any convention of cut-off from the present. The whole point of that novel was the relation between necessary and desirable plans for the future and at once the ways in which they get distorted and frustrated and the even more complex ways in which they relate to what is already lived and known and valued. In *The Volunteers* I used a degree of cut-off from the present, to get an action in which both received and abstract values were tested without the familiar context of supporting and reliable institutions embodying them: a possible near future, I then thought, and with whatever variation of date and detail, I am not yet persuaded it was other than closely possible.

In any real future tense, then, what we call imagination seems more like the usual accounts of it than in either present or past tenses. We speculate, we project, we attempt to divine, we figure. The actual writing that goes with that dimension is in its turn distinctive: more general; more immediately accessible to ideas; often more angular and more edged; relatively low in the kind of saturation by detailed and unlooked-for experiences so common and ordinarily so valued in the other tenses. I do not want to turn a contrast of kinds into some order of merit. Each kind of writing does quite different work. But if that is a recognizable kind of imagination – over a range from the secular and political to the solidly traditional and the surprisingly private visions and divinations – there is a problem in using not just the same word but the same concept, pointing to the same general process, in the other tenses. The problem is already there, however, in the everyday range of the word. The mental concept of something not present to the senses, which corresponds to future-writing and to many kinds of fantasy, coexists in the language with the sense of empathy, of feeling our way into a situation which in a general way we know but which we can come to know as it were from the inside – a sense which I think is not far from the idea of discovering and being moved by a structure of feeling within what is already nominally and even carefully known. Yet if the word can be applied to either process, the real processes are still different, and the key difference, as it matters in writing, seems to me essentially a matter of real tense.

There are periods in a culture when what we call real knowledge seems to have to take priority over what is commonly called imagination. In our own image-conscious politics and commerce there is a proliferation of small instrumental professions which claim the sonorous titles of imagination and creativity for what are, when examined, simple and rationalizer processes of reproduction and presentation. To know what is happening, in the most factual and down-to-earth ways, is indeed an urgent priority in such a world. A militant empiricism claims all; in a world of rearmament and mass unemployment seems rightly to claim all. Yet it is now the very baf-flement and frustration of this militant empiricism, and especially of the best of it, that should hold our attention. It can quickly identify its enemies among the hired image-makers, the instrumental projectors of the interests of wealth and power. But now, very clearly, there are other deeper forces at work, which perhaps only imagination, in its full processes, can touch and reach and recognize and embody. If we see this, we usually still hesitate between tenses: between knowing in new ways the structures of feeling that have directed and now hold us, and finding in new ways the shape of an alternative, a future, that can be genuinely imagined and hopefully lived. There are many other kinds of writing in society, but these now – of past and present and future – are close and urgent, challenging many of us to try both to understand and to attempt them.

Notes

1. This article is based on lectures 'delivered at University College of Wales, Aberystwyth 1978' (*Writing in Society*, p. i). Ned Thomas recalls inviting Raymond Williams to Aberystwyth in Dai Smith, Ned Thomas and Daniel G. Williams, 'The Exchange', *Planet: The Welsh Internationalist*, 195 (Summer 2009), 58. See also Jeremy Hooker, *Welsh Journal* (Bridgend: Seren, 2001), pp. 187–8.

2. Raymond Williams's views on William Shakespeare (bapt. 1564–1616) merit further study. A chapter in *Drama in Performance* (London: Muller, 1954) is dedicated to *Antony and Cleopatra*, and Shakespeare appears several times as a point of comparison in *Drama from Ibsen to Eliot* (London: Chatto & Windus, 1952). In *Politics and Letters* (London: New Left Books, 1979) and in 'The Importance of Community' in this volume, Williams recalls a reveal-ing episode that took place when the scholar L. C. Knights was lecturing on Shakespeare at Cambridge, with Williams, his friend Wolf Mankowitz and F. R. Leavis in attendance: 'When Knights said that nobody now can understand Shakespeare's meaning of neighbour, for in a corrupt mechanical civilization there are no neighbours, I got up and said I thought this was only differentially true; there were obvious successive kinds of community,

and I knew perfectly well, from Wales, what neighbour meant. Mankowitz
– that was characteristic of our relationship, which was very close – then
attacked me bitterly for sentimental nonsense. Leavis was nodding approv-
ingly while he was doing so' (p. 67). On F. R. Leavis, see 'Community',
n. 7. On L. C. Knights, see 'The Importance of Community', n. 3. Cyril
Wolf Mankowitz (1924–98) was an English writer, playwright and screen-
writer, of Russian-Jewish descent. Dai Smith discusses Williams's friendship
with Mankowitz in *Raymond Williams: A Warrior's Tale* (Cardigan: Parthian,
2008), pp. 240–6.

3. Henry Home, Lord Kames (1696–1782), was a judge, philosopher, and a
central figure of the Scottish Enlightenment.
4. Charles Robert Darwin (1809–82) was an English naturalist best known for
his contributions to the science of evolution.
5. Williams is referring here to *The People of the Black Mountains*. See 'The Welsh
Trilogy and *The Volunteers*', n. 24.
6. Aldous Leonard Huxley (1894–1963) was an English writer and philosopher, and author of *Brave New World* (1932). George Orwell, pen name of
Eric Arthur Blair (1903–50), was an English novelist, essayist, journalist and
critic, and author of *1984* (1949). Raymond Williams develops some of
these present ideas in 'Utopia and Science Fiction', *Problems in Materialism
and Culture* (London: Verso, 1980), pp. 196–212.
7. Ursula Kroeber Le Guin (1929–2018) was an American author best known
for her science fiction works set in her Hainish universe, and the Earthsea
fantasy series. Her utopian novel *The Dispossessed* appeared in 1974.

REGION AND CLASS
IN THE NOVEL

Douglas Jefferson and Graham Martin (eds),
*The Uses of Fiction: Essays on the Modern
Novel in Honour of Arnold Kettle* (Milton Keynes:
Open University Press, 1982), pp. 59-68.

Collected in Raymond Williams, *Writing in
Society* (London: Verso, 1984), pp. 229-38.

I am not sure when certain novels, or kinds of novel, began to be called 'regional'. My estimate is that the distinction began to be significant only in the late nineteenth century, and to be confident only in the twentieth century. At first sight it seems a simple distinction; it indicates a novel 'set in' or 'about' such regions as the Lake District or South Devon or mid-Wales. But then as distinct from what? There are three possible answers, each ideologically significant. First, that certain places are 'regions', with a recognized local or provincial character, while certain other places are not. Second, that certain novels are 'regional' in the sense that they tell us primarily, or solely, about such places and the life lived in them, rather than about any more general life. Third, that one kind of novel is 'regional' because it is 'about' or 'set in' some specific social life, as distinct from novels which address broader and more permanent kinds of human experience.

We can look more closely at each of these answers. The first has direct political significance. A 'region' was once a realm or kingdom or country, in the sense of *regere* = to rule, but it was also, with the characteristic political ambiguity of such divisions of the earth, a specific part of a larger ruled area: a diocese, a district, a bounded tract, in the sense of *regere* = to direct. The latter sense became common in English from the sixteenth century in church government, though the former, more absolute, sense persisted in natural and metaphorical descriptions. It was then obviously as a function of increasingly centralized states, with a newly formalized centralization of government and administration continuously 'delegating' and 'devolving' limited kinds of authority, that 'region' came to take on its modern meaning of 'a subordinate area', a sense which is of course compatible with recognition of its now 'local' – 'regional' – characteristics.

And then what is striking, in matters of cultural description, is the steady discrimination of certain regions as in this limited sense 'regional', which can only hold if certain other regions are not seen in this way. This is in its turn a function of cultural centralization; a modern form of the 'city-country' discrimination. It is closely connected with the distinction between 'metropolitan' and 'provincial' culture, which became significant from the eighteenth century. Yet this is no longer a distinction of areas and kinds of life; it is what is politely called a value-judgement but more accurately an expression of centralized cultural dominance.

One entertaining form of this cultural description is the expression 'Home Counties' derived from the assize circuit – the 'Home Circuit' – centred on London, and taking on wider significance in the nineteenth century. The point can be tested by asking whether a novel 'set in' or 'about' the Home Counties, or 'set in' or 'about' London or some district of London – Chelsea, Hampstead, or Bloomsbury – would be described as 'regional' in a way comparable to descriptions of similar novels 'set in' or 'about' the Lake District or South Devon or mid-Wales – or, shall we say, Dorset or 'Wessex'? At this level, the description is plainly ideological. The life and people of certain favoured regions are seen as essentially general, even perhaps normal, while the life and people of certain other regions, however interestingly and affectionately presented, are, well, regional.

The second possible answer is obviously, in many mouths, a mere variant of this and, because less explicit, more pretentious. Experience is not, a priori, more general or more significant because it occurs in London or Paris or New York rather than in Gwynedd or the Carse of Gowrie or Anatolia. Yet, at a different level, there is a real point here: a distinction which, as we shall see, is important also in considerations about 'class' in fiction. For there is indeed a kind of novel which is not only set in its own place but set in it as if there were no others. As a matter of fact this is at least as likely to be true of a New York or California or Home Counties novel as of the more readily perceived type, in which what happens in, say, the Lake District (compare the novels of Constance Holm) is seen as happening, even in the twentieth century, as if this were indeed an essentially self-subsistent life, which in none of its major characteristics is influenced or determined by social relations extending beyond it and penetrating into it. To be sure, the most important cases of this kind are particular types of late-bourgeois fiction – the *rentier* novel, the corporation novel, the university novel – in which absorption in the details of an essentially local life depends, ultimately, on not seeing its relations with a more general life: the work which is at the source of the rentier income; the market and power relations which are the true substance of the corporation's internal operations and manoeuvres; the wider processes of learning and resources and access which constitute a particular kind of university.

Yet that there is a form of encapsulation which is distinctly 'regional' cannot be doubted. It is indeed a popular form. Much twentieth-century rural fiction has this fly-in-amber quality. Its essential strategy is one of showing a warm and charming, or natural and even passionate, life, internally directed by its own rhythms, as if rural Britain, even in its most remote and 'unspoiled' parts, had not been shot through and through by a dominant urban industrial economy. Or, as a variant of this, the 'region' is so established, in autonomous ways, that pressures on it can be seen as wholly external: that other life against this region.

I suppose I am particularly conscious of this because I can see that it catches up certain actual social processes; much of the pressure has indeed been that way. But the truly regional novel, in this limiting sense, has initially so isolated its region, and thus projected it as internally whole – 'organic' – that it is unable to recognize the complex internal processes; including internal divisions and conflicts, which factually connect with those wider pressures. I know that I wrote *Border Country* seven times to find that alternative form in which these internal processes and divisions have their real weight, and in *The Fight for Manod* I found that form very consciously and explicitly, though it is still, deliberately, a novel about a particular region. To put the matter more generally, the fiction in which to explore and clarify the problems of 'regionalism' is, of course, pre-eminently Hardy's. Some metropolitan idiots still think of Hardy as a regional novelist because he wrote about Wessex – that strange, particular place – rather than about London or the Home Counties. But at a more serious level, the distinction is very clear inside Hardy's work, as between, on the one hand, *Under the Greenwood Tree* and even *Far From the Madding Crowd*, which can be seen as regional in an encapsulating and enclosing sense, and *The Woodlanders* or *Tess of the D'Urbervilles*, which are set even more deeply in their region but which are not in any limiting sense 'regional': what happens in them, internally and externally – those two abstractions in a connected process – involves a very wide and complex, a fully extended and extensive, set of relationships.[1]

The third answer, at its only serious level, can be connected with this point. At its trivial conventional level it is merely a late-bourgeois prejudice: that novels are not 'about' or 'set in' kinds of social life; novels are about people – individuals – living sexually, spiritually, and above all privately. The very idea of a novel which recognizes a wider social life is pushed away. Indeed, it is lucky – though luck now is ambiguous – if it is not put on a different shelf as Sociology. Yet at the same time, not in those late-bourgeois terms but more generally, we do have to distinguish one reasonable sense of regionalism in fiction: a sense which indicates that a novel is indeed more about a region or a way of life than about those people in relationships who inhabit or constitute it.

It is not a matter of simple categorization. The question of people in relationships – their degree of realization, individuation, space and time for development – is of course historically and socially variable, and the only relevant distinctions are in turn historical and social. The late-bourgeois isolation of private individuals, whose lives can be closely and intimately explored as if there were no wider social life, is evidently dependent on the social existence of individuals in whom power or money has created the possibility of practical distancing or displacement. In other communities and classes there is no such firm distancing or displacement, but of course it can then happen that a novel so concentrates on the most general features that it is unable to recognize – a recognition involving the simultaneous existence of real pressures and some space – the individual people who inescapably embody and enact these general features. More significantly it can fail to recognize those real areas of experience and relationship which, while they must coexist with and are usually influenced or are at times determined by the most general and common situations and processes, are still not reducible to the most general and common terms: for example, sexual and spiritual experiences (to retain these conventional descriptions), which are not only or 'merely' functions of the social situation. 'Regional' is not the most obvious word for those many novels which effect such reductions, but the factor of subordination of certain kinds of experience to the most general 'way of life' is common between certain directly regional types and more recognizable 'documentary' or in a genuinely specifying sense 'sociological' novels.

It is at this point that we can make a useful transition from the concept of 'region' to the concept of 'class' in fiction. It is particularly relevant to the idea of 'the working-class novel'. There are, evidently, uses of this description which are strictly comparable with uses of the 'regional' description: assigning certain novels to a deliberately limited area; indicating their limited status by this kind of 'narrowness' or by their limiting priority of 'social' over 'general human' experience. On the other hand, yet in some overlapping ways, such novels have been valued in the labour and socialist movements, just because they declare their identity in such ways. The undoubted neglect of majority working experience, and of the majority of working-class people, within the bourgeois fictional tradition, seems to justify the simple counter-emphasis. A whole class, like whole regions, can be seen as neglected. The implication of its marginality or, as often, its inferiority of status or interest, is rejected by deliberate selection and emphasis. A programme in defence of working-class fiction is then proposed in terms which in effect accept elements of the 'regional' definition, but with some of its values transposed.

The issue has again to be considered historically. The 'working class novel', in the broadest sense of fiction which includes substantial elements of working-class experience, has to be seen as from the beginning different in kind from the regional novel. Thus the earliest novels of this type – the English industrial novels of the 1840s

– were not written from within these class regions. On the contrary they were written by visitors to them, by sympathetic observers, or by people with some special though still external mode of access. This is very unlike the regional novel, which is from the beginning characteristically written by natives. It is a major fact of nineteenth-century cultural history that the many talented working-class writers did not, with only the occasional exception, include novelists. This had primarily to do with the available forms of the novel, centred predominantly on problems of the inheritance of property and of propertied marriage, and beyond these on relatively exotic adventure and romance. These offered few points of entry for working-class writers, unless they left their class and pursued individual careers through conventional themes. Where most working-class writers turned, instead, was (apart from essays, pamphlets, and journalism, directly related to class causes) to autobiography and memoirs, or to popular verse.

However, one paradoxical effect of the social base of the first industrial novelists was that *class relations* were at issue from the beginning. Through all the observable ideological manoeuvres and shifts, Elizabeth Gaskell, Dickens, Kingsley, Disraeli, George Eliot and others were continuously and intensely concerned with the active relations between as well as within classes.[2] A problem in the definition of 'class' is then especially relevant. A class can indeed be seen as a region: a social area inhabited by people of a certain kind, living in certain ways. That is indeed its ordinary descriptive sense. But a Marxist sense of class, while indeed and inevitably recognizing social regions of this kind, carries the inescapable and finally constitutive sense of class as a formation of social relationships within a whole social order, and thus of alternative and typically conflicting (in any case inevitably relating) formations.

Thus to see a class on its own, however closely and intimately, is subject to the same limitations as seeing a region on its own, and then to some further limitations in that certain of the crucial elements of class – that it is formed in and by certain definite relations with other classes – may then be missed altogether. We can find examples of this in, the late nineteenth-century 'Cockney School' of fiction, with some precedents in Gissing, where much of the real life of the East End of London is effectively written, but characteristically in isolating – and then often in externally 'colourful' or 'melodramatic' – ways.[3] For one of the essential constituents of East End life was the existence – pressing and exploiting but of course by definition not locally and immediately visible – of the West End. Without that relation, the most vigorous depiction of specific localities and characters lacks a decisive dimension.

This is relatively easy to see, theoretically, but that is not – as in structuralist analysis – the end of the matter. For what is really in question is practice, and the conditions of practice. These can be observed, in their actual and complex development, in the twentieth century.

In England there are the very different examples of Tressell and D. H. Lawrence.[4] What is distinctive about Tressell is that *The Ragged Trousered Philanthropists* is founded, from the beginning, on a view of class relations. All his observations and fictionalizations of working-class life are even determined by that, to the extent of the deliberate adoption of caricatured and rhetorical modes. In one sense this connects with the older mode of the sympathetic observer – and the link with Dickens is clear – but the observational mood has changed. This is a participating and exposed observer, seeking transformation rather than reconciliation.

Yet the element of externality persists, as can be seen by the strictly literary contrast with Lawrence, who has turned out to be typical of at least two generations of 'working-class writers' in the specific conditions of his practice. For Lawrence was born into at once a working-class family and a densely settled locality (in both respects, it seems, unlike Tressell/Noonan). 'Working-class life' is then from the beginning mediated by the experiences of family and locality, with their particular and powerful immediacies. Thus Lawrence is never in any danger of writing a reductive novel about working-class life, since what first materialized was not the class but family, neighbours, friends, places. Of course he eventually saw some of the true class relations, but significantly only when he was already moving away from them – as in *The Rainbow* and *Women in Love*. And by that time he was already primarily interested – from a determination in the conditions of his practice quite as much as from his personal and ideological predilections – in individuals who were moving out and away from their origins. Thus, in his later fiction, both the working-class and the general complex of class relationships are displaced: the former to childhood and adolescent experience, without significant attention to the continuing conditions of adult working-class life; the latter, almost wholly, to generalities of an ideological kind, often fictionalized by a kind of back-formation, in ideologically 'representative' figures such as Gerald Crich.

This is an analysis, not a criticism. These particular conditions of practice have continued to be powerfully determining, and especially in the matter of fictional form. Thus the direct inheritance from Lawrence is a series of fictions of escape and flight, or at best of retrospect. Yet much of this is still represented as 'working-class fiction' *tout court*.

Yet some other moves were possible, within these conditions. They are well exemplified in the Welsh industrial novel. This began with the work of Joseph Keating (see *The Flower of the Dark*, 1917), but with all the marks of the nineteenth-century difficulties. Keating was a working miner who later became a journalist. His novels include some of the finest direct descriptions of colliery work that we have, but in *The Flower of the Dark* these are inserted in, and in effect overwhelmed by, a bourgeois romance of a familiar nineteenth-century kind.[5] It was really not until the 1930s that the best form of the 'working-class family' novel was found, in Gwyn Jones's *Times Like These* (1936). This is remarkably close and convincing, and it is free of the (largely ideological) distances between the class and the particular family which disfigure Lawrence. On the other hand, as Gwyn Jones came to recognize, the limitation to a single family has a certain effect of closure, even where the action is that under economic pressures the family is broken up and dispersed. However, that this general social action can be shown, as again and very powerfully in T. Rowland Hughes's *Chwalfa* (1946), is a significant advance on the fiction of individual (an individual writer's) escape or flight.[6]

In the 1930s there are two Welsh examples of quite different directions, each attempting to move beyond the class as (family and locality) region. There is the work of Jack Jones, socially panoramic as in *Rhondda Roundabout* (1934), family-based but through generations and therefore through history as in *Black Parade* (1935). There is also the world of Lewis Jones, in *Cwmardy* (1937) and *We Live* (1939), again family-based but with the difference that the class element and indeed the class struggles now have explicit presence in the experience of the Miners' Federation and the Communist Party. It is significant that each of these new directions was found by an adult working-class writer, as distinct from writers who had been born in the working class but had moved out of it.[7]

The common view of these Welsh novels as regional – indeed as doubly regional Welsh and working-class – is to a large extent simple prejudice. Yet there are still basic obstacles, even in these new forms, to any full realization of class relations. To any actual working class, within its locality, other classes are very selectively and often quite misleadingly represented. The local class enemy is usually the Manager, or more broadly the local petty bourgeoisie. The dominant bourgeoisie is less visible and indeed is often, at this stage of capitalist development, physically absent. Thus class relations materialize either in very local (internal or working-class and petty-bourgeois relations) or in very general and fully ideological ways. The short-cut to full class relations via the political party, as in Lewis Jones, thus has its (in factual terms) substantial as well as local historical and political difficulties. Even with the fine perspectives of history, as in *Black Parade*, the very strength of class and locality cuts off certain moving forces in its very constitution, because they are distant and alien, in the fiction as often in the fact. It is ironic that the best historical fiction about the Welsh working class has been written (though with its own kinds of fault and limitation) by a sympathetic outside observer, who could read as well as experience the history: Alexander Cordell (see *The Rape of the Fair Country*, 1959).[8] The form does much, but with still significant and weakening connections to the historical romance. The way in which the form avoids some of the local difficulties as well as some of the hardest local recognitions can be seen in a comparison with the most important novel of this whole phase, Gwyn Thomas's *All Things Betray Thee* (1949), which significantly is centrally concerned with the problems of writing – speaking, singing – this complex experience: the clear objective reality as subjectively – but by a collective subject – experienced.[9]

Given the generations of neglect, there is more than enough room for hundreds of working-class novels which are still, in effect, regional novels: of a district, of an industry, of an enclosed class. But the central creative problem is still that of finding forms for a working-class fiction of fully developed class relations. The problem has in some ways become more objectively difficult. Further tendencies in monopoly capitalism have removed to an even greater distance the decisive individuals and functions and institutions by which most working-class life is formed. To realize such relations substantially – as distinct from the alternative modes of projection and extrapolation, as characteristically now in science fiction – is then especially difficult. Changes inside the working class, in types of community and in both general and individual mobility, provide both problems and opportunities. It is becoming virtually impossible, wherever the writer stands, to write serious enclosed fiction, except in retrospective and residual modes. Thus just as the limited 'regional' novel is passing out of serious consideration and possibility, in advanced capitalist societies (though it is still being effectively written in post-colonial and intermediate societies), so the limited 'working-class' novel shows its limits ever more clearly.

But then there is still great need for those works, rooted in region or in class, which can at once achieve that close living substance (in marked contrast to what is now happening, through etiolation, in metropolitan and international bourgeois fiction) and yet seek the substance of those finer-drawn, often occluded, relations and relationships which in their pressures and interventions at once challenge, threaten, change and yet, in the intricacies of history, contribute to the formation of that class or region in self-realization and in struggle, including especially new forms of self-realization and struggle.

The formal and technical problems, for the novelist, are very severe, but if we are looking for a direction – and not to be doing so, in the present state of fiction, is, incomprehensible – this is our best road, or, more probably, our best set of connecting paths. Historically, in any case, regions and classes are only fully constituted when they fully declare themselves. There is still much for novelists to contribute to those decisive declarations.

Notes

1. On Thomas Hardy, see 'Marxism, Poetry, Wales', n. 10.
2. These are the 'industrial novelists' of *Culture and Society*. See 'The Welsh Industrial Novel', n. 4.
3. On Gissing, see 'The Welsh Industrial Novel', n. 6.

4. On Tressell and D. H. Lawrence, see 'The Welsh Industrial Novel', nn. 8 and 7 respectively.

5. On Joseph Keating, see 'The Welsh Industrial Novel', n. 11. *Flower of the Dark* appeared in 1917. 'Thomas' Keating appears erroneously in the version of this essay in *Writing in Society*, p. 236.

6. On Gwyn Jones, see 'The Welsh Industrial Novel', n. 13. On Glyn Jones, see 'Freedom and a Lack of Confidence', n. 3. On T. Rowland Hughes, see 'The Welsh Industrial Novel', n. 14.

7. On Jack Jones, see 'The Welsh Industrial Novel', n. 16. On Lewis Jones, see 'The Welsh Industrial Novel', n. 15.

8. On Alexander Cordell, see 'The Welsh Industrial Novel', n. 19.

9. On Gwyn Thomas, see 'Community', n. 11.

WORKING-CLASS, PROLETARIAN, SOCIALIST: PROBLEMS IN SOME WELSH NOVELS

※

H. Gustav Klaus (ed.), *The Socialist Novel in Britain: Towards the Recovery of a Tradition* (Brighton: The Harvester Press, 1982), pp. 110-21.

※

1

First they had to be recovered, those novels by working-class writers, and those others about working-class life, which had been read out of the literary tradition and even the literary record. The recovery is by no means yet complete, but real progress has been made: as part of the research of a new generation, from the 1950s, in cultural studies and social history; also in the research of scholars from outside Britain, who at times moved more confidently past the native cultural blocks that had been set in place.

But recovery only as research, a new department of academia, is at best the beginning of the story. Significant recovery begins when at least some of the novels are put into active circulation again, for the readers and the children and successors of the readers among whom and sometimes for whom they were written.

There is then one difficulty. A certain recirculation, of selected examples, had already occurred. Where, you might ask, from the 1950s onwards, were the working-class novels of the 1930s? Why, there on the shelves, in paperback editions: Walter Greenwood's *Love on the Dole*; Richard Llewellyn's *How Green Was My Valley*. These stood for the others, were the most representative, the most successful, the best.[1]

Few knowing the wider body of work would consent to any of those or similar adjectives, except 'successful'. The success was a success is a success. But as this began to be said, the work of recovery became, and not only from educated habit, internally evaluative, discriminatory, critical. Read *Chwalfa* and *Black Parade* so that you can learn to 'place' *How Green Was My Valley*. Read *All Things Betray Thee* to find a mode beyond any of these. And so back to literature, and to criticism.[2]

But not entirely. For the work of recovery is also, indeed sometimes exclusively, a political impulse. Already *The Ragged Trousered Philanthropists*, now also *Cwmardy* and *We Live*, have direct political interest.[3] New questions then: the political line; its difficulties; its contrasts with the non-political, the non-aligned, the romanticised, the reactionary. Simple questions, or at least simple answers, since we know in hindsight what the correct line might, could, should have been.

Yet in the end questions as difficult as those other, persuasively simple, critical questions: how well written; how vigorous; how convincing. Intellectually difficult questions, and the answers depending, in large part, on the position from which they are asked. A familiar position: what did those working-class writers, that generation, do for us? The only question that is easily admitted into bourgeois discourse on this topic: did they do enough for us? Did they serve us well?

'Piss off', would they say, if they were here to speak for themselves? That is not the language of an intervention in a discourse. 'Go blow your own trumpet, fight your own battles, write your own novels.' That is getting more like it. It is the beginning of the discipline of working-class culture. But only the beginning. Active solidarity, rather than informed retrospective sympathy. No room then for reckoning mistakes? For learning the lessons of history? 'Well yes, admitted. In our own time we blew up the old buggers who stood in our way. And honoured a few of them, come to that.' So that we could do better. Try to do better. We didn't manage too much of it. How about you?

2

The simplest descriptive novel about working-class life is already, by being written, a significant and positive cultural intervention. For it is not, even yet, what a novel is supposed to be, even as one kind among others. And changing this takes time. As late as the 1830s the English middle class had still to persuade themselves that their own lives were interesting enough for a novel. The aristocracy, its romances and its scandals, that was where the blood flowed. Flows. Commerce, family, the individual picking his way: how to make these fictionally moving? It was done; had in part been done already while many writers and readers still wondered if it was possible, or concluded it was impossible. But in the end done so thoroughly that impressed readers will have no other: serious fiction, refuse all substitutes.

Or now the other way round: the bourgeois novel; the classic realist text. Change commerce to industrial labour and it is not nearly enough; the family is still there, and the individual picking his way. They have not done enough for us: where is the class? A question asked, but more practically, in these actual novels. A place, a community, a type of work, families, collective actions, failures to act, solidarities, divisions, factions, struggles, local victories, defeats, changes of mind, emigrations. Who wants a class like that?

Because we are here we shall write about ourselves. To try to get it clear and to let others know about it. If they don't like it that's up to them.

3

That they have not, in general, liked it, and for an ever-lengthening list of reasons, we shall have to live with, die with. We. We die, we live. History moves on; our history and that bigger history made for, imposed on us. Can we not then ask, with respect, about the practical problems and about the changes? Ask, whether they like it or not, so that, still being here, we may know a little better what we have done and failed to do, and what we could still do and try to do.

Because we are here. Because the Depression, suddenly, is not a historical period, for the recovery of documents and memoirs. Because it has come back, is again being imposed on us, and we thought that could never happen. Not a literary or historical experience. Unemployment, closures; political defeats and divisions; advice to emigrate; anger.

It is being lived as well as written. It was always being lived as well as written.

4

The terms are often in everyday practice interchangeable: working-class, popular, industrial, proletarian, radical, socialist, regional, Welsh. They are confused as terms because they are confused as experience and practice. Thus we endure their confusion, necessarily endure. But then to change we must think about them, begin to make some distinctions for ourselves.

Popular: yes and no. We had to write the life of a people. Popular in that sense, yes. Popular in the other sense: not really. We were read by some, but most even of those we wrote about were at the cinema and then the television, or reading penny dreadfuls and twopenny loves.

Regional: yes, we were admitted as that. New exotics for the English to read about. Funny people the Welsh. Talking and singing like mad. And yes suffering of course. 'Something must be done.'[4]

Welsh: yes and no. It was a special problem for us. We had a literature, *in* Welsh, that was perhaps the oldest continuous body of writing in Europe. Except that by the twentieth century it was no longer our majority language, and as part of the same history Wales had changed, had a majority of urban and industrial workers, was to that extent separate from the life within which the received forms were generated: tribal, feudal, pastoral, religious; a many-sided tradition which did not, however, include realist prose narrative. By the twentieth century that may have been old to the English; it was new to us.

Industrial; well, certainly. But there is the problem. There were novels about English industrial life from the 1840s: *Mary Barton, North and South, Hard Times, Shirley* and so on. A Welshman grouped them as English industrial novels.[5] He was right and wrong. As a group they had been read out of the tradition; it was right to insist on the group. But then 'industrial'; that is so many things. It was textiles, that group: the first wave of the Industrial Revolution. Except that there were already iron and coal as their base: iron and coal that were already, by the 1840s, changing the face of Wales. If you look at the range of work that was represented in nineteenth-century novels, you will find, on the one hand, the full middle-class spectrum of businesses and professions; on the other hand a very limited working-class range, with the textile mills predominant. Agricultural labour made some head-way; rural and urban craftsmen were there; in the city, and especially London, a wide variety of occupations, including the humblest, and among them the sweatshops. But of industry, in its developing sense, comparatively little was visible. Nobody was writing novels which more than glanced, if that, at the ironworks, the rapidly developing coalmines, the docks, the shipyards, the chemical works, the engineering shops. Or if they were, we have still to recover them.

This is the groundwork for analysing the remaining terms: radical and socialist; working-class and proletarian. For on the one hand there was already, by the 1830s, a self-organizing and self-conscious working class, predominantly radical in politics, only beginning to be touched by socialism but – as at Merthyr and elsewhere – already moving at times into local insurrection.[6] By the 1890s this was a much more general movement, with established unions and the beginning of a move into parliamentary representation. These phases of organization and conflict can be found in English novels from the 1840s. In novels written by middle- or upper-class observers, some of them initially sympathetic but predominantly to working men or women as individuals within a total condition, rather than to a class marked by its own forms of independent organization. Almost invariably there is hostility to the active factors of class, even alongside sympathy with the conditions of the class. And because this is so, class relations are elements of the organization of such novels, but relations as seen from outside the working class. This tendency actually strengthened during the century. There can be a shared radicalism – the old working-class/middle-class alliance – in Mrs. Gaskell, in Mark Rutherford; even, in mediated ways, in Kingsley and George Eliot.[7] But, as the active working class developed, the specific hostility of Dickens – still enclosed within a generalized radicalism – became the active hostility and contempt of Gissing. The subtitle of his *Demos* was *A Story of English Socialism*. The conscious class issue, in its modern form, had been joined.[8]

On the other hand, all through the nineteenth century, there were working-class writers. Only they were rarely writing novels. Verse of several kinds, and some vigorous work-songs. In prose, pamphlets, memoirs, autobiographies. That is either writing in the direct service of the cause, or writing as a record of it. Or, as in the increasingly popular form of the autobiography, of which hundreds of examples are still being recovered, the story of an exceptional man who had served the cause, or had become important through the cause, or who had 'risen' from the class to some other eminence. A mixed history, but the accessible form individual, even when middle-class fiction was already, in its own terms, social.

5

Novels by writers born or still living in the modern working class are then predominantly a twentieth-century phenomenon, occurring up to a century after the economic and political formations of the class. And still, in the earliest phase, over a narrow spectrum of working-class life. *The Ragged Trousered Philanthropists* includes building workers in a seaside town; at the outside edge of modern industrial organization. The socialist who mocks and instructs them, and who so memorably shows up their exploiters, is an immigrant. So, significantly, was the writer.

Then the first example of one of the two main kinds of working-class writer: (i) the writer born in a working-class family, moving out of it typically through education and his profession as writer; (ii) the working-class adult who writes a novel. Noonan (Tressell) becomes an example of (ii). The central English example of (i) is D. H. Lawrence. And with Lawrence comes a central sector of working-class life: coalmining.[9]

Eighty years on, with the spectrum remarkably broadened, we have not yet mapped these emergences. We shall have to do this, if we are to answer all the questions about working class and proletarian, socialist and anti-socialist or 'neutral'. I know only one map in reasonable detail: that of the Welsh. It raises all the questions. The answers come less readily.

6

The first novelist I know of who had worked in a coalmine was Joseph Keating (born Mountain Ash, 1871).[10] He left the mine at sixteen, became a clerk and a journalist, published novels from the 1890s. He shows us some of the difficulties. He describes colliery work with remarkable power. But he centres his fiction in a different class, of coal-owning families and managers, or the old landed families. He had a shrewd sense of what novels then were.

270

Yet beyond these difficulties (which I have discussed in more detail in 'The Welsh Industrial Novel') Keating marks a specifically Welsh situation. For reasons internal to its social history, the writers and intellectuals of twentieth-century Wales are much more often working class in origin than their twentieth-century English counterparts. Thus the novels of Welsh working-class life are, in great majority, written in one way or another from inside the class.

In one way or another: that is where the problems start. But first a necessary word about class. As people organizing and organized by work, and by the specific fact of selling their labour, the working class is very widely extended, with relative strength or weakness in particular trades but still with a national form. There are then variable degrees of relation between this economic class and different types of community. In the coalfields, in the docks, in the shipyard areas there are special kinds of community formed by the relative singularity and uniformity of employment. The majority are workers but also neighbours, inter-related families, inhabitants of a particular locality: in social relations which in no way contradict, which on the contrary strengthen, their economic ties. Is it then only a coincidence that it is in just such places, where different kinds of social relations strengthen the economic ties of class, that socialist consciousness has been and is to this day strongest? At the other extreme, as now in south-east England, there are millions of workers, the majority organized in unions, who live in more heterogeneous communities and who work in a variety of jobs which have physical contiguity but no other visible integration. In such areas, socialist consciousness has been and still is weakest. And then there are not only the extremes; there is a very complex range of intermediate cases.

For the novel, several consequences. In fact most of the working-class novels have come from the coalfields, the shipyard areas, the docksides, together with the continuing examples from the textile mills. But they come not only with these advantages, of the inspiring consciousness of a working-class community, but with the associated disadvantages – or are they disadvantages?; that is now where the argument turns.

First, that the very intensity of the community can be self-enclosing. It is the only and sufficient thing to write. But then the working-class novel can become a 'regional' novel: 'regional' not in the prejudicial sense of metropolitan criticism, where anything that is not London or Home Counties is 'regional' = 'provincial'; 'regional' in that more serious sense that the novel is written as if the region were autonomous. For Welsh mining families, in a novel, that can be in effect so; they are miners, Welsh, neighbours, families, members of chapels or parties, in one broad defining dimension. And one part of this dimension is working-class consciousness, in these terms. But then a working class, at its most general, and in any socialist perspective, is really a formation within a much wider system: not only the much wider national and international economy; but also the relations between classes, including that other alien class, those other alien or indeterminate or irrelevant classes. The stronger the sense of class singularity, in that defining place, the more difficult, in fictional terms, the true sense or presence of a differently defining system.

So a number of possibilities: the descriptive novel, not now by the sympathetic outside observer, but from within the class community. Thus not 'objective realist fiction', in the bourgeois mode, but subjectively descriptive, with the class community as subject. For example Gwyn Jones's *Times Like These*. Or is it? For the most accessible fictional centre, grounded in the reality of this kind of class community – the community of workers always within the community of families – is of course the working-class family, all the levels meeting or seeming to meet there. But can a family then represent a class? In these local terms, yes. In wider terms, including especially the more systematic elements, no. But then to follow the system, in any normal fictional terms, would be to go beyond the community which is the immediate subject and inspiration. Hence the predominant feelings: suffering; strain; pressures on the family to break up, emigrate, losing the community and the family – and becoming, where you can, economic man; indeed, the family and community feeling is at its strongest and most moving when it is being broken and dispersed by economic depression. Compare the structure of feeling of Rowland Hughes's *Chwalfa*, in another intense locality, the quarrying villages of North Wales: the full dimension and its breaking, dispersal.[11]

Second possibility: the wider system is not realized in the novel, because that would involve going beyond the boundaries of the community which forms it. Only local representatives and subordinates of the alien class are at all visible. But there is then internal struggle, not only with these, but between different versions of the nature of the system, as they affect and run through this intense local life. The struggle within the class, as between militant socialism, reformism, subordinate adjustments, collaboration. A struggle highlighted in certain major events, notably strikes, and crucially in South Wales the General Strike of 1926 followed by the months of the miners' lockout. For examples, Lewis Jones's *Cwmardy* and *We Live*. Socialist novels, as distinct from working-class novels? That change of emphasis is right but especially in *We Live* carries the marks of its specific formation.[12] The identification of the system is not only locally generated and fought out; it is also attached to imported, unrealized, versions of what is happening elsewhere. And then what really happens elsewhere can kick back to blur the internal version. A lived and substantiated movement can become a party line. But only at that level. In the main the novels have moved much closer to the class as subject, though for economy still centrally the class as family, as distinct from the other possibility; the family as class.

Third possibility: historical formation. The advantages of locality retained and even strengthened; new perspectives made possible by moving through periods and generations, a working class being made, and changing, rather than simply, descriptively and substantially, present. For example, Jack Jones's *Black Parade*. The same Jack Jones who in *Rhondda Roundabout* had sketched the internal variety rather than the class uniformity or the mainly political diversity of the people of the valley. In neither kind socialist, for there are other destinations of that turbulent and diverse history. But in *Black Parade* powerful; a novel of the making, the struggles, the defeats of a class.[13] An ironic question, aside. Can the initial form of the socialist novel – its committed perspective added to the descriptive local identity – include defeats (of which there were many) except as springboards for new struggles or as lessons for final victory? The commitment, as in Lewis Jones, is inspiring: The victory, or even the avoidance of further defeats, is still due. The problem reaches to the known boundary of the novel as a form.

Fourth possibility: the process of composition itself. The composition of a history, and the composition of a writing of that history. For example, Gwyn Thomas's *All Things Betray Thee*.[14] Most of the localizing marks taken out. The particulars of struggle given a general form. At the centre of the novel the problem of finding a voice to articulate them. The hesitations, the actual limits, of art; the final committed articulation almost inarticulate, but moving because it has included the struggle in its most general form. A struggle which includes finding the voice of the history, beyond either the flattened representations or the applied ideological phrases.

7

Each of these possibilities was worth attempting and achieving. And each is still a possibility, given the vast area of unrecovered, unwritten, popular and labouring and working-class experience.

But in the period since the 1950s some new problems, within some new opportunities. Among 'working-class writers' there has been a heavy shift of proportion between the two kinds: those born in the working class but moving out, in some sense, through education and writing; working-class adults beginning to write. The drift of the culture, and of the organization of publishing, have worked to multiply the former, through now two or three generations; to diminish the latter, though in some vigorous local developments of community publishing it is clear that many of them are still there, waiting for openings. Some political differences also. The Left in the 1930s, and especially the Communist Party, consciously sought adult working-class writers, and made openings for them: with some disadvantages, in the consequent political direction, but still releasing new cultural forces. The postwar Left has not done this, in any central way. The Labour Party and the unions have failed, throughout, even to see that the cultural struggle is a major element of all political and economic struggles. It is only on the fringe, in radical community publishing, that this has been recognized; but then indeed as yet on the fringe; marginally.

And meanwhile a quite different major force has been unleashed. In the general advancement of the working class, and in a rapidly expanding cultural market – led by radio and television but with important effects in print, there is now major commercial production in the area of working-class life and for working-class publics. Once this has happened, the problem of distinctions within the general category, 'working-class writing', becomes acute. Especially the problem of the meaning of 'socialist' or 'proletarian' writing within this now general category.

We can try to distinguish some kinds.

(a) The novel of working-class childhood, and of the move away from it.
(b) The novel of a past period of working-class life, typically just at the edge of living memory; unconnected to the present.
(c) The novel of contemporary working-class life, naturalized, depoliticized, reproductive.
(d) The novel of working-class–middle-class encounters, within newly mobile and mixed communities.

We cannot yet make any full inventory, but it seems clear that (a) has been predominant in the literature of the period. It corresponds to a typical social movement of the majority of writers who enter this area at all. From *Sons and Lovers* on, it is a significant English form.[15] The working-class childhood is strongly written; the move away from it is given equal force. It is less common in Welsh writers. Thus Gwyn Jones, sharing the same, apparent trajectory of educational mobility, centred not on the individual move away, but on the broader and persistent family experience. For much the same reasons I wrote *Border Country* and *Second Generation* against this pattern, including the childhood and the mobility but making them interact with a persistent adult working-class life.

There has been important work in (b), which again fits the trajectory of the socially mobile writers. Through education and research, combined with local and family memories, they can recover a period. Compare *When the Boat Comes In* and *Days of Hope*, finding an outlet first now in television, and then moving to print.[16] It is often moving, valuable work. But it connects to the present in mood and idea rather than in social experience. Hence the numerous weak commercial forms of the same apparent kind: what it was like yesterday; not like today. Poverty as nostalgia reaches through the cultural spectrum, even into advertising. Of course a simple, decent, wholesome poverty. A distinct ion then within this kind: the distinction between period and historical fiction. Period fiction is enclosed in its time, is an object – often colourful – of spectacle.

Historical fiction, even where it makes no deliberate connections, or is not fully consequent, has movement and challenge.

Work in (c) is the predominant commercial form. It has many local reproductive fidelities. It extends to relatively vigorous 'low life' fiction. The treatment of politics is often the key. Naturalistically it can indeed be seen as marginal; much of that has happened, in the wider history, though it was never for long as central and general as some work in type (b) suggests, or as in the work which came out of exceptional crisis – the Welsh novels of the 1930s. Marginality is one thing; the eccentricity, comicality, of politics – the 'local red' – is another. A great deal of this.

Commercial work also in (d), at simple levels of contrast of life-styles, often overlapping with (a). In any serious way still comparatively rare. The pulls of (a), (b) and (c) are much stronger.

8

Some criteria then perhaps. There is a still workable descriptive classification of working-class fiction. Very simple. The majority of characters and events belong to working-class life. For some time yet, given the persistent dominance of other classes in fiction, a distinction worth making.

But only to lead on to further distinctions, as above. And for some of us as an impulse to distinguish socialist writing within the expanded general form.

Easily done? The author, or a decisive character, offers a socialist interpretation of what is happening, what happened, what might have happened, what could yet happen. Heavily warned off by the dominant culture. No preaching in novels. No ideas in novels! To hell. Do it.

But interlocked with this necessary defiance, some harder decisions. An interpretation of what? Look at the kinds again. In (a) the necessary socialist shift; what ought to have been a more general human shift. The working class is not a childhood family, although of course it includes that experience. The socialist writer has to interpret not only the childhood but the mobility and the immobility and the consequent problems of relationship, at every level from the most directly personal to the social and economic and political.

In (b) the simplest mode of interpretation, but with dangers. Not just the heroic period, as inspiration. The working class is not a past

276

tense. At this stage, for a socialist writer, the necessary inclusion of interpretation of defeats and failures, and the relations between these and subsequent adaptations. Possible only in the historical novel, whether like *Black Parade* or the quite different *All Things Betray Thee*. Overridden by the period novel. A reflection for socialist writers. We have many period novels. We have a few historical novels. We have only the beginnings of a historical materialist novel, yet it ought to be one of our three major forms.

Nothing in (c), as it stands, but an obvious need for work which can recognize, without either stabilizing, promoting or recommending, the altered political and social conditions of the now exceptionally diverse contemporary working class. The inclusion of continuing struggles within what is frankly recognised, also, as in majority a predominantly reproductive mode. The interactions between these, especially those starting now, as the new slump presses on the new acceptances.

Much for socialists in (d). The purity of 'working-class fiction' refused, sometimes, for the exploration of class relations and class developments, and for that difficult contact, beyond local interactions, with what is truly systematic, the working class visibly within a system. Recognitions indeed of the working class still making itself, though now in diverse ways. Recognitions also of it being made, remade, deprived of its identity for a bargain. The risk, here, of proletarian pieties. Stick to the fact not the idea of a proletariat, and seek forms in which the changes can be shown and interpreted, rather than the received shapes imposed. Changes within the class, but then also the contradictory class locations: not only intellectuals but technicians, some managers and administrators; these not only in their subjective traverse from working-class childhood to adult relocation or contradiction; also in their objective trajectory, towards contesting places in a contested and precarious and at once determined and determinable system. Socialist writing of classes and between classes, and of people moving and changing in and between classes and class gaps and class contradictions. Beyond piety to realism.

9

A reach exceeding our grasp? Not exceeding *our* grasp. From historical objects – working-class writers of the 1930s – to historical subjects: our fathers, our comrades, who worked and would expect us to work. Learning from them to change and go on.

Notes

1. Walter Greenwood (1903–74) was a novelist. *Love on the Dole* (London: Cape, 1933) was based on his experience growing up in a radical working-class family in Salford. On Richard Llewellyn, see 'West of Offa's Dyke', n. 5.
2. On *Chwalfa*, see 'The Welsh Industrial Novel', n. 14. On *Black Parade*, see 'The Welsh Industrial Novel', n. 17. On *All Things Betray Thee*, see 'Community', n. 11.
3. On *The Ragged Trousered Philanthropists*, see 'The Welsh Industrial Novel', n. 8. On *Cwmardy* and *We Live*, see 'The Welsh Industrial Novel', n. 15.
4. 'Something must be done' were reported to be King Edward VIII's words when he visited the south Wales coalfield in 1936.
5. That 'Welshman' is of course Williams himself. See 'The Welsh Industrial Novel', n. 4.
6. Williams is referring to the Merthyr Rising (1831). See 'Wales and England', n. 8.
7. Mark Rutherford, the pseudonym of William Hale White (1831–1913), whose novel *The Revolution in Tanner's Lane* (1887) draws a sympathetic portrayal of dissenting circles, radical politics and working-men's lives in the early nineteenth century. On Gaskell and Kingsley, see 'The Welsh Industrial Novel,' n. 4. On Eliot, see 'The Welsh Industrial Novel', n. 5.
8. On Dickens, see 'The Welsh Industrial Novel', n. 4. On Gissing, see 'The Welsh Industrial Novel', n. 6.
9. On Noonan (Tressell), see 'The Welsh Industrial Novel', n. 8. On Lawrence, see 'The Welsh Industrial Novel', n. 7.
10. On Joseph Keating, see 'The Welsh Industrial Novel', n. 11.
11. On Gwyn Jones, see 'The Welsh Industrial Novel', n. 13. On T. Rowland Hughes, see 'The Welsh Industrial Novel', n. 14.
12. On Lewis Jones, see 'The Welsh Industrial Novel', n. 15.
13. On Jack Jones, see 'The Welsh Industrial Novel', n. 16.
14. On Gwyn Thomas, see 'Community', n. 11.
15. On D. H. Lawrence, see 'The Welsh Industrial Novel', n. 7. Williams discusses *Sons and Lovers* (1913) and compares Lawrence with Lewis Grassic Gibbon (1901–35) in *The Country and the City* (London: Chatto & Windus, 1973), pp. 264–5.
16. *Days of Hope*, broadcast in 1975, was a television series made by left-wing director Ken Loach and Jim Allen. It depicted the decades leading up to the 1926 General Strike. *When the Boat Comes In* was a television series created by James Mitchell and directed by Paul Ciappessoni and Gilchrist Calder, set in post-Great War Tyneside and first shown in 1976.

A WELSH COMPANION

※

The Guardian (27 February 1986).
Review of Meic Stephens (ed.), *The Oxford
Companion to the Literature of Wales*
(Oxford: Oxford University Press, 1986).[1]

※

There is a vernacular literature on this island, from what maybe the sixth to what is certainly the twentieth century which a majority even of literary specialists are content to know little about. Only the fact of several centuries of political domination, and of a consequent cultural indifference, often punctuated by aggression, can begin to explain this.

But there is then an obvious danger of withdrawn and resentful enclosure and submission. The most encouraging fact of the last hundred years of Welsh writing and scholarship, and especially, in a rising momentum, of the last twenty, is that a new cultural identity, exploring and valuing its past but also fully engaged with its real present, has been so vigorously asserted.

In scholarship the historians led the way, pushing through to a distinctive Welsh history in the centuries of English political control. This Companion, on the literature of Wales, shows a similar initiative. There can be endless arguments about the possibility of combining the long history of writing in Welsh with an account of Welsh writers who from inheritance or choice have written mainly or exclusively in English. Yet it is a mark of the new confidence that it has now been carefully and authoritatively done.

Of nearly twelve hundred writers discussed in this work, the majority wrote in Welsh. There are also accounts of Welsh prosody and of distinctive forms and genres. Yet we can turn a few pages from William Thomas, whose bardic name was Islwyn, to Dylan

Thomas, Gwyn Thomas, R. S. Thomas, all writing in English but still, through their differences, identifiably Welsh.[2]

Anyone who follows the course of literary argument in Wales will know the test entries to look out for. Thus there is a relatively brief, relatively cool entry on Richard Llewellyn (Lloyd) whose *How Green Was My Valley* was internationally selected as the definitive novel of the Welsh Depression. The entries on T. Rowland Hughes, Kate Roberts, Idris Davies, Jack Jones, Lewis Jones, Gwyn Jones, Gwyn Thomas offer a more native perspective.[3]

It is in this sense of the continuities and discontinuities of a people that so much modern Welsh writing, in Welsh and in English, can be distinctively centred: a refusal to separate moral and social (including political) concern.

There are also convincing entries on those difficult cases of English writers who have written about Wales, from Borrow and Arnold to Kilvert and Cordell.[4] The tone here is just and discriminating, as also in the interesting and difficult case of the Welsh or Silurist Henry Vaughan.[5] Yet the main informative thrust of the book is on the writers in Welsh, and the Welsh sense of their own history, from Dafydd ap Gwilym to Daniel Owen and from the Three Oppressions to the Blue Books.[6]

I have to declare an interest in this volume, as one of its many subjects, but I can still thoroughly welcome it. I am also especially glad that an edition in Welsh is being published by the University of Wales Press, at the same price.

Notes

1. On Meic Stephens, see 'The Arts in Wales', n. 1.
2. William Thomas, 'Islwyn' (1832–78), was a Welsh language poet and Christian clergyman, born in the Sirhywi Valley, Monmouthshire. On Dylan Thomas, see 'Community', n. 12. On Gwyn Thomas, see 'Community', n. 11. On R. S. Thomas, see 'West of Offa's Dyke', n. 7.
3. On Richard Llewellyn's *How Green Was My Valley*, see 'West of Offa's Dyke', n. 5. On T. Rowland Hughes, see 'The Welsh Industrial Novel', n. 14. On Jack Jones, see 'The Welsh Industrial Novel', n. 16. On Lewis Jones, see "The Welsh Industrial Novel', n. 15. On Gwyn Jones, see 'The Welsh Industrial Novel', n. 13. On Gwyn Thomas, see 'Community', n. 11. Kate Roberts (1891–1985) was a Welsh-language author; in English, see Katie Gramich, *Kate Roberts* (Cardiff: University of Wales Press, 2011). Idris Davies (1905–53) was a poet of the working-class experience in his native

Rhymni. Kate Roberts and Idris Davies are discussed in Daniel G. Williams, 'Welsh Modernism', in Andrzej Gasiorek et al. (eds), *The Oxford Handbook of Modernisms* (Oxford: Oxford University Press, 2010), pp. 797–816.

4. On George Borrow, see 'The Welsh Industrial Novel', n. 1. On Matthew Arnold, see 'Community', n. 2. Robert Francis Kilvert (1840–79), known as Francis or Frank, was an English clergyman renowned for his diaries that reflect rural life in the 1870s. On Alexander Cordell, see 'The Welsh Industrial Novel', n. 19.

5. Henry Vaughan (1621–95) was a Welsh Anglophone poet, author, translator and physician, knows as 'the Silurist'. See M. Wynn Thomas, *Corresponding Cultures: the two literatures of Wales* (Cardiff: University of Wales Press, 1999), pp. 7–44.

6. On Dafydd ap Gwilym and Daniel Owen, see 'Wales and England', n. 4. The 'Three Oppressions' refers to a tradition that the early history of Britain consisted of successive invasions by alien peoples; the *Coraniaid* (possibly based on the Romans), the *Gwyddyl Ffichti* (Picts) and the *Saeson* (English). See Rachel Bromwich (ed.), *Trioedd Ynys Prydein / The Triads of the Island of Britain* (1961; Cardiff: University of Wales Press, 2014). The 'Blue Books' were the three volumes published by the British government on the state of education in Wales in 1847. The reports commented on much beside education, and blamed the Welsh language and religious Nonconformity for the deceitfulness and immorality of the people. See Gwyneth Tyson Roberts, *The Language of the Blue Books: the Perfect Instrument of Empire* (Cardiff: University of Wales Press, 1998).

ALL THINGS BETRAY THEE

■

Introduction to Gwyn Thomas, *All Things Betray Thee*
(1949; London: Lawrence & Wishart, 1986), pp. iii–x.

■

All Things Betray Thee is so unusual a novel, and in many ways so unlike Gwyn Thomas's better-known writing, that some words of introduction may be especially necessary.[1] In a summary of its action it appears comparatively straightforward. In the late summer of 1835 a travelling harpist, Alan Hugh Leigh, arrives in one of the new towns of the ironmasters looking for his friend, the singer John Simon Adams. He has seen, on his travels, people driven from their old villages as the great estates enclosed their lands, and knows how they have moved in their many thousands to 'the new noisy centres where cloth, iron, coal were creating new patterns of effort, reward, unease'. But it has always been his own plan to move fast enough, at the edge of these changes, to stop the forces they have released laying their hands on him. He expects to find his friend in the same mood, but two years in the uproar of the iron town Moonlea have changed him. There is a recession in the iron trade and some of the furnaces will be closed down. There is unrest and much talk of agitators and of violence. Adams the singer is now a popular leader, and slowly, unwillingly, even accidentally, Leigh the harpist is drawn into what becomes a bloody conflict. There is fighting and a rising, which is suppressed by the yeomanry. The story ends with the harpist leaving Moonlea.

The action thus barely described is important in itself. In its broadest outline it can be related to the extraordinary Merthyr Rising of the same period, and the anger of that remembered history is clearly an element in the novel.[2] But in several significant ways Gwyn Thomas chose a kind of story-telling which removes it from the ordinary shape of a historical novel. Thus, taking first one small indicative point, the novel is flooded with unmistakably Welsh language and feeling, and the general landscape of those first turbulent iron towns is retained, yet there is an evidently deliberate excision of local Welsh references and names. Moreover the convention of one kind of historical novel is retained, in the use of an account by someone coming relatively strange to the events, but in its handling, as we shall see, is transformed. And then, most strikingly, for within a few pages of the beginning it demands recognition from the reader – a recognition which if withheld can be disabling – the events, though vividly described, are in effect themes for what is the real movement of the novel: a pattern, a composition, of voices, in which what is being said is both of and beyond its time.

It is a remarkable experiment, which needs to be set not only within Gwyn Thomas's development as a writer but within the broader course of Welsh writing from the 1930s. Many forces worked to make Welsh writers of this period adopt different perspectives from most contemporary English writers whose language they now both shared and used for themselves.

First, in an unusually large number of cases – and certainly by comparison with what was most publicly happening in England – these writers were by family or upbringing or direct participation exposed to the full social crisis of poverty, depression and the disintegration of communities: exposed also to the movements that responded to these events: the positive movements of self-organization, protest and political militancy; and those other movements, of emigration for a chance of work or the different ground gained through the openings of higher education.

Secondly, in both their received tradition and their local contemporary stance, they were not persuaded by that dominant English pressure, now crude, now subtle, to leave the pain and anger and intricacy of this crisis to politicians, economists, sociologists, historians, keeping literature to what was said to be its true deep concern with private lives and private feelings. In every year since that stance was gained, Welsh writers emboldened by what their colleagues were doing have encountered the indifference or the anxious correction of the English literary establishment, and some of them, since a good harpist can play many tunes, have found ways of going round about and offering new, often consciously comic, alternatives. If the wisdom of attachment to a people was not acceptable, the wit of a lyrical semi-detachment might be, though the rhythms of other songs still hammered in the mind.

In different phases, different modulations of the central stance seemed able to connect. There could be the steady construction of these lives and times from inside: in pity and hopelessness – the move for sympathy; or in struggle and optimism – the move for shared change. Very different from these, there could be the historical reconstruction: the sweeping colourful narrative of what was, in sober truth, an epic history: the transformation, at once the exaltation and the depression, of an active and eloquent people.

There is a sense in which *All Things Betray Thee* might be seen to belong to this second kind, but we do not have to read far into it to be disconcerted if that form is our expectation. For although the form of the epic history is there in outline, the substance is con-sciously different. Some readers might suppose the novel an attempt at that kind of historical reconstruction, which fails. But if we wait and listen to what it is actually doing we will find a story which is as much part of the crisis as the most dramatic events.

For in and through the action this is essentially a story of how to live with, live through, pity and anger: not by displacing them but by recognizing them without the props of their projections. The occa-sions for pity and anger are explicit, but the problem, reaching deeply into the minds of writer and reader, is how to speak of them, how to write of them, in ways that do not rely only on the stimulus of external events. What is being distilled, that is to say, is the experience of absolute connection with a place, a people, a history, which in the terms of ordinary narrative are often disconnecting, disintegrating, removing and disrupting.

What is then being written is the inner experience of that histori-cal movement which was always more than depression and protest: a movement which experienced defeat, confusion, the deepening of uncertainty, and within these the heartfelt problems of those who could move, near or far, from the core of the tragedy, who knew and could sometimes realise a common longing for quiet and settlement and a different music, but who also could never really be themselves except within the shapes of this more general and more demanding life.

All Things Betray Thee is a moment of transition in Gwyn Thomas's writing, but it is best now seen, in wider terms, as a moment of unusual achievement. As such, if the composition of its voices is heard, it is an irreplaceable instance of a deep underlying problem in thought and feeling but also specifically in writing. The point to grasp is that shift of convention from observer to participant – the underlying movement of the story itself – which makes the harpist's history of the history at once a recognition of what that history truly is and an intricate construction of the often unforeseen and unwanted but finally inevitable connections with it, in the depths of the mind.

This is why, in this tradition, Welsh writers cannot accept the English pressure towards a fiction of private lives: not because they do not know privacy, or fail to value the flow of life at those levels that are called individual, but because they know these individuals at what is always the real level: a matter of inevitable human involvement, often disconcerting, which is at once the mode and the release of the deepest humanity of the self. This is a lesson painfully administered by the history of their own people; a lesson not to be forgotten if the most explicit pressures are distanced or temporarily removed, or while the music calls to a kind of life which everyone would prefer.

The point is clear in the last words of the novel:

I turned, walking away from Moonlea, yet eternally towards Moonlea, full of a strong, ripening, unanswerable bitterness, feeling in my fingers the promise of a new, enormous music.

It is doubtful if foreseeably that music will be heard, but it is the impulse, the general creative direction, that is affirmed. It is a step on from that anonymous dedication which Longridge affirms:

Men like John Simon Adams and myself, we are not much more than leaves in the wind, bits of painful feeling that gripe the guts of the masses. From the cottages, the hovels, the drink shops and sweat mills, anger rises and we are moved. No choice, Mr Connor, save perhaps the last-minute privilege of adjusting the key of the scream we utter.

For it is possible to move beyond that honourable commitment, in which revolt is dependent on how events are moving, and when others can say, in retrospect: 'they should have waited. They were in too much of a hurry. Has death some special call that lures these lads its way?' The larger music is of a longer history, rising and falling but still available to be composed:

> We state the facts, now softly, now loudly. The next time it will be softly for our best voices have ceased to speak. The silence and the softness will ripen. The lost blood will be made again. The chorus will shuffle out of its filthy aching corners and return. The world is full of voices, practising for the great anthem but hardly ever heard. We've been priv-ileged. We've had our ears full of the singing. Silence will never be absolute for us again.

This is said from the experience of defeat, but also from a pride in the struggle which was defeated. Beyond both, which fall and rise over the years, there is the certainty of composition: not only the remaking of lost blood, but the memory of voices which is also a finding of voices: the vast struggle out of silence into a chorus which is at once being practised and composed.

Many voices contribute to this steady composition. In the movement itself there are disputes, evasions, offered alternatives, and powerful voices still speak confidently over and above them. But what comes through in the end is a connection which is the true promise of that music. It is a connection to the past and to the future, but in the intricacy of its own movement it is always primarily of the present: that endlessly repeated present in which the issues and the choices are personally active. The immediate location is 1835 but the connection is beyond it: to 1986 if we can hear it.

> Today is always a muck of ails, shifts and tasks, a fearsome bit of time to stare at and tackle. A man always hates to make a hostile grab at the fabric of the existence he actually knows. But yesterday's beliefs are nice, smooth drumsticks, and they are often brought to tap out reassurance against fears to which we have no answer.

The connection with those moments of hesitation and false reassurance is necessary, as part of the final composition. It is the same when the harpist, believing that his mobility is freedom, rejects all those who have walked into the great social trap. He gets the hard answer:

> They walked into what you call traps because they find a lot more shelter and a bit more food in the trap than elsewhere, even though they might finish up in the trap with no room or chance to do anything but wait patiently to be pecked to hell.

It is a break-out from the traps that is celebrated, and such a celebration is not cancelled even by repeated defeats. For instead of the simple voluntarism of skipping round the traps, the harpist learns both necessity and the necessity, within those hard terms, of the struggle beyond it.

Thus the uncertainties, the despairs, even the hard cynicism or the soft evasion that accompany this apparently never-ending struggle, have lodged deep in this writer's mind: deep enough to settle for, as the dominant culture was recommending and organizing; but also so deep that they can be shared, articulated, and finally transformed as they enter the whole composition of this novel. The beliefs are strong because they have been tested to near-destruction. The music can be felt in the fingers because the singing has been heard and silenced but also remembered; it is there to be practised and developed for the next time.

In this way the voices of the novel speak quite especially to our own period: voices full in their immediate and at first hearing (the reading is often best with hearing) strange rhythms – an eloquence and a rhetoric, a wit and a bathos. The composition is so unlike almost all other novels of its time that it might go on being set aside, for simpler or more obviously encouraging modes and tones. Yet I believe it will be seen, beyond its period, as a quite exceptionally authentic work: authentic in embodying that historical moment, which continues now to include us, in which what is being lived and felt through is the full experience of struggle: not only its causes and its courage, but its defeats and the slow music of its renewal.

Notes

1. On Gwyn Thomas, see 'Community', n. 11.
2. On the Merthyr Rising, see 'Wales and England', n. 8.

PEOPLE OF THE BLACK MOUNTAINS

Planet: The Welsh Internationalist, 65
(October/November 1987), 3-13.[1]

For the past twenty years Raymond Williams has divided his time between the academic world of Cambridge and the village of Craswall in the Black Mountains. Born and raised in Pandy, near Abergavenny, the Mountains and their people have always had a deep fascination for him. During the past seven years he has been at work on a novel about the area which is now nearing completion.

What gave you the idea for the book?
The idea was to write what I thought of as a true historical novel, meaning that most works we call historical novels are in fact period novels – that is, they go back into some time in the past, then interestingly recreate the period, remaining enclosed within that period. What interested me was the movement of history through a particular place which connected not only one period with another but, in a sense, all the periods with the present, and with a present understanding of them. There was in the Black Mountains such an available continuity, and in a place that meant a good deal to me and which I'd grown up in.

At the same time, the things that had happened to the area, although local, were not so in any limiting sense. The shifts that happened there reflected shifts that had occurred in European culture as a whole – shifts in ways of livelihood, technology, types of family, and so on. But what also interested me was that for 1500 years it was a military frontier, a place where, repeatedly, different cultures encountered each other – and not just one culture and one invader, but that whole succession through Celts, Romans, Saxons, Vikings, Normans, and after them the quite different pressure of the central-ized English State. All this was a movement of a very general kind which at the same time I could localize in a place with a strong character of its own and among people who are identifiable and with whose lives I am in any case bound up.

The form of the novel is a fairly simple one at first sight, in that there is a young man, Glyn Parry, who has grown up with his mater-nal grandparents in a Black Mountains village, because of the divorce of his parents when he was a small boy. At the beginning of the novel he comes back late one evening and finds that his grandfather is up on the mountains. The grandfather has always made it a rule of the house that anyone who walks on the mountains leaves a record of his route, in case anything happens. It is late, the grandfather is not back, and Glyn sets out to retrace, from the home end, the grand-father's walk. So running through the novel, there is Glyn, walking the mountains by moonlight, looking to find his grandfather along the way. But once he is on the mountain strange things, shall we say, begin to happen. Glyn feels the pressure of the past (which I think many people walking in these mountains have had), a sense almost of the presence of the past as well as a very strong physical sense of the place. The convention of the novel is simply that while he is walking, which serves as a link passage throughout, the lives of people over a long span of time are narrated in their own terms. When it is their lives, Glyn is not present; yet one could assume that in some sense it might be happening in his mind from what he knows of the hills – though the plot is not made dependent on that. In the link passages he reflects on these stories, thinking all the way about the history and the nature of the place, and the different ways in which people have made a livelihood there, or failed to make one. He is reflecting in the present, but the lives of these people are happening very much in their own time and in their own terms.

Does the novel follow a chronological order?
It follows chronology over an immense span of time, because it begins with the hunters in very changing physical conditions, from the time

when the mountains were on the edge of the great ice sheet and they were hunting at the edge of the ice for deer and horse, through a time after the ice when the country became very open and there were herds of grazing animals, then on into the period when it was heavily forested and the hunting was in the forest. So although these early chapters are all concerned with hunting, they take place under very different conditions. And this is one of my points – that although one thinks of the Black Mountains as a very permanent age-old place, it has actually gone through these traceable physical changes.

The novel then runs on through different periods. From that stage each episode is like a short story, moving from one group of people in a particular situation to another. The continuity, apart from the link through Glyn's search for his grandfather, is in the continuity of the place, and also in certain themes I am trying to follow, concerned with continuities – and discontinuities – in the ways people have lived in this same place over such a very long period of time.

The Black Mountains have always seemed to me to have a strange kind of anonymity, as if age after age of settlement has left little or no trace.
Glyn's grandfather had been a telephone engineer who lived and worked in the area all his life, but he is also a sort of amateur historian and collector, so that his house is full of things he has picked up at different times, and Glyn thinks at the beginning of the novel what an extraordinary gap there is between this collection of information and materials picked up, and the sense when you are up in the hills that there is nothing at all – that you can feel absolutely alone and that the place is absolutely empty. The contrast between these two things is very strongly in his mind. Now in a way this is one of the themes that runs through the novel. It is there in the fact of a man looking for his grandfather, which can be seen as the search so many people are engaged in, of trying to situate their own lives by looking for their immediate ancestors. The whole journey is a search for his ancestors in that way, but all the time there is a contrast between what is available – which is very scattered and discontinuous – and the physical reality of the place, which, as you say, in most of its contacts seems untouched. In fact the records of every period are there, but you have to know about them before you see them.

What kind of records do you mean – archaeological records?
It is very curious. You have the tools of the Middle Stone Age
hunters which have been found, but typically only if some hillside
is ploughed up for forestry and the peat which has overlain them
for thousands of years is disturbed. Once you get to the New Stone
Age, there is a whole line of dolmens along the north-western slopes.
Several of the more important ones have been excavated, and you
can learn a lot from them. At the same time, when you go to see
them they are so small and so grown back into the mountain, as it
were, that it is the same theme again – they are there, but you have
to know about them before you see much in them. Just over the
top here there is a very good Beaker cist burial of a young man on
whom there was an autopsy, so we actually know in general terms
what he looked like; and probably there is a woman in the other cist
beside him. Then there are the Iron Age hill forts, hill villages; the
little Celtic churches with circular enclosures – Craswall church has
still got its old circular enclosure which is probably from the sixth
or seventh century. Then of course, really biting into the place, you
have the Norman castles; three different orders of monastery; you
have some of the early woollen mills: and from that time on all the
usual records of houses, and many more written records of people.

What kind of written records, apart from parish registers?
There are several very good sources. One is that it happens that the
Llandaf charters, so well analysed by Wendy Davies, survive for the
eastern half of this area and its edges, so that, for instance, we have
the original charter of gift of a church like Clodock and the story of
the martyrdom which is attached to it – which I take with a certain
scepticism, but nevertheless it is there.[2] From the Norman period you
have lots of surviving estate papers; you can discover the wage of a
day's mowing or a day's nut collecting, or the various fines and prices
on a particular estate. There is an excellent study by R. R. Davies at
Aberystwyth of the lordships which covered the north-western half
of the Black Mountains.[3] There are the writers who start from then:
Geoffrey of Monmouth is not far away;[4] Giraldus travelled through
and left a record;[5] and there are Walter Map and Adam of Usk who
are full of stories about the neighbourhood.[6]

Indeed, as one goes on, it is a quite different problem from the early part of the book where one had to learn the general conditions and pick up certain archaeological evidence. Now you have abundant historical evidence. But the key point throughout for me is that the novel presents a history written very much, as it were, from below. The people chosen as the central characters are the working people of the mountains. In the earlier period you know what the economy was like, you know to some extent what the society was like, but they are anonymous, and the people you can choose as the leading characters of your stories are naturally of those communities. As you get on into historical records, the bias is immense towards the chiefs, the kings and lords. But at best they appear off stage in the novel. They are there – and it would be wrong not to have them there because their power was very real – but always the generation of each story is of people making a living in the place, having to relate to that kind of power. Because that is the other thing which strikes me so much about historical novels – just because there are abundant records, everything is written from the level of the dominant class, and the others are, so to say, off stage. Now in terms of the original idea of my book, it had to be written from the point of view of the people who were using this often very unpromising land to make a living.

But the lords in the Middle Ages were also off stage in the sense that the land in the Black Mountains was so poor that estates there would have been marginal to their centres of power.

Well this is so in a way, and yet when you get stories like the one of a convoy of carts filled with bullion setting off from the Mortimer estates, which included estates in these mountains, for London, with an escort of archers; or the story of 400 herd of cattle being driven from an estate here to the lord's estate in Essex, well before the drovers' trade – you realize these men were siphoning off, collecting surplus value even from a marginal land, and they were putting it, of course, into richer places elsewhere.

Given the historical sweep of the novel, it sounds as if it is going to be immensely long.

It is long, and I considered when I was planning it whether to make it a series of three or to have it as one big novel. I think the difficulty with a series is that the writer, and perhaps even the publisher, assumes that people will get them all and in the right order – and read them in the right order. But this rarely happens. However, this is a single story and I think it needs to be told that way, because there is a continual intercutting from the present to the past, so that to organize it differently it would have had to have been conceived differently from the beginning. Certain events are linked, through, for example, surprising re-emergences, while people with the same names appear in different stories over a gap of time and often in at least comparable situations. There is also the characteristic fact that people forget what has happened to their ancestors, often indeed have false ideas about them or have been given false ideas – particularly the latter in the modern period, because the amount of false history is enormous. So you have these two elements running throughout. There is historical continuity, and there is continuity of situation again and again, with a lot of the stories devised in such a way that the same kind of emotional situation recurs but in very different social and economic conditions, so that people put the same feeling into what are different worlds.

But I'm not writing a history; it is a novel, and I claim imaginative rights over it, though I have tried to keep to one strict rule, and that is that there is nothing in it which goes against what is factually known. But I'm much more interested in generating enough understanding of the period to be able to say: right, that is the base of the society, now what is it like just to live and fall in love, or get in a quarrel or a fight, in those quite different conditions?

In an interview published in The New Left Review *on your childhood in Pandy, the interviewer phrased his questions in terms of the abstracting language of sociology.[7] As someone who grew up nearby, I found it an alienating experience to follow a discussion about a community I knew well in this abstracted and theoretical way. Is this why you yourself have mostly written fiction about your home area?*
Well, that's it. Scholarly historians have to deal with the provable and they have to deal with generalized evidence, but the people can

hardly be there except the few who are, I think, the least interesting, the people who were the exploiters, the lords and so on. And really the whole novel is an effort to put back these actual lives into what would otherwise be a generalized history or simply abstract sociology. I know enough theoretically to be fascinated by some of these very early societies, how they were socially organized, but I want to understand enough to be able then to ask: what is it, for example, to face a problem of female infanticide; or somebody's reaction to an arranged marriage; or a story I have just been writing of the difference when two men are killed in an accident and one is free and the other unfree? What happens to the widows in each case?

It has theoretical fascination, but I am interested in those people who, with many comparable feelings and situations, are nevertheless living within that frame; and it seems to me that if you can say, well, look, this is not about somewhere else, this is not like reading the anthropology of some distant island, this happened here, it is a fine thing to realize. These are probably genetically one's ancestors and yet they lived in these very different conditions, and that is why the book is not merely structured chronologically but is linked to the present by a young man asking himself what it is to have grown up in this place.

In your researches, have you discovered when the Welsh language ebbed from the Black Mountains?
I think the agreed date is the 1840s–1850s. Of course, by then it is already socially differentiated. It is very much in the Nonconformist farming families that Welsh survives longest. There are votes in various chapels, and churches, in the mid nineteenth century about whether to hold services in Welsh or English. The nature of such a vote indicates, first, that it was a problem but, second, that there was still enough Welsh for it to be an issue; and you find that the vote goes one way in this place and one way in that. You can also tell from the naming of farms, because after a certain date – but then this is often a matter of who owned the estate – you will get an English name given to a farm, while in other cases the Welsh name will have survived.

Then sometimes the Welsh name will clearly have survived into a period where the words didn't mean anything anymore, and so you get them locally pronounced in English ways, though still spelt as a very evident Welsh name. To take an example, there is a hill above Longtown called Mynydd Fyrddin, which at a certain point some people started calling Money-Farthing. By that time Mynydd Fyrddin had almost gone. But on the other hand you get a Maes Coch which has probably been there for millennia. And people still know how to pronounce their own place even if that is all the Welsh they have.

Do you think the people of the Black Mountains consider themselves Welsh?
The thing I always heard, and still hear, is that they talk about both the English and the Welsh as other peoples. This is a very curious thing. It is probably changing – I mean from my childhood – but I have heard both groups talked about as if they were other than the people here, which is clearly impossible. I suppose it is the sort of thing that happens in a border area, that people can't quite orientate. When they talk about London here, they are talking about a foreign capital. It is very distant. On the other hand, you hear people saying: 'Ah, he's ever so Welsh' – meaning he is from further west!

That presumably is a function of the loss of the language, but also of the fact that the Black Mountains with their extraordinary scarp slopes on three sides have until recently been geographically very isolated.
That's right. In fact an interesting thing which keeps coming up as an image in the novel is that this is a kind of massif which these waves of invasion go around – right back, oddly, to the last Ice Age, when the ice went all around it and ground at it up to 1200 feet, but above 1200 feet it could not get. And if you take the various invasions, they were always around it; they controlled it, but they did not penetrate it. So *penetrating* is another theme that keeps recurring – what it is to be ruled from outside, and the difference between that and actually being penetrated. I have found, working it through, that there is a real difference, to be ruled, often in very harsh ways, but not penetrated.

I've often thought about the Roman signal station on the hill above Fforest Coal Pit. That is really as far as the Romans penetrated, and a member of the garrison there must have had a strong sense of isolation, of being on the real edge of the Empire.

On the real edge. I could have written the whole set of middle stories just about battles, because we actually defeated the best part of a Roman legion over at Clyro, catching them by surprise and coming down out of the mountains. The battles take place at key points of entry, on the edge. Often of course the people from the mountains would come down and take part in them; or sometimes they would not come down. There is a wonderful moment in the Wars of the Roses where because of the accidents of inheritance Yorkist and Lancastrian estates were scattered in a totally arbitrary way over the mountains with their strong common physical sense. I have a story of requisitioning of cattle by both Yorkist and Lancastrian armies, and whenever they come to what was called a Yorkist lordship, it just so happened that Lancastrians have arrived and taken off the cattle to the neighbouring lordship, and vice versa! Of course what was happening in each case is that when they saw the requisitioning forces coming, people passed their cattle along to their neighbours and families, because there could be nothing more ludicrous and alien than subdividing an area merely because on the map and by title one part was Yorkist and another Lancastrian.

What you are doing, it seems to me, is providing an imaginative vision of the Black Mountains – something which, when I read Wordsworth or Faulkner, I always feel a need for, in an area which is geographically and culturally as unique as Westmorland or Mississippi.

I think that it needs to be in an imaginative form. When I came back here to live, twenty years ago, at first I simply read the books about the area. I found them (guide books and so on) useful, but they did not have the feel of the place for me, in the sense, as you say, of *imaginatively* creating the Black Mountains. When I am writing the stories I sometimes think – well, I have described the place before. But different kinds of weather and light, even in a single day, make the mountains look so different, and this sense of the place, as place, almost irrespective of history, is very important. I find that I have to keep describing it in all its different moods and colours and lights. I see something and – I have never done this in writing before – down it goes in a notebook: some particular effect of mist or cloud or the colour the hills turn in a particular season. Then I use that in a story.

In the end, though, it is people in association with the hills that seem to be the focal point of your feelings for the Black Mountains – and of the novel. Yes. There is a historical example of this which I find very moving. When the Romans were here, there grew up a little Romano-British town, a trading town, just west of Hereford, called Magnis, and clearly it traded with the mountains for woollen cloaks which were highly valued in the Empire. We happen to know that a cloak of Black Mountain wool of a traditional kind was sought after as a luxury item all over Europe. It also traded in horses, because horses run right through the history of the mountains, a particular breed of ponies which has been used for everything – from being hunted to being used as pack horses, down to pit ponies, and now pony trekking. Now when the site of the trading post was excavated, there was not much left, because most of it had been bodily removed to Hereford. But they did find one shallow grave with a tiny skeleton, obviously by physical type what we would call a Neolithic woman, a very short, dark, broad-shouldered, heavily-muscled woman in her sixties, with all the signs of very hard physical labour all her life – evidently, a slave, almost certainly from the mountains, who had been in one of these fairly elaborate houses in Magnis. A man who later became a famous forensic pathologist did the autopsy, and he was obviously moved by this extraordinary damaged person, half of whose face had atrophied. This is a case where the story almost writes itself, because we know that woman, the history is there, the reality of this very confident refined Romano-British town with its mosaics and so on, and with the mountains as a reservoir of people to be servants, which they went on being through centuries. The story comes out of her. I only have to give her a name, and the thing has happened.

People have asked me a lot, which is it, a history or a novel? Well, it is unambiguously a novel, but using history. For there is a sense, I would say, in which history which is both recorded and unrecorded

can only find its way through to personal substance if it then becomes
a novel, becomes a story.

Notes

1. The interview is with John Barnie (1941–), who was at the time assistant
   editor of *Planet*. Barnie is a poet, critic and native of the border town of
   Abergavenny. See Matthew Jarvis (ed.), *Wired to the Dynamo: poetry & prose
   in honour of John Barnie* (Tanygrisiau: Cinnamon Press, 2018).
2. See Wendy Davies, *An Early Welsh Microcosm: Studies in the Llandaff Charters*
   (London: Royal Historical Society, 1978). Raymond Williams is buried at
   Clodock, in the Parish Church of St Clydawg.
3. See R. R. Davies (1938–2005), *Lordship and Society in the March of Wales,
   1282–1400* (Oxford: Clarendon Press, 1978).
4. Geoffrey of Monmouth (*c.*1090–1155) was a Latin writer, believed to have
   been born in the vicinity of Monmouth, and author of *Historia Regum
   Britanniae* (History of the Kings of Britain) (*c.*1136).
5. Giraldus Cambrensis (Gerald De Barri) (*c.*1146–1223) was the finest Latin
   writer to be born in Wales. See Brynley F. Roberts, *Gerald of Wales* (Cardiff:
   University of Wales Press, 1982), and Michael Richter, *Giraldus Cambrensis
   and the Growth of the Welsh Nation* (Aberystwyth: National Library of Wales,
   1972).
6. Walter Map (*c.*1140–*c.*1209) was a Latin author, from the border country,
   probably Herefordshire. Adam of Usk (1352?–1430) was a chronicler. Further
   information can be found in R. R. Davies, *The Revolt of Owain Glyndŵr*
   (Oxford: Oxford University Press, 1995), pp. 107–8, 284–5.
7. Barnie is referring to the chapter on 'Boyhood' in *Politics and Letters* (London:
   Verso, 1979), which is included in this volume.

POLITICS

▪ ▪ ▪

GOING INTO EUROPE

Encounter, 20 (March 1963), 13.[1]

When the Summer arguing about the Common Market was at its muddiest, I was camping in Provence and seeing only the French papers. Of course I read what 'the English' were thinking, and I was glad that on a technicality, having been born across the Welsh border, I needn't feel bound by it. Then I looked away through the pines at the other tents in view, nationally identifiable only by the car signs. During the weeks we were there, we saw French, German, Austrian, Italian, Swiss, Belgian, Dutch, Swedish, British. I asked myself if I was one of the 'Europeans' who had been identified as a party. That I was in fact European I did not doubt. I feel myself European in ways that make sense of the complex British experience. When I oppose contemporary middle-class English assumptions in social and literary thinking (and that I have been guilty of this I have been made well aware, in your own pages), I base myself partly on Welsh experience, where I still find immediate contact, and partly on elements of the European tradition, in which I have always felt more at home. I know that I would feel utterly isolated and hopeless in England, if I had only contemporary middle-class Englishness to measure myself by. But then that is the complexity, because the 'Europeans', as a party, seem to me of that essence. They talk of the Common Market in terms of internationalism, and become old-Statesmanish lyrical about wine and sun and pavement tables. These, as adventures, don't even begin in my own mind, for they are already, except for the lyricism, taken for granted. I mean that I can't feel, meeting Western Europeans, that there is any *international* problem at all. There are interesting differences, between and within national groups, but no more than I find with Scots or Yorkshiremen. A basic community and culture and habit is effectively there, at the level of ordinary living. When there are conflicts of loyalty and ideas, I find myself lining up across the national groups: against Home and Adenauer and with Sartre and Dolci.[2] The only *international* challenge I know is with Africans and Indians and Latin-Americans. When anyone talks of getting beyond limited frontiers and local habits, it is to those continents that I look.

I react against 'European' as an adventure and a gimmick. The problem is how we, as Europeans, are going to behave to each other and to the rest of the world. I shall judge the Common Market terms from that basic standpoint; at the moment they look unacceptable, internationally, quite apart from the fact that even Europeans will be excluded from the arrangements: the Austrians, Swiss, and Swedes, from that camp in Provence, to say nothing of the Hungarians and Poles and Yugoslavs. This doesn't mean I can line up with, for example, Mr Gaitskell or the Forward Britain Movement.[3] All that is gone anyway, and if it's only a thousand years of history I resent being excluded from it: we were here before that, and Europeans have been arriving ever since.

It's too complicated and detailed to go through, in the sort of comment you asked for. But briefly, I want to see the Common Market judged by European standards. If it divides even Europe, not accidentally but as a matter of policy, I am against it. If it disgraces Europe, by breaking our complex and delicate links with the non-European peoples to whom we are in living debt, I am against it. If it is a tired, painted cartel, seeking to substitute efficient consumption for the democratic and socialist traditions which are Europe's major contributions to humanity, I am against it. But I am only against as a European, and I recognise the European responsibility to put our house in order, to co-operate with each other and with the rest of the world. It will be a bloody tragedy if we betray Europe by being pseudo-Europeans, or by being so 'English' that we find ourselves in the wrong century facing the wrong problems. Still, to have two parties, locked in amplified combat and both wrong, is what we've had to get used to for years. It's time for a change, don't you think?

Notes

1. This is from the fourth and final part of an 'inquiry into British attitudes on the European question' conducted by the journal *Encounter* in 1962–3. The purpose was to record the views of 'our intellectuals' (from W. H. Auden to Peregrine Worsthorne) on entry into the Common Market. By the time Raymond Williams's response appeared in the March edition, General De Gaulle and the French government had adjourned the accession negotiations due to alleged incompatibilities between European and British economic interests. The United Kingdom joined the European Economic Community in 1973 and voted to stay in the EEC in 1975. For Raymond Williams's views in the 1970s, see 'Going into Europe – Again?', *Encounter*, 36 (June 1971), 13; and 'The Referendum Choice', *The New Statesman*, 89 (30 May 1975), 719.

   Edited initially by Irving Kristol (1920–2009) and Stephen Spender (1909–95), *Encounter* was founded in 1953 and funded by the Congress for Cultural Freedom, an anti-communist cultural organisation supported by the United States. In 1967, it was revealed that the source of funds was in fact the CIA. See Frances Stonor Saunders, *Who Paid the Piper? The CIA and the Cultural Cold War* (London: Granta, 1999).

2. Alexander Frederick Douglas-Home (1903–95) was Conservative Prime Minister of the United Kingdom from 1963 to October 1964. Konrad Hermann Joseph Adenauer (1876–1967) served as the first Chancellor of the Federal Republic of Germany (West Germany) from 1949 to 1963. From 1946 to 1966, he was the first leader of the Christian Democratic Union (CDU). Jean-Paul Sartre (1905–80), French philosopher. See 'Marxism, Poetry, Wales', n. 5. Danilo Dolci (1924–97) was an Italian social activist, educator and poet.

3. Hugh Gaitskell (1906–63) was Leader of the Labour Party from 1955 until his death at the start of 1963. The Forward Britain Movement was a broadly Eurosceptic campaign group with links to the British Labour party, formed in the context of Conservative Prime Minister Harold Macmillan's application to join the Common Market.

THE IMPORTANCE
OF COMMUNITY

Radical Wales, 18 (Summer 1988), 16-20.
Collected in Raymond Williams, *Resources of Hope*
(London: Verso, 1989), pp. 111-19; also published
under the title 'Homespun Philosophy' in 'Borderlands',
a *New Statesman and Society* supplement (19 June 1992).
Originally a lecture given to the Plaid Cymru
Summer School at Llandudno, 13 July 1977.

L ate evening, and the television humming in the corner. A programme, not by a Welshman, on last year's National Eisteddfod.[1] Between listening and drowsing, the balance was tipped when I heard one phrase which I thought first was a misreading of the script. He said at the end of that account of the Eisteddfod – which was very sympathetic, sentimental, selective – he said suddenly: 'Here we have a nation trying to become a people.' I suppose verbal analytic training is an inevitable part of the kind of literary education I had. I thought 'Well, he's reversed the terms, an understandable error.' He wasn't reading from autocue, he was simply reading from a script. But a *nation* trying to become a *people*! It must have been written as a *people* trying to become a *nation*. But then I thought, if you counterpose either term you see that each is problematic. This is not the most difficult problem in the terms with which we now try to do our political thinking. But 'nation' and 'people', just to start with, indicate the problems – problems of history, problems of perspective – which are right inside the very terms that are necessary methods of exchange in the most urgent political issues.

A *nation* once was unproblematic, with its strong connections with the fact of birth, the fact that a nation was a group of people who shared a *native* land. This meaning was overridden but never destroyed, by the development of the *nation-state*, in which what really matters is not common birth or the sharing of native land, but a specific independent kind of political organization. A *people*, on the other hand, was always slightly problematic: a mutual term to indicate a group which then at a certain point went through a very significant development in which there were people and there were others within the same place who were not people or who were not *the* people. There was a very significant use in radical politics in the eighteenth and nineteenth centuries in which you set *the people* against what? – against the system, against the ruling class, against them. That use, a very specifying use, a very uniting use, disappeared, I suppose, or became much more difficult when you got to the era of electoral politics and found that all parties were claiming this appellation of the people. It lost that earlier social specification.

In orthodox modern political thought, these earlier terms – *nation* and *people* – have often been replaced by the simple abstract term *society*. Its uses are familiar, yet it, too, is not as simple as it may look. If you look through an eighteenth-century writer, for example, and see how he uses the word 'society', you'll find that in one paragraph he will mean what we would now have to express as 'company' or simply 'being with other people' – society as our active relations with others, being in society as distinct from being alone or being withdrawn. He will in the next paragraph be likely to use 'society' to mean what I suppose we now generally take it to mean – the systematic set of political and general arrangements by which a given people live: society as a social *system*. And this simultaneous use of the same term for quite different meanings has a piece of history in it which may be crucially relevant in the attempt to think nationalist politics in our generation. The term 'society' began with a very strong stress on direct relations with other people, specifically physical relationships of contiguity, contact, relating. It was a word that was consciously opposed to the word 'state' – 'state' with all its implications of the power structure, the display centre of decision and authority. This had been the contribution of a developing middle class: to find or try to find a term which was alternative to state, which should nevertheless express something which was not a private construction but a public one. The attempt to counterpose *society* to *the state*, to insist that there was a whole area of lived relationships which was other than that centre of power and display: this was a very crucial phase. But then in its turn 'society' moved towards that meaning which it had originally opposed. In the course of the nineteenth century, and now again today, we are trying to find terms which represent an emphasis of certain kinds of direct and directly responsible relationships, as against a centre of power and display.

Now the word which touches the nerve, the word which has had to carry most of the freight of this very difficult sense of direct and responsible relationships – this word is 'community'. I want to talk about some of the meanings of community at the point where I think they are becoming extremely problematic and yet when the issues inside the term have never been more important. Community is unusual among the terms of political vocabulary in being, I think, the one term which has never been used in a negative sense. People never, from any political position, want to say that they are against community or against the community. You can have very sophisticated individualist arguments about the proper sphere of society, but the community, by contrast, is always right. I think on the one hand we should be glad that this is so, on the other hand we should be suspicious. A term which is agreed among so many people, a term which everybody likes, a notion which everybody is in favour of – if this reflected reality then we'd be living in a world very different from this one. So what is the problem inside the term, what is it that allows people to at once respond very positively to it and yet mean such very different things by it? Here I have to go back over some of the phases of my own understanding of this word and try to relate it to some direct aspects of social experience. I happened to grow up in a very small rural community right on the Welsh–English border. I didn't realize until many years later that many of the ideas that I had absorbed in that particular situation, and had later expressed, were in a sense common property throughout a very wide area of Welsh social thought. And the difficulty, if you lived on that border, of knowing who you were in terms of any larger grouping, certainly prevented me from seeing in the first stage that this had a relation to Welsh social thought. It was pointed out to me by some Welsh

commentators that this was so; it was much more often and more
rudely pointed out by English commentators, who described my
first definitions of community in terms which showed that in one
sense they knew where they came from. One called it 'chapel rhetoric', with that particular single image of the Welsh. Someone more
recently called it 'radical eisteddfodism'.[2] That would be a very curious notion actually: a festival at once strongly cultural and distinctly
professionally competitive. But I'll let that pass.

That original experience was in a way so special and in other
ways so marginal. What it meant for me was, first, the experience of
a relatively stable community, which had acquired a certain specific
identity in opposition to certain external forces mainly on the land
issue, and then which practised – and I felt the great importance of
this – within that kind of scattered rural society, certain habits which,
I came to recognize when I moved away from it, could certainly
not be taken for granted. If I could give an example of this. When
I went to Cambridge I heard a lecture by Professor L. C. Knights
on the meaning of the word 'neighbour' in Shakespeare.[3] He said
that the word 'neighbour' in Shakespeare indicated something that
no twentieth-century person can understand, because it signified
a whole series of obligations and recognitions over and above the
mere fact of physical proximity. And F. R. Leavis was leaning against
the wall and nodding vigorously (it was the time when this was the
going position in Cambridge) and everybody was saying: Yes, in the
twentieth century nobody understands the meaning of 'neighbour'.[4]
Well, then I got up, straight from Pandy, so to say, and said I knew
perfectly well what 'neighbour', in that full sense, means. That got
hissed – it was a remark so against the common sense that here was
something in literature which was not now socially available: the
notion of that kind of recognition of certain kinds of mutual responsibility. Now this was not to idealize my own place. I do not mean
that people – and above all perhaps to this audience I do not need
to explain – I do not mean that people all liked each other. I do not
mean that people didn't play dirty tricks on each other sometimes. I
do not mean that people didn't have disputes. I mean that there was
nevertheless a level of social obligation which was conferred by the
fact of seeming to live in the same place and in that sense to have a
common identity. And from this sense there were acts of kindness

beyond calculation, forms of mutual recognition even when they were wild misinterpretations of the world outside. My father had to go to the local pub to stop them taking up a collection for me when I won a scholarship to Cambridge. He had to explain to them that having won a scholarship I had enough money to go. People assumed that going to a strange place like that ... I mean the one thing they could identify about Cambridge was that you'd need a lot of money up there. And so a collection was taken up, to try to look after me.

This was entirely within that sense of neighbour, of community. But it was still – as I soon realized when I moved out – so marginal a case, there were so few places like that I subsequently went to, that I had to learn to see a whole range of other possible meanings. And it did come to seem to me that a very different kind of community was actually physically quite close to where I'd grown up, but which I'd not known so well. A community that didn't depend at all on this sense of relative stability, relative custom, but a community that had been hammered out in very fierce conflict, the kind of community that was the eventual positive creation of struggles within the industrialization of South Wales. The connections between these very different kinds of community – rural and industrial – have still not been sufficiently explored: how much of one went into the other, the very complex interlocks inside those struggles, the very complex conflicts inside them, in the earlier stages, between the older tradition and the new. I think probably we are still in the early phase of understanding this.

For there is, of course, a habit of mutual obligation which easily becomes the ground on which exploitation is possible. If you have the sense that you have this kind of native duty to others it can expose you very cruelly within a system of the conscious exploitation of labour. And it is for a long time a very powerful appeal, one that is still repeatedly used in politics, that you have this kind of almost absolute obligation to 'the community', that the assertion of interest against it is merely selfish. Yet what happened in South Wales, as strongly as anywhere in the world, still seems to me an immense achievement. Out of some of the most bitter and brutal struggles came the intense sense of a community of a different kind: the notion of a much more collective community than any I'd been used to, which cast its institutions in collective forms and which did propose to change society radically but to change it in a very particular direction; to attempt to establish from these received and new notions of mutuality and brotherhood, a total society which was possible, one which seemed, if you read the earlier arguments, only just around the corner. You only really had to go to London and pronounce them, it sometimes seemed, and it would happen.

I am reminded in that sense that Robert Owen's proclamation of cooperation, a century and a half before, had also come out of Wales.[5] Owen had that same sense that once it was announced it would be seen as so obviously just, so obviously a higher kind of living, that he even took it as a plan to the prime minister and was very surprised when they said 'Well, I don't think that we can do that quite now.' We have all had this sense of shock, that this is not a message which is instantly received. But that association between a specific understanding of community in terms of the extending obligations of neighbourhood, very much attached to a place, moving on through the sense of a community under stress, under attack, through conflict, finding its community and its collective institutions and attempting to move on from that to a political movement which should be the establishment of higher relations of this kind and which would be the total relations of a society: that association, for all its difficulties, has been a most significant part of the history of Wales. But the difficult thing within it, and it had been the difficulty with the earlier term of society, is that because it had begun as local and affirmative, assuming an unproblematic extension from its own local and community experience to a much more general movement, it was always insufficiently aware of the quite systematic obstacles which stood in the way. If you think back, for example, to that change of meaning in the word 'society', it can seem a loss. It was indeed in one sense a grave loss, that 'society' lost its sense of immediate direct relation to others and became the general abstract term for a whole social-political system. It is undoubtedly a loss, and yet that abstraction was a crucial way of understanding the nature of a quite new historical phase which was presenting problems which could not be negotiated, let alone understood, if the sense of something quite systematic and distant, something which was not in that sense accessible in any direct local mode, was established. This I think was the experience that we're repeating with our attempts to extend new meanings of community towards a whole movement, and it is particularly a problem that is mixed up with our very specific assertion, which is one of national community. Because what the abstraction of society represented, given the losses, was the perception that there were now fundamental and systematic historical changes, above all in the mode of production but carrying with them virtually every other kind of institutional change. Something had happened which put certain of the basic elements of our social life beyond the reach both of direct experience and of simple affirmation, affirmation followed by extension. In came, necessarily, the politics of negation, the politics of differentiation, the politics of abstract analysis. And these, whether we liked them or not, were now necessary even to understand what was happening.

The thing that always seems to me significant is that almost contemporary with this new abstract meaning of the word 'society' was the quite necessary invention of statistics as a mode of understanding our actual social environment. Everybody knows the limitations of statistics, they are too well-known to be argued, but there was a moment in that historical development when it would have been mere ignorance and we would have lived like people in the dark, without the statistics. As indeed we still would if we hadn't that kind of necessary access to things that are indeed our common life but which are not accessible by means of direct observation and experience. Certain things which are now profoundly systematic, which happen in complex ways over very large areas, and which we had to understand in ways that, by comparison with the simple affirmatives extended from experience through community to the making of new societies, seem and indeed often are distant and dehumanized: the apparent opposites of community. The system of ownership, for example, in the modern economy, which cannot be observed, which has to be consciously discovered. New characteristic social relations which have, in a sense, to be discovered, not only by factual enquiry but by very complex interpretation, discovering all kinds of new systems and modes. And these things which are the determining tendencies in modern history can be put into conflict with those other affirmative notions which, whether they come from older kinds of rural communities or from militant working-class communities, are always more closely tied to experience. And around them still centres the notion of community, contrasted now with what? Often I found, as this argument continued, contrasted with 'real politics' or 'practical politics'. That is to say, people would point out that to attempt to build a modern society in terms of the values of rather simple communities was simple idealist nonsense. A modern community – a word they still sometimes appropriate because they know what a positive charge it carries – simply could not be built in the model of these simpler earlier ways of life. And of course that is right. Then again there were people who said that the idea of community is always in its affirmations and in its pieties weakening, because it is less capable of perceiving an enemy, it is less capable of identifying what is truly hostile to it. It contains within it complacencies which really do lack the practice of politics in a modern world at once as extensive and as hard as this one. These are the objections being made in this phase of the revival of community and nationalist thinking. I think they have to be taken at their full and proper weight. They have to be superseded rather than pushed aside as simply the talk of our opponents. Because it must be the case that the projection of simple communities, even on the smaller scale of a new national independence, is a projection of reductions rather than of expansions, a projection of simplifications rather than of the kind of complex liberation which genuine community and new national politics could be.

It is evident also that the hostile and opposing elements to this new kind of politics are very strong, are very identifiable there and that they are not only in some distant power centre. This was my saddest discovery: when I found that in myself – and of course by this time I had been away and through a very different experience – in myself that most crucial form of imperialism had happened. That is to say, where parts of your mind are taken over by a system of ideas, a system of feelings, which really do emanate from the power centre. Right back in your own mind, and right back inside the oppressed and deprived community, there are reproduced elements of the thinking and the feeling of that dominating centre. These become the destructive complexities inside what had once seemed a simple affirmative mood. Nor can we simply react by saying that the values of community, which are strong and affirmative, are superior to those values of the power centres and the identification of power centres, the identification of destructive actual relationships, actual forms of ownership, actual ideas and feelings which are oppressing us. Where we have now got, it seems to me, within the politics of change in the centres of the metropolitan counties, is that we have learned all too harshly and bitterly the truth of this latest phase, the phase of negation, the phase of knowing that you have to go beyond the simple community, the phase of the quick identification of enemies, the phase also of very conscious and prolonged political abstraction. If we merely counterpose to that the forms of a simpler kind of politics, I very much doubt if we shall engage in the central struggle. On the other hand, if that negative politics is the only politics then it is the final victory of a mode of thought which seems to me the ultimate product of capitalist society. Whatever its political label it is a mode of thought which really has made relations between men into relations between things or relations between concepts.[6] And yet to re-establish the notion of politics as relationships between men, to re-establish the ideas of community politics, would mean superseding, going beyond, that kind of politics rather than merely in turn negating it.

Now this is what interests me so much about the present political situation, that reaching the end of that kind of politics which I'm sure we are, reaching also the end of that kind of radical politics, we are finding certain signs of the possibility of going beyond, carrying the kind of affirmatives of community through those negotiations into a different kind of politics. And those signs, here and now, are very specifically national. I live in Cambridge among young radical students who would not recognize many of the analyses that are made about the condition of a dependent or deprived nation within Britain or any of the other deprived nations and regions of Europe. Yet they start from very similar but less negotiable feelings: feelings of social distance, of alienation, of political frustration and powerlessness. But the steps that they can then take, they find extremely difficult. It seems to me that what is happening – and this is what gave me a very strong sense of retracing a journey and finding that I'd come back to the same place but that place had changed – is the possibility in nationalist politics of making new affirmatives through necessarily confronting all the forms of negation, not simply to identify these as enemies but to see them as the whole complex of forces that at first sight we are against but that are parts of what has meanwhile happened to a whole human historical phase which in fact also includes us.

The moment when we move from a merely retrospective nationalist politics to a truly prospective politics, we begin that affirmative thinking which some of the most developed and intelligent left politics in certain other centres of Europe has truly lost. For however sophisticated, however militant that politics may be, it has lost something at its heart which is recognized again and again by those who are inside it: the sense of what any of this liberation is for, the sense of what the struggle would be able to attain, the sense of what that human life would be, other than merely Utopian rhetoric, which is the object of all the preoccupied conflict and struggle and argument. That sense has been so truly lost in so many of those areas, especially through the complications of the modern history of socialism, that what is now being contributed, I think still very incompletely, but what is being contributed and almost alone is being contributed from the new nationalist movements, is a re-connection inside the struggle, including the negations, but also the sense of an objective which has the possibility of affirmation. And if I read the nerves of my contemporaries rightly, I realize how exhausted those nerves are after the extraordinarily confused and frustrating politics of the last thirty years. The new moment of affirmation is to me the quite crucial ingredient and at present it is coming from the periphery. It is the renewal of a crucial ingredient without which politics will be only the capitalist interplay of interests, and that would be the end of politics in any sense which would have been understandable by me when I first started looking at political life.

And so the movement curiously is from an initial naivety, which I remember very well not understanding – as I still sometimes can't understand – how it could be that people should not want to live in real community. I mean, is it not so clearly a much better way to live? What on earth is stopping us? And still I went back a year ago to the fiftieth anniversary of the General Strike at the National Union of Mine-workers' conference at Pontypridd.[7] As people talked about it, it seemed incredible that there had not been socialism in Britain for fifty years. What on earth was stopping us? I found out; we have all found out. But in the course of finding out, what has been learned is in so many ways so negative that the renewal of effort back in those metropolitan centres is a matter of fibre, is a matter of emotional strength quite as much as it's a matter of intellectual ability or organizing capacity. That then is the thing which I see as the importance of the renewal of national politics, and especially here in Wales. It would be absurdly flattering to say that it has done more yet than feel at the edges of what this new kind of affirmative and liberating politics could be, but it almost alone is attempting it.

Notes

1. On the Eisteddfod, see 'Welsh Culture', n. 1.
2. The phrase is Anthony Barnett's, in 'Raymond Williams and Marxism: A Rejoinder to Terry Eagleton', *New Left Review*, 1/99 (September/October 1976), 50. 'Williams is in some ways consciously Welsh – a nationality which embodies traditions of strong inter-class affiliations and smallman radicalism with a particularly strong if ambiguous communal emphasis. "Radical eisteddfodism", then, might be closer to the mark than "populism", were it not for Williams's refusal of nostalgia. Before rejecting this Welsh note of harmony, other British socialists might reflect on the fact that within the UK it is possibly only in Wales that socialism has been to date a mass popular ideal' (50–1). Ioan Bowen Rees was one of the first to identify the Welsh radicalism informing Williams's thought, in *The Welsh Radical Tradition* (Cardiff: Plaid Cymru, 1961), pp. 37–8.
3. Lionel Charles Knights (1906–97) was a Shakespeare critic and, for twenty-two years, a member of the editorial board of the influential periodical *Scrutiny*. In *Politics and Letters* (p. 92), Raymond Williams notes that he 'read and re-read' Knights's *Drama and Society in the Age of Johnson* (London: Chatto & Windus, 1937). On the significance of this, see Stefan Collini, *The Nostalgic Imagination: History in English Criticism* (Oxford: Oxford University Press, 2019), p. 91.
4. On F. R. Leavis, see 'Community', n. 7.
5. Robert Owen (1771–1858) was a factory reformer, Utopian socialist and writer from Newtown/Y Drenewydd. See Noel Thompson and Chris Williams (eds), *Robert Owen and his Legacy* (Cardiff: University of Wales Press, 2011).
6. The phrasing here comes from Karl Marx's analysis of the commodity where he notes that while there is a physical relation between physical things, it is different with commodities for 'the commodity-form, and the value-relation of the products of labour within which it appears, have absolutely no connection with the physical nature of the commodity, and the material [*dinglich*] relations arising out of this. It is nothing but the definite social relation between men themselves which assumes here, for them, the fantastic form of a relation between things.' Karl Marx, *Capital: Volume 1* (1867; Harmondsworth: Penguin, 1990) p. 165.
7. Williams delivered 'The Social Significance of 1926' (collected in this volume) at Pontypridd in 1976.

ARE WE BECOMING
MORE DIVIDED?

Radical Wales, 23 (Autumn 1989), 8–9.
The text of a talk prepared
for Granada television in 1976.

One of the first things people think of when it is said, sadly, that we are becoming more divided, is the growth of nationalist movements in Scotland and Wales: a growth that has led to arguments about what is called devolution. But it depends where you are, where you are seeing this growth from.[1]

In Scotland and Wales it could be said that we are becoming more united, though there is still plenty of fierce division and argument. The point is, I suppose, that many forms of unity are forms of division, separation, from other groups. I find it ironic that some of the angriest opponents of Scottish and Welsh nationalism are also angry opponents of British membership of the European Community, in which a wider unity is being sought. The truth is that very few people believe in unity or in division as abstract social and political principles. What most people believe in, simultaneously, is the kind of unity they've got used to and the kind of divisions, separations, they've got used to. And some people get so attached to these versions that they go through an emotional crisis when anybody proposes that either the existing unities or the existing divisions and separations should, in a changing world, be looked at again.

Of course there are always important practical arguments about the advantages and disadvantages of any existing or proposed form of unity or, to give division its more favourable name, independence.

Those are the arguments that we should really be having, and it can be reasonably expected that from our varying situations and experiences we shall often disagree, even divide. But there is now an unmistakable undertone of something else: an implication of radical disloyalty, even treason. 'The break-up of the United Kingdom', some people say, their voices almost cracking with real or rehearsed emotion. But take this 'United Kingdom'. I know it is officially called that, in the language of draftsmen and diplomats, and there is a kind of administrative and commercial shorthand in which it is reduced to 'UK', in the way that some people say 'HQ'. But very few of us who live on this island think of it, first, as the 'United Kingdom'. The more usual name now is Britain, in fact a very old name. The first known reference to these islands was to the 'Pretannic Isles', hundreds of years before Christ. In its Welsh form, as 'Prydein', the name has come down through the centuries. But many of us can remember, and often still hear, the most common modern name for this island and its society: England. If you travel abroad and say 'Britain' most people know where you come from, but what they say back, and say to each other, in English or in their own languages, is 'England'. Politicians have now had to learn to say 'Britain' to avoid losing Scots and Welsh votes by their old generalizing references to 'England' as including everybody. 'Scotland' is now almost always referred to separately, though there is still an amorphous administrative unit called 'England and Wales'.

But you can see what has happened, historically. A particular dominant version of this island, its people and its society was spread through the world at the time of the domination of a particular ideology and a particular class. You can still find, in many other countries, a deep conviction about 'the typical Englishman', who wears a bowler hat and rides to hounds, of course, not always at the same time. Indeed I remember a well-travelled Belgian asking me, after seeing the Beatles and then seeing some of our travelling football supporters, what had happened to the English, who were well known not only to wear bowler hats rather than long hair but to be emotionally reserved and even repressed, whereas now ... I'm not sure that he believed me when I told him that what he had known was not a people but a class, and that though there had been historical changes, there had been millions of us here all along who were nothing like that class image, an image which had been projected as 'England' and through that as a whole people.

Now you can see how this applied to the Welsh and the Scots who have after all been here a long time – since before the English, if that's the argument – but who, as a matter of fact, like the majority of the English, have had to put up with a version of who they are, what their interests are, what their energies and their resources should be used for, in the name of this unity called 'England' or, more artificially, the 'United Kingdom'. Not just the version abroad, but the more effective version, at home. Take the question of language. It wasn't only that the minority languages of Welsh and Gaelic were harshly discriminated against, a process that hastened changes that were happening anyway, with the spread of industrial society. It was also that a version of English, the majority language, was projected at the rest of us with the implication and indeed the instruction that those of us who did not make all its particular sounds, or its omissions of sound – sounding the letter 'r' is a particular example – were, as English speakers, inferior. I have heard English people, in the same kind of confusion between correctness and their own local habits, going around Wales and amusing themselves by imitating, usually very badly, what they call a Welsh accent.

In fact this singular image of England and the English, as well as overriding all our actual diversity, has been a main source of all sorts of division, especially trivial division, within our society. It is ironic when its perpetrators turn round and tell us that we are wrong to promote what they call disunity because all this means in practice is that other people are asserting their own identity, their own interests, and their own still-forming ideas of how their common life should be governed.

The central point about Scottish and Welsh nationalism is perhaps this: that in Scotland and Wales we are beginning to find ways of expressing two kinds of impulse that are in fact very widely experienced throughout British society. First, we are trying to declare an identity, to discover in fact what we really have in common, in a world which is full of false identities or, to put it another way, in which important kinds of meaning – the meaning of community, for example – are much harder to find, in real terms, than they have seemed to be in the past. And second, but related to this, we are trying to discover political processes by which people really can govern themselves – that is, to determine the use of their own energies and resources – as distinct from being governed by an increasingly centralised, increasingly remote and also increasingly penetrating system: the system that those who run it, for their own interests, have decided to call 'Unity'.

Now I'd be the first to say that there are problems in satisfying these impulses by simply saying that we are Scots or Welsh, or that we want Scottish or Welsh independence. Mixed in with these impulses, in the nationalist movements, are all kinds of other ideas and feelings, and especially a weak kind of romanticism which, selecting a particular version of history, or even just bits and pieces of the past, makes both the Scots and the Welsh more different from the English than they really are, and the Scots or the Welsh or of course the English more like each other than they really are. The historical fact is that the different peoples who have come to these islands over several thousands of years have moved and fought and intermarried and been united and been divided in extraordinarily complex ways. At the same time there have been significant periods in which distinctive Scots and Welsh cultures have established themselves, and other significant periods – the Industrial Revolution is the most obvious example – in which the decisive changes worked through the whole society and we divided, in response to them, mainly in other ways, for example in the decisive formation of modern social classes. Simply to seize some moment of the past, or to create a tourist version of a wholly distinct people, with bits and pieces of local colour, is no basis for a significant nationalist movement. But then what I have noticed is that these elements were most prominent when the nationalist movements were weak, defensive and even hopeless, and that what is happening now is the more realistic and more truly creative definition of what a modern Scotland, a modern Wales, both is and can become. In Wales, for example – and I think this would be even more true of Scotland – we have always been aware of the deep differences between industrial South Wales, rural North and West Wales, and the very specific border country from which I myself come. We don't get past that by inventing a pseudo-historical or romantic Welshness; indeed that would only divide us further. We get past it by looking and working for unity in the definition and the development of a modern Wales, in which the really powerful impulses – to discover an effective modern community and to take control of our own energies and resources – can be practically worked through. That is what I mean by saying that the nationalist movements, while they can be seen from one position, as working to divide, must be seen from another position as working to unite.

And then I think this has special relevance to the English. Some people talk about the English backlash against Scots and Welsh nationalism, but this covers two very different responses. There is of course the 'unity' backlash, in which the dominant system and all its agents and organizations want to stop other groups of people working out their own future in their own ways. That sort of backlash has simply to be fought and defeated. But there is also what I would call the 'why not us?' backlash and this, I believe, every genuine nationalist would welcome. England has recently been divided into regions, some of them paper regions, dreamed up by bureaucrats. It is a problem for many English people, with strong local and regional needs and loyalties, that they want the same things as the Scots and Welsh nationalists – to deepen their effective community, to control their own future – but don't have available, in such apparently simple ways, the effective definitions from which they can start. This means, among other things, that a nationalist movement isn't the only way, often isn't the way at all, to work for these things. But unless in one way or another people can get effective positive control of their own places and their own lives, this complex industrial society will smash itself up, with increasing hatred and bitterness, not in spite of but because of the imposed and artificial unity which the existing system is now fighting to maintain. Division, as I said, is someone else's name for independence. Once you are not controlled, in advance and systematically, by others, you soon discover the kinds of co-operation, between nations, between regions, between communities, on which any full life depends. But it is then your willing and not your enforced co-operation. That is why I, with many others, now want and work to divide, as a way of declaring our own interests certainly, but also as a way of finding new and willing forms of co-operation: the only kind of co-operation that any free people can call unity.

Note

1. This piece could be considered Williams's contribution to the debate taking place in the late 1970s between Tom Nairn (1932–) and Eric Hobsbawm (1917–2012) in the pages of *New Left Review*. See Tom Nairn, 'The Twilight of the British State', *New Left Review*, 101–2 (February–April 1977), 3–61, reprinted in Tom Nairn, *The Break-Up of Britain* (London: New Left Books, 1977); Eric Hobsbawm, 'Some Reflections on the Break-up of Britain Thesis', *New Left Review*, 105 (September–October 1977), 1–23.

THE CULTURE OF NATIONS

Raymond Williams, *Towards 2000*
(London: Chatto & Windus, 1983), pp. 177-99.

1

There was this Englishman who worked in the London office of
a multinational corporation based in the United States. He drove
home one evening in his Japanese car. His wife, who worked in a
firm which imported German kitchen equipment, was already at
home. Her small Italian car was often quicker through the traffic.
After a meal which included New Zealand lamb, Californian carrots,
Mexican honey, French cheese and Spanish wine, they settled down
to watch a programme on their television set, which had been made
in Finland. The programme was a retrospective celebration of the
war to recapture the Falkland Islands. As they watched it they felt
warmly patriotic, and very proud to be British.[1]

2

The contradictions in what is meant by nationality, and even more by
patriotism, are now very acute. If they are more noticed and thought
about by some people than by others, they are still not of a kind to
be projected only to those who are most evidently and practically
confused. There is a strongly effective continuation of relatively old
ideas of nationality, and beyond these of race, while at the same time
there is an extraordinary and yet widely accepted penetration and
coexistence of powerful international and paranational forms. These
are to be found not only in the obvious cases of world markets in
food and in manufactured commodities, but also in active membership of a political and military alliance and of a paranational economic
community. Each of these has radically altered the nature of sovereignty, yet that idea is still quite centrally retained. Our couple may
well not have noticed the American aircraft, armed with nuclear

weapons, flying high above their house from an English base, or the new heavier lorries on the bypass, whose weight has been determined by an EEC regulation, yet, regularly, systematically, these are there.

'Contradiction' is a curious analytic term. It can be applied quite easily to cases where people actually say contradictory things, or act on contradictory beliefs. If somebody says that his country means everything to him, but that as a consumer he must buy what he wants at the most suitable price and quality, whatever its national origin, the element of contradiction is obvious. But the term has been extended to much more difficult cases, when it is not so much what people say and believe that is contradictory but when actual forces in a society are pulling in opposite or at least different directions and thus creating tensions – and instabilities. The former cases, of verbal or everyday practical contradiction, can be met by arguments. They are what most of us come to notice, at various points in our lives, when we have to decide what we really (most) believe. The other kinds of 'contradiction' are not so readily dealt with. Indeed it is already assuming a lot to say that they are simple contradictions. The mental model by which we test coherence or compatibility may be simply what we are putting into the situation, and what looks contradictory, in its selected terms, may in fact be no more than an unfamiliar system, which in its own terms is coherent enough. There is then still a problem of the things we say about it, which may be muddled or locally contradictory. But the system itself, not only creating but also containing and managing tensions and instabilities, is not something that can be refuted by argument alone.

This is now the case, I believe, in these central problems that are indicated by talk of 'nationality', 'patriotism' and – for it is part of the same complex – 'internationalism'. There are innumerable muddles and stupidities, and there is some very powerful political and cultural exploitation both of these and of the genuine difficulties. But in general these are problems of the surface of politics and culture. They would be relatively easily solved if the underlying and obscured problems of contemporary societies, on which they feed, were not so great.

3

It is human nature to belong to a society, and to find value in belonging to it. We are born into relationships, and we live and grow through relationships. There is a whole range of such forms, variable in different places and times, but any actual forms are close and specific to those who are living in and through them. Intellectual analysis, of an historical or comparative kind, can show very quickly how 'limited' or 'local' any such form may be. But while in times of pressure and change this wider perspective is encouraging, showing us that it is possible for people to find meaning and value in many different kinds of relationship and society, it can also be an effective evasion of the actual problems which, with such meanings and values as they have, people are trying to resolve.

Thus in several modern intellectual systems there has been rapid progress to forms of universality – what is believed to be true of all people everywhere – which are then used to define what most people are still trying to live by as mere local illusions and prejudices. Genuine progress towards establishing the universality of social situation by class is offered as a way of dissolving stubborn self-definitions by nationality, or religion. A presumed universality of situation by primary relationships, as in psychoanalysis, is offered as a way of enlightening and questioning forms of relationship which are, nevertheless, being continually reproduced. Each of these systems, with other similar systems, clearly affects the ways in which many people have learned to think about their relationships, but, except in certain very specific groups, they have nowhere come near to realising their own apparent logic, by which the offered universalities would prevail over more local forms.

Yet this is only half the story. The real 'universalities' – large forms which do succeed in prevailing over more local forms – are not to be found in intellectual systems but in actual and organised relationships which achieve, over the relevant areas, effective power. This is the way to look at the urgent modern problem of the 'nation'. It is ineffective and even trivial to come back from a demonstration of the universality of the human species and expect people, from that fact alone, to reorganise their lives by treating all their immediate and actual groupings and relationships as secondary. For the species meaning, and the valuation of human life which it carries, is in practice only realised, indeed perhaps in theory only realisable, through significant relationships in which other human beings are present. No abstraction on its own will carry this most specific of all senses. To extend it and to generalise it, in sufficiently practical ways, involves the making of new relationships which are in significant continuity – and not in contradiction – with the more limited relationships through which people do and must live.

Thus there is little point in jumping from 'the nation' to a projected 'internationalism'. Instead we have to move first in the other direction, to see what in practice this widely accepted 'universality' now amounts to. 'All modern peoples have organised themselves as nations'. Have they? The artificialities of many forms of modern 'nationality' and 'patriotism' have often been noticed. Some relatively detached or mobile people see them as merely 'backward' or 'primitive', and have a good laugh about them, until some war makes them weep. But the real point of entry for analysis is that the artificialities are functional. That is to say, they are neither backward nor primitive but contemporarily effective and deliberate forms. That they are now increasingly artificial, with very serious effects on what is also residually quite real, is then the central point.

4

'Nation', as a term, is radically connected with 'native'. We are born into relationships, which are typically settled in a place. This form of primary and 'placeable' bonding is of quite fundamental human and natural importance. Yet the jump from that to anything like the modern nation-state is entirely, artificial. What begins as a significant and necessary way of saying 'we' and 'our' (as so much more than 'I' and 'mine') slides by teaching or habit into bland or obscuring generalities of identity. The strongest forms of placeable bonding are always much more local: a village or town or city; particular valleys or mountains. Still today in societies as different as Wales and Italy people say where they come from, where they were formed or belong, in these insistently local ways. It is of course possible to extend these real feelings into wider areas: what are often spoken of now as 'regional' identities and loyalties. But that term, 'region', illuminates a very different process. A 'region' was once a realm, a distinct society. In its modern sense, by contrast, it is from the beginning a subordinate part of a larger unity, typically now a part of a 'nation'. What has then happened is that the real and powerful feelings of a native place and a native formation have been pressed and incorporated into an essentially political and administrative organisation, which has grown from quite different roots. 'Local' and 'regional' identities and loyalties are still allowed, even at a certain level encouraged, but they are presumed to exist within, and where necessary to be overridden by, the identities and the loyalties of this much larger society.

It is of course true that some of these wider identities and loyalties have been effectively achieved through real relationships. Even where, as in the great majority of cases, the larger society was originally formed by violent conquest, by repression, by economic domination or by arbitrary alliances between ruling families, there are usually generations of experience of living within these imposed forms, and then of becoming used or even attached to them. What is still in question, however, is the projection of those original 'native' and 'placeable' feelings to the forms of a modern state. Nothing is now more striking, for example, than the images of 'England' which are culturally predominant. Many urban children, when asked what is really 'England', reply with images of the monarchy, of the flag, of the Palace of Westminster and, most interestingly, of 'the countryside', the 'green and pleasant land'. It is here that the element of artifice is most obvious, when the terms of identity flow downwards from a political centre, and yet when the very different feelings of being 'native' and being 'loyal' are invoked and in this way combined.

In nations with long and complex histories the procedures of invocation and combination are deeply embedded in the whole social process. Yet it is an evident historical fact that the processes of political combination and definition are initiated by a ruling class: indeed to say so is virtually tautologous. The building of states, at whatever level, is intrinsically a ruling-class operation. The powerful processes that then ensue, in the complex transitions from conquest and subjection to more embedded formations, necessarily take place, however, over much wider social areas. War stands out as one of the fundamentally unifying and generalising experiences: the identification of an alien enemy, and with it of what is often real danger, powerfully promotes and often in effect completes a 'national' identity. It is not accidental that talk of patriotism so quickly involves, and can even be limited to, memories and symbols of war. Meanwhile the assembly of armies, from diverse actual communities into this single and overriding organisation, is one of the most notable processes of actual generalisation and unification.

In modern societies, engaged in the transition from a subject people to a civil society, education of every kind, in churches and then mainly in schools, exerts more regular pressures. When children start going to school they often learn for the first time that they are English or British or what may be. The pleasure of learning is attached to the song of a monarch or a flag. The sense of friends and neighbours is attached to a distant and commanding organisation: in Britain, now, that which ought to be spelled as it so barbarously sounds – the United Kingdom, the 'Yookay'. Selective versions of the history underlying this impressed identity are regularly presented, at every level from simple images and anecdotes to apparently serious textbook histories. The powerful feelings of wanting to belong to a society are then in a majority of cases bonded to these large definitions.

It is often the case that this bonding moves at once from the smallest social entity, within the family, to the available largest, in the nation-state. These are offered as non-contradictory. Indeed they are rationalised as levels, the personal and the social. Many other kinds of bonding may then occur: distinction by streets or by parts of a town or village; distinction by gender and age-group; distinction by city or region. Many kinds of active 'local' or 'regional' groups, and of more passive groups of fans or supporters, grow up around these and carry powerful feelings. But typically they are unproblematically contained within the initial bonding between 'family-individual' and 'nation', which in all important and central cases is felt either to be an extension from them (as in particularised army regiments) or to override them.

It is a matter of great political significance that in the old nation-states, and especially the imperial states, scepticism and criticism of such bonding has come almost exclusively from radicals. They have seen, correctly, that this form of bonding operates to mobilise people for wars or to embellish and disguise forms of social and political control and obedience. It is true that opposition comes also from incompletely assimilated or still actively hostile minority peoples who have been incorporated within the nation-state, but this characteristically takes the form of an alternative (Irish or Scots or Welsh or

Breton or Basque) nationalism, relying on the same apparent bonding though within a political subordination. The complex interactions between such nationalisms and more general radicalisms have been evident and remarkable, though in general it is true that unique forms of national-radical bonding, unavailable by definition in the larger nation-state, come through and have powerful effects. It is sadly also true that not only the majority people, with 'their own' nation-state, but also many among the minority peoples, regard this kind of nationalism as disruptive or backward-looking, and are even confident enough to urge 'internationalism' against it, as a superior political ideal. It is as if a really secure nationalism, already in possession of its nation-state, can fail to see itself as 'nationalist' at all. Its own distinctive bonding is perceived as natural and obvious by contrast with the mere projections of any nationalism which is still in active progress and thus incomplete. At this point radicals and minority nationalists emphasise the artificialities of the settled 'commonsense' nation-state and to their own satisfaction shoot them to pieces from history and from social theory.

The political significance is then that radicalism becomes associated, even in principle, with opposition to 'the nation'. In the old nation-states this has been profoundly damaging, yet it can be understood only by reference to the history and formation of actual social orders. For what has been most remarkable in the twentieth century has been the successful fusion of nationalism and political revolution, including armed struggles, in many other parts of the world, from Cuba to Vietnam. The conditions of such fusion evidently derive from a pre-existing colonial or semi-colonial status, in which relatively direct and powerful bonds of identity and aspiration are formed as against both foreigners and exploiters. There are then usually major problems, at a later stage, in relations with other national-revolutionary states, and the elements fused in the struggle enter a new stage in which the bonding can no longer be taken for granted. Meanwhile the political problem, for radicals back in the old nation-states, who are quick to identify with the national-liberation struggles of the ex-colonial peoples, lies in their fundamental attitudes to their own nation. For again and again, hurling themselves at the mystification of social reality by the ruling definitions of the nation and patriotism, they have found themselves opposed not only by the existing rulers and guardians but by actual majorities of the people in whose more fundamental needs and interests they are offering to speak.

There are many false ways out of this basic problem. All of them depend on subjection to the existing terms of the definitions. Contemporary social democrats, in particular, do their calculations and emerge with an amazing and implausible mix of patriotism, internationalism and social justice, drawing on each principle as occasion serves, or rhetorically proclaiming their compatibility or even identity. All this shows is their profound subordination to the forms of existing interests. The increasing irrelevance of social-democratic politics, in the old nation-states – indeed the transformation of social democracy itself, under a merely confusing retention of an old name, which in different conditions had more significance and coherence – is a direct result of this basic subordination.

For what they will not challenge, except in selected marginal ways, is capitalism itself. Yet it is capitalism, especially in its most developed stages, which is the main source of all the contemporary confusions about peoples and nations and their necessary loyalties and bonds. Moreover it is, in the modern epoch; capitalism which has disrupted and overridden natural communities, and imposed artificial orders. It is then a savage irony that capitalist states have again and again succeeded in mobilising patriotic feelings in their own forms and interests. The artificialities of modern nationalism and patriotism, in states of this kind, have then to be referred not to some intellectually dissolving universality, but to the precise and powerful functions which, necessarily in the form of artifice, they are now required to perform.

5

Both in its initial creation of a domestic market, and in its later organisation of a global market, the capitalist mode of production has always moved in on resources and then, necessarily, on people, without respect for the forms and boundaries of existing social organisations. Whole communities with settled domestic forms of production, from farming to brewing and clothmaking, and from small manufacturing to local services, were simply overridden by more developed and more centralised and concentrated capitalist and capitalist-industrial forms. Communities which at simpler levels had relatively balanced forms of livelihood found themselves, often without notice, penetrated or made marginal, to the point where many of their own people became 'redundant' and were available for transfer to new centres of production. Capitalist textile-production, ironmaking, mining, grain production and a host of other industrial processes set in train immigrations and emigrations, aggregations and depopulations, on a vast scale. Typically, moreover, people were moved in and out on short-run calculations of profit and convenience, to be left stranded later, in worked-out mining valleys or abandoned textile towns, in old dockyard and shipbuilding areas, in the inner cities themselves, as trade and production moved on in their own interests.

Through these large and prolonged dislocations and relocations, which are still in progress in every part of the world, the older traditional forms of identity and community were dislocated and relocated, within enforced mobilities and necessary new settlements. It is significant that William Cobbett, observing just these processes in one of their most decisive stages, is in effect the last authentic English radical: a man in whom love of birthplace, love of country, and root-and-branch opposition to the whole social order, could be authentically integrated. Even in him there were tensions, underlying his radical change of political direction as his idea of the old England encountered the reality of the new. In all later periods, the kind of continuity which Cobbett still saw as ideal, from home and birthplace to county to country – none in tension with or cancelling the other – was increasingly unavailable. What took its place was an artificial construction, which had increasingly to be defined in generalising and centralised images because the only effective political identity still apparently compatible with the dislocating and relocating processes of industry was now at that deliberately distanced level.

But this was still only an early stage. What was done within the first industrial societies was soon also being done, at an accelerating pace, in every accessible part of the world. Whole tracts of land, where people had been living in their own ways, were ripped for minerals, ores, gems, fertilisers. Whole forests, in which people and animals had been living, were felled and exported. Simple subsistence farming communities were dispossessed and reorganised for plantations of rubber and cotton and sugar and coffee and tea, or for any and every kind of export-oriented monoculture which the physical conditions of the land, irrespective of the needs and preferences of its inhabitants, indicated for profit. The long forced trade in human beings, moving them as slaves into new kinds of work, was succeeded by various kinds of economic forcing, in which whole communities and peoples, or by selection their young men and women, had to emigrate to the new centres of work and subsistence.

Some of these developments struck back into the old economies, depressing or ruining other traditional kinds of production, and forcing new internal emigrations from what had been made into 'marginal areas'. Flows of people following these externally induced flows of trade and wealth broke up, at either end, the older types of settlement and community in which identity had been directly engaged. Moreover, as in the first industrial societies, it was never a movement once for all, into some new adjustment. As production and trading advantages shifted, vast numbers had to move yet again, or be left stranded in the debris of a worked-out economy. Massive movements of this kind are still occurring, in thousands of authorised and unauthorised emigrations and immigrations, and in the desperate trails from land dispossessed by agribusiness to the shanty towns on the edges of the already densely populated cities.

What is really astonishing is that it is the inheritors and active promoters, the ideologists and the agents, of this continuing world-wide process who speak to the rest of us, at least from one side of their mouths, about the traditional values of settlement, community and loyalty. These, the great disrupters, not only of other people's settlements but of many of those of their own nominal people, have annexed and appropriated, often without challenge, many of the basic human feelings about a necessary and desirable society. They retain this appropriation even while their hands are endlessly busy with old and new schemes in which the priorities are wholly different: schemes through which actual people and communities are depressed or disappear, under the calculations of cost-benefit, profit and advantageous production.

It is an outrage that this has happened and been allowed to happen. Yet while we can protest and fight in these terms, we can only analyse and understand if we bring in another dimension, which is now probably decisive. Instead of looking only at the promoters and agents of this vast dislocation and relocation, we have to look also at the changes that have happened and are still happening in the minds of those to whom, in effect, all this has been done.

6

Most human beings adjust, because they must, to altered, even radically altered conditions. This is already marked in the first generations of such shifts. By the second and third generations the initially enforced conditions are likely to have become if not the new social norms – for at many levels of intensity the conditions may still be resented – at least the new social perspective, its everyday common sense. Moreover, because so many of the shifts are enforced by a willed exploitation of new means of production and new products, sometimes ending in failure but much more often increasing goods of every kind, there are major if always unequal material advantages in the new conditions. Capitalism as a system, just because of its inherent one-dimensional mobility, can move on very rapidly from its failures and worked-out areas, leaving only local peoples stuck with them. By its very single-mindedness it can direct new and advantageous production in at least the short-term interests of effective working majorities. In any of its periodic crises it can make from one in ten to one in three of a numbered people redundant, but while it still has the other nine or the other two it can usually gain sufficient support or tolerance to continue its operations. Moreover, identified almost inextricably with positive advantages in improved products and services, it not only claims but is acclaimed as progress.

Thus while on an historical or comparative scale its forced operations are bound to be seen as arbitrary and often brutal, on any local and temporarily settled scale it flies with the wings of the dove. It brings factories and supermarkets, employment and affluence, and everything else is a local and temporary difficulty – out of sight, out of time, out of mind – or is the evident fault, even the malign fault, of those who are suffering. In any general examination, the system is transparent, and ugly. But in many, and so far always enough, local perspectives it is not only the tolerated but the consciously preferred order of real majorities.

For now from the other side of its mouth it speaks of the consumer: the satisfied, even stuffed consumer; the sovereign consumer.

Sovereign? That raises a problem, but while the production lines flow and the shopping trolleys are ready to carry the goods away, there is this new, powerful social identity, which is readily and even eagerly adopted. It is at best a radically reduced identity, at worst mean and greedy. But of course 'consumer' is only a general purpose word, on the lines of 'citizen' or 'subject'. It is accepted only as describing that level of life: the bustling level of the supermarket. When the goods from the trolley have been stowed in the car, and the car is back home, a fuller and more human identity is ready at the turn of a key: a family, a marriage, children, relatives, friends. The economic behaviour of the consumer is something you move out to, so as to bring the good things back.

There is then a unique modern condition, which I defined in an earlier book (*Television: Technology and Cultural Form*, 1974) as 'mobile privatisation'. It is an ugly phrase for an unprecedented condition. What it means is that at most active social levels people are increasingly living as private small-family units, or, disrupting even that, as private and deliberately self-enclosed individuals, while at the same time there is a quite unprecedented mobility of such restricted privacies. In my novel *Second Generation* (1964) I developed the image of modern car traffic to describe this now dominant set of social relations in the old industrial societies. Looked at from right outside, the traffic flows and their regulation are clearly a social order of a determined kind, yet what is experienced inside them – in the conditioned atmosphere and internal music of this windowed shell – is movement, choice of direction, the pursuit of self-determined private purposes. All the other shells are moving, in comparable ways but for their own different private ends. They are not so much other people, in any full sense, but other units which signal and are signalled to, so that private mobilities can proceed safely and relatively unhindered. And if all this is seen from outside as in deep ways determined, or in some sweeping glance as dehumanised, that is not at all how it feels like inside the shell, with people you want to be with, going where you want to go.

Thus at a now dominant level of social relations, systems quite other than settlement, or in any of its older senses community, are both active and continually reproduced. The only disturbance is when movements from quite outside them – movements which are the real workings of the effective but taken-for-granted public system – slow the flow, change the prices, depreciate or disrupt the employee-consumer connection: forcing a truly public world back into a chosen and intensely valued privacy.

The international market in every kind of commodity receives its deep assent from this system of mobile-privatised social relations. From the shell, whether house or car or employment, the only relevant calculations are the terms of continuing or improving its own conditions. If buying what such calculations indicate, from another nominal 'nation', leads directly or indirectly to the breaking or weakening of other people's shells, 'too bad' do we say? But the connections are not often as direct as that. They work their way through an immensely complicated and often unreadable market system. The results emerge as statistics, or as general remarks in television. Mainly what is wrong, we usually conclude, is what all those other shells are doing.

The fiercest drives of the modern international capitalist market are to extend and speed up these flows across nominal frontiers, these mutual if uneven penetrations that are properly called (including by some of the most surprising people) 'aggressive marketing'. If there is a fen of tended strawberries or an orchard valley of apples, each corning to fruit, it is of positive advantage, we are told, that at the crucial moment an entrepreneur who might be your neighbour ships in foreign strawberries or apples at a lower price, leaving your produce to be ploughed in or to rot. What is visible and wretched (and an annual occurrence) in grown natural produce is as wretched but less visible when it happens to every other kind of production. Thus a planned penetration or disruption of other people's economies, by the strongest national economies and by the multinational companies which are already operating without respect to frontiers, is offered as unambiguously in the general good. If you suffer from it, many more others benefit. All you have to do or can do is cut your costs and improve your product. If you cannot sufficiently do either, you must become redundant; go bankrupt; get out of the way of the leaner and fitter; join the real world.

It is an evil system, by all fully human standards. But what has then to be asked is why 'it' still has need of nations, of loyalty and patriotism, of an exaltation of flags and frontiers when the frontiers are only there to be economically dismantled and the flags, if the calculations come out that way, are quickly exchanged for flags of convenience? Why, in sum, in a modern free-trade capitalist international economy, have 'nations' at all?

7

The most dedicated consumer can only ingest so much. For other human needs, beyond consumption, other relationships and conceptions of other people are necessary. Similarly the market, great god as it is, can only exchange so much. It can produce and sell weapons, but it cannot, in any generally effective way, protect people. It can move and regulate producers and consumers, but it cannot meet all the essentially non-profitable human needs of nurture and care, support and comfort, love and fidelity, membership and belonging.

Where then will these needs be met? The current orthodoxy rules off many of them as private, not public matters at all. Yet it is surely a public matter that there are now in materially rich societies so many neglected, deprived, emotionally dissatisfied and emotionally disabled people; so many problems of loneliness and of unbearable while undrugged depressions, tensions, despairs. Leave all that to the market? But the decision-makers know, even if some of them keep working to forget, that this would be unacceptable and dangerous. It is a matter then of where the lines are drawn. A welfare state, a health service, an education system: the mainstream political parties move through these with differences of degree. It is where something national – 'national assistance' – is still necessary but at levels to be negotiated, subject always to the needs of 'the economy'. Protection? Now that is another matter. Even the market itself, to say nothing of its luckiest beneficiaries, cannot stand unprotected among so many random and unpredictable individual wills. Thus 'law and order'; armed forces called a 'defence force' even when some of their weapons are obviously aggressive: these, unambiguously, are the real functions of a state. And then the basis of a state is a nation, and the circle is squared.

It can, be seen either way: as a cynical retention of just those nation-state powers which defend the existing social and economic order and head off, at minimum cost, movements of discontent which its enemies might exploit; or as a more generous if still limited recognition that there are social purposes which must still be sustained, if necessary by protection from the market. It matters very much which of these interpretations is at any particular time more true – for indeed, as purposes and methods, they vary and fluctuate. But it matters even more to see that on either interpretation there is a nation-state which does not even claim to be a full society. What it actually is, whether cynically or generously, is a deliberately partial system: not a whole lived order but a willed and selected superstructure.

This is the functional significance of its artifices. It is significant that the aggressive radical Right who are now in power in so many countries combine a pro-State rhetoric and practice, in military forces and a heavily policed law-and-order, with an anti-State rhetoric and practice in social welfare and the domestic economy, and in international monetary and trading exchange. This can be said, in a comforting way, to be a 'contradiction', but it is better seen as an open and class-based division of powers which is a genuine adjustment to an intensely competitive and profoundly unstable late capitalist world.

The national statism is to preserve a coherent domestic social order, both for general purposes and as a way of meeting the consequences of its commitment to open 'international' competition. It permits the ruin of certain 'national' industries by exposure to full transnational competition, but it does this as a way of enforcing transnational efficiency in what remains: the efficiency, indeed, of 'the Yookay', no longer a society but a market sector. At the same time it permits and even encourages the outflow of socially gathered capital (in pension funds and insurance and in the more general money market) to investment in whatever area of the global economy brings the highest money returns. So far as it can, against the established interests of communities and workers who are still its political electorate, it withdraws what it sees as distorting or enervating support for its own 'national' enterprises.

Thus an ideal condition is relentlessly pursued. First, the economic efficiency of a global system of production and trade, to include a reorganised and efficient 'national' sector within an open and inter-penetrating market flow. But at the same time a socially organised and socially disciplined population, one from which effort can be mobilised and taxes collected along the residual but still effect-ive national lines; there are still no effective political competitors in that. It is to this model of 'a people' that the rhetoric of an increasingly superficial and frenetic nationalism is applied, as a way of over-riding all the real and increasing divisions and conflicts of interest within what might be the true nation, the actual and diverse people.

I repeat that this is a genuine adjustment to late twentieth-century conditions. It is a conscious programme to regulate and contain what would otherwise be intolerable divisions and confusions. Moreover, there is no way back from it to some simple and coherent national-ism. Some alternative programmes are now being offered, combining a recovery of full political and military sovereignty with a national economic recovery plan, including heavy domestic investment and controls on the export of capital and on selected imports. It is at first sight very surprising that this fails to strike any resonant 'national' chord. But this is the real complication, that this kind of emphasis on the nation-state taking control of a national political and economic life contradicts very openly the practices and ideals of market mobility and free consumer choice. To substantiate 'nationality' at the neces-sary depth, for alternative policies, means drawing on resources in active social relations which both mobile privatisation and consum-erism and the most superficial and alienated versions of nationalism and patriotism have seriously weakened.

Thus 'nationalisation' is not perceived as connected to 'national-ism'. It is widely seen as an alien intrusion, from the other side of the statist coin. Meanwhile 'patriotism' has been so displaced to its func-tional images – the monarchy, the heritage, the armed forces, the flag – that alternative policies not only do not connect with them but by talking about other emphases and priorities often literally contradict them. Thus a 'nationalising' programme can be perceived as 'unpat-riotic' – 'unBritish', 'unAmerican' – while a transnational strategy, pursued even to the point where a national economy loses heavily within unrestricted competition, is by its structural retention of the most artificial national images perceived as the 'patriotic' course.

8

What headway can be made against such intolerable confusions? Little or none, I judge, by the familiar intellectual jump to this or that universality. It is not in the mere negation of existing social perceptions that different forces can be generated. It is in two positive and connected initiatives: first, the cultural struggle for actual social identities; and second, the political definition of effective self-governing societies. I will first consider these separately.

What is most intolerable and unreal in existing projections of 'England' or 'Britain' is their historical and cultural ignorance. 'The Yookay', of course, is neither historical nor cultural; it is a jargon term of commercial and military planning. I remember a leader of the Labour Party, opposing British entry to the European Community, asserting that it would be the end of 'a thousand years of history'. Why a thousand, I wondered. The only meaningful date by that reckoning would be somewhere around 1066, when a Norman-French replaced a Norse-Saxon monarchy. What then of the English? That would be some fifteen hundred years. The British? Some two thousand five hundred. But the real history of the peoples of these islands goes back very much further than that: at least six thousand years to the remarkable societies of the Neolithic shepherds and farmers, and back beyond them to the hunting peoples who did not simply disappear but are also among our ancestors. Thus the leader of a nominally popular party could not in practice think about the realities of his own people. He could not think about their history except in the alienated forms of a centralised nation-state. And that he deployed these petty projections as a self-evident argument against attempts at a wider European identity would be incomprehensible, in all its actual and approved former-European reorganisations, if the cultural and historical realities had not been so systematically repressed by a functional and domineering selective 'patriotism'.

All the varied peoples who have lived on this island are in a substantial physical sense still here. What is from time to time projected as an 'island race' is in reality a long process of successive conquests and repressions but also of successive supersessions and relative integrations. All the real processes have been cultural and historical, and all the artificial processes have been political, in one after another dominative proclamation of a state and an identity. It is obvious that there can now be no simple return to any of what may be seen as layers of this long social and physical process. But it should be equally obvious that this long and unfinished process cannot reasonably be repressed by versions of a national history and a patriotic heritage which deliberately exclude its complexities and in doing so reject its many surviving and diverse identities. Thus the real inheritance of these hundreds of diverse and unevenly connecting generations cannot be reduced to a recent and originally alien monarchy or to a flag which in its very form records their enforced political unification. The consequences of the long attempts to suppress or override a surviving and remade Irish identity ought to show, clearly enough, the bloody stupidity of the prevailing versions of patriotism. Yet characteristically the consequences are functionally projected to the Irish themselves, butts of hatred or of complacent jokes. Again, it is a common ruling-class cultural habit, carefully extended by most schools, to identify with the Roman imperial invaders of Britain against what are called the mere 'native tribes'. Can such people monopolise 'patriotism'? In practice yes, since many of those whose actual ancestors were slaughtered and enslaved have reconstructed them in the images dispensed by their conquerors: savages in skins; even, in comic-strip culture, cavemen.

I do not know how far any real knowledge of the physical and cultural history of the peoples of this island might prevail against the stupidities of this narrow orthodox perspective. I cannot believe that it would make no difference, and I am encouraged by the growing positive interest in these misrepresented and obscured pasts. But at any time what has also to be faced is the effective stage of their current integration. It is here that there is now a major problem in the most recent immigrations of more visibly different peoples. When these interact with the most recent selective forms of identity – 'the true-born Englishman' who apart from an occasional afterthought is made to stand for the whole complex of settled native and earlier-immigrant peoples; or the imperial 'British', who in a new common identity used economic and military advantages to rule a hundred peoples across the world and to assume an inborn superiority to them – the angry confusions and prejudices are obvious.

At the same time many generations of formerly diverse peoples have experienced and adapted to a differently rooted though overlapping social identity, and as at all earlier stages of relative integration are at best deeply uncertain of, at worst openly hostile to, newcoming other peoples. This is the phenomenon now crudely interpreted as 'racism'. It is not that there is no actual racism: it flows without difficulty from the most recent selective forms, as it flowed also, in modern times, against the Irish and the Jews. But it is a profound misunderstanding to refer all the social and cultural tensions of the arrival of new peoples to these ideological forms. The real working of ideology, both ways, can be seen in that most significant of current exchanges, when an English working man (English in the terms of the sustained modern integration) protests at the arrival or presence of 'foreigners' or 'aliens', and now goes on to specify them as 'blacks', to be met by the standard liberal reply that 'they are as British as you are'. Many people notice the ideological components of the protest: the rapid movement, where no other terms are available, from resentment of unfamiliar neighbours to the ideological specifications of 'race' and 'superiority'. But what of the ideology of the reply? It is employing, very plainly, a merely legal definition of what it is to be 'British'. At this strict level it is necessary and important, correctly asserting the need for equality and protection within the laws. Similarly, the most active legal (and communal) defence of dislocated and exposed groups and minorities is essential. But it is a serious misunderstanding, when full social relations are in question, to suppose that the problems of social identity are resolved by formal definitions. For unevenly and at tunes precariously, but always through long experience substantially, an effective awareness of social identity depends on actual and sustained social relationships. To reduce social identity to formal legal definitions, at the level of the state, is to collude with the alienated superficialities of 'the nation' which are the limited functional terms of the modern ruling class.[2]

That even some socialists should reply in such terms – socialists who should entirely depend on deeply grounded and active social identities – is another sign of the prepotence of market and exchange relations. One reason is that many minority liberals and socialists, and especially those who by the nature of their work or formation are themselves nationally and internationally mobile, have little experience of those rooted settlements from which, though now under exceptionally severe complications and pressures, most people still derive their communal identities. Many socialists are influenced by universalist propositions of an ideal kind, such as the international proletariat overcoming its national divisions. Many liberals are

influenced by North American thought, where for historical reasons a massively diverse mobility was primarily integrated at legal and
functional levels. There can then be a rapid intellectual supersession
of all the complex actualities of settled but then dislocated and relocated communities, to the point where some vanguard has a clear set
of general 'social' positions only to find that the majority of its nominally connected people have declined to follow it. When this turns,
as sometimes, to abusing them, there is a certain finality of defeat.

A socialist position on social identity certainly rejects, absolutely,
the divisive ideologies of 'race' and 'nation', as a ruling class functionally employs them. But it rejects them in favour of lived and formed
identities either of a settled kind, if available, or of a possible kind,
where dislocation and relocation require new formation. It happens
that I grew up in an old frontier area, the Welsh border country,
where for centuries there was bitter fighting and raiding and repression and discrimination, and where, within twenty miles of where I
was born, there were in those turbulent centuries as many as four different everyday spoken languages. It is with this history in mind that
I believe in the practical formation of social identity – it is now very
marked there – and know that necessarily it has to be lived. Not far
away there are the Welsh mining valleys, into which in the nineteenth
century there was massive and diverse immigration, but in which,
after two generations, there were some of the most remarkably solid
and mutually loyal communities of which we have record. These are
the real grounds of hope. It is by working and living together, with
some real place and common interest to identify with, and as free
as may be from external ideological definitions, whether divisive or
universalist, that real social identities are formed. What would have
seemed impossible, at the most difficult stages, either in that border
country or in those mining valleys, has indeed been achieved, though
this does, not mean that it happens naturally; there are other cases,
as in the north of Ireland, where history and external ideologies still
divide people and tear them apart.[3]

This connects with the second emphasis: on the redefinition
of effective self-governing societies. It is now very apparent, in the
development of modern industrial societies, that the nation-state,
in its classical European forms, is at once too large and too small
for the range of real social purposes. It is too large, even in the old

342

nation-states such as Britain, to develop full social identities in their real diversity. This is not only a problem of the minority peoples – Scots or Welsh or Irish or West Indian – but of the still significantly different cultures which are arbitrarily relegated to 'regions'. In this situation, imposed artificial definitions of 'Britishness', of 'the United Kingdom' and 'The Yookay', of the 'national interest' and of 'nationwide' lines of communication, are in practice ways of ratifying or overriding unequal social and economic development, and of containing the protests and resentments of neglected and marginalised regions and minorities within an imposed general 'patriotism'. The major economic and political divergence of the North and the South-East of even the supposedly unified and clamorous 'England' is an obvious current example.

It is clear that if people are to defend and promote their real interests, on the basis of lived and worked and placeable social identities, a large part of the now alienated and centralised powers and resources must be actively regained, by new actual societies which in their own terms, and nobody else's, define themselves. All effective socialist policies, over the coming generations, must be directed towards this practice, for it is only in the re-emphasis or formation of these full, active social identities that socialism itself – which depends absolutely on authentic ideas of a society – can develop. In particular, it is only in these ways, as identifiable communities and regions are broken by movements of the national or international market, that there is the possibility of overcoming those reductive identities as mobile consumers which positively depend on advantage and affluence.

At the same time it is obvious that for many purposes not only these more real societies but also the existing nation-states are too small. The trading, monetary and military problems which now show this to be true, and which have so heavily encroached on the supposed 'sovereignty' of the nation-states, would not disappear in any movement to placeable communal self-management. It is not necessarily true that they would become more difficult. Many of the toughest trading and monetary problems flow directly from the system of international capitalist competition, and quite new forms of planned external trade would be possible in societies which genuinely began from the interests of their own people rather than from the interests of a 'national' ruling class integrated in and serving the international economy. The military problems are also very difficult, but it can now be seen that it is the arbitrary formation of generalised hostile blocs, overriding the diversities of real popular interests, which increasingly endangers rather than assures our necessary defence and security.

We cannot say, at any level, that these placeable self-managing societies could be 'sovereign'. Even to say that they could be 'autonomous' is taking a very limited sense. What has really to be said is different: that we have to explore new forms of *variable* societies, in which over the whole range of social purposes different sizes of society are defined for different kinds of issue and decision. In practice some of this now happens, as in the supposed 'division of powers' between local, regional, national and international bodies. But this is a false kind of division. The local and regional are in practice, as their names indicate, essentially subordinate to and dependent on the national. What goes through to an international level is first centralised or simply substituted by this national system ('it is felt *in London*'; '*Britain* has refused to ratify the Law of the Sea'). Meanwhile many of the most effective international forms – not only the multinational corporations but also the World Bank and the International Monetary Fund – are in effect wholly irresponsible to any full actual societies; indeed it is often their specific business to override them.

A variable socialism – the making of many socialisms – could be very different. There would be an absolute refusal of overriding national and international bodies which do not derive their specified powers directly from the participation and negotiation of actual self-governing societies. At a different level, there would be a necessary openness to all the indispensable means of mutual support and encouragement, directly and often diversely (bilaterally as well as in variable multilateral groupings) negotiated from real bases. Moreover, much of this negotiation would be at least in part direct, rather than through the necessarily alienating procedures of 'all-purpose representatives'. The true advantages of equal exchange, and of rooted contacts and mobilities, would be more fully realised in this variable socialism than in the current arbitrary mobilities, or in any merely defensive reversion to smaller societies and sovereignties.

To bring together these two emphases – on the cultural struggle for actual social identities, and on the political redefinition of effective self-governing societies – is, I believe, to indicate a new and substantial kind of socialism which is capable both of dealing with the complexities of modern societies and also of re-engaging effective and practical popular interests.

Very much remains to be done by way of detailed discussions and proposals, but we cannot in any case live much longer under the confusions of the existing 'international' economy and the existing 'nation-state'. If we cannot find and communicate social forms of more substance than these, we shall be condemned to endure the accelerating pace of false and frenetic nationalisms and of reckless and uncontrollable global transnationalism. Moreover, even endurance is then an optimistic estimate. These are political forms that now limit, subordinate and destroy people. We have to begin again with people and build new political forms.

Notes

1. The Falklands War (Spanish: *Guerra de las Malvinas*) was a ten-week undeclared war between Argentina and the United Kingdom in 1982, disputing two British-dependent territories in the South Atlantic: the Falkland Islands and its territorial dependency, South Georgia and the South Sandwich Islands. See Stuart Hall, 'The Empire Strikes Back', in *The Hard Road to Renewal: Thatcherism and the Crisis of the Left* (London: Verso, 1988), pp. 68–74. 'More scandalous than the sight of Mrs Thatcher's best hopes going out with the navy has been the demeaning spectacle of the Labour front bench leadership rowing its dinghy as rapidly as it can in hot pursuit' (p. 74).

2. This passage is the basis for Paul Gilroy's influential accusation that Williams endorsed 'the presuppositions of the new racism'. Paul Gilroy, *'There Ain't No Black in the Union Jack': the Cultural Politics of Race and Nation* (1987; Chicago: Chicago University Press, 1991), p. 50. This critique relies on the occlusion of Williams's Welsh-European identity. See my Introduction and Afterword to this volume for an alternative interpretation.

3. This paragraph is a striking example of what Stefan Collini describes as the 'omnivorous present' in Williams's work, that is, the way in which the past continues to be seemingly alive in the present. See Stefan Collini, *The Nostalgic Imagination: History in English Criticism* (Oxford: Oxford University Press, 2019), p. 173. Williams theorises this process in the distinction made between residual, emergent and dominant forces in *Marxism and Literature* (Oxford: Oxford University Press, 1977), pp. 121–7.

DECENTRALISM AND THE POLITICS OF PLACE

Raymond Williams, *Resources of Hope*
(London: Verso, 1989), pp. 238-44.
First published in a slightly shorter form
as 'Nationalisms and Popular Socialism',
Radical Wales, 2 (Spring 1984), 7-8.[1]

*In your recent writing the questions of territory, national movements, and
so on have figured prominently. Does this mean that for you national
movements are essentially progressive forces?*
It is important to make a distinction about nationalism in the context of the unitary British state. There are two kinds of nationalism.
There is that nationalism which reinforces the idea of the traditional
nation-state. This nationalism has been given added impetus under
the Thatcher governments as we saw at the time of the Falklands/
Malvinas episode.[2] But this kind of nationalism is also shared
by the Labour Party, as was so vividly revealed by their support for
the British intervention in the South Atlantic. The other kind of
nationalism is that which questions the whole basis of the unitary
British state. I think that the first kind of nationalism is reactionary
and the second is progressive. This argument starts from the analysis
that existing nation-states of the size of Britain are both too small
and too large for useful politics. They are too small because of the
nature of the international economy and the structure of military
politics. The average nation-state simply cannot be independent.
And if it pretends to be, it has to carry this off through a falsification
which seeks to cover up the fact that it is subordinated to the larger
thing and driven by wider forces than those which can be internally

controlled. This dishonesty leaves the nation-state morally and politically extremely vulnerable.

The argument that the nation-state of Britain is too large derives from the given unevenness of development and the diversity of areas within. These conditions make it impossible to have policy-making in a general sense dominated by a single centre. Then you ask the question: What are the genuine alternative units capable of developing a politics speaking to the interests of the people rather than the unjustified units of a presumed nation-state? Where there is a national entity such as Wales or Scotland, there is already a measure of self-definition, a real base. But it does not only occur in such places. There may well be another base to be found in large cities such as London and Liverpool. These are refusing to submit their perceived interests to the nation-state interest. This is a pragmatic analysis on my part – there is an objective need for alternative definitions having relevance to definable numbers of people.

Places like London are having their attempts to satisfy real popular needs stopped by the central machine. This of course reproduces the case that has been made in Wales and Scotland for a long time. There are perceived needs, there is the possibility of political majorities which are not to be mocked, we are talking of large numbers of people – yet they are all reduced to the subordinate sense of 'locality'. This is doubly wrong when the nation-state is both subordinating, yet not large enough to manage, its own affairs.

Does this open up the prospect of alliances between the new urban Left and the old depressed industrial regions?
Yes, although clearly it first raises the prospect of competition between the newly depressed cities and the older depressed regions. Yet all these places are suffering. But one thing is clear, they may agree on the causes of their suffering but you can't make much of an alliance out of negatives; the only real basis of alliances is agreement on positive proposals for transcending the negatives. This needs nothing less than the reconstruction of the Left on a new basis. Left policy would no longer be attached to the nation-state itself. Whether the Labour Party can do that given its attachment to the nation-state remains in serious doubt. But electoral defeat has provided the basis

for recasting the Left – there is a new political activity in the cities and regions. These are natural units of government which also relate to wider issues.

There are of course, massive problems in Wales and Scotland, where the Labour Party has a mixed record, especially because of its attachment to a centralized nation-state and associated policies. The politics of alliances are very difficult and it would be impossible for the national movements of Wales and Scotland to work with old-style Labourist policies, but not so much so with the new urban Left. The real problem with traditional politics is that where alliances have existed they have been leadership alliances and thus of very limited usefulness. It's basically no good if only the leadership engages in alliance-building; if alliances are to happen they will come from the people rejecting leadership and building a popular base. A problem of the Left is that, often, ideas are good; leadership, even, may be satisfactory, but there is an inadequate popular base.

This seems to me to be one of the problems with the Hobsbawm thesis, which has become rather popular in left intellectual circles of late.[3] I mean the idea that there needs to be some form of agreement between opposition parties to prevent them cutting their own throats and keeping a Thatcher government in virtually permanent office. It is, once again, an alliance of negatives, the priority being to unite against an immediate evil rather than concentrating upon the development of a truly popular programme with mass support from below. Then, a popular front, as it were, might be a feasible proposition. I think territorially based popular mobilization may be a way forward here.

Reading Towards 2000 *one is struck by the extent to which a policy of decentralist socialism is argued for. Can you say something about the development of this conviction in your thinking?*
In the 1960s and 1970s I felt close to the arguments being put forward by nationalists leading up to and during the devolution debate. I even joined the Welsh party for a year or two; however, I found it difficult to discharge my obligations living at a distance from Wales. I felt my thinking on culture and community was more reflected there than in the Labour Party then or now. When I said this I didn't fully

realize the complexities of nationalism in Wales, especially its trad-itional difficulty with adhering to fully socialist principles of common ownership. The support it gets from rural areas is clearly not based on a demand for the common ownership of land, for example. I was told at the time by those inside and outside that I was idealizing it, but many of its ideas remain closer to me than those of the contem-porary Labour Party. I think there was just a coming together – a tendency and a movement on the ground developing against cen-tralism. But, of course, it's not just in that context that I've found shared ideas; I find I'll also come across it with one kind of Swede, Yugoslav, or American. I saw socialism differently from the English Fabian or English Marxist intelligentsia – I still get rebukes from them for being too community-conscious and not universal enough. But, of course, English middle-class universality is something of a contradiction in terms!

You've mentioned the significance of Wales for your thinking on the question of decentralism, but Wales is a subject to which you've often returned in your more general analyses. What, for example, has the Welsh experience of capitalism taught you in particular?
Well, really, that's how I learnt it in large part. I was in a border position, close to a formative industrial experience but also seeing what happened to rural Wales. It was a simultaneous transformation producing curious effects. There was a new Wales of the industrial valleys, and the old Wales of emptying rural areas. The relations between them have always been fraught and this uneasiness is repro-duced in Welsh political thinking, which is very complex here. But there is now the possibility of getting beyond this division based on competition between the urban and the rural areas of Wales. Both these separated orders are becoming relatively old. There was the question of how to relate the new boisterous South Wales to the old rural Wales, but when you get the particular experience of continu-ing depression affecting both, there is the possibility of transcending the old divisions. I'm particularly struck by the situation of rural Wales where strange things are occurring – outside financial capital is putting pressure on farmers, the Common Market fragments the farming community along deeper class lines.

There is, of course, a problem here, that of arriving at a point where unity is being stressed through more negatives. Nevertheless this fracturing of the old urban and rural bases is going on and it is powerful outside interests that are responsible equally for the sufferings both of urban and rural societies.

You've stressed the importance of 'bonding' in Politics and Letters *and* Towards 2000. *Is the kind of bonding you write of in older industrial regions necessarily tied to their particular experience and therefore of only limited general relevance?*
This is very difficult and I admit I'm uncertain. Bonding in traditional societies – as studied anthropologically – is very evident. You can pick out the economic, political and cultural elements of bonding. There is a most complex relationship between socialism and bonding for the following reason. What socialism offered was the priority of one kind of bonding – trade unionism, the class bond – this cancelled all other bonds. This, of course, accounts for the hostility to nationalism and the irrelevance of religious movements, as well as the curious attitude towards the family on the part of some socialists. So there are other bonding mechanisms in reality which are beyond either national consciousness or class consciousness. One crisis for socialism comes from this. Where economic bonding had occurred and socialism had developed to as high a point as was then known, has it always been the case that bonds of other kinds were analytically suppressed? For, historically, it seems to me to be more and more true that where centres of proletarian consciousness developed, their strength really drew from the fact that all the bonds were holding in the same direction. This has become much clearer to me from the experience of the women's movement, where more than one kind of bonding has made for exceptionally penetrative political practice and significant success. Aspects of the peace movement come to mind from a similar non-territorially particular viewpoint. But to return to your question, there is a possible way out of the analytical problem of an overnarrow emphasis on the bond of economic experience. This was always the specialized version of socialism. A new theory of socialism must now centrally involve *place*. Remember the argument was that the proletariat had no country, the factor which differentiated it from the

property-owning classes. But place has been shown to be a crucial element in the bonding process – more so perhaps for the working class than the capital-owning classes – by the explosion of the international economy and the destructive effects of deindustrialization upon old communities. When capital has moved on, the importance of place is more clearly revealed.

In writing about 'bonding' you have drawn heavily on the experience of established regional communities such as Clydeside and South Wales. It could be argued that you romanticize proletarian cultures, especially in the light of their subordination of women and often narrow focus on wage struggles. How would you respond to such a criticism?
The old socialism excluded the reality of women and families. Women gave generations of support to their men and received no recognition for it. This must change and the lessons to be learnt from the analyses of the women's movement are that it will change, and if socialists are not to lose a substantial part of their potential constituency they had better come to terms with the problem very quickly.

As far as the wage-bargain is concerned – what elsewhere I've called militant particularism – I can see why these men did it. I'll explain why obliquely. I'm doing a new novel at the moment. It starts in the 1930s with a meeting between some Oxbridge socialists and representatives of the Welsh working class, although most of it is set in the postwar period.[4] In researching the novel I came across a quotation from Arthur Horner, the miners' leader from Wales, who said that 'labour is a commodity like any other. Employers have to buy it, so I want to control it.'[5] This is understandable, but of course it reproduces the language of capital. When you're in organized bargaining of this kind it leaves you with no moral basis against, for example, monetarist arguments. Monetarists can say 'Fine, we don't want labour now, and if that's the strong point of your argument, we can steer around it without any difficulty.' Without the first stress being on people rather than money, you have not a strong movement but a shell. So when, as in the 1983 election, the Conservatives said 'there is no alternative', some of their ground had been prepared for them already.

The implication then is that you believe in incomes policy?
There are bound to be incomes policies. Official left thinking has
occurred in compartments. Wages policy has been not to have a
wages policy. Welfare expenditure cannot somehow rise in a separate compartment. There is an increasing proportion of nonworking
population and the unemployed. Policy has to be general – integrated
– or it is opportunist. You can't run an economy on a humanized
version of market forces, then bring out the welfare policies like
Crosland suggested, any longer. I've increasingly taken the view
that, at this stage of internationalized production, there's no way
that growth is going to produce the satisfaction of people's needs.[6]
Simply, some are made affluent by it while others are made poorer.
Of course, there's a need for short-term measures to stimulate the
economy, but to think that this can be done without attending to
the distortions of market relations – in wage as well as other kinds of
market exchange – is to think fifty years in arrears.

*You clearly see the need for some degree of centralization in aspects of
economic management. But what are the mechanisms for gaining mass
popular support for socialism, given the diversity of places to which you
have drawn attention? Is the cultural level given an added importance now,
and what is the nature of a politics of culture?*
I'm conscious of this difficulty. What depresses me is that the setting for these ideas is the need for the mobilization of scattered
movements and interests. Yet the intellectual Left is concentrated
in London – it is distant from these concerns. But when people's
ideas move closer on a set of issues, history teaches us that they can
be given powerful expression despite geographical and intellectual
distance. Ideally, a new movement comes out of new ideas being
specified in particular places – then there may be a model being
expressed which is adaptable to the interests of other places and scales
of operation. These can be ideas relating to long- or short-term real
interests and the policies which express them. It is perfectly clear
that ideas have to federate – it's in the nature of the analysis. The
difficulty comes not least because of the existence of the old Labour
Party nationalism, its tradition of metropolitan centralism (what I've
referred to in a more general context as metropolitan provincialism)

and its tradition of short-term electoral politics, and leadership geared to precisely that. It is difficult to produce ideas for a single place; it needs lots of people with skills being brought together. This is very difficult, especially as intellectuals will work in campaigns such as disarmament, the ecological movement and on questions of the economy. But there is little bringing together of these energies. It would happen more quickly – this bringing together – if it happened in a place. There are no shortcuts, but to some extent the Greater London Council has focused this in London.[7] It could be a model.

What do you see as the future for decentralized political mobilization, given the strong centralizing forces operating in such areas as the mass media?
This is difficult. All I'd say is we're entering a phase of cultural politics with both more risks and opportunities. The monopoly of centralized public broadcasting authorities coinciding with current nation-state electoral politics is going to be overtaken by a rough international force with the coming of cable TV. I see the public authorities as the agents of a centralized, perniciously *mass* media as represented in absurdities such as *Nationwide* or *Sixty Minutes*. The operators of cable are not, of course, in the business of decentralized socialism. But there are real possibilities and opportunities for entry into cable at a time when the centralized forces are weakening. Small organizations, parties, interest groups could get time at low cost. The Left has to see this as an opportunity as well as a threat. Greater dispersion does mean the flooding in of foreign material. But in somewhere with a distinctive linguistic and cultural base such as Wales, this happens now anyway. Getting a policy on community cable is acting positively. The Left must move out of its old phase. The new political economy of TV will be smaller audiences, such as Channel 4 experiences, based on communities of interest. If we can work it out, we can connect to these multichannel networks. This is one of the most interesting and possibly rewarding challenges faced by decentralist politics for the future.

Notes
1. The interview was conducted by Philip Cooke, at the time a reader in Town Planning at the University of Wales College of Cardiff, and a member of

the editorial collective of *Radical Wales*. The interview took place in January 1984.

2. On the Falklands War, see 'The Culture of Nations', n. 1.

3. Eric Hobsbawm (1917–2012) was a leading Marxist historian. See 'Are We Becoming More Divided?', n. 1. See also the essays collected in Eric Hobsbawm, *Politics for a Rational Left* (London: Verso, 1989). For Williams's critique of Hobsbawm's position, see 'Socialists and Coalitionists' (1984), in *Resources of Hope* (London: Verso, 1989), pp. 175–85.

4. The novel was published as *Loyalties* (London: Chatto & Windus, 1985).

5. Arthur Lewis Horner (1894–1968) was a Welsh trade union leader and Communist politician, President of the South Wales Miners Federation (SWMF) from 1936, and General Secretary of the National Union of Mineworkers (NUM) from 1946. See Nina Fishman, *Arthur Horner: A Political Biography: Volume 1 1894–1944; Volume 2 1944–1968* (London: Lawrence & Wishart, 2010).

6. Charles Anthony Raven Crosland (1918–77), known as Anthony or Tony Crosland, was a British Labour Party politician and author.

7. The Greater London Council (GLC) was the top-tier local government administrative body for Greater London from 1965 to 1986. The socialist Ken Livingstone (1945–) led the GLC from 1981 until 1986, offering a starkly different political vision to that espoused by the 1979–90 Conservative government of Margaret Thatcher (1925–2013).

THE PRACTICE OF POSSIBILITY

New Statesman (7 August 1987), 19–21.

Collected as 'The Politics of Hope: an interview', in Terry Eagleton (ed.), *Raymond Williams: Critical Perspectives* (Cambridge: Polity Press, 1989), pp. 176–83; and as 'The Practice of Possibility', in Raymond Williams, *Resources of Hope* (London: Verso, 1989), pp. 314–22.[1]

You retired from the chair of drama at Cambridge University in 1983, after a long career on the political Left which still continues. You fought Fascism in Europe, and took a major role in the creation of the early New Left and the early years of CND. Since then you've been involved in a whole series of socialist interventions, both inside and outside the Labour Party, and your intellectual work – what you've come to call 'cultural materialism' – has transformed the thinking of generations of students and workers in the cultural field.

It would have been nice to have been able to present you on your retirement, not with a gold clock, but with a socialist society. It's arguable, however, that such a goal is now as remote, if not more so, as at any time in your political career. Instead we are witnessing the most viciously anti-working-class regime of most people's political memory, the laying of the groundwork of a police state, and an apparently baffled left opposition. Militarily speaking we live in the most terrible danger. Could I ask you, then, whether after so long a struggle you now feel in any sense disillusioned? What are your political thoughts and hopes, immediately after the election of a third Thatcher government?

Disillusionment, not at all; disappointment, of course. Yet looking back it seems to me I absorbed some of these disappointments quite early on, so the recent ones didn't come as so much of a surprise.

Indeed I was so thrown out of my early expectations, as a young man and a soldier in the war, by the events of 1947 that I went into a kind of retreat for a year or two, trying to work out a different kind of intellectual project, which also involved a sense of what a different political project might be. This was a time, remember, when the expectations of a Labour government, which had been the whole perspective of my childhood, had been not just disappointed but actively repulsed: the priority of the military alliance with the USA over Labour's quite real achievements in welfare, the use of troops against groups of striking workers and so on. So the crisis for me was an early one; and perhaps this partly explains why the crisis of 1956 didn't come as so much of a shock for me as it did for some of those intellectuals who had stayed in the Communist Party. There was then a sense of reinvigoration in the late 1950s, which carried on throughout the sixties in the various attempts at some new gathering of left forces. When that went down, in 1970, there was of course a sense of setback and defeat; but I think that whole history had prepared me emotionally and intellectually for the failures which the Left was then to go through.

When all of this passed into the period of open reaction of the Thatcher governments, it seemed to me that the Left was repeatedly trying to reconstitute the very limited kind of hope that I'd repeatedly seen fail. The rhetoric of victory in 1945 is in a sense fair enough, but it shouldn't convince anyone unless it is immediately qualified by the realities of 1947–8. The rhetoric of the (supposedly) successful Labour governments of the 1960s is for me similarly qualified by the events of 1968 – that very confused time in which the attempt to feed new currents of ideas and feelings into the labour movement was not merely ignored but, again, actually repulsed.

Today, it's clearer to me than ever that the socialist analysis is the correct one, and its correctness has been in my view repeatedly demonstrated. But the perspectives which had sustained the main left organizations were simply not adequate to the society they were seeking to change. There was always the attempt on the Left to reconstitute old models: the notion of 'uniting Britain', to take an example from recent electoral rhetoric, or of an autonomous sovereign economy – as if what's happened in international capitalism over the past forty years simply hadn't happened. When they fight in these terms, what can and should be fought for becomes much more difficult to define.

What then should be fought for? Are you suggesting a wholly different strategy for the Left?
The strategy is all still to be found, but what blocks it, I'm saying, is this old model of creating a relatively powerful, united Britain with a 'successful' sovereign economy. That, I think, is what history has ruled out. And one consequence of this has been a retreat to certain areas, traditional strongholds of labour: Scotland, Wales, the north of England. But the shape of a genuine strategy would be to pass beyond this idea of altering such situations only in Britain. To adopt at least a West European perspective, where there are many people and regions in similar situations, penetrated and distorted by international capitalism and the military alliance. Any useful strategy would involve a great building up of autonomy in such regions in Britain, but instead of orienting that to the British state, looking out for the connections which can be made to Western Europe, at least in the first instance.

The obvious block to this is the electoral system which imposes the need for a national party – 'national' on this superannuated model of the British state. There follows the necessity for a coalition of left forces which everyone knows is impossible to sustain honestly. The range of opinion from liberal to far left is just too broad. Socialists want to take part in defeating something uniquely vicious, and so must be friendly to the Labour Right, or to Liberals, Social Democrats, even progressive Tories; but if you do so pretending that you share their perspective then you fail in one of your most basic duties: telling the truth as you see it.

Meanwhile a major obstacle to any socialist strategy is that the Left makes repeated attempts to remake the whole Labour Party in its own image, as distinct from maintaining, within present constraints, a socialist element. In practice, this has prevented the Labour Party from achieving the kind of unity it needs for the limited jobs it has to do. But it also means a limitation on the amount of absolutely straight socialist argument and propaganda, under the pretence of consensus. When one hears a Labour candidate, as mine did, talking about loyalty to NATO, building up a fine fleet and the rest, one knows one simply isn't living in the same world with people with whom otherwise one's prepared to be comradely and cooperative, for specific objectives. Yet while the Left still sees the wholesale conversion of a social democratic party to a socialist party as its objective, there's an important sense in which it silences itself.

If we had proportional representation, what we would rapidly get is a realignment of the centre. People talk of a realignment of the Left, but what's already beginning to happen is actually a realignment of the centre. Now such a realignment of the centre, which I think is bound to happen, just isn't the Left's business. Socialist analysis and propaganda must be made in its own terms. If there was a realignment of the centre which took the Labour Party into some unambiguous social-democratic phase, there would be in altered electoral conditions a space for some federation of socialist, Green and radical nationalist forces. This would not be insignificant electorally, and above all it would be able to speak up without equivocation for its view of the world, which at present doesn't get through politically very far. It would be dreadful for the Left in the Labour Party to try to break it up, weaken it even further, and there's no simple question of a breakaway. But in the situation I'm describing, there will be a possibility of the Left speaking in its own voice; and in a political situation as hard as this, that's not to be discounted.

Indeed; though as the crisis of capitalism has tightened, we've been witnessing a steady haemorrhage of intellectuals from the far Left. Individuals, groups, journals, whole parties have moved inexorably to the right, and this at a time – a bitter irony – when in a sense there's never been so obviously, so devastatingly what one might describe as a 'total global system', which demands an appropriately radical response. To affirm such a truth in an age of postmodernist fragmentation, however, is becoming increasingly unfashionable. To mention social class in certain so-called left circles is to be unceremoniously shown the door. Defeatism and adaptation, however 'dynamically' and modernistically tricked out, seem instead the order of the day. I once heard you refer in a nicely sardonic phrase to those who 'make long-term adjustments to short-term problems'. I wonder whether it was this treason of the clerks that you had in mind?
Well, the strength of our enemies isn't to be doubted; yet the most intelligent operators of the system itself know just how profoundly unstable it is. The whole future of a US-led, anti-Communist, anti-Third-World alliance is coming under pressure, if only from its own

internal divisions and the increasing inability of the USA to dominate it. The international financial system is a helter-skelter economy based on frightening credit expansion and credit risk, which would have terrified an earlier generation of orthodox bankers and financiers. To say this, of course, isn't to advocate some policy of waiting for the crash; for one thing such crashes aren't automatic, and for another thing they're just as likely to produce a hard Right well beyond anything we've seen so far – those who talk of the hard Right in Britain haven't really seen one. But if the system is that unstable, this clearly isn't a world to adjust to. It's not a world in which one has to settle for belonging to an eccentric minority who believe there are old socialist texts and ideas which must be kept alive, in an all too powerful and successful system. Powerful, yes; successful, no.

Meanwhile what's happened in so-called 'actually existing socialism' in Eastern Europe has done the Left more damage than can be properly accounted for. It's been a key feature in many intellectual desertions, and one difficult to argue against since of course one endorses the denunciation of terror, while recalling that such terror is in fact historically outweighed by the long, systematic terror of the Right. If it were a reason to desert socialism, because such terrible things have happened in its name, it would be a reason to desert every system we know. The Eastern European societies, however, aren't going to remain in their present condition; they know they can't sustain themselves without radical change. And this will be a positive factor for socialist intellectuals in the West.

It would sometimes seem today that a commitment to class struggle on the one hand, and a celebration of difference and plurality on the other, have been lined up on opposite sides of the left political fence. Yet both ways of thinking would seem to have subtly coexisted in your own work almost from the beginning. You've always deeply suspected closed, monolithic theories and strategies, and from the outset your socialism has stressed difficulty, complexity, variety; yet, not least in your development over the past decade or so, in the very period of some other left intellectuals' sail-trimming or simply renegacy, you would seem to hold firmly to a class perspective. How do you see the relation between these two emphases?

I've always been very aware of the complicated relationships between class and place. I've been enormously conscious of place, and still get an extraordinary amount of emotional confirmation from the sense of place and its people. Now the key argument in Marxism was always whether the proletariat would be a universal class – whether the bonds it forged from a common exploitation would be perceived as primary, and eventually supersede the more local bonds of region or nation or religion. On the one hand the recognition of exploitation continually reproduces class consciousness and organization on a universal basis. On the other hand, I don't know of any prolonged struggle of that kind in which these other issues haven't been vital, and in some cases decisive. So I'm on both sides of the argument, yes: I recognize the universal forms which spring from this fundamental exploitation – the system, for all its local variety, is everywhere recognizable. But the practice of fighting against it has always been entered into, or sometimes deflected, by these other kinds of more particular bonds.

Which of course vitally include gender. In your book The Long Revolution, *right back in 1961 and long before the resurgence of the contemporary women's movement, you identified what you saw then as four interlocking systems within any society, and named one of them as the 'system of generation and nurture'. Yet your theoretical work would seem to have preserved a relative silence on those issues; instead, perhaps, they have tended to take up home in your fiction, in which the family, generation and their connections to work and politics have figured prominently.*
That's true. It's really all in my second novel, *Second Generation*; that's what it was really all about. But at about the same time I was writing *The English Novel from Dickens to Lawrence*, where I describe the Brontë sisters as representing interests and values marginalized by the male hegemony. Not only that, however, but representing human interests of a more general kind which showed up the limits of the extraordinary disabling notion of masculinity. I remember how I used to embarrass students in my lectures – you will doubtless remember this – by suggesting it would be interesting to locate the historical moment when men stopped crying in public. The suppression of tenderness and emotional response, the willingness to admit what isn't weakness – one's feelings in and through another; all this is a repression not only

of women's experience but of something much more general. And I suppose I found it easier to explore that in more personal terms, in my novels. That's no real excuse; I ought to have been doing this in my other work too; but by the time I came to understand it in that way it was already being done by a lot of good people who were no doubt making more sense of it than I could have done.

The media, or communications as you prefer to call them, have long formed a centrepiece of your work. Although the whole concept of 'media' is surely much too passive to convey the enormous power of these institutions. The editors of the Sun, Mail *and* Express *were surely infinitely more important to Thatcher in the election than any members of her inner circle, and ought to be buried in Westminster Abbey. I mean as soon as possible. How are we to go about combatting this formidable source of political power?*
Well, one can talk of course of education – of arming people's minds against that kind of journalism. But there's now been a sustained cultural attempt to show how this manipulation works, which has hardly impinged on its actual power. I don't see how the educational response can be adequate. The manipulative methods are too powerful, too far below the belt for that. These people have to be driven out. We have to create a press owned by and responsible to its readers. The increasing concentration of power in the media has been a process strangely unresisted by socialists, by the labour movement as a whole, who have actually let go of key sectors. When I was concentrating on this kind of cultural analysis in the 1950s I was sometimes told by good Marxist friends that it was a diversion from the central economic struggle. Now every trade union and political leader cries 'the media, the media'. It was correctly foreseen that this, in electoral politics, was where the battle would be fought, but the response to that was very belated. The proposals which I put forward in my book *Communications* in the early 1960s, for a democratic control of the media, still seem to me a necessary programme.

You have turned increasingly to Wales both in your fictional and political work; you still have close, active relations, personally and politically, with Wales. Is this marginality a source of strength in your work? Or is it

simply convenient to have, so to speak, a different passport and identity
when one sallies forth among the middle-class English natives?

I think some of my Welsh friends would be kind enough to say that
if I have some importance for them it's precisely because I came out –
because I went among the English, and got a hearing, even recognition,
in their own institutions. When you're part of one of these disadvan-
taged nationalities you can be very bitter about people who have gone
off and made it elsewhere, but it can be different if you also know
they still relate to you, even if one has crossed the border rather than
remained inside it. In that sense I don't altogether regret crossing the
border, though there are times when I do. Coming from a border area
of Wales in any case, the problem for me has always been one of what
it was to be Welsh – I mean in some serious sense, rather than in one of
the exportable stage-Welsh versions. I suppose there was some group I
thought of as the real Welsh, secure in their identity, who would come
out in force and flail this returning migrant with all his doubts.

The response I've had, especially from young Welsh people, has
been precisely the opposite: thank God someone has come out and
asked who are we, what are we? All my usual famous qualifying and
complicating, my insistence on depths and ambiguities, was exactly
what they already knew. And this experience of ambiguity and contradiction hasn't only equipped us in Wales to understand our own
situation better; it's also equipped us, emotionally and intellectually,
to understand the situation of increasing numbers of people – including the once so self-assured, confident English. It's easier for us, in
other words, to put questions to those simple, confident, unitary
identities which really belong to an earlier historical period.

Let me return finally to where we began, with the question of disappointment
or despondency. What you say about the need to reject any kind of
disillusion strikes me as absolutely right. Your work has always seemed to me
distinguished by a kind of steady, profound humanism, which it would be
too facile to describe as optimism. Beneath your political writing has always
run this confident trust in human capacities – capacities so steadfast and
enduring that not to see them finally triumph in some political future would
seem not only unthinkable but, as it were, blasphemous. Perhaps I share that
belief; but let me put to you, in the spirit of devil's advocacy, an alternative

scenario. The historical record shows that such capacities have so far always been defeated. History, as Walter Benjamin might have put it, is more barbarism than progress; what you and I might consider moral and political virtue has never ruled any social order, other than briefly and untypically.[2] The real historical record is one of wretchedness and unremitting toil; and 'culture' – your and my speciality – has its dubious roots in this. How then are we to undo such a history with the very contaminated instruments it has handed us? Is socialism, in other words, anything more than a wishful thinking which runs quite against the historical grain? To put the point more personally: how far is your own trust in human creative capacities in part the product of an unusually warm and affectionate working-class childhood, of which it's in some sense the nostalgic memory?

It's true that much of my political belief is a continuation of a very early formation. I can't remember any time when I haven't felt broadly speaking as I do now, except for the period of retreat I mentioned in the 1940s, which in a sense was a kind of cancellation of the certainties I'd assumed in childhood. I ceased then to be simply a product of that culture. I don't know what I became a product of, since I couldn't accept the offered alternatives. Out of that period of radical dislocation was rebuilt what was, and I think still is, an intellectual conviction. Though of course it can't ever be only that. The crisis which came to me on the death of my father, who was a socialist and a railway worker – I haven't been able to explain this to people properly, perhaps I explained it partly in my novel *Border Country* – was the sense of a kind of defeat for an idea of value. Maybe this was an unreasonable response. All right, he died, he died too early, but men and women die. But it was very difficult not to see him as a victim at the end. I suppose it was this kind of experience which sent me in the end to the historical novel I'm now writing, *People of the Black Mountains*, about the movements of history over a very long period, in and through a particular place in Wales.[3] And this history is a record of all you say: of defeat, invasion, victimization, oppression. When one sees what was done to the people who are physically my ancestors, one feels .it to be almost incredible.

What do I get from this? Simply the confidence of survival? Yes, that in part. There's been a quite extraordinary process of self-generation and regeneration, from what seemed impossible conditions. Thomas Becket once asked a shrewd, worldly-wise official on the Marches about the nature of the Welsh.[4] 'I will show you the curious disposition of the Welsh', said the official, 'that when you hold the sword they will submit, but when they hold the sword they assert themselves.'[5] I like the deep, poker-faced joke of that. The defeats have occurred over and over again, and what my novel is then trying to explore is simply the condition of anything surviving at all. It's not a matter of the simple patriotic answer: we're Welsh, and still here. It's the infinite resilience, even deviousness, with which people have managed to persist in profoundly unfavourable conditions, and the striking diversity of the beliefs in which they've expressed their autonomy. A sense of a value which has won its way through different kinds of oppression in different forms.

If I say, estimating, for example, whether we'll avoid a nuclear war, 'I see it as 50–50', I instantly make it 51–49, or 60–40, the wrong way. That is why I say we must speak for hope, as long as it doesn't mean suppressing the nature of the danger. I don't think my socialism is simply the prolongation of an earlier experience. When I see that childhood coming at the end of millennia of much more brutal and thoroughgoing exploitation, I can see it as a fortunate time: an ingrained and indestructible yet also changing embodiment of the possibilities of common life.

Notes

1. The interview was conducted by Terry Eagleton (1943–), at the time lecturer in Critical Theory at the University of Oxford, and took place in July 1987.
2. Walter Benjamin (1892–1940) was a leading German-Jewish man of letters, and Marxist literary and cultural critic. Forced out of Berlin into exile by the Nazis in 1933, Benjamin took his own life in flight from the Gestapo in 1940. Hannah Arendt translated and edited a useful collection of writings as *Illuminations* (New York: Schocken Books, 1968).
3. On *People of the Black Mountains*, see the interview with John Barnie in this volume.
4. St Thomas Becket (?1118–70) became Archbishop of Canterbury in 1162, and was assassinated on King Henry II's orders in the cathedral at Canterbury on 29 December 1170.
5. This is how the joke appears in print. I assume that it should be reversed, with the Welsh asserting themselves without the sword and submitting while they hold it; a comment on the Welsh tendency to revolt when oppressed, but unwillingness to take power for themselves when given the opportunity. This would be in keeping with Williams's emphasis on cultural survival.

NATIONAL COMMUNITY AND GLOBAL HUMANITY

I

As you head northwest out of Wales on the A465 – that 'straight wide motor road where the lorries race' – take a left turn as you reach his native Pandy onto an unnamed country lane. By following that track for fifteen minutes through a patchwork of fields, past oaks, hollies, elms and thorns, you will arrive at the Parish Church of St Clydawg.[1]

It is said that Clydawg, king of this area in the fifth century, was killed on a hunting expedition by a rival for the hand of his betrothed. On the day of his funeral, the oxen pulling his cart refused to cross the river and he was buried at this spot near the bank of the Mynwy. His subjects considered Clydawg a martyr and would gather to worship at his tomb. A church dedicated to St Clydawg has existed here since the sixth century. As was the practice in Wales, the village that grew around the church was called a Llan (enclosure). This was Llan y Merthyr Clydawg. Today it is known, contracted and Anglicised, as Clodock.

You probably won't have realised it, but you crossed from Wales into England on the way here from Pandy. This is now Herefordshire. It was once the kingdom of Ewias and a part of Wales until the boundary was changed during the reign of Henry VIII. The parish remained under the jurisdiction of the Welsh Church until 1858, when it was included in the Diocese of Hereford. *Cymraeg* was spoken here until the mid-nineteenth century. It is in this 'received and made and remade' place that you will find the grave of Raymond Williams.[2]

The grave is in the new cemetery, on the other side of the road from the church. Make sure that you enter the church itself before leaving, for there is more than the gravestone to remember him by. As you enter, look up at the wall above the gallery stairs. You will see a large, beautiful, eighteenth-century Decalogue restored in 1989, as the small plaque beneath it tells us, 'In Memory of Professor Raymond Williams'. Given the relatively little attention paid to religion in Williams's writings and his refusal as an adolescent 'to be confirmed', which 'caused no crisis in the family', this seems on first acquaintance, in terms of location (in a church) and content (the Ten Commandments), a somewhat incongruous memorial.[3] Yet despite his father's hostility to religion and his own shifting Communist and socialist beliefs, Raymond Williams did attend chapel with his grandmother as a child, and 'went to Church' when slightly older.[4] His appeal to be released from call-up to the Korean War was based on a pacifism rooted in the 'atmosphere of Christian instruction' in which he was brought up.[5] In the shadow of that Decalogue, we might ask whether Raymond Williams's 'Welsh Trilogy' of novels should be considered a manifestation of the 'exodus politics' that Michael Walzer argues is at the root of revolutionary thought in the West? Following the tripartite structure of Walzer's analysis, is not *Border Country* an exploration of the 'house of bondage', *Second Generation* a documentation of 'murmurings in the wilderness', and *The Fight for Manod* an attempt at imagining a 'free people'?[6] What significance should we give the fact that, in Williams's novel *The Volunteers*, the Welsh are described as the 'Jews of Britain'?[7] The relationship between the universal and particular in Raymond Williams's thought may be the key to answering these questions.

II

On 11 April 1962, Hannah Arendt wrote to Raymond Williams to tell him how much she had enjoyed and profited from reading his review of her book *Between Past and Future*.[8] Williams's piece, in which he paid 'a more than ordinary tribute' to Arendt's work, appeared in *The Kenyon Review* in 1961. He described Arendt's latest study as a 'worthy and natural successor to *The Human Condition*', and as a profound meditation on 'the breakdown of tradition in our time, and the consequent effects of the loss of this natural bridge between past and future'.[9] He found much in the book to be 'genuinely clarifying', but wished 'there could be a genuine encounter between what seem to me the patterns of thought of a particular society and similar local patterns elsewhere'. Williams was addressing a tendency that he identified in Arendt's work of assuming that the American experience, where the bonds of society were allegedly being eroded by a devastating 'consumer culture', could be generalised into a truth about the contemporary world. While acknowledging that 'very powerful consumption tendencies' had appeared in Britain, Williams presented himself as a member of a group of critics who saw this as 'a particular stage of capitalism' that could be resisted and was 'capable of being beaten back'. His American contemporaries, on the other hand, seemed unable to 'look at capitalism with any sense that it is transient and replaceable'. No meaningful dialogue across the Atlantic could happen, argued Williams, if 'the processes of American society are held, consciously or unconsciously, to be universal processes'. It is only through the acceptance of the particularity and non-generalisable nature of national cultures that 'a genuine encounter' between 'a particular society and similar local patterns elsewhere' could take place.[10]

Williams's review of *Between Past and Future* amounts to a critique of the ways in which dominant groups and formations seek to pass off their particularisms as universals, and in this respect is an early articulation of one of his abiding concerns. He was – as the essays in *Who Speaks for Wales?* testify repeatedly – interested in the continuities and particularities of cultures, and on the mechanisms by which people resist domination and assimilation. He noted in 1977 that, because of 'the great continuity of the language and the awareness of the difference in the past', the Welsh retain 'the sense, which I think is very important at this stage in the twentieth century, that it is possible to *be* a different people'.[11] This defence of particularism is rarely mounted from an anti-universal position, however. C. L. R. James's observation, in a review of *Culture and Society*, that the basis of Williams's world-view 'seems to be the semi-religious "brotherhood of man"' deserves further consideration, for Williams's concern with the particular co-exists with his desire (that I emphasised in the introduction) to make connections in the name of a cultural 'wholeness', a 'common culture' or a 'general interest'.[12] Hannah Arendt, whom Williams names in the short list of acknowledgments in *Modern Tragedy* and whose *On Violence* he would later review, is an useful complement to Williams for my purposes in this afterword, concerned as I am with the tension between the universal and the particular in his writings on Wales.[13] This tension informs Arendt's work and is central to her argument that the 'concept of human rights can again be meaningful only if they are redefined to mean a right to the human condition itself', which depends upon belonging to some human community'.[14] Both Williams and Arendt ultimately came to suggest that a tolerant world is one of many particular communities and citizenships, and that dreams of universalist global orders have tended to underpin totalitarian regimes. They came to this conclusion by somewhat different routes.

Born into a secular Jewish family in Hanover in 1906, Hannah Arendt witnessed the rise of Nazism, was stripped of her German citizenship in 1937 and, having been briefly imprisoned by the Gestapo, fled Germany to Czechoslovakia and Switzerland before settling for a period in Paris. When Germany invaded France in 1940, she was detained by the French as an alien. In 1941 she escaped and made her way, via Portugal, to the United States where she remained for the rest of her life.[15] Arendt was profoundly aware of the way in which dominant discourses could obliterate the histories of others. Writing on 'Moses or Washington' in 1942, she noted that while 'Christian humanity' had 'appropriated' Jewish history for itself, 'reclaiming our heroes as humanity's heroes',

> there is paradoxically a growing number of those who believe they must replace Moses and David with Washington or Napoleon. Ultimately this attempt to forget our own past and to find youth again at the expense of strangers will fail – simply because Washington's and Napoleon's heroes were named Moses and David.[16]

In evoking 'our own' past, Arendt is asserting her Jewish identity as a vehicle for challenging forms of French and American exceptionalism. Arendt had found herself denied human rights in 1940 at the very moment when, stripped of her German citizenship, she was reduced to being human 'in general' and thus in most need of the protection of those 'universal human rights' which belong to individuals independently of citizenship. But, deprived of the particular socio-political identity that accounted for citizenship, the Jews of 1940s Europe found that they were no longer recognised as human at all. 'The world', noted Arendt in a chilling sentence, 'found nothing sacred in the abstract nakedness of being human'.[17]

Reasserting her connection with Moses and David was one response to this scenario. The other was to trace the roots of authoritarian thought. Her *The Origins of Totalitarianism* contains a remarkable chapter on 'The Decline of the Nation-state and the End of the Rights of Man'. It is here that Arendt makes a distinction between universal, pre-political, human rights possessed by every human being 'as such', and the specific political rights that one may acquire from being a political citizen of a particular nation. For Arendt, the loss of citizenship is the loss of 'the right to have rights' resulting in a 'political death'. Those in this condition 'may become objects of charity or benevolence', but they have no 'first-order' claims as citizens, 'they become non-citizens with respect to justice'.[18] The conclusion that Arendt reaches is that universal 'human rights' can only find expression within particular forms of national citizenship. There is no usable concept of human nature that can be accessed independently of particular communities. In the midst of the mass murders of the Second World War, Hannah Arendt dissociated 'race' from 'nation', 'racism' from 'nationalism', and made the case for a universalism that is rooted in the particular. Her focus was on the nation as a polity with legal and civic structures that could secure an individual's 'right to have rights'.[19]

Raymond Williams's emphasis was quite different. He argued that it was a mistake to suppose that formal definitions could resolve the problems of social identity:

> To reduce social identity to formal legal definitions, at the level of the state, is to collude in the alienated superficialities of 'the nation' which are the limited functional terms of the modern ruling class.[20]

Throughout his chapter on 'The Culture of Nations' (1983), the 'artificial' political structure of the nation-state is contrasted with an alternative form of identity variously designated as 'deeply grounded', 'settled', 'real' and 'residual'. There is some irony that Williams should be memorialised in the form of a 'Decalogue' in Clodock church, for he regarded a nation defined by laws and the tendency to espouse legal forms of national citizenship as deriving from a 'mobile' and 'detached' intellectual class.[21] What Williams offered in place of legal constitutionalism was a 'socialist position' that

> rejects, absolutely, the divisive ideologies of 'race' and 'nation' as a ruling class functionally employs them. But it rejects them in favour of lived and formed identities either of a set-tled kind, if available, or of a possible kind, where dislocation and relocation require new formation.[22]

For Williams, there is no usable concept of human nature that can be accessed independently from particular 'lived and formed identi-ties'. For Arendt, there is no usable concept of human nature that can be accessed independently from the legal and political structures of particular national communities. Despite the former focusing on cultural identity and practice, and the latter on the political structures of the state, they come to compatible conclusions.

One of the reasons that their arguments lead to similar endings, is that they share the same beginning. The celebrated section on the 'Rights to have Rights' in *The Origins of Totalitarianism* begins with a discussion of the Irish critic of the French Revolution, Edmund Burke. Burke is often seen as a foundational figure for conserva-tive thought in Britain, but in an illuminating account of Raymond Williams as a 'left Burkean', Henry Louis Gates Jr. notes that the reactionary critic of enlightenment universalism and the French Revolution may also be considered a father of cultural relativism and anti-colonialism.[23] Burke criticised the modern colonial state, cam-paigned against the British administration in India, and led an eight year prosecution of Warren Hastings, governor of Bengal and head of the East India Trading company. Luke Gibbons has emphasised the ways in which Burke, informed by Irish history, described the violence, both material and cultural, that colonialism inflicted upon subject peoples, 'whether generated by religious bigotry in Ireland, the plunder of Warren Hastings in India, or the sordid excesses of British military policy during the American Revolution'.[24] Burke's emphasis on particular cultures and traditions as opposed to the universalistic discourse of 'the rights of man' make him an important inspiration for Arendt:

> These facts and reflections offer what seems an ironical, bitter and belated confirmation of the famous arguments with which Edmund Burke opposed the French Revolution's Declaration of the Rights of Man. They appear to buttress his assertion that human rights were an 'abstraction', that it was much wiser to rely on an 'entailed inheritance' of rights which one transmits to one's children like life itself, and to claim one's rights to be the 'rights of an Englishman' rather than the inalienable rights of man. According to Burke, the rights which we enjoy spring 'from within the nation', so that neither natural law, nor divine command, nor any concept of mankind such as Robespierre's 'human race', 'the sovereign of the earth', are needed as a source of law. The pragmatic soundness of Burke's concept seems to be beyond doubt in light of our manifold experiences.[25]

Arendt traces the roots of her argument that human rights are best articulated and defended in relation to particularistic traditions back to the writings of Burke.

Raymond Williams's *Culture and Society* (1958) begins with Burke. For Williams, Burke establishes the tradition of deploying culture as a means of critiquing industrial society. As the following quotation suggests, Burke also seems significant for articulating a definition of national belonging:

> [Burke] prepared a position in the English mind from which the march of industrialism and liberalism was to be continually attacked. He established the idea of the State as the necessary agent of human perfection, and in terms of this idea the aggressive individualism of the nineteenth century was bound to be condemned. He established, further, the idea of what has been called an 'organic society', where the emphasis is on the interrelation and continuity of human activities, rather than on separation into spheres of interest, each governed by its own laws.

A nation is not an idea only of local extent, and individual momentary aggregation; but it is an idea of continuity, which extends in time as well as in numbers and in space. And this is a choice not of one day, or one set of people, not a tumultuary and giddy choice; it is a deliberate election of the ages and of generations; it is a constitution made by what is ten thousand times better than choice, it is made by the peculiar circumstances, occasions, tempers, dispositions, and moral, civil, and social habitudes of the people, which disclose themselves only in a long space of time.

Immediately after Burke, this complex which he describes was to be called the 'spirit of the nation'; by the end of the nineteenth century, it was called a national 'culture'. Examination of the influence and development of these ideas belongs to my later chapters.[26]

But in fact, 'these ideas', at least as they relate to the 'nation' which seems to be the subject of Burke's thoughts here, do not return in Williams's later chapters. Nor for that matter do they appear in *The Long Revolution*, the 1961 sequel to *Culture and Society*. Indeed, while the idea of nationhood is an explicit concern of the novels, and of the essays on Wales and Welshness that Williams began to write in the early 1970s, it is not until *Towards 2000* (1983) that he engages with national identity both theoretically and at length. His argument in that book, published five years before his death in 1988, is that the 'legal (and communal) defence of dislocated and exposed groups and minorities is essential'. But he notes that 'it is a serious misunderstanding, when full social relations are in question, to suppose that the problems of social identity are resolved by formal definitions. For unevenly and at times precariously, but always through long experience substantially, an effective awareness of social identity depends on actual and sustained social relationships.'[27]

For Williams and Arendt, the form that a common humanity would take was not a globally individualist universalism, but it would be based on the universalising claim that every individual is inseparable from his or her local communal or national particularity. Humanity must be developed within local communities as part of a shared value common to all local, particular communities in order to guarantee, universally, a human 'right to have rights'. This model, as Mark Greif has noted, would seem to require a form of supra-national, planetary or species-level guarantee, some sort of over-law or world government to ensure that all communities lived up to their ethical and moral responsibilities.[28] 'Politically,' stated Arendt, 'before drawing up the constitution of a new body politic, we shall have to create – not merely discover – a new foundation for human community as such.'[29] In response to 'political forms that now limit, subordinate and destroy people', stated Raymond Williams, 'we have to begin again with people and build new political forms'.[30] 'Much harder than making the institutions that are required,' noted Williams, 'is having the feelings that make the institutions work.' He concluded that, 'I think there is a very rich resource for that in Wales'.[31]

III

What kind of 'forms' would these be, and with which 'people' should we 'begin'? What kind of 'feelings' would allow the institutions to work? These questions, revolving around Arendt's emphasis on the frames of political decision-making and Williams's emphasis on the cultural constitution of community, bring me back to the influential charges of racism and essentialism made against Williams by Paul Gilroy, which I discussed in the introduction.[32] There are omissions in my defence of 2003 that I would now wish to address. Gilroy's harshest critique derived from two aspects of Williams's analysis of national identity in *Towards 2000*, to which I return again in what follows. The first was the fact that Williams based his discussion of race on a scenario in which 'an English working man (English in the terms of sustained modern integration) protests at the arrival or presence of "foreigners" or "aliens" and now goes on to specify them as "blacks"'.[33] On this evidence, Gilroy alleges that 'Williams does not appear to recognize black as anything other than a subordinate moment in an ideology of racial supremacy'.[34] The second aspect of Williams's analysis that Gilroy found troubling was that though Williams recognised the danger of the 'jump from resentment of unfamiliar neighbours to the ideological specifications of "race" and "superiority"', his focus was not on the world view of 'the English working man' but on the 'ideology' of the 'standard liberal reply' to his protestations: 'they are as British as you are'. The British liberal's reply, for Williams, was 'to reduce social identity to formal legal definitions, at the level of the state', and was to ignore the power and legitimacy of people's 'communal identities'.[35] For Gilroy, this focus on the 'reply' amounted to a 'refusal' on Williams's part 'to examine the concept of racism'.[36] For the purpose of analysis, it is useful to address these aspects of Williams's argument in turn.

My main counter argument, in the introduction, to Gilroy's accusations of racism and essentialism was to note that Williams did not endorse or defend the words of the 'English working man'. Williams does not deny 'the indispensability of citizenship rights for immigrants', for he states explicitly a few lines earlier that 'a merely legal definition of what it is to be "British" [...] is necessary and important, correctly asserting the need for equality and protection within the laws'.[37] Furthermore, Williams located the 'real grounds of hope' in the experience of the 'Welsh mining valleys, into which in the nineteenth century there was massive and diverse immigration, but in which, after two generations, there were some of the most remarkably solid and mutually loyal communities of which we have record'.[38] I would still wish to emphasise that Williams was never opposed to immigration, and that the comparison of his thought with the overt racism of Enoch Powell is misleading. I would now supplement that argument with an analysis of the ways in which what Williams described as the 'remarkably solid and mutually loyal communities of which we have record' were partially created through a process by which a white working class defined itself against a racial 'other'. Though there was a historical and contemporary black presence, especially in Butetown and the Cardiff docklands (where a major race riot took place in 1919), immigration into south Wales primarily involved white ethnic groups. This was an aspect of the critique that I failed to address in the introduction, and it is worth doing so now in relation to the narratives informing Welsh cultural history on which Raymond Williams drew and to which he contributed.

In his discussion of 'race and the making of the American working class', David Roediger registers the crucial contribution made by the 'new labour historians' of the 1960s, 1970s and 1980s in showing the extent to which workers, even in periods of economic depression or political oppression, were historical actors who made their own political choices and created their own cultural forms. He notes, however, a hesitancy on the part of Leftist historians to explore 'working class "whiteness" and white supremacy as creations, in part, of the white working class itself'.[39] Roediger's work emerges from the ethnically and racially diverse communities of industrial America, but it is worth keeping in mind his observation that 'even in an all-white town, race was never absent' when analysing the constitution of identities in industrial, 'American', Wales.[40] The Welsh Labour historians on whom Raymond Williams mainly drew for his understanding of Welsh history – notably Gwyn A. Williams and Dai Smith – rejected views of working-class societies as unthinking victims of political or cultural hegemonies. Yet, as the Wales-based African American ethnographer Glenn Jordan has noted, the cultural forms and political values that emerged from those societies were not always progressively subversive:

> South Wales miners, and mining communities, are famous for their socialist traditions and internationalism, including their virtual hero worship of Paul Robeson. But there is another, long-established tradition in the south Wales Valleys: the working-class community as breeding ground for racism.[41]

As I sought to trace in my *Black Skin, Blue Books* (2012), the dominant forms of Welshness evolved and were defined in the nineteenth century in relation to an imperial discourse of 'blackness'. The infamous government 'Report on the State of Education in Wales' of 1847 (the 'blue books' of my title) saw the Welsh language described as 'the language of slavery' keeping the Welsh 'under the hatches', and the Welshman described as living in 'an underworld of his own' as 'the march of society goes completely over his head'.[42] Linguistic and religious deviancy from Anglophone and Anglican norms were clothed in a language of 'slavery' and 'servitude'. Significant sectors of the Welsh bourgeoisie in the Victorian era responded to these attacks by seeking to prove their 'whiteness'; to re-model themselves and their people as practical, business-like, English-speaking Britons. Indeed 'gwyn' ('white') is one of the keywords of the Welsh ideology of social uplift.[43] In the United States, this was the story of how 'the Irish became white' (in Noel Ignatiev's phrase), and on mainland Europe, of how Breton peasants became Francophone Frenchmen (to adapt Eugen Weber's formulation).[44] In the twentieth century black-face minstrelsy was a widely noted feature of the popular culture of Welsh industrial societies, and a feature of the Welsh industrial novels of Jack Jones and Gwyn Jones (discussed by Raymond Williams in this volume).[45] During the long months of the lockout in 1926, that forms the backdrop to the childhood memories of Williams's *Border Country*, mining communities found expression in bands such as the 'Seven Sisters Black Natives', the 'Carolina Coons' and the blackfaced 'Graig Miners'.[46] South Wales exemplifies Susan Gubar's observation that race-changing conventions 'enabled artists from manifold traditions to relate nuanced comparative stories about various modes and grada-tions of othering'.[47] I have argued elsewhere, in a discussion of Paul Robeson's reception, that the emergence of a coherent and politic-ally empowering working-class movement from the ethnic (especially linguistic and religious) diversity that characterised Welsh industrial society gave rise to forms of black masculinity in popular culture that functioned as images of otherness.[48] As Tiffany Willoughby-Herard notes, the process of social uplift for 'poor whites' in many contexts involved a process of racial 'decontamination'; having been defined or associated with 'blackness' in Victorian discourses of class and empire, 'progress' for white minorities was measured by their distance from a black 'other'.[49] While what W. E. B. Du Bois described as the 'wages' of whiteness allowed an assimilationist route for white ethnicities, this was never available to their black contemporaries.[50] The rise of white 'ethnics' up the social hierarchy in the United States was, in Walter Benn Michael's terms, 'less an effect of the triumph over racism' than it was 'an effect of the triumph of racism'.[51] Blackface minstrelsy can be read as an embodiment of this dynamic in popular culture in the United States and, albeit in a muted form, in Wales.

If a discourse of increasing 'whiteness' reflected the racial logic of assimilation, minority nationalisms in Europe and anti-assimilationist white subcultures in the United States sought to adopt, rather than reject, the mask of blackness as a means of differentiating them-selves from mainstream norms. Indeed, when the African American novelist Richard Wright deployed the 'white negro' concept for the first time in his 1957 work *Pagan Spain*, he was not describing a process of passing as white but emphasising the 'impurity' of a Spanish history that included pagan, Catholic, Jewish, Muslim, African and Moorish strands.[52] As forms of separatist nationalism developed on the peripheries of the French and British states, and as various American subcultures would question the ideology of uplift undergirding American assimilationism, white minorities would begin to develop the implications inherent in Wright's analysis by re-appropriating the 'blackness' that they had been desperate to reject a generation earlier.[53] Raymond Williams would have been familiar with Norman Mailer's essay on 'The White Negro', which problematically both exemplified and analysed this use of 'blackness' as a marker of difference by the Beat poets and hipsters of the 1950s, for he reviewed an anthology of articles from the journal *Dissent* in which it was re-published.[54] Williams was never to appropriate the black mask in this primitivist manner, but he did note in his review of Ned Thomas's *The Welsh Extremist* that

> it seems to be true that in late capitalist societies some of the most powerful campaigns begin from specific unabsorbed (and therefore necessarily marginal) experiences and situations. Black Power in the United States, civil rights in Ulster, the language in Wales, are experiences comparable in this respect to the student movement and to women's liberation.[55]

Indeed, the title of that review, 'Who Speaks for Wales?', may owe something to Robert Penn Warren's widely read and reviewed *Who Speaks for the Negro* (1965).[56] Williams also drew explicitly on Michael Hechter's work on nationalism when writing on Wales, most notably the volume *Internal Colonialism: the Celtic Fringe in British National Development*.[57] Hechter noted that the intention of his major work of comparative historiography was to explore 'intergroup relations' in the 'long run' offered by the British Isles in order to understand the African American experience. Hechter's work may usefully remind us that it is necessary to distinguish between 'alternative strategies for the liberation of oppressed minorities – assimilationism versus nationalism'.[58] Indeed, it was an awareness of the Welsh experience 'of subjection to English expansion and assimilation historically' that 'alerted' Raymond Williams to 'the dangers' of his earlier emphases in *Culture and Society* and *The Long Revolution* on a 'common culture' as the basis for 'a persuasive type of definition of community, which is at once dominant and exclusive'.[59]

A distinction needs to be made, then, between the assimilation-ist fear of blackness characteristic of white minority discourses of uplift into 'British' or 'American' norms, and the minority national-ist's embrace of blackness and desire to make broader comparisons with other anti-colonial movements as a strategy to counter and resist assimilationism.[60] The assimilationist's wish to 'decontaminate' and the minority nationalist's desire to 'associate' are both problem-atic, however, albeit for different reasons. The former is based on a racial hierarchy of inferiority and superiority and racist fear of 'con-tamination'. The latter draws on strains of ahistoric and romantic identification and functions to ventriloquise the voices of racialised others thus potentially (if never wholly) denying them the power to speak for themselves.[61] Nowhere is this danger more apparent than in the use of 'colonialism' to describe the Welsh experience, especially as Wales is today a first world nation whose industrial his-tory is intimately tied to the economy and practice of the slave trade and Empire.[62] It is also true, however, that Welsh literary and intel-lectual history constitutes one of the longest documented traditions of resistance to domination and assimilation.[63] I would still endorse what I said then about the colonial question in relation to Wales in the introduction to this volume, and would reiterate my observation that Williams perceived the continuation of that history of colonial oppression and imperial collaboration in his own psyche. 'My saddest discovery', he notes, was

> when I found that in myself [...] that most crucial form of imperialism had happened. That is to say, where parts of your mind are taken over by a system of ideas, a system of feelings, which really do emanate from the power centre.[64]

It needs to be acknowledged, however, that the nature and terms of the colonial debate is transformed once Wales itself is defined in multicultural terms, as a crucible of difference in its own right as opposed to being one racial ingredient contributing to the British melting pot. Charlotte Williams responds pithily to the challenge that the existence of a range of hyphenated Welshnesses poses for the narrative of Welsh colonial oppression: if the 'Welshman' is a 'black man at heart', where does that leave 'the black man who is Welsh or the Welshman who is black'?[65] Answering that question requires an engagement with the diverse histories that constitute the contemporary Welsh people, but it does not necessarily entail a rejection of nationalism. Werner Sollors has noted that the 'very language used to create national unity and a sense of coherence' via the assimilationist 'melting pot' can also serve 'to support the ethnogenesis of regional and ethnic groups that could challenge national unity'.[66] Minorities may resist assimilation by claiming a distinctive 'pot' or 'bowl' of their own, thus emphasising their own internal diversity and ability to integrate others. Indeed – in a strain of thought that can be related to Arendt's emphasis on the role of the nation to confer rights to the individual – the desire to foreground their hybrid, multicultural credentials has been a characteristic of the most significant strains within minority nationalisms. Williams never presented his arguments in the terms of contemporary multicultural debates, but his emphasis in the essays collected in this volume is consistently on the internal diversity of the nation. If Wales, as Williams notes, tends to be viewed as 'unusually singular' from an English perspective, he reverses the gaze in *Border Country*, where it is on the Welsh side of the border that identities become unstable, that variousness and openness replace an Englishness that is depicted in terms of its reserve and insularity.[67] 'The least known fact, by others, about contemporary Welsh culture and politics,' notes Williams, 'is that there are harsh and persistent quarrels within a dimension that is seen from outside as unusually singular.'[68] Wales in this respect illustrates his broader argument that '[o]ne place is as real and as potentially interesting as another, only metropolitan centralization and cultural imperialism would have it otherwise'.[69]

It is in relation to this argument that we should address Raymond Williams's problematic shift of focus in 'The Culture of Nations' from the ideology informing the 'English working man's protests at the arrival or presence of "foreigners" or "aliens"' to the ideology of the 'standard liberal reply that "they are as British as you are"'.[70] As I argued in the Introduction, Williams is not turning to the ideology of the 'standard liberal reply' in order to ask 'how long is long enough to become a genuine Brit' as Gilroy alleges, and neither is Williams's question informed by a 'discomfort' when faced with 'those who were not settled, not truly English, not part of the nation' as Henry Louis Gates, Jr. suggests.[71] It is only by ignoring Williams's self-defined Welsh-Europeanism that such readings become possible, and indeed what Gilroy and Gates wholly ignore in their respective histories of cultural studies in England is that the figure whom they both suggest inaugurated that tradition was a member of a minority himself. This is not a trivial matter, for the occlusion of Williams's Welsh identity leads to misleading accounts of his work. Williams's intention in turning to the ideology of the reply is to reject the kind of ahistorical, assimilationist conception of Britishness that Gilroy perceives, a few pages later, in a Tory election poster of 1983 in which a picture of a black male in an ill-fitting suit was captioned 'Labour says he's black. Tories say he's British'. 'Blacks are being invited,' states Gilroy 'to forsake all that marks them out as culturally distinct before real Britishness can be guaranteed.'[72] This is precisely Williams's point. To focus on the ideology of 'the standard liberal reply' is to expose the way in which Britishness is rendered empty and contentless in order that it may function as the universal-neutral space where difference may be rendered irrelevant and cultural particularism transcended.[73]

Slavoj Žižek, who notes that 'when some procedure is denounced as ideological [...] one can be sure that its inversion is no less ideological', would approve of Williams's revisionist reversal, for it is in keeping with the Slovenian's argument regarding the 'self-denial of white identity' in the contemporary arguments relating to decolonisation:[74]

And this is why white liberals so gladly indulge in self-flagellation: the true aim of their activity is not really to help the others but the *Lustgewinn* brought about by their self-accusations, the feeling of their own moral superiority over others. The problem with the self-denial of white identity is not that it goes too far but that it does not go far enough: while its enunciated content seems radical, its position of enunciation remains that of privileged universality.[75]

To 'decolonise' Britishness means that we not only follow Edward Said, Gauri Viswanathan, Paul Gilroy and others in demystifying the myth of cultural homogeneity, cohesion and insularity (a discourse that equates 'Britishness' with the 'Englishness of the home counties' as Williams notes in this volume) by making Empire and its legacies central to 'national' history.[76] It also requires us to demystify forms of British universalism. Jed Esty usefully identifies the reasons why this pincer manoeuvre is required:

> In colonial modernity, Englishness represented both an insular wellspring of distinctive values and an almost blank Arnoldian metacultural capacity to absorb and govern the cultures of its periphery. The English difference was, then, both a cultural essence and an essential culturelessness.[77]

Decolonisation involves an insistence on the multicultural history and reality of the British against monocultural myths, and a critique of the ways in which Britishness poses as the realm of the universal. Esty sees this dual process exemplified in the writings of Stuart Hall, whose work combines multicultural and multi-ethnic studies of England that challenge monolithic myths of national identity, while also recognising the importance of addressing 'a conception of "Englishness" which because it is hegemonic does not really represent itself as an ethnicity at all'.[78] These emphases are manifest in Williams's writings in this volume; the emphasis on the diversity of 'lived and formed identities either of a settled kind, if available, or of a possible kind, where dislocation and relocation require new formation' on the one hand, and the rejection of 'the alienated superficialities of "the nation"' on the other.[79] Indeed, the advantage of a minority nationalist position for Williams is that it allows for an insight and emphasis on 'the artificialities of the settled "commonsense" nation-state', allowing the critic 'to shoot them to pieces from history and from social theory'.[80] Williams endorses Sartre's point when 'writing about the Basques' that 'we're dealing with an entirely different' kind of nationalism 'when it is a case of the marginal or absorbed or oppressed nationality, the sense of difference from some particular dominant large nation-state or of course empire'.[81] The question that arises here is what happens if the nationalist project succeeds, and subordination comes to an end in the form of a political state? Is the minority doomed in such a scenario to adopt the 'discourses of sameness' characteristic of those coercive universalisms that deny the particularistic differences of others?[82]

This question leads us to a final step in the argument. The 'standard liberal reply' that 'they are as British as you are' expresses a desire that the majority should be tolerant enough to allow minorities to transcend their particularities in embracing a capacious Britishness. What this seemingly tolerant gesture forecloses is the possibility of a distinctive universalism rooted in the experiences of minorities; a 'Welsh' or 'black' universalism, say. The liberal assimilationist reply rightly rejects racist intolerance, but hides a fear that minorities may not wish to part with their particularities, may not wish to assimilate into a pre-defined Britishness, but would rather forge a distinctive universalism of their own. This form of the universal would not require the erasure of its particularism by the black, or Jewish, or Welsh-language community. It would require an embrace of what Žižek describes as the 'determinate negation' which bears the mark of what it negates. Thus, while the 'standard liberal reply' to the particularism of a movement such as Black Lives Matter would be to emphasise that 'all lives matter' (a variant of 'they are as British as you are' in Williams's scenario), a more far-reaching response would acknowledge

> that while this principle is true, in today's concrete constellation, the violence to which blacks are exposed is not just a neutral case of social violence but its privileged, exemplary case – to reduce it to a particular case of violence means to ignore the true nature of violence in our society. This is the Hegelian 'concrete universality': we can formulate the universal dimension only if we focus on a particular case which exemplifies it.[83]

This is very close to what Raymond Williams meant when he spoke of 'militant particularism' and 'real universalities'.[84] In this crucial dimension of his thought, the logic of movements based on class, ethnicity and nation are structurally related. Writing in 1981 of the 'unique and extraordinary character of working-class self-organization', Williams noted that

[i]t has tried to connect particular struggles to a general struggle in one quite special way. It has set out, as a movement,
to make real what is at first sight the extraordinary claim
that defence and advancement of certain particular interests,
properly brought together, are in fact the general interest.[85]

The movement of this argument, from the particular to the general,
is repeated in the attempt at seeking a response to the 'intolerable
confusion' regarding nationhood and identity. Little, notes Williams,
is to be gained from the 'familiar intellectual jump to this or that
universality'. But this does not entail a rejection of the universal:

The real 'universalities' – large forms which do succeed in
prevailing over more local forms – are not to be found in
intellectual systems but in actual and organised relationships
which achieve, over the relevant areas, effective power. This
is the way to look at the urgent modern problem of the
'nation'. It is ineffective and even trivial to come back from
a demonstration of the universality of the human species
and expect people, from that fact alone, to reorganise their
lives by treating all their immediate and actual groupings and
relationships as secondary. For the species meaning, and the
valuation of human life which it carries, is in practice only
realised, indeed perhaps in theory only realisable, through
significant relationships in which other human beings are
present. No abstraction on its own will carry this most
specific of all senses. To extend it and to generalise it, in
sufficiently practical ways, involves the making of new relationships which are in significant continuity – and not in
contradiction – with the more limited relationships through
which people do and must live.[86]

For the solidarities forged in a particular struggle to become mean-
ingfully practical requires their extension and generalisation into a
new form of society. For Williams, political engagement needs to
be grounded in a militant particularism that exemplifies a broader
universal truth. The Civil Rights and Black Lives Matter movements in the United States draw on the specificity of the African

American experience to articulate a programme of universal justice; the most far-seeing strains of the feminist and ecological movements project their particularisms forwards into wide-ranging reconstructions of society with the aim of benefitting all. This process – where the particular crisis of a community 'under stress, under attack' becomes extended into a 'political movement' that addresses 'the total relations of a society' – is identified by Raymond Williams as also being 'a most significant part of the history of Wales'.[87] To the envisaged 'federation' of movements mobilising particular energies for universal ends, he adds the 'radical nationalist forces' of 'Irish or Scots or Welsh or Breton or Basque'.[88] It will have been noticed by readers of this volume that the essays in it typically follow a trajectory from the particular to the general. In concluding his thoughts on Welsh nationalism in the opening, titular essay Williams notes that 'challenging, personally and publicly, and from wherever we are, the immense imperatives which are not only flattening but preventing the realities of identity and culture', is a cause 'better than national and more than international, for in its varying forms it is a very general human and social movement'.[89] The 'Welsh essays' collected in this volume are not, then, the products of Williams's withdrawal 'into the redoubt of his Welshness', nor do they represent a search for solace in a 'Celtic commune'.[90] They represent Williams's attempt at articulating a universalism that does not erase the particular.

IV

Turn around and, with the Decalogue behind you, step back out of the serene silence of the Parish Church of St Clydawg. The light will momentarily dazzle your unaccustomed eyes but, as they come back into focus, you will be reminded that this place is surrounded by the long ridges of the Black Mountains. It is a fitting location to end. Raymond Williams began his unfinished, posthumously published *The People of the Black Mountains* by placing his 'right hand', 'palm downward', on the 'layered sandstone' of this landscape, feeling that 'the generations' were 'all suddenly present'.[91] In doing so, was he acknowledging that the desired reconciliation of national community with universal humanity remained – like the promised land from Mount Nebo – out of reach?

Notes

1. Raymond Williams, *The Country and the City* (London: Chatto & Windus, 1973), p. 4.
2. Raymond Williams, *People of the Black Mountains 1: The Beginning* (London: Chatto and Windus, 1989), p. 2. An informative pamphlet 'The Parish Church of St Clydawg' prepared by the Longtown Outdoor Education Centre can be picked up at the Church.
3. See 'Boyhood', p. 106.
4. See 'Boyhood', p. 106.
5. Dai Smith, *Raymond Williams: A Warrior's Tale* (Cardigan: Parthian, 2008), p. 329.
6. Michael Walzer, *Exodus and Revolution* (New York: Basic Books, 1985).
7. Raymond Williams, *The Volunteers* (1978; London: Hogarth Press, 1985), p. 72.
8. Hannah Arendt, 'Letter to Raymond Williams', April 11, 1962. Raymond Williams Papers, Swansea University.
9. Raymond Williams, 'Thoughts on a Masked Stranger', *The Kenyon Review*, 23/4 (Autumn, 1961), 698–702 (698).
10. Williams, 'Thoughts on a Masked Stranger', 701–2.
11. See 'Marxism, Poetry, Wales', p. 175
12. J. R. Johnson [James's pseudonym], *Marxism and the Intellectuals* (Detroit: Facing Reality Publishing Committee, 1962), n.p. See the Introduction to the present volume, p. 24.
13. Raymond Williams, *Modern Tragedy* (1966. London: Hogarth Press, 1992), n.p. Raymond Williams, 'Violence and Confusion', *The Guardian*, 25 June 1970.
14. Hannah Arendt, *The Origins of Totalitarianism* (New York: Harcourt Brace, 1951), p. 439. This is taken from the first edition, the passage was deleted from later editions.
15. See Richard J. Bernstein, *Why Read Hannah Arendt Now* (Cambridge: Polity Press, 2018), pp. 1–8.
16. Hannah Arendt, *The Jewish Writings*, ed. Jerome Kohn and Ron H. Feldman (New York: Schocken Books, 2007), pp. 149–50.
17. Hannah Arendt, *The Origins of Totalitarianism* (1951; London, Penguin, 2017), p. 392.
18. Nancy Fraser, 'Reframing Justice in a Globalising World', *New Left Review II*, 36 (November/December 2005), p. 77. 'Political death' is Fraser's term.
19. Arendt, *The Origins of Totalitarianism* (2017), p. 388.
20. See 'The Culture of Nations', p. 341; Raymond Williams, *Towards 2000* (London: Chatto & Windus, 1983), p. 195.
21. See 'The Culture of Nations', p. 326.
22. See 'The Culture of Nations', p. 342.
23. Henry Louis Gates Jr., *Tradition and the Black Atlantic: Critical Theory in the African Diaspora* (New York: Basic Books, 2010), pp. 28–32.
24. Luke Gibbons, *Edmund Burke and Ireland* (Oxford: Oxford University Press, 2003), p. 88.

25. Arendt, *The Origins of Totalitarianism* (2017), pp. 391–2.
26. Raymond Williams, *Culture and Society* (1958. London: Hogarth, 1992), p. 11.
27. See 'The Culture of Nations', p. 341.
28. Mark Greif, *The Age of the Crisis of Man: Thought and Fiction in America 1933–1973* (Princeton: Princeton University Press, 2015), p. 94.
29. Hannah Arendt, *The Origins of Totalitarianism* (1951), p. 434.
30. See 'The Culture of Nations', p. 345.
31. See 'Marxism, Poetry, Wales', p. 175.
32. Gates Jr. repeats Gilroy's argument in *Tradition and the Black Atlantic*. See Daniel G. Williams, *Wales Unchained: Literature, Politics and Identity in the American Century* (Cardiff: University of Wales Press, 2015), pp. 93–111, for a counter-argument.
33. Paul Gilroy, *'There Ain't No Black in the Union Jack': The Cultural Politics of Race and Nation* (Chicago: The University of Chicago Press, 1987), pp. 49–51. Williams, 'The Culture of Nations', p. 341.
34. Gilroy, *'There Ain't No Black in the Union Jack'*, p. 50.
35. See 'The Culture of Nations', p. 341.
36. Gilroy, *'There Ain't No Black in the Union Jack'*, p. 50.
37. See 'The Culture of Nations', p. 341.
38. See 'The Culture of Nations', p. 342.
39. David R. Roediger, *The Wages of Whiteness: Race and the Making of the American Working Class* (London: Verso, 1991), p. 9.
40. Roediger, *The Wages of Whiteness*, p. 3. 'American Wales' was Alfred Zimmern's term for industrial south Wales in Zimmern, *My Impressions of Wales* (London: Mills and Boon, 1921); quoted by Dai Smith, *Aneurin Bevan and the World of South Wales* (Cardiff: University of Wales Press, 1993), p. i.
41. Glenn Jordan, '"We Never Really Noticed You Were Coloured": Postcolonialist Reflections on Immigrants and Minorities in Wales', in Jane Aaron and Chris Williams (eds), *Postcolonial Wales* (Cardiff: University of Wales Press, 2005), pp. 70–1.
42. Quoted in Daniel G. Williams, *Black Skin, Blue Books: African Americans and Wales 1845–1945* (Cardiff: University of Wales Press, 2012), pp. 26–8. See also Gwyneth Tyson Roberts, *The Language of the Blue Books: The Perfect Instrument of Empire* (Cardiff: University of Wales Press, 1998), p. 203.
43. See Hywel Teifi Edwards, *Codi'r Hen Wlad yn ei Hôl 1850–1914* (Llandysul: Gomer, 1989); Daniel Williams, 'The Welsh Atlantic: Mapping the Contexts of Welsh-American Literature', in Marc Shell (ed.), *American Babel: Literatures of the United States from Abnaki to Zuni* (Cambridge MA: Harvard University Press, 2002), pp. 343–68.
44. Noel Ignatiev, *How the Irish Became White* (New York: Routledge, 1995); Eugen Weber, *Peasants into Frenchmen: Modernization of Rural France, 1870–1914* (Stanford: Stanford University Press, 1976).
45. See my discussion in *Black Skin, Blue Books*, pp. 188–93.

46. See Hywel Francis and Dai Smith, *The Fed: A History of the South Wales Miners in the Twentieth Century* (1980; Cardiff: University of Wales Press, 1998), p. 58.

47. Susan Gubar, *Racechanges: White Skin, Black Face in American Culture* (Oxford: Oxford University Pres, 1997), p. 48.

48. Williams, *Black Skin, Blue Books*, pp. 193, 204.

49. Tiffany Willoughby-Herard, *Waste of a White Skin: The Carnegie Corporation and the Racial Logic of White Vulnerability* (Oakland: University of California Press, 2015), p. 153.

50. W. E. B. Du Bois, *Black Reconstruction in America, 1860–1880* (1935; New York: First Free Press, 1998), pp. 30, 700.

51. Walter Benn Michaels, 'Plots Against America: Neoliberalism and Antiracism', *American Literary History*, 18/2 (Summer 200), 288–302 (290).

52. Richard Wright, *Pagan Spain* (1957; Jackson: University Press of Mississippi, 2002), p. 162.

53. This is particularly a characteristic of Welsh-language pop music of the 1970s and 1980s. See Daniel G. Williams, 'Cyflwyniad', *Canu Caeth: Y Cymry a'r Affro-Americaniaid* (Llandysul: Gomer, 2010), p. xv. For the United States, see Eric Lott, *Black Mirror: The Cultural Contradictions of American Racism* (Cambridge MA: Harvard University Press, 2017).

54. Raymond Williams, 'Grammar of Dissent', review of *Voices of Dissent: A selection of Articles from Dissent Magazine*, in *The Nation*, 188 (1959), 174–5

55. See 'Who Speaks for Wales', p. 48.

56. Robert Penn Warren, *Who Speaks for the Negro?* (New York: Random House Publishing, 1965).

57. Michael Hechter, *Internal Colonialism: the Celtic Fringe in British National Development 1536–1966* (1975; New Brunswick NJ; Transaction Publishers, 1999). See the reference in 'Wales and England', p. 74, and discussion in 'For Britain: See Wales', p. 141.

58. Hechter, *Internal Colonialism*, pp. xxvi–xxix.

59. Raymond Williams, *Politics and Letters: Interviews with New Left Review* (London: Verso, 1979), p. 118–19.

60. See Hechter, *Internal Colonialism*, pp. xxviii–xxix.

61. For a subtle analysis of forms of allegorisation and appropriation in relation to Jewish identity, see Daniel Boyarin, *A Radical Jew: Paul and the Politics of Identity* (Los Angeles: University of California Press, 1994), chapter 9.

62. This is a case made by Chris Williams in 'Problematizing Wales: An Exploration in Historiography and Postcoloniality', in Aaron and Williams, *Postcolonial Wales*, pp. 3–17. See also Chris Evans, *Slave Wales: The Welsh and Atlantic Slavery 1660–1850* (Cardiff: University of Wales Press, 2010).

63. See Jane Aaron, 'Bardic Anti-colonialism', in Aaron and Williams, *Postcolonial Wales*, pp. 137–58; Richard Wyn Jones, 'The Colonial Legacy in Welsh Politics', in Aaron and Williams, *Postcolonial Wales*, pp. 23–38.

64. See 'The Importance of Community', p. 313.

65. Charlotte Williams, *Sugar and Slate* (Aberystwyth: Planet, 2002), p. 176.

66. Werner Sollors, *Beyond Ethnicity: Consent and Descent in American Culture* (New York: Oxford University Press, 1986), p. 99.
67. See Daniel G. Williams, 'To Know the Divisions: the identity of Raymond Williams', in *Wales Unchained*, pp. 99–105.
68. See 'Community', p. 78.
69. See 'Freedom and a Lack of Confidence', p. 240.
70. See 'The Culture of Nations', p. 341.
71. Gilroy, *'There Ain't No Black in the Union Jack'*, p. 49. Gates Jr., *Tradition and the Black Atlantic*, p. 42.
72. Gilroy, *'There Ain't No Black in the Union Jack'*, p. 59.
73. See 'The Culture of Nations', p. 341.
74. Slavoj Žižek, 'Introduction: The Spectre of Ideology', in Žižek (ed.), *Mapping Ideology* (London: Verso, 1994), p. 4.
75. Slavoj Žižek, *Like a Thief in Broad Daylight: Power in the Era of Post-Humanity* (London: Allen Lane, 2018), p. 134.
76. See 'Region and Class in the Novel', p. 255.
77. Jed Esty, *A Shrinking Island: Modernism and National Culture in England* (Princeton: Princeton University Press, 2004), p. 196.
78. Esty, *A Shrinking Island*, p. 196.
79. See 'The Culture of Nations', p. 341.
80. See 'The Culture of Nations', p. 329.
81. See 'Marxism. Poetry, Wales, p. 169.
82. See Daniel Boyarin and Jonathan Boyarin, 'Diaspora: Generation and the Ground of Jewish Identity', Kwame Anthony Appiah and Henry Louis Gates Jr. (eds), *Identities* (Chicago: University of Chicago Press, 1995), p. 319.
83. Slavoj Žižek, 'Foreword: The Importance of Theory', in Zahi Zalloua, *Žižek on Race: Towards and Anti-Racist Future* (London: Bloomsbury, 2020), p. xii.
84. Raymond Williams, 'The Forward March of Labour Halted?' (1981), in Robin Gable (ed.), *Resources of Hope* (London: Verso, 1989), p. 249; see 'Wales and England', p. 74; 'Decentralism and the Politics of Place', p. 351.
85. Williams, 'The Forward March', p. 249.
86. See 'The Culture of Nations', p. 325.
87. See 'The Importance of Community', p. 311.
88. See 'The Practice of Possibility', p. 358; 'The Culture of Nations', pp. 328–9.
89. See 'Who Speaks for Wales?', p. 49.
90. Patrick Parrinder, *The Failure of Theory* (Brighton: The Harvester Press, 1987), p. 78; James A. Davies, '"Not going back, but... exile ending": Raymond Williams's fictional Wales', in W. J. Morgan and P. Preston (eds), *Raymond Williams: Politics, Education, Letters* (London: Macmillan, 1993), p. 207.
91. Raymond Williams, *People of the Black Mountains*, pp. 1–2.

INDEX